The New National Accounts

Dedicated to the memory of
Nicholas Coope (1980–1998)
Son of Cousin Jennifer and Christopher
reliable and cheerful bushwalking companion
a loss deeply shared

The New National Accounts

An Introduction to
the System of National Accounts 1993
and the European System of Accounts 1995

Dudley Jackson

Edward Elgar

Cheltenham, UK • Northampton, MA, USA

© Dudley Jackson 2000

Published by
Edward Elgar Publishing Limited
Glensanda House
Montpellier Parade
Cheltenham
Glos GL50 1UA
UK

Edward Elgar Publishing, Inc.
136 West Street
Suite 202
Northampton
Massachusetts 01060
USA

A catalogue record for this book
is available from the British Library

Library of Congress Cataloguing in Publication Data

Jackson, Dudley.
    The new national accounts : an introduction to the system of national accounts 1993 and the European system of accounts 1995 / Dudley Jackson.
        Includes index.
        1. National income—European Union countries—Accounting. 2. National income—Accounting. I. Title.

HC240.9I5 J33 2000
339.34—dc21

00–029364

ISBN 1 84064 157 6

Typeset by Robert Hood
Printed and bound in Great Britain by Bookcraft (Bath) Ltd.

Contents

Figures

Tables

1 The Economy and the Sequence of Accounts

1.1 Introduction

Starting in 1998, all the countries of the world will be changing their national income accounts to conform to the international standard conventions, terminology and structure of accounts of the United Nations *System of National Accounts 1993* (the conventions, definitions of concepts, terminology and structure of accounts in this document will be referred to as 'the SNA93' (with the definite article and printed in roman) while the document explaining and defining those conventions and concepts and so on will itself be referred to as '*SNA93*' (without the definite article and printed in italics)). *SNA93* refers to the SNA93 as 'the System', and occasionally I use this term as well.

Additionally, the member states of the European Union are obliged to produce national accounts in conformity with Eurostat *European System of Accounts ESA 1995* (the conventions and so on of which will be referred to as 'the ESA95' and the document itself as '*ESA95*'). The implementation of the ESA95 is in consequence of Council Regulation (EC) No. 2223/96 of 25 June 1996 on the European system of national and regional accounts in the Community (*Official Journal of the European Communities*, No. L 310, Volume 39, 30 November 1996) according to which the ESA95 'constitutes a version of the SNA [93] adapted to the structures of the Member States' economies, [and] must follow the layout of the SNA [93] so that the Community's data are comparable with those compiled by its main international partners'.

The ESA95 is thus based on, and is consistent with, the SNA93 but is occasionally (for European Community purposes) more specific and prescriptive in various details. The best way to think of the ESA95 is that it is a *standard for compliance* with the SNA93. This book is an introduction to both the SNA93 and the ESA95, and so I refer generally to 'the SNA93/ESA95'.

New balance of payments statistics will also be produced in conformity with the International Monetary Fund *Balance of Payments Manual Fifth Edition* (the conventions and so on of which will be referred to as 'the BPM5' and the document itself as '*BPM5*'). The SNA93 and the BPM5 are fully consistent, each with the other, and this book makes occasional reference, where required, to the BPM5.

An introduction to the new system of national accounts is necessary even for those familiar with the old system of national accounts because there is considerable change both in the overall structure of national accounts and also in particular detail within the accounts, with many new concepts and altered definitions and consequential new terminology.

This book explains *everything* from the beginning and assumes no prior knowledge of national accounts and of national accounting concepts. This means that the book is suitable for non-economists as well as economists.

In order to illustrate the explanations the book uses, side by side where possible, comparative data from the United Kingdom and from Australia as befits the aims of international standardisation intended by the SNA93 and the ESA95. However, this is for illustration only, and any reader from another country is recommended to find parallel illustrations from his or her own country's national accounts compiled on the SNA93/ESA95 basis, while any reader from the United Kingdom or Australia should update the illustrations here given.

The reader will note that I quote both from *SNA93* and also from *ESA95* but (save in a very few instances where the ESA95 is more restrictive and/or more detailed than the SNA93) no special significance should be attached to this other than that I have selected whichever seems to me best suited to advance my explanation (the only 'competition' between *SNA93* and *ESA95* is a competition in the clarity and usefulness of definitions and explanations). For the same reason, I occasionally use the Office for National Statistics, *United Kingdom National Accounts Concepts, Sources and Methods 1998 Edition* (abbreviated as *UK NACSM*). (The corresponding publication for the Australian national accounts had not been published at time of writing.)

This book is intended as a 'stand-alone' introduction for the general reader – economists and non-economists alike – to the new national accounts. Most readers are not likely to have ready access to *SNA93*, *ESA95*, *BPM5* or *UK NACSM* and for this reason I usually quote, where required, official definitions or explanations in full (noting whenever a definition is quoted in part only). For the reader wishing to pursue more specific interests I also provide, where useful, additional references to paragraphs in *SNA93*, *ESA95*, *BPM5* and *UK*

NACSM, but these additional references are for this category of reader only and may safely be ignored by the general reader. That is, fully following the argument of this text does *not* depend upon reading the unquoted material in these additional references to *SNA93, ESA95, BPM5* or *UK NACSM*.

In Chapter 1, Section 1.2 gives my broad definition of 'economics' as a background to understanding what a system of national accounts sets out to achieve. Section 1.3 explains the basic concept of a sector of the economy, and Section 1.4 explains the basic concepts of transactions and related flows, including especially balancing item flows. Sections 1.5 and 1.7 provide a map of the SNA93/ESA95 and a guide to the rest of the book, with an intervening explanation in Section 1.6 of the classification of economic assets used by the SNA93/ESA95.

1.2   The economy and the SNA93/ESA95

Economics is the study of transactions by transactors, of the balancing items resulting from those transactions, of the economic assets and liabilities resulting from those transactions and of the decision-making underlying those transactions.

It follows from this – the only comprehensive and worthwhile definition of 'economics' – that the classification of transactions, transactors and assets and liabilities are each fundamental to economics.

It also follows from my definition of the subject matter of economics that microeconomics is the study of the transactions, balancing items, assets and liabilities of an individual transactor, while macroeconomics is the study of aggregates of transactions, of the resulting aggregate balancing items, of aggregates of assets and liabilities and of the aggregate influences of all these aggregates, all pertaining to groups of transactors.

The main purpose of a system of national accounts is to provide a full record of the working of an economy. An economy, or rather the working of an economy, may be described in terms of the transactions of the transactors, of the resulting balancing items, and of the assets and liabilities of transactors.

A transactor is any entity who or which engages in transactions. Instead of the term 'transactor' the SNA93/ESA95 uses the term 'institutional unit' and deals only with institutional units. This could be a cause of initial difficulty because real people – you and me – seem to disappear from the System, yet everyone is familiar with his or her own transactions – say, in shopping. So where do all the real people fit in?

My explanation of the concept of a transactor is given in Figure 1.1.

The concept of a transactor can be divided between natural persons taken individually and institutional units. An institutional unit is an elementary – that is, basic or irreducible – economic decision-making centre. An institutional unit is characterised by the following three attributes.

1. An institutional unit has a pattern of behaviour that is both regular and distinctive from the behaviour of institutional units of a different type.
2. An institutional unit makes its own decisions independently of other institutional units; in the jargon, an institutional unit has 'decision-making autonomy'.
3. An institutional unit does, or could in principle, keep a complete set of (a) flow accounts for 'its' transactions (including, where relevant, the transactions of the institutional unit's natural persons taken as individuals), and (b) balance sheets of assets and liabilities (including, where relevant, the assets and liabilities owned or owed by the institutional unit's natural persons taken as individuals).

Institutional units can then be divided into two main categories: households; and legal persons.

The SNA93 definition of a household is:

> a small group of persons who share the same living accommodation, who pool some, or all, of their income and wealth and who consume certain types of goods and services collectively, mainly housing and food (*SNA93*, para. 4.132).

In the United Kingdom, the definition of a household used in the population census is:

> A *household* is either:
>
> (a)   one person living alone; or
> (b)   a group of people (who may or may not be related) living, or staying temporarily, at the same address, with common housekeeping (Office of Population Censuses and Surveys/General Register Office for Scotland, *1991 Census Definitions Great Britain* (HMSO, 1992), para. 3.11).

The ESA95 definition of a household is based on the SNA93 definition but amplifies that definition by noting that households can also function as

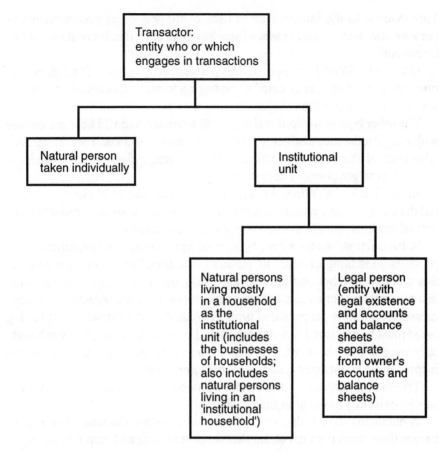

Figure 1.1   Transactors and institutional units

producing units in addition to functioning as consuming units (*ESA95*, para. 2.75).

Nearly all persons live in households, sharing 'household' income (earned by an individual member or individual members of the household), participating in 'household' consumption (items for household consumption being bought by individual members of the household), and sharing 'household' assets (with legal ownership of each asset being vested in an individual member or individual members of the household).

Because of such pooling of income and sharing of consumption and assets by the members of the household, the SNA93/ESA95 has, in regard to natural persons, to take an 'institutional unit' – or 'household' – view of their affairs.

This extends to the business enterprises of the self-employed, particularly because the income and assets of the business are effectively those of the household.

Under the SNA93, persons living permanently, or for a long period of time, in an institution are treated as belonging to an 'institutional household' which is treated as a household.

The other type of institutional unit I call a 'legal person'. These are entities with a legal existence distinct from their owner or owners or from the persons who control them. These institutional units range from private business enterprises to government departments.

In this book, we follow the System's 'institutional unit' view of affairs, but the reader should remain aware that this view includes the transactions of natural persons, but always taken as members of a household.

A transaction occurs when, by mutual agreement, one institutional unit provides something of value to another institutional unit (but noting that in this context 'another institutional unit' may on occasion include the same institutional unit acting in a different capacity or role). A transaction is always measured as a flow per period of time. For example, the transaction of buying bread must be measured, say, as bread bought *per week*, even if bread is bought only once during the week. For another example, the transaction of earning income must be measured, say, as income *per month*.

Transactors may also own stocks of assets or owe stocks of liabilities. Stocks exist at a moment in time.

A balancing item is the result of subtracting either the total of one set of transactions from the total of another set of transactions (each set relating to the same – identical – period of time) or the total of one set of stocks from the total of another set of stocks (each set relating to the same date in time).

As such, a balancing item is an accounting construct, derived from sets of transactions (totalled) or from sets of stocks (totalled), and is not itself an observable independent transaction or an independent stock. A balancing item is not independent of the transactions or stocks from which it derives. It follows from this that fully to understand a balancing item requires, as a necessary prerequisite, an understanding of the transactions or stocks from which the balancing item is derived. (The failure, common in economics, to observe this principle is the source of a great deal of confusion.)

Although balancing items are accounting constructs (and in this sense 'artificial'), balancing items are economically significant. Some of the more important balancing items in accounts containing flows are:

gross value added/gross domestic product
gross operating surplus
gross mixed income
gross disposable income
gross saving
net lending or net borrowing
current external balance.

For accounts containing stocks, known as 'balance sheets', the important balancing item is:

net worth

where net worth, as the difference between total assets owned and total liabilities owed, is a measure of wealth.

Transactions are flows and any balancing item calculated from transactions is itself a flow.

A flow occurs *during* a period of time, and the magnitude of the flow has meaning only with reference to that specified period of time. For example, income is a flow per period of time, and the magnitude of the income flow has meaning only with respect to a specified period of time. A labourer may have an income of £10 000 per annum; a barrister may have an income of £10 000 per week. The two magnitudes each only have meaning with respect to its specified period of time. (What would you reply to someone who told you that the labourer and the barrister had 'the same' income because each received £10 000?!)

Transactors can also own a stock of assets or can owe a stock of liabilities. A stock has existence *at* a moment (or date) in time. To illustrate, on 1 January 1999, both the labourer and the barrister might have (a stock of) assets of £2000 in a bank account deposit. At that date, the stock of their respective bank deposit assets can be compared.

Accounts which record stocks are known as balance sheets. Balancing items can also be calculated from stocks. For example, the balancing item calculated by subtracting an institutional unit's total stock of liabilities owed (at a certain date) from the institutional unit's total stock of assets owned (at that same date) is a balancing item known as the institutional unit's net worth (at that same date). This obviously important balancing item is a measure of the institutional unit's wealth. Note that net worth is not an independently existing stock in the way that a bank deposit is an independently existing stock.

In the economy there are a variety of types of institutional units, transactions, stocks of assets and stocks of liabilities. Each of these needs to be classified systematically. The SNA93/ESA95 is based on such classifications. Therefore, learning about the SNA93/ESA95 involves a great deal of learning about these classification systems and accordingly this book is much concerned to explain these classifications fully. It is not possible to understand the SNA93/ESA95, even at an introductory level, unless one understands the various systems of classification on which the new national accounts are based.

A grouping of institutional units, each grouping comprising a similar type of institutional unit, is known as a *sector* of the economy. The sectors of the economy depend upon a systematic classification of institutional units.

The system of national accounts established under the SNA93/ESA95 record and report for each sector of the economy separately and for the economy as a whole:

1.   aggregates of transactions with balancing items; and
2.   aggregates of stocks of assets and of liabilities with balancing items.

The accounts for transactions are arranged in a sequence, where the balancing item on one account is carried down to the account next in sequence. The balancing items thus form the connections between the accounts in the sequence.

In order to understand all this fully, the next section explains the SNA93/ESA95 sectors of the economy, and the sections following explain the SNA93/ESA95 sequence of accounts with intervening explanations of the concept and types of transactions and of the SNA93/ESA95 classification of assets and liabilities.

1.3   Sectors of the economy

A sector of the economy is a grouping of institutional units where the grouping is based on a similarity or similarities among the institutional units so grouped together.

Figure 1.2 shows my basic classification scheme for institutional units with, towards the bottom of the diagram and in bold, the five SNA93/ESA95 (resident) sectors of the economy. I start with a global view of all the institutional units in the world. From the point of view of a particular economy, there is one important similarity of type to consider: is the institutional unit a resident of the particular economy or is it not a resident?

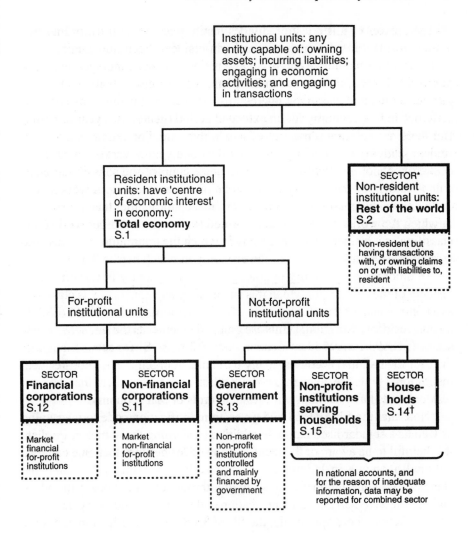

Figure 1.2   Sectors of the economy

The answer to this question divides institutional units globally into two groups: resident institutional units and non-resident institutional units.

An institutional unit is classified as a resident of an economy when it has 'a centre of economic interest' in the economic territory of that country. The phrase 'a centre of economic interest' usually means engaging in economic activities in that economy for an extended period (generally a year or more). But there are commonsense exceptions to this rule. For example, a foreign student studying in a country for more than one year nevertheless retains a centre of economic interest in his or her home country and so is classified as a non-resident of the country in which he or she is studying. A worker who daily or weekly crosses a frontier to work in a country other than the country in which the worker's household is located (known as a 'border worker') is classified as a resident of the economy in which the household is located and is, conversely, a non-resident of the economy in which he/she works.

An embassy of a country operating in another country is classified as a resident of the country for which it is an embassy and conversely is classified as a non-resident of the country in which it is operating. In the SNA93/ESA95 all non-resident institutional units are grouped together as the *rest of the world* sector (SNA93/ESA95 identification code S.2 with 'S' for sector), but note that, for the national accounts of any particular economy, these non-resident institutional units are taken into consideration only to the extent that the non-resident units have dealings with resident units of that economy.

(Note that the SNA93/ESA95 gives an identification code to everything as well as a standardised name. In addition to learning the names in English, it is helpful to be aware of the identification codes because then one can read national accounts in languages other than English simply by using the standardised code numbers. Accordingly, throughout this book I introduce and use the SNA93/ESA95 identification codes. In each and every table, and in each figure where applicable, the SNA93/ESA95 identification codes are always given in addition to the names of the items. The SNA93/ESA95 identification codes are usually alpha-numeric and comprise: (i) a letter of the alphabet (chosen as a mnemonic – as in the case of 'S' for 'sector' – and generally upper-case followed by a full point); and (ii) a number in a hierarchical system of numbering.)

The rest of the world is treated as a sector pertaining to the economy only insofar as there are transactions between residents and non-residents or only insofar as residents own claims on or owe liabilities to non-residents. Transactions between residents and non-residents may be called 'international transactions' or 'external transactions'; assets and liabilities involving, on the one hand, a resident and, on the other hand, a non-resident may be called 'international assets' and 'international liabilities'.

In the SNA93/ESA95, accounts for international transactions are known as *external accounts* and these tend to be summary accounts. There is also published, in a separate publication, a set of accounts known as *balance of payments* accounts; these are the detailed accounts for international transactions and for international assets and liabilities. The balance of payments accounts are published according to the conventions and nomenclature of the International Monetary Fund, *Balance of Payments Manual Fifth Edition*, this system of balance of payments accounts being referred to as the BPM5. The BPM5 is based on the SNA93 and is therefore consistent with the SNA93.

The balancing items in these balance of payments accounts are, as we shall see in subsequent chapters, very significant to an economy. (For future reference, note that there are five almost synonymous terms: 'international', 'external', 'rest of the world', 'foreign', and 'abroad'. There is also the term 'overseas' which is no longer used in any context. The use of these five terms is not definitively standardised under the SNA93/ESA95 as implemented in countries' national accounts; however, the context usually makes it very clear what is intended. The use of these five terms will be exemplified in Chapter 5 on external transactions, but until then the reader should be prepared to encounter any one of the five.)

Any particular economy is defined in terms of, and is constituted by, its resident institutional units with an identification code starting with 'S.1'.

I divide resident institutional units into two main categories: those institutional units whose fundamental purpose is to make, or at least to try to make, a profit; and those institutional units whose fundamental purpose is other than to make a profit. In Figure 1.2, I call the former 'for-profit institutional units' and the latter 'not-for-profit institutional units'. I use these terms not only to draw attention to the purpose, or intention, as the basis of the classification but also to differentiate between these terms (which are not used in the SNA93/ESA95) and the term 'non-profit institution' which is used in the SNA93/ESA95 but in a more restricted sense. The difficulties of classifying non-profit institutions will be discussed separately in due course.

For-profit institutional units are classified into two formally designated sectors of the economy: *financial corporations*, S.12, and *non-financial corporations*, S.11. (But note that there is an awkward category of unincorporated businesses owned and run by households which make a 'profit-type' income for their owners and which are included in the household sector.)

A corporation is a legal entity – an institutional unit – distinct from its owners (other institutional units) which is created in order to make a profit for its owners by producing goods or services for sale in the market or by engaging in financial transactions.

Financial corporations are corporations mainly engaged in financial activities, such as deposit-taking and on-lending the money so received (the activity technically described in economics as 'financial intermediation'), or in auxiliary financial activities, such as giving investment advice (where the auxiliary's activities are closely related to financial intermediation), or in insurance and pension funds (these are those corporations which are, as a fundamental description of their activity, concerned with the pooling of risks).

Non-financial corporations are those corporations who are market producers producing goods and non-financial services.

Under the prescriptive conventions of the ESA95, the term 'market producer' means that the producer covers more than half the costs of production from sales receipts.

Not-for-profit institutions are classified into three formally designated sectors of the economy: *general government*, S.13; *households*, S.14; and *non-profit institutions serving households*, S.15.

General government comprises: central (that is, nationwide) government; state governments (where applicable); and local governments. In the term 'general government' the force of the word 'general' is to exclude any for-profit corporation owned by general government (at any level – central, state, or local). Note that general government, S.13, includes the social security funds of general government.

The household sector contains all the resident persons in the economy mainly living in households, but also including persons living long-term in institutions such as retirement homes, hospitals, prisons, and so on. The household sector also includes household businesses in those cases where the accounts and balance sheets of the household and of the household's business cannot meaningfully be separated and distinguished one from the other. But partnerships are treated as distinct institutional units and are allocated either to non-financial corporations or to financial corporations, depending upon activity.

A non-profit institution is a legal or social entity which produces goods or services but whose status does not permit it to be a source of profit, income, or financial gain to the institutional units who are its members or who finance or control the non-profit institution.

The rules for classifying non-profit institutions are shown in Figure 1.3. It is important to understand at the outset that non-profit institutions include

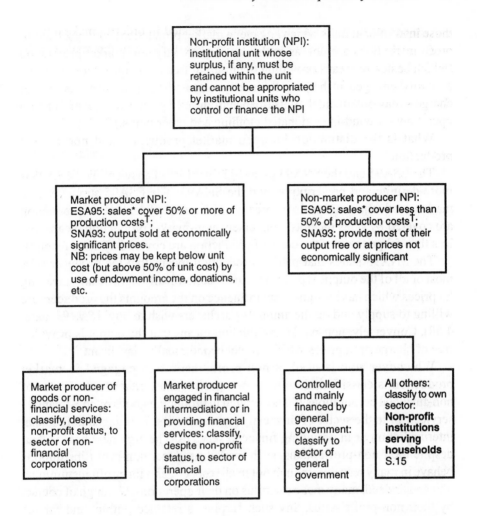

* Sales include subscriptions by business members to a non-profit institution created to serve the interests of business (in this case, subscriptions are treated as payments for services and not as transfers) but does not include other subscriptions, e.g., by households or by businesses for philanthropic purposes, where subscriptions are treated as transfers.
† Production costs are the sum of intermediate consumption, compensation of employees, consumption of fixed capital and other taxes on production.

Figure 1.3   Classification of non-profit institutions

those institutional units which engage in market production; conversely, non-profit institutions are not, as such, confined to only non-market production (which basically means providing their output free of charge). (For example, a charity engaged in helping the needy – providing these services free of charge – may obtain much of its finance from selling – in a market production operation – second-hand donated clothing and other items.)

What is the distinction between market production and non-market production?

The ESA95 and the SNA93 give slightly different answers. The ESA95 is more definite and prescriptive than the SNA93. The ESA95 stipulates that market production means that more than 50 per cent of the costs of production are covered by sales receipts; conversely, non-market production means that less than 50 per cent of the costs of production are covered by sales receipts.

The SNA93 states that market production means that the producer sells most or all of the output at prices that are 'economically significant', meaning 'at prices which have a significant influence on the amounts the producers are willing to supply and on the amounts purchasers wish to buy' (*SNA93*, para. 4.58). Conversely, non-market production means that the output is provided free of charge or at prices which are not economically significant.

Whichever rule is used, a non-profit institution engaged in market production is classified, despite its non-profit status, either to the sector of non-financial corporations if it is engaged in producing goods or non-financial services, or to the sector of financial corporations if it is engaged in financial intermediation or in providing financial services. The argument here is that, despite their non-profit status, such market producer non-profit institutions behave in many respects, though not in all respects, as a for-profit institutional unit and, indeed, many make a surplus on their operations, although of course, by their non-profit status, any such surplus is retained within, and for the benefit of, the non-profit institution itself.

A non-profit institution engaged in non-market production is classified to the sector of general government if it is controlled or mainly financed by general government, and this classification occurs regardless of who established or runs the non-profit institution. All other non-profit institutions engaged in non-market production are classified to their own distinct sector of the economy: non-profit institutions serving households, S.15.

Examples of non-profit institutions serving households are: churches; Girl Guides Association; Oxfam; Red Cross; RSPCA; trades unions.

Non-profit institutions serving business are classified either to the sector of non-financial corporations (for example, the Confederation of British

Industry) or to the sector of financial corporations (for example, the British Bankers' Association), depending upon the activities of their members.

Returning to Figure 1.2, the end-result of the classification of resident institutional units is that there are five sectors, mutually exclusive and jointly exhaustive, to one of which each resident institutional unit in the economy must be allocated:

Financial corporations, S.12
Non-financial corporations, S.11
General government, S.13
Households, S.14
Non-profit institutions serving households, S.15

The two sectors of non-financial corporations, S.11, and financial corporations, S.12, except for the central bank, may be subclassified according to whether they are in public (that is, government) ownership, private national ownership, or are foreign controlled.

1.4   Transactions and flows

Economic activity is measured by transactions and by the resulting balancing items. A transaction occurs when, by mutual agreement, one institutional unit provides something of value to another institutional unit. The phrase 'by mutual agreement' is to be understood as extending to taxes and fines imposed by or under law. A transaction is always an independent, stand-alone flow existing in its own right by virtue of the economic activity to which it relates. A transaction is also regarded as occurring when an institutional unit, acting in one capacity, provides something of value to itself acting in another capacity. For example, if a dairy farmer, acting as producer, provides some milk to the dairy farmer's household, acting as consumer, then a transaction has occurred.

I classify transactions in either of two different ways. In the first instance, any transaction may be either *requited* or *unrequited*. In the second instance, any transaction may be either *monetary* (actual in cash or an obligation to pay cash in the future) or *non-monetary* (no cash changes hands in the present or the future, so a cash value has to be estimated or imputed). I put these two classification systems together to give the two-by-two, or four category, classification system for transactions shown in Figure 1.4.

Across the top of Figure 1.4, I put the requited/unrequited classification. This is a mutually exclusive and jointly exhaustive classification: any

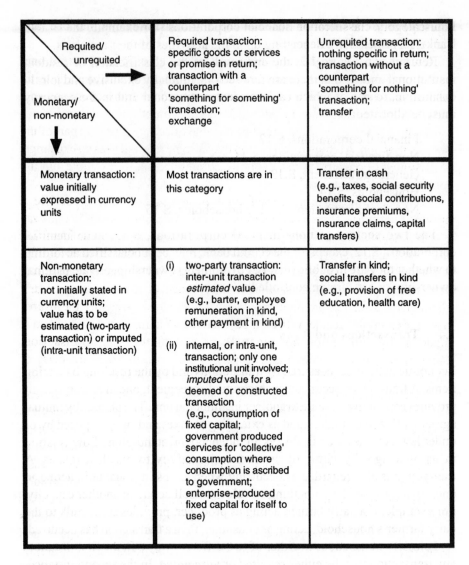

Requited/ unrequited → Monetary/ non-monetary ↓	Requited transaction: specific goods or services or promise in return; transaction with a counterpart 'something for something' transaction; exchange	Unrequited transaction: nothing specific in return; transaction without a counterpart 'something for nothing' transaction; transfer
Monetary transaction: value initially expressed in currency units	Most transactions are in this category	Transfer in cash (e.g., taxes, social security benefits, social contributions, insurance premiums, insurance claims, capital transfers)
Non-monetary transaction: not initially stated in currency units; value has to be estimated (two-party transaction) or imputed (intra-unit transaction)	(i) two-party transaction: inter-unit transaction *estimated* value (e.g., barter, employee remuneration in kind, other payment in kind) (ii) internal, or intra-unit, transaction; only one institutional unit involved; *imputed* value for a deemed or constructed transaction (e.g., consumption of fixed capital; government produced services for 'collective' consumption where consumption is ascribed to government; enterprise-produced fixed capital for itself to use)	Transfer in kind; social transfers in kind (e.g., provision of free education, health care)

Figure 1.4   The basic classification of transactions

transaction must be either one or the other. Down the left side of Figure 1.4, I put the monetary/non-monetary classification. This, too, is a mutually exclusive and jointly exhaustive classification: any transaction must be either one or the other. Combined, the two systems of classification make a two-by-two, four-category classification scheme, and any transaction fits into one, and only one, of the four categories.

A requited transaction occurs where something specific to an institutional unit is provided as a counterpart in return for something also specific to an institutional unit. There is a two-way reciprocity in the transaction, and so a requited transaction may be identified as a 'something for something' transaction. Each 'something' must be capable of being viewed as part of the *same* transaction. A requited transaction may also be referred to as an exchange.

Requited (monetary) transactions are commonplace; for example, buying something in a shop.

Conversely, an unrequited transaction occurs where nothing specific is provided in return. There is no reciprocity; the transaction is purely one-way – without a counterpart – and so an unrequited transaction may be identified as a 'something for nothing' transaction. An unrequited transaction is referred to in the SNA93/ESA95 as a *transfer*. The concept of an unrequited transaction, or transfer, includes such transactions as the payment of an insurance premium: although the insurance premium provides in return coverage against the insured risk (for example, accident, fire), a payment of a claim, if any such claim is made, is by convention not regarded as part of the *same* transaction; accordingly both premiums and claims (which are an awkward class of transactions) are treated as transfers in the SNA93/ESA95.

Unrequited (monetary) transactions usually occur in relation to government; one example is the payment by the government of a social security benefit to a household. But some unrequited (monetary) transactions occur in relation to non-profit institutions serving households (for example, donations to charities) and to insurance corporations (for example, insurance premiums).

A non-monetary transaction occurs whenever a transaction is not initially stated in units of currency. In some cases the non-monetary transaction involves two different institutional units and is called an inter-unit transaction, such as a barter transaction or the provision of free education by the government, and in these cases a value in currency units must be *estimated* for the transaction. (In Chapter 3, we will consider how the monetary value of output provided free of charge, such as education, may be estimated.)

In other cases, the non-monetary transaction involves only one institutional unit; that is, the transaction occurs within the same institutional unit. This is called an internal transaction or an intra-unit transaction.

In the case of an intra-unit transaction, the institutional unit, acting in one capacity or role, supplies something of value to itself in another capacity or role. It is analytically necessary to distinguish the two roles played by the same institutional unit because we can then both construct a transaction – that is, we can pretend or deem that there has been a transaction – and also *impute* a monetary value to this deemed transaction.

Note that for a non-monetary transaction, the SNA93 differentiates between *estimating* a value for a two-party non-monetary inter-unit transaction and *imputing* a value for a (non-monetary and constructed) intra-unit transaction.

Imputed intra-unit transactions are important in the economy and in national accounting. One example of an important imputed transaction, to be discussed in the next section and in Chapter 6 (Section 6.8), is the consumption of fixed capital. Another example of an important imputed transaction is the provision by the government of such collective services as law and order (to be discussed in Chapters 3 and 6).

Unrequited monetary transactions are called 'transfers in cash'. Examples of these would be payment by government to households of social security benefits and payments by institutional units to government of taxes on income. Taxes are an unrequited payment because in return for the taxes the government does not as a *quid pro quo* provide any service *specifically* to the tax-paying institutional unit as part of the same transaction.

Unrequited non-monetary transactions are known as 'social transfers in kind'. For example, the provision by the government of free education is a social transfer in kind from the government to those institutional units (that is, persons in a household) receiving the education.

Transactions may also be subject to other classifications, in particular the division between current and capital transactions. Current transactions relate to the production of goods and services, the generating and distributing and redistributing of income, and the use of income for current purposes of consumption or saving.

Capital transactions deal with the acquisition and disposal of assets and with the incurring and redemption of liabilities.

Covering both current and capital transactions we may also classify transactions under the following headings: transactions in products (goods and services); distributive transactions arising from transactions in products; redistributive transactions affecting the distributive transactions; transactions relating to finance involving financial assets and liabilities; and transactions not elsewhere specified, such as the important transaction of consumption of fixed capital.

We have been discussing transactions, the recording of which is the main business of national accounts. However, national accounts deal with things other than transactions. Transactions are flows, but there are flows other than transactions in the national accounts and the national accounts also deal with stocks of assets and liabilities. The classification of assets will be discussed later in this chapter. The basic classification of national accounts flows is shown in Figure 1.5.

There are three basic types of flows in the System: transactions; balancing items; and what I call 'non-transaction changes in assets and liabilities'. (A fourth type of flow may occur in real-world national accounts: a statistical discrepancy flow which 'reconciles' two aggregate flows, each differently calculated, which should in principle be equal but which turn out in practice, because of the exigencies of compiling national accounts, not to be equal. The statistical discrepancy flow is not included in Figure 1.5 because it is not part of the System as such.)

The distinguishing characteristic of transaction flows is that each transaction is an independent flow existing in its own right (even if estimated or imputed). This is because each transaction arises from an 'event' (or economic activity) which occurs in the real world, such as the purchase of bread or the receipt of wages. Here we must understand the word 'event' to include such things as the consumption of fixed capital or the construction of capital equipment 'in-house' the value of either being measured by an imputed transaction.

The basic classification of transactions has already been described in Figure 1.4, and subsidiary classifications of transactions (current/capital; transactions in products/ distributive transactions/financial transactions, and so on) have already been mentioned.

The word 'current' should be understood generally in terms of recurrent, regularly repeated, ongoing transactions. Capital transactions are those concerned directly with the acquisition and disposal of assets and with the incurring or redemption of liabilities and in this sense are not 'recurrent'. For instance, a household buys bread on a recurrent basis (a current transaction) but does not buy a new dwelling on a recurrent basis, so the latter is a capital transaction. In addition, of course, the acquisition of a dwelling is distinguished as a capital transaction because it adds to the transactor's stock of assets. Current transactions and their balancing items are grouped into what are known as current accounts. Capital transactions, their balancing items and non-transactions changes in assets and liabilities are grouped into what are known as accumulation accounts.

Transactions in products (where 'products' means goods and (non-employee) services) can generally be broken down into an identifiable quantity

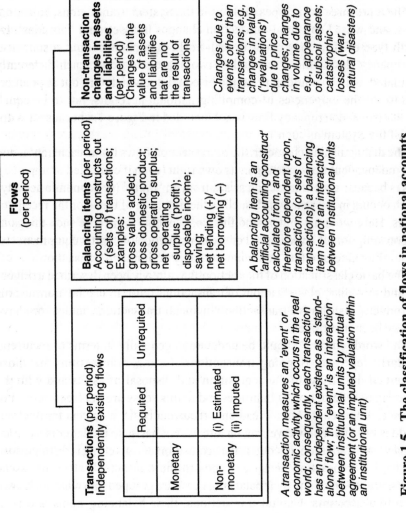

Flows
(per period)

Transactions (per period)
Independently existing flows

	Requited	Unrequited
Monetary		
Non-monetary	(i) Estimated (ii) Imputed	

A transaction measures an 'event' or economic activity which occurs in the real world; consequently, each transaction has an independent existence as a 'stand-alone' flow; the 'event' is an interaction between institutional units by mutual agreement (or an imputed valuation within an institutional unit)

Balancing items (per period)
Accounting constructs out of (sets of) transactions;
Examples:
gross value added;
gross domestic product;
gross operating surplus;
net operating
   surplus ('profit');
disposable income;
saving;
net lending (+)/
net borrowing (−)

A balancing item is an 'artificial accounting construct' calculated from, and therefore dependent upon, transactions (or sets of transactions); a balancing item is not an interaction between institutional units

Non-transaction changes in assets and liabilities
(per period)
Changes in the value of assets and liabilities that are not the result of transactions

Changes due to events other than transactions; e.g., changes in value ('revaluations') due to price changes; changes in volume due to e.g., appearance of subsoil assets; catastrophic losses (war, natural disasters)

Figure 1.5   The classification of flows in national accounts

of the product and an identifiable price or unit value for the product. It is an important characteristic of these transactions that each has quantity units of its own with prices to match.

The distinguishing feature of balancing item flows is that each balancing item is *not* an independent flow, existing in its own right, but is an 'artificial' accounting construct derived by subtracting one transaction (or set of transactions) from another transaction (or set of transactions). For example and provisionally, the flow of household saving per period is an accounting construct derived by subtracting household consumption expenditure (one set of transactions flows) from household disposable income (resulting from another set of transactions flows). Saving is thus not an independent 'event' with its own stand-alone existence and does not comprise quantity units with a matching price as does, say, the purchase of bread. Nevertheless, saving (per period) is a flow of considerable importance and may well be the focus of economic decision-making by the household.

(In the following chapter the distinction between transactions flows and balancing item flows will be fully illustrated.)

The distinguishing feature of the flows which I call 'non-transaction changes in assets and liabilities' is that these flows measure changes in assets and liabilities that are *not* the result of transactions. For example, the value of your stock of shares in a company may increase either because during a period you purchase more of those shares (this is a transaction change in the value of your stock of shares) or because the price of those shares increases (this is a non-transaction change in the value of your stock of shares). Non-transaction changes in the value of assets and liabilities arise from two basic causes: changes in the *price* of the asset or liability (changes which are called 'holding gains or losses'); or other changes in the volume of assets and liabilities. Other changes in the volume of assets or liabilities may arise from such events as the economic appearance of non-produced assets (for example, an increase in reserves of sub-soil assets) or catastrophic losses such as may occur due to natural disasters or war. (Although mention must be made of non-transaction changes in assets and liabilities in any complete classification of flows, it may be some while before there is sufficient data to incorporate these flows fully into the national accounts.)

In order to understand all these classifications of flows, we must consider in turn the accounts for current transactions and the accounts for capital transactions. This we do in the sections following, also considering the meaning and classification of assets and liabilities en route.

1.5   A map of the SNA93/ESA95: (1) The current accounts

The usefulness of a map lies in the reduction of scale and judicious simplification of detail. (There is no usefulness in a map of a scale of 1 to 1!) This section and the two following provide my simplified map, on a reduced scale and with much simplification, of the SNA93/ESA95.

Some (less important) accounts are omitted from the map, and many details relating to transactions are omitted. This is inescapable if the map is to be useful in showing, more or less at a glance, the route from the beginning of the accounts to the end of the accounts, thus providing an introduction to the structure of the SNA93/ESA95 as a whole.

One important SNA93/ESA95 account is omitted from Figure 1.6 because it is a summarising account without a balancing item which stands apart from the other accounts. This is Account 0 Goods and services account. The goods and services account is applicable only to the entire economy because it shows the supply and use of resources by the whole economy; conversely, the goods and services account is not applicable, as the other accounts are, to sectors of the economy. The goods and services account is explained and discussed in Chapter 3.

Figure 1.6 provides my map of the sequence of accounts in the SNA93/ESA95. The 'legend' of the map is that a route, relating to transactions and to balancing items, is plotted through the accounts by lines; the accounts are given as boxes in bold; the SNA93/ESA95 names of the accounts are given in capitals also with their code numbers (comprising roman and arabic numerals); balancing items, both for flows and stocks, are given by their SNA93/ESA95 names in italics. All of the foregoing are common to the SNA93 and the ESA95.

At this beginning stage, some of the terms will be unfamiliar to the reader (even to the reader already versed in economics and national income accounting because some of the terms are newly introduced by the SNA93). As we go through Figure 1.6, I will give a very brief, but provisional, explanation of each term. As we progress through the book, each of these introductory provisional explanations will be supplanted by a full and comprehensive technical explanation, after which each provisional explanation should be set aside.

To help the reader initially to grasp what is going on, Figure 1.6 can be thought of as applying to an individual institutional unit. This helps to make the transactions more understandable. Initially, we shall conduct the explanation in terms of a non-financial corporation engaged in production, and then, at a convenient juncture, we shall switch to an explanation in terms of a household. However, two points must immediately be made: first, that the SNA93/ESA95 accounts apply to *sectors* of the economy – that is, to aggregates of institutional units; and, second, that the full sequence of accounts applies to each and every sector.

The first two things to understand about the SNA93 are that the System is constructed as (1) a *sequence* of (2) *connected* accounts. This is made clear in the official documents at the outset in the following two quotations:

> The System is built around a sequence of interconnected flow accounts linked to different types of economic activity taking place within a given period of time, together with balance sheets that record the values of the stocks of assets and liabilities held ... at the beginning and end of the period (*SNA93*, para. 1.3).

> The [SNA93/ESA95] system is built around a sequence of inter-connected accounts. The full sequence of accounts ... is composed of current accounts, accumulation accounts and balance sheets (*ESA95*, para. 1.61, with my interpolation in square brackets).

The purpose of these accounts, in sequence and as connected, is to record, and thereby *describe*, the results of economic activity.

Grouping transactors into sectors, the accounts must provide a complete record of each sector's transactions relating to what may be broadly described as 'getting and spending' and, because 'spending' is a somewhat limited word, to this phrase we should add 'and acquiring and holding assets and possibly incurring liabilities'.

So the accounts are nothing mysterious: all they do is describe getting and spending and acquiring and holding assets and possibly incurring liabilities. And the sequence of the accounts is simply intended to describe this in a logical order, starting from the obvious fact that in order to spend one has generally first to get.

The accounts are connected by virtue of the fact that we can describe an unbroken route from 'getting' to 'acquiring and holding assets and possibly incurring liabilities'.

The sequence of accounts is also systematic in order to ensure that, by the time we reach the end of the sequence of accounts covering a particular period, all transactions during that period will have been accounted for and nothing will have been left out. The record of the transactions for that particular period is thus a *complete* record.

Current accounts

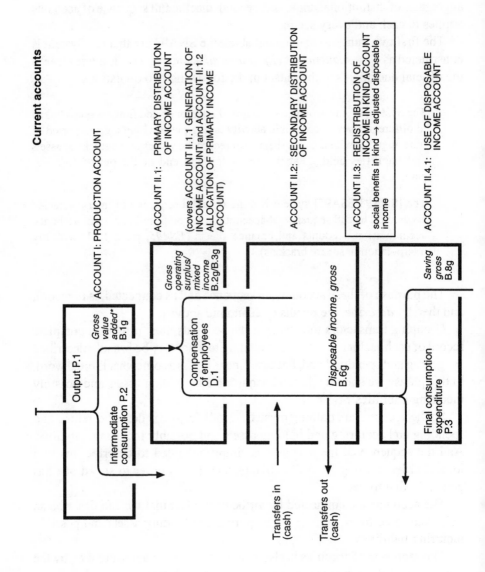

ACCOUNT I: PRODUCTION ACCOUNT

ACCOUNT II.1: PRIMARY DISTRIBUTION OF INCOME ACCOUNT

(covers ACCOUNT II.1.1 GENERATION OF INCOME ACCOUNT and ACCOUNT II.1.2 ALLOCATION OF PRIMARY INCOME ACCOUNT)

ACCOUNT II.2: SECONDARY DISTRIBUTION OF INCOME ACCOUNT

ACCOUNT II.3: REDISTRIBUTION OF INCOME IN KIND ACCOUNT social benefits in kind → adjusted disposable income

ACCOUNT II.4.1: USE OF DISPOSABLE INCOME ACCOUNT

Output P.1

Intermediate consumption P.2

Gross value added B.1g

Compensation of employees D.1

Gross operating surplus/ mixed income B.2g/B.3g

Disposable income, gross B.6g

Final consumption expenditure P.3

Saving gross B.8g

Transfers in (cash)

Transfers out (cash)

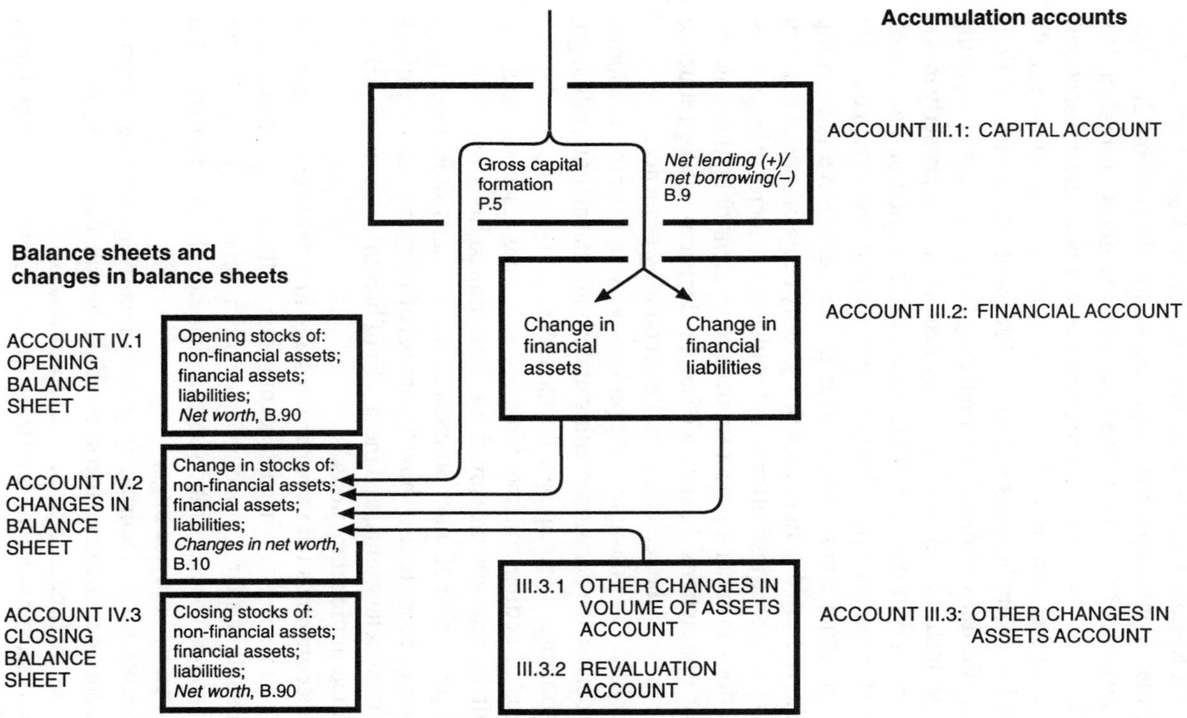

Accumulation accounts

ACCOUNT III.1: CAPITAL ACCOUNT

ACCOUNT III.2: FINANCIAL ACCOUNT

ACCOUNT III.3: OTHER CHANGES IN ASSETS ACCOUNT

Gross capital formation P.5

Net lending (+)/ net borrowing(−) B.9

Change in financial assets

Change in financial liabilities

III.3.1 OTHER CHANGES IN VOLUME OF ASSETS ACCOUNT

III.3.2 REVALUATION ACCOUNT

Balance sheets and changes in balance sheets

ACCOUNT IV.1 OPENING BALANCE SHEET

Opening stocks of: non-financial assets; financial assets; liabilities; *Net worth*, B.90

ACCOUNT IV.2 CHANGES IN BALANCE SHEET

Change in stocks of: non-financial assets; financial assets; liabilities; *Changes in net worth*, B.10

ACCOUNT IV.3 CLOSING BALANCE SHEET

Closing stocks of: non-financial assets; financial assets; liabilities; *Net worth*, B.90

Upper case and numerals denote names and code numbers of SNA93/ESA95 accounts.
Italics denote SNA93/ESA95 balancing items.
* Aggregates to gross domestic product.

Figure 1.6   A map of the SNA93/ESA95

25

It is important to note that the accounts are purely descriptive in their recording and that, conversely, the sequence of the description does not necessarily imply anything about the sequence of decision-making by institutional units nor anything about the sequence in time of the transactions. Recording transactions and describing decision-making are two entirely different things. For example, in the sequence of accounts the last transactions to be recorded are the transactions of accumulating financial assets or repaying debt. However, an institutional unit could very reasonably and properly make, as its very first priority, a decision at the outset of the period on how much debt it wishes to (or has to) repay during the period. The consequence of this would be that all other transactions, prior in the descriptive accounting sequence, are then adjusted to fit in with this priority decision, and at the very end of decision-making the institutional unit could seek to increase its income-earning transactions in order to meet its debt repayment obligations in the light of its other transactions. In such a case, the decision-making sequence would be the reverse of the recording in the accounting sequence.

The SNA93/ESA95 is designed comprehensively to describe economic activity, not to analyse the decision-making underlying that activity, although, of course, the former is a prerequisite for the latter.

The activities of getting and spending and acquiring assets or incurring liabilities result in, and are measured by, flow transactions expressed in monetary units per period of time. So most of the accounts show these flow transactions. Some accounts also show the stocks of assets owned (of various types), valued in monetary units, and the stocks of liabilities owed (of various types), also valued in monetary units.

Each flow account deals with a particular stage in the sequence and, most importantly, the balancing item in each account shows the *result* of that stage.

The accounts fall into three broad groups: current accounts; accumulation accounts; and balance sheets (with changes in balance sheets). In Figure 1.6 these are indicated by bold headings.

Current accounts are for recurrent (regularly recurring) flow transactions relating to production, income, income redistribution (involving current transfers) and current (that is, non-capital) spending.

Accumulation accounts are for flow transactions which maintain or add to assets or which incur or redeem liabilities or which relate to these (capital transfers) and also for non-transaction changes in assets and liabilities.

Balance sheets show the value of stocks of assets owned or liabilities owed (and we here include the account which summarises the changes in the balance sheets).

The flow of gross saving is the end-result of the entire sequence of current accounts and links the current accounts with the accumulation accounts. Briefly, the sequence of current accounts shows how the flow of gross saving arises, and the sequence of accumulation accounts shows how the flow of gross saving is used and, if need be, supplemented.

The balance sheets show, in terms of stocks of assets and liabilities, the results of past and present flows of gross saving and other finance, and the balance sheets also allow for the impact on asset and liability values of revaluations such as capital gains and devaluations such as as capital losses.

We turn now to the sequence of accounts depicted in Figure 1.6. Note that each account is given its proper SNA93/ESA95 name and identification code.

The production account, Account I, shows the first stage of 'getting'. The account has, as an inflow or resource, the output resulting from the production of goods and services. The identification code for output is P.1; 'P.' signifying transactions in products; '1' is an identification number among the various types of transactions in products. A resource is a transaction which adds to the amount of economic value. Conversely, a use is a transaction which reduces the amount of economic value.

Provisionally, output can be understood as sales receipts. (As we shall see in the next chapter, 'output' has a broader meaning than 'sales receipts'.)

If, from output we subtract, as a use, the cost of materials and non-labour and non-capital services used up in producing output – this cost being known as intermediate consumption, P.2 – we are left with the balancing item of *gross value added*, B.1g (in this code number, 'B.' denotes a balancing item, '1' is an identification number among the balancing items, and the 'g' attached as a suffix signifies that it is measured gross of the consumption of fixed capital; balancing items can also be measured net of the consumption of fixed capital, in which case the suffix 'n' is used instead of the suffix 'g').

The concept of gross value added is explained fully in the next chapter, but, as its name implies, gross value added measures the value which has been added to the materials and so on which have been worked on during the process of production. As Chapter 2 explains, gross value added taken over all resident producers aggregates to the total known as 'gross domestic product'.

For the moment, what is important to understand is that gross value added, the balancing item on the production account, is the *result* of production. From an economic point of view, production is undertaken to give the result of positive gross value added.

Consequently, in the words of the SNA93:

> The production account ... is designed to emphasize value added as one of the main balancing items in the System (*SNA93*, para. 2.108).

We need briefly to deal with the meaning of the word 'gross' in the term 'gross value added'. In general, the word 'gross' should be read as 'gross of ...' meaning 'including ...' or 'before deduction of ...'. So the term 'gross value added' should be read as 'value added gross of ...' or 'value added including ...' or 'value added before deduction of ...'. The elision, '...', means that a missing term has to be supplied, and in this instance the missing term is the SNA93/ESA95 term 'consumption of fixed capital, K.1'.

The SNA93/ESA95 uses the term 'consumption of fixed capital' in preference to the more common term 'depreciation' because consumption of fixed capital in the way imputed for the national accounts needs to be distinguished from depreciation allowed for tax purposes or historic cost depreciation which may be shown in the accounts of businesses. Depreciation may in some instances coincide with consumption of fixed capital but the ESA95 recommends:

> Consumption of fixed capital ... should be estimated on the basis of the stock of fixed assets and the probable average economic life of the different categories of those goods. ... The stock of fixed assets should be valued at the purchasers' prices of the current period. ... Consumption of fixed capital is calculated according to the 'straight-line' method, by which the value of a fixed asset is written off at a constant [annual] rate over the whole lifetime of the good [fixed asset] (*ESA95*, para. 6.04, with my clarifying interpolations in square brackets).

Consumption of fixed capital is an imputed flow transaction which measures, in monetary terms, the cost incurred, during a period, of using fixed capital owned by the producer. Consumption of fixed capital is thus a cost of production, but (see Figure 1.4) it is a non-monetary requited transaction. It is a non-monetary transaction because there is no initial monetary valuation to the intra-unit transaction; it is a requited transaction because the imputed cost requites, and is requited by, the services of owned fixed capital as part of the same transaction.

One straightforward way of imputing consumption of fixed capital is the straight-line or linear method recommended by the ESA95. To illustrate this method consider a motor vehicle, to be used as a taxi, with an acquisition cost of £20 000 when new, and with a working life of four years, and (to keep things as simple as possible) a zero scrap value at the end of four years. The up-front acquisition cost, an actual transaction known as gross fixed capital formation, provides the taxi enterprise with the ability to provide taxi-rides for four years. It is not sensible to apportion the entire £20 000 to the first year of providing taxi-rides (with a consequent zero apportionment in each of the following three years).

One reasonable method of annually apportioning the acquisition cost is to do it *pro rata*, apportioning £5000 (= £20 000/4 years) to each year. This allocates the cost of using fixed capital *pro rata* in a linear or straight-line way (so called because the value: Acquisition cost *minus* Cumulated annual (depreciation) cost, decreases linearly along a straight line: £15 000 (at end-Year 1), £10 000 (at end-Year 2), £5000 (at end-Year 3), and finally to £0 (at end-Year 4)).

When this calculation is done with respect to the acquisition cost in the current year, the annual imputed cost is called 'consumption of fixed capital'. (A full discussion of the concepts of fixed capital and consumption of fixed capital (but there called 'depreciation') may be found in Chapter 1 of my book *Profitability, Mechanization and Economies of Scale* (Ashgate, 1998).)

Intermediate consumption is defined to *exclude* consumption of fixed capital. Consequently, when intermediate consumption is subtracted from output (sales receipts), the consumption of fixed capital will not have been taken into the subtraction and consequently the value added so calculated is gross of the consumption of fixed capital, or before deduction of the consumption of fixed capital. Hence the (synonymous) terms 'gross value added' and 'value added, gross'. In a separate calculation, consumption of fixed capital may be deducted from gross value added, and this then gives net value added. (This additional calculation is not shown in Figure 1.6.)

Generally, the word 'net' is the opposite of 'gross' and 'net' accordingly means 'net of ...' or 'excluding ...' or 'after deduction of ...'. However, as we shall see, 'net' is also used in other ways, so it is a word always to be wary of.

Balancing items for flows connect accounts, and gross value added is carried down from the production account to the account next in sequence where it is entered as a resource (that is, as a resource to be used). This next account in the SNA93/ESA95 sequence is the primary distribution of income account, Account II.1. Gross value added is the resource for the distribution of what are known in the SNA93/ESA95 as *primary incomes*.

Primary incomes are those incomes which accrue to institutional units as a result either of their direct involvement in the process of producing value added or of their ownership of assets required for purposes of production. Primary incomes are those incomes which are paid or taken directly out of value added. All primary incomes are requited transactions (see Figure 1.4).

The primary distribution of income account shows the types of primary income and enables the calculation of the balancing item of gross operating surplus/gross mixed income.

One main type of primary income is the requited monetary transaction of compensation of employees, D.1 (the prefix alphabetical code is 'D.' for 'distributive transactions' with the identifying number '1'). Compensation of employees is the (gross of income tax) wages and salaries paid to employees plus any employer contributions on behalf of employees (such as to a pension fund or for health insurance) plus the value of any benefits in kind to employees (such as free meals at the workplace).

When compensation of employees is subtracted from gross value added, the total balancing item is known as gross operating surplus/mixed income. Which is which (gross operating surplus or gross mixed income) depends upon the nature of the institutional unit receiving this residual primary income.

If the institutional unit is an unincorporated enterprise owned by a household or households in which a member or members of the household or households work without receiving a wage or salary, then the income is called *gross mixed income*, B.3g, because the income is a mixture of compensation for labour input and profit for ownership of the enterprise. For example, in the case of a self-employed hairdresser, the income of the hairdresser is a mixture of return for labour and return for ownership of the business.

Gross operating surplus, B.2g, comprises all other types of balancing items left over from gross value added after compensation of employees has been paid and is what accrues to an independent business. The gross operating surplus is the gross income which the institutional unit obtains from its own use of its own production facilities. (This also means that for an owner-occupier household which is engaged in 'producing' accommodation services for itself the balancing item is identified as gross operating surplus (and not as mixed income).)

In order to apportion the residual primary income – the total balancing item on the primary distribution of income account – between gross operating surplus and gross mixed income, information is required about the status of the institutional unit receiving the residual primary income. For present purposes we do not need to be concerned with this, so Figure 1.6 simply depicts the combined total as B.2g/B.3g.

In the SNA93/ESA95 sequence of accounts, the next main account which follows the primary distribution of income account is the secondary distribution of income account, Account II.2.

The secondary distribution of income account shows, for any sector and for the economy as a whole, how primary income is affected by redistribution, both in being subtracted from by cash transfers payable (such as payment of income tax to government) and also in being added to by cash transfers receivable (such as receipt of social security benefit from government). Transfers payable (out) are recorded in the secondary distribution of income account as a 'use', while transfers receivable (in) are recorded as a 'resource'. The receipt of primary income is also a resource for the secondary distribution of income account.

The balancing item on the secondary distribution of income account is called 'disposable income', B.6. (For simplicity, in Figure 1.6 this balancing item is shown only in relation to compensation of employees. Gross operating surplus/mixed income is subject to a similar secondary distribution of income, mainly through income tax as a transfer out, but to keep things simple this route is terminated in Figure 1.6 and the discussion is continued in terms of a household.)

Taking the household sector as an illustration, we have the following definitional equation:

$$\underset{\text{item}}{\underset{\text{Balancing}}{\begin{array}{c}\text{Disposable}\\\text{income, B.6}\end{array}}} = \underbrace{\underset{\text{Resources}}{\begin{array}{c}\text{Primary}\\\text{income}\end{array} + \begin{array}{c}\text{Transfers}\\\text{receivable (cash):}\\\text{e.g., social}\\\text{benefits, etc.}\end{array}}} - \underset{\text{Uses}}{\begin{array}{c}\text{Transfers payable}\\\text{(cash): e.g., current}\\\text{taxes and social}\\\text{contributions, etc.}\end{array}}$$

For the household sector, the cash transfers in are mainly (but not entirely) from general government while the (cash) transfers out are mainly (but not entirely) to general government. Accordingly, an important descriptive function of the secondary distribution of income account is that the account clearly articulates the interaction, with regard to redistribution of income, between that sector and the government. We shall examine this in detail in Chapter 6.

Given that governments have significant policies on the redistribution of primary incomes, it is necessary for the System to be structured so that there are distinct accounts which provide macroeconomic data on such redistribution as it affects each sector of the economy.

However, redistribution involving cash transactions is only one part of the interaction between government and other sectors. The other part is that the government also supplies directly to institutional units many benefits in kind, such as education (free of charge) or health care (ditto).

Thus, the System also has another account to deal with benefits in kind. This account is the redistribution of income in kind account, Account II.3. The net result of this account is to show what the System calls adjusted disposable income, gross, B.7g, where, in simplified terms for households:

Adjusted disposable income, gross	=	Disposable income, gross	+	Net value of social transfers in kind

To illustrate, in the United Kingdom in 1997, household adjusted disposable income, gross was 16 per cent greater than disposable income, gross (£642 362 million versus £554 641 million respectively), and this indicates the considerable extent to which the household sector benefitted from the net value of social transfers in kind (data from Office for National Statistics, *United Kingdom National Accounts The Blue Book 1999 edition*, tables 6.1.4 and 6.1.5, pp. 208 and 210).

Returning from the redistribution of income in kind account, the balancing item disposable income, B.6, is carried down from the secondary distribution of income account to the account next in sequence: the use of disposable income account, Account II.4.1. For the household sector the use of disposable income account shows how disposable income gross (as a resource but with an adjustment which is explained in Chapter 7) is divided between, on the one hand, *final consumption expenditure*, P.3, as a use and, on the other hand, the residual balancing item, *saving, gross*, B.8g, also as a use.

For households, final consumption expenditure is the value of goods and services used by households to meet their needs for current consumption (expenditures on such things as food, clothing, housing accommodation, electricity, furnishings, health, transport and recreation).

Gross saving is the balancing item remaining out of disposable income (that is, after-tax/after-benefit income), after this consumption expenditure has been met. For households (with some detailed adjustment, here omitted but discussed in Chapter 7, relating to pension funds):

Saving, gross = Disposable income, gross − Final consumption expenditure

The System's sequence of current accounts is designed to show the balancing item of saving (gross or net) as the end-result of the current accounts and with this balancing item the current accounts conclude.

Saving (gross or net) is the connection between the current accounts (for flows) and the accumulation account (also for flows). The current accounts, taken as an entire sequence, show how the flow of saving arises. The accumulation accounts, also taken as an entire sequence, show how the flow of gross saving, supplemented by borrowing if need be, is used to finance the accumulation of assets and/or the the repayment of debt. (For the economy as a whole, supplementation to gross saving, if needed, comes from the rest of the world in the form of foreign borrowing.)

The following schematic diagram summarises where we have come from and where we are going and emphasises the significance of saving:

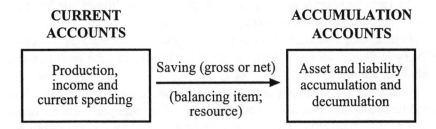

CURRENT ACCOUNTS		ACCUMULATION ACCOUNTS
Production, income and current spending	Saving (gross or net) ⟶ (balancing item; resource)	Asset and liability accumulation and decumulation

Transactions in assets and liabilities are recorded in the accumulation accounts. So before we can continue along our route map through the SNA93/ESA95, we need to consider the definition and classification of types of assets and liabilities. This is done in the next section, following which we consider the accumulation accounts and their related balance sheets.

1.6   Economic assets and financial liabilities

The accumulation accounts for flows deal with the acquisition and/or disposal, during the period, of economic assets and with the incurring and/or redemption, during the period, of financial liabilities. What are economic assets and what are financial liabilities?

An economic asset is any entity which satisfies each and every one of the following three conditions; it must be an entity:

1. which functions as a store of value; and
2. over which an ownership right is enforced by institutional units, whether the right be individual to a unit or collective to a community; and

3.   from which economic benefits may be derived by its (individual or collective) owner, either through holding the asset or through using the asset over a period of time.

A financial liability is a counterpart to some (but not all) types of financial assets. We need therefore to consider the SNA93/ESA95 classification of economic assets. My arrangement of this classification is shown in Figure 1.7. (Table 7.12, pp. 398–400, shows this classification applied to the recording of assets and liabilities in the Australian economy.)

An economic asset is any (very general) 'thing' – or 'entity' in the official definition – which is valuable, which is the subject of ownership rights, and which provides an economic benefit to its owner. The economic benefit is either income or a possible holding gain (capital gain).

The term 'economic asset' is used to exclude other 'things' or 'entities' which might be considered assets.

Human beings are excluded from the purview of *economic* assets because slavery is illegal: an institutional unit cannot legally enforce an ownership right over a human being.

Natural assets that do not or cannot satisfy each and every one of the three conditions are excluded from economic assets. For example, regular rainfall is a very important environmental asset to farmers and a warm sunny climate is a very important environmental asset to the tourist industry, but neither can count as an economic asset.

Among economic assets the System makes a broad distinction between *financial assets/liabilities* (code AF for 'Assets: Financial') and *non-financial assets* (code AN for 'Assets: Non-financial'); the significance of the letter 'A' in 'AF' and 'AN' is that it denotes a stock.

A financial asset, AF, is an economic asset which is either:

1.   a means of payment; or
2.   a financial claim; or
3.   an economic asset which is closely similar in nature to a financial claim but is not a financial claim.

What does all this mean? A means of payment is a reasonably straightforward concept. It is anything which can be used to discharge obligations and is generally acccepted as discharging obligations. There are two main categories of means of payment: first, *monetary gold and special drawing rights* (SDRs) [with the International Monetary Fund], AF.1 – used by governments (central banks) in international transactions; and, second, *currency and deposits*, AF.2, used by all institutional units.

Monetary gold and special drawing rights (SDRs) constitute the one category of financial asset for which there is no corresponding counterpart financial liability: monetary gold is gold owned by monetary authorities as an asset and as part of foreign reserves (all other gold is treated either as valuables, AN.13, or as inventories, AN.12, if held for use in production). Special Drawing Rights are international reserve assets created by the International Monetary Fund and allocated to official holders (central banks) to supplement reserve assets.

Currency and deposits are financial assets used to make payments; these have a counterpart financial liability: a liability of the government (central bank) for currency (notes and coin); and a liability of banks for deposits.

Financial claims are those claims which entitle their owners, technically known as creditors, to receive either a payment or a series of payments (generally specified by contract) from other institutional units, technically known as debtors, who have incurred the counterpart financial liabilities. At the time of receiving the payment or payments (more exactly, repayments), the creditors do not have to do anything in return for the (re)payments. The creditor's claim is extinguished when the debtor has paid *all* the requisite sum or sums specified in the contract.

There are three broad categories of financial claims: *securities other than shares*, AF.3; *loans*, AF.4; and *other accounts receivable/payable*, AF.7.

Securities other than shares are securities that may normally be traded in financial markets and that give their owners the *unconditional* right to receive a stated fixed sum of payment on a specified date (such as bills) or the *unconditional* right to receive money income (interest) and (almost always) the right to repayment of principal (bonds and debentures).

Loans are financial assets created when creditors lend to debtors but the financial instrument is not one that is normally traded in financial markets.

Other accounts receivable/payable are trade credit, advances for work in progress, and other items due to be paid (for example, salary arrears). Other accounts receivable constitute financial assets; other accounts payable constitute financial liabilities. The two are given together because they may be quoted as a net item (receivable net of payable).

Economic assets which are close to financial claims but are not financial claims (because they differ from financial claims in several important respects) are *shares and other equity*, AF.5, and *insurance technical reserves*, AF.6. The institutional unit issuing (originating) such a financial asset (for another institutional unit to hold as an asset) is considered in the System to have incurred a counterpart liability, but the liability is of a peculiar sort.

Shares form an entitlement to the residual value of an enterprise (that is, a claim on what the enterprise would realise if all its assets were sold and all outstanding financial claims against it were settled), and to a payment of a dividend if, and only if, the enterprise makes a profit out of which it can, and does, declare a dividend. (Contrast this with the unconditional right to interest income which the owner of securities other than shares has.) The proprietor's net equity in a business owned by the proprietor is a component of AF.5. Note that the shareholder is not entitled to repayment of the finance subscribed by way of shares.

Insurance technical reserves are, largely, the claims which households are (eventually) entitled to make on life insurance/assurance funds and on pension funds. This also includes prepayment of non-life insurance premiums.

As we shall see, insurance technical reserves are a form of financial asset that is very important to households. For example, each year households pay considerable amounts into pension funds in order to accumulate financial assets from which, eventually, a pension may be paid in retirement.

In Figure 1.7's classification, each financial asset except for monetary gold and special drawing rights, AF.1, has a counterpart financial liability, generally referred to as a liability for short. Consequently, categories AF.2 to AF.7 inclusive are each a category of financial assets of one institutional unit and at the same time a (counterpart) category of liability for another institutional unit.

To illustrate, category AF.4 loans has one institutional unit, the creditor, for whom the loan is a financial asset, and another institutional unit, the debtor, for whom the loan is a liability. Currency is a liability of the issuing government (central bank); a bank deposit is a liability of the bank; securities other than shares are a liability of whomsoever issued the security; shares are regarded as a liability of the institutional unit who issued the shares; and insurance technical reserves are a liability of the life insurance institution or pension fund.

A share is a peculiar type of asset/liability. A share is simply 'an ownership right on the liquidation value of the corporation, whose amount is not known in advance' (*ESA95*, para. 7.52). The nature of this liability for the enterprise is so structured that the share-owner assumes the risk of the enterprise (no profit – no dividend; failure of the enterprise – loss of asset), but at the same time the share-owner benefits from the success of the enterprise (high profit – high dividend; success (growth) of the enterprise – capital gain).

The other main division of economic assets is *non-financial assets*, AN. In turn, non-financial assets are divided between *produced assets*, AN.1, and *non-produced assets*, AN.2. Produced assets comprise those assets which have come into existence as outputs of production processes. Non-produced assets are those assets which have come into existence in ways other than through processes of production.

Produced non-financial assets are classified in three main categories: *fixed assets*, AN.11; *inventories*, AN.12; and *valuables*, AN.13.

Fixed assets and inventories (but not valuables) are coterminous with the word 'capital' as this word is generally used in economics. The definition of 'capital' is: *a produced means of production*. There are two ways in which a produced means of production can be used in production.

First, the produced means of production may be capable of a repeated, on-going use in the process of production. Such capital is known (after Adam Smith) as 'fixed capital', or, synonymously, 'fixed assets', AN.11.

Second, the produced means of production may be capable of only a once-for-all, or once-over, use in the process of production. Such capital is known as 'inventories', AN.12 – Adam Smith's term 'circulating capital' having dropped out of use, but he intended 'fixed' and 'circulating' to be opposite terms, so knowing about this helps to explain the adjective 'fixed' in the terms 'fixed assets' and 'fixed capital'.

To illustrate: a dressmaker's sewing machine – a produced means of production – is a fixed asset (because the sewing machine is capable of repeated use in the process of production); a dressmaker's stock of dress fabric – also a produced means of production – constitutes inventories (because a piece of dress fabric has a once-over use in the process of production).

Inventories are sub-divided into: *materials and supplies*, AN.121 (materials and supplies consists of goods that an enterprise holds in stock with the intention of using them as intermediate inputs into its own production process (these goods are not intended for reselling without further processing)); *work in progress*, AN.122 (work in progress consists of goods and services that are partially completed – that is, not yet sufficiently processed to be in a state in which the good or service is normally supplied to another institutional unit, and whose production process will be continued in a subsequent accounting period by the same producer; if the good is a structure or machinery or equipment not intended for (eventual) supply to another institutional unit but is intended for retention for the producer's own use, the (incomplete) good is not classified to inventories (AN.12) but is classified instead to tangible fixed assets (AN.111)); *finished goods*, AN.123 (finished goods consist of goods

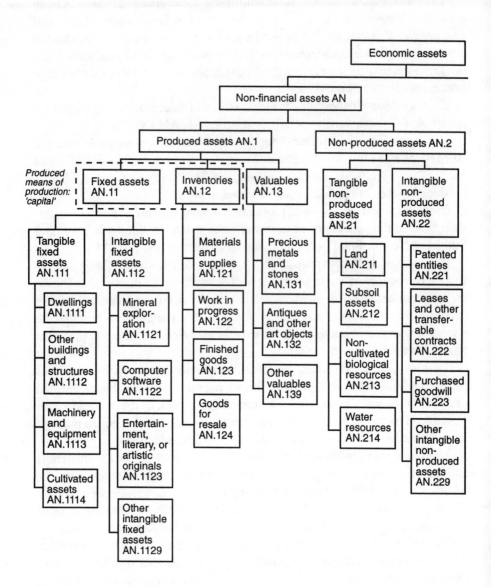

Figure 1.7   The SNA93/ESA95 classification of economic assets

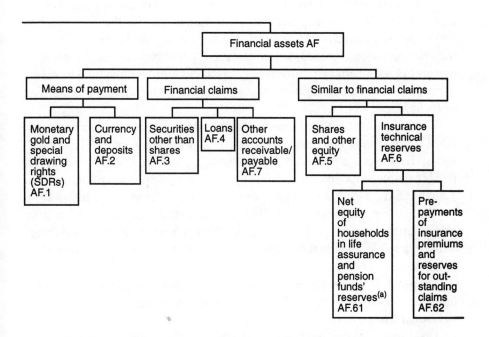

(a) Wording used in the *Blue Book*; *SNA93*: AF.61, 'Net equity of households on life insurance reserves and on pension funds'; *ESA95*: AF.61, 'Net equity of households in life insurance reserves and in pension funds reserves'.

produced as output that their producer does not intend to process further before supplying them to other institutional units); and *goods for resale* without further processing, AN.124 (goods for resale consist of goods acquired by enterprises, such as wholesalers and retailers, for the purpose of reselling them to their customers without further processing other than presenting them for resale in ways that are attractive to their customers (so goods for resale may be transported, stored, graded, sorted, washed, packaged, and so on by their owners but not otherwise transformed)). Inventories are required for the process of production but the quantitatively important part of the capital stock consists of fixed assets, AN.11.

Fixed assets are divided into two main categories: *tangible fixed assets*, AN.111; and *intangible fixed assets*, AN.112. Anything in either of these categories has the common characteristic of being a produced means of production that is capable of having a repeated, ongoing use in the process of production. Tangible fixed assets are distinguished from intangible assets as follows.

The general meaning of 'tangible' is 'perceptible by touch' and a more particular meaning of 'tangible' is 'property with respect to a physical thing' with 'intangible' having the contrasting meaning of 'property with respect to a right'.

Tangible fixed assets are categorised as: *dwellings*, AN.1111; *other buildings and structures*, AN.1112; *machinery and equipment*, AN.1113; and *cultivated assets*, AN.1114.

Dwellings comprise anything that is used entirely or primarily as a principal residence of a household together with any associated structure such as a garage. Houses, units, mobile homes, caravans, houseboats and barges are all dwellings. The cost of site preparation is also included in the value of a dwelling.

Other buildings are all non-residential buildings while structures are all things (other than dwellings and non-residential buildings) which are constructed in, on, or under a fixed location. Structures are mainly civil engineering structures: roads, railways, airport runways, bridges, harbours, dams, water-supply pipelines, sewers, power lines, mine shafts, tunnels. But note that any major improvement to land, such as a drainage system, is classified with land, AN.211, because any such improvement directly and integrally affects, and becomes part of, the value of the land.

Machinery and equipment comprises all transport equipment used commercially and all machinery used in production. The list of types of machinery is very long as each industry has its own special type of machinery.

In order to be classified under tangible *fixed* assets, a cultivated asset must be a cultivated asset that is capable of a repeated, on-going use in the process of production. A dairy cow is classified under tangible fixed assets, but a beef steer (being capable of only a once-over use in the process of producing beef) is classified under inventories (work in progress). Cultivated tangible fixed assets include breeding livestock, sheep for wool, animals used for transport or draught power, animals used for racing or entertainment, plants such as fruit-, nut-, sap-, resin-, leaf- or bark-producing trees or vines (capable of yielding repeatedly).

Intangible fixed assets is a category used to classify economic assets that are a result of production, that are capable of repeated use in the process of production, but which have rather the character of a 'right' than of a tangible 'thing'. Distinct types of intangible fixed assets are the knowledge resulting from mineral exploration, computer software, and entertainment, literary or artistic originals.

Mineral exploration results in valuable knowledge, quite costly to achieve, of where, and where not, to mine for minerals; mineral exploration knowledge is capable of an ongoing use in the process of mining, and this knowledge is clearly a saleable asset for whomsoever possesses it. Yet it clearly cannot be categorised as a tangible asset. Accordingly the category of intangible asset fits it best.

The same applies to computer software. A programme to run a computer is clearly an extremely valuable asset to be used in the process of production, is capable of repeated, ongoing use in the process of production, and is itself the result of a process of production. Yet it is in itself intangible, and so is better classified separately from the (tangible) hardware which the software runs.

Entertainment, literary, or artistic originals (films, sound recordings, manuscripts) also are fixed assets, but their value consists more in the rights which can be enforced over them.

Valuables, AN.13, are goods of recognised considerable value which are held as a store of value and are not used in production. These include items such as precious metal, precious stones, works of art, or antiques. Many households in developing countries may systematically accumulate quite significant quantities of such assets to hold as a store of value and even pension funds have been known to acquire works of art as an investment.

All this being said, much of what would be considered the 'wealth of the nation' comprises tangible fixed assets. This category is quantitatively the dominant part of produced assets, and expenditure on acquiring tangible fixed assets is very important to the growth of the economy.

Non-financial non-produced assets, AN.2, fall into two categories: *tangible non-produced assets*, AN.21; and *intangible non-produced assets*, AN.22.

Tangible non-produced assets occur in nature and comprise land, subsoil assets such as minerals, non-cultivated biological resources such as fisheries within territorial waters, and water resources such as aquifers and ground water resources. To be classified in this category these economic assets must be capable of having some (exclusive) ownership right enforced over them, and must be capable of bringing a benefit to their owners.

Intangible non-produced non-financial assets are basically of the nature of legal and social constructs, and are created by either a legal or an accounting process. For example, although an inventor may produce an invention, an asset for the inventor only comes into existence with the granting of a patent right. The patent right is thus classified as an intangible non-produced (that is, legally created) non-financial asset.

This completes our brief consideration of the classification of economic assets. We have to know about this classification system for the following three reasons. First, accumulating economic assets is an extremely important part of the economic behaviour of institutional units and the stock of assets so accumulated is extremely important to the economy as well as to the institutional units.

Second, having a systematic classification for economic assets is the only way we can be sure that we have covered all assets and is therefore the only basis for a comprehensive description of economic assets and of asset accumulation.

Third, systematic comprehensive description is a foundation for analysis, and the analysis of asset accumulation is a very significant part of economics, of management accounting, and of management science.

We are now in a position to continue our consideration of the sequence of accounts in the SNA93/ESA95.

1.7   A map of the SNA93/ESA95: (2) The accumulation accounts and the balance sheets

A flow transaction which results in the acquisition or creation of a fixed asset, AN.11, is known in the SNA93/ESA95 as 'gross fixed capital formation', P.51 (where the 'P.' signifies a transaction in a product).

A flow transaction which results in the acquisition of inventories, AN.12, is known in the SNA93/ESA95 as 'changes in inventories', P.52.

If a fixed asset or an item of inventory is *bought* by an institutional unit it is valued at purchasers' prices (the term 'purchasers' prices' is explained in Chapter 3 and for the moment need be of no concern as it is not presently material to understanding the concepts of fixed capital formation and changes in inventories). If an asset is *produced* by an institutional unit for its own use (and so is not the subject of any market transaction), then it is valued either at basic prices (also explained in Chapter 3) or at its cost of production.

A flow transaction which results in the acquisition of valuables is known in the SNA93/ESA95 as 'acquisitions less disposals of valuables', P.53. Acquisitions are valued at actual or estimated prices payable by the institutional unit which acquires the valuable.

The total of flow transactions comprising gross fixed capital formation, changes in inventories, and acquisitions less disposals of valuables, is known in the SNA93/ESA95 as 'gross capital formation', P.5.

Transactions relating to non-produced non-financial assets are reported in the SNA93/ESA95 as acquisitions less disposals of non-produced non-financial assets, K.2. Because of their peculiar status as relating to non-produced economic assets, this total is handled separately, but must nevertheless be taken into the reckoning. Transactions in land are important but land is in fixed supply within an economy so the acquisition of land by one institutional unit means its disposal by another institutional unit and overall the two transactions cancel each other, except for the transfer costs.

Gross saving is the balancing flow which connects the current accounts and the accumulation accounts, so gross saving is brought down to the first of the capital accounts, Account III.1 Capital account: Account III.1.1 Change in net worth due to saving and capital transfers. Account III.1.1 also takes into the reckoning capital transfers receivable and capital transfers payable, because, as with gross saving, these capital transfers (to be explained in Chapter 7) affect the ability of the institutional unit to finance the acquisition of assets.

The purpose of the capital account is to record the transactions acquiring *non-financial* assets during the period (net of any disposals during that period). Accordingly, these acquisitions (less disposals) are recorded in the account under the obvious heading 'Changes in assets'.

The flow of gross saving is the main source of finance to pay for these changes in assets, so the flow of gross saving is reported under the counterpart heading 'Changes in liabilities and net worth'. This is a rather peculiar heading: why should gross saving be counted a change in liabilities? This heading can be explained as follows (ignoring consumption of fixed capital).

If the gross saving is from a producing unit – an enterprise – then the flow of gross saving will add to the net worth of the enterprise but the net worth of the enterprise is a *liability to* the other institutional units which are the owners of the enterprise; conversely, of course, the net worth of an enterprise is an *asset of* the owners of the enterprise. Thus, for enterprises, the flow of gross saving constitutes a change in a *liability*, and of course corresponding to this liability the enterprise will own the fixed and other assets acquired.

If the gross saving is a flow from a household or government, then that flow of gross saving adds directly to the net worth of the household or government, because households and governments are not owned by other institutional units in the way that enterprises are owned. So, in this case, gross saving is directly a change in net worth.

Hence the heading in the capital account for gross saving: 'Changes in liabilities and net worth'. On the capital account, the flow of gross saving may be supplemented by capital transfers; these transfers (in) are payments received as a 'gift' – that is, without the creation of a future obligation. Generally, the transfers are from general government to enterprises to assist with gross fixed capital formation.

When the flow of total gross capital formation plus acquisitions less disposals of non-produced non-financial assets is subtracted from the flow of gross saving (supplemented by capital transfers, if these exist), the resulting balancing item on the capital account is called 'net lending (+)/net borrowing (–)', B.9. (The meaning of this name will be explained in Chapter 7.)

The balancing item on the capital account, net lending (+)/net borrowing (–) is carried down to the next account in the sequence of accounts: Account III.2: Financial account.

The financial account is the account for the acquisition and disposal of financial assets and for the incurring or redemption of financial liabilities, all occuring through transactions (and only through transactions). The financial account shows the types of financial assets and liabilities – the types of 'financial instruments' – which are the subject of such financial transactions.

Note that in Figure 1.6, the box for the financial account III.2 has only one opening for bringing down net lending (+)/net borrowing (–) from the capital account, but unlike all the other accounts for flows the financial account has no exits for balancing or other items.

This is because the financial account is the last account, in the sequence of accounts, to have transactions between institutional units. The financial account brings to a close all the accounts for transactions and so it has no distinct balancing item. The financial account simply shows what happens to the final B.9 balancing item in the descriptive sequence of accounts.

However, although we have finished with transactions, we have not finished with all the accounts because the SNA93/ESA95 contains four more main accounts. These accounts all deal with matters which are not transactions.

First, some financial assets may increase or decrease in value because their value, at a point in time, is determined on the market for assets where prices of assets can rise or fall. Such price changes lead to changes in the value of assets and these changes are not due to any transactions but are due to revaluations of assets.

It is also the case that some assets may occasionally (and exceptionally) be reduced in value by 'catastrophic losses', such as hurricanes, floods or war, while some assets may occasionally be discovered, such as a new deposit of gold or a new oilfield. Again, such changes in the value of assets are not due to transactions.

Such changes in asset values are recorded in the SNA93/ESA95 in Account III.3: Other changes in assets account. Account III.3 is sub-divided into two sub-accounts: Account III.3.2 for changes in the value of assets due to revaluations; and Account III.3.1 for (non-transactions) changes in assets due to factors other than revaluations.

Second, the SNA93/ESA95 records, in Account IV.1: Opening balance sheet, the values of all the types of assets and liabilities at the beginning of the period.

A balance sheet is a statement of the values of the economic assets (both non-financial and financial) and of the financial liabilities owed at a particular date. The values recorded are at the prices prevailing on that particular date.

For any particular sector (or indeed any particular institutional unit), the balancing item in the balance sheet has a very great significance. The balancing item which exists at a moment in time because it is the difference between two stocks, is called *net worth*, B.90.

The following equation defines the balancing item in the balance sheet:

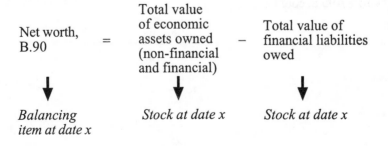

Net worth is a measure of wealth. It is easy to see what net worth means for an individual institutional unit, for example your household. Your household's net worth is the total value of all the assets (non-financial and financial) that your household owns net of (or minus) the value of all the financial liabilities your household owes.

This concept of net worth can be extended to a sector of the economy. A sector's net worth is the total value of all assets (non-financial and financial) owned net of the value of all financial liabilities owed.

For the economy as a whole, net worth is the value of all the non-financial assets owned by resident institutional units plus the value of financial assets owned, by resident institutional units, in the form of monetary gold, Special Drawing Rights and claims on non-resident institutional units, *minus* the value of financial liabilities which resident institutional units owe to non-resident institutional units.

Third, in Account IV.2: Changes in balance sheet, the SNA93/ESA95 brings together: (1) the transactions from the capital account (which affect the value of stocks of non-financial assets); (2) the transactions from the financial account (which affect the value of the stocks of financial assets and liabilities); and (3) the events from the Other changes in assets accounts (which can affect the value of any type of economic asset).

Fourth and finally, when the changes in assets and liabilities described in Account IV.2 are added to the asset values and liability values of the opening balance sheet, Account IV.1, the result is Account IV.3: Closing balance sheet, which gives the values, at end-of-period prices, of all the assets and liabilities existing at the end of the period.

Comparing the net worth of the closing balance sheet with the net worth of the opening balance sheet then shows the change in net worth during the period.

This concludes our map of the SNA93/ESA95. The next chapter explains the balancing item on the production account, gross value added and its related SNA93/ESA95 accounts.

2 Gross Value Added and Gross Domestic Product

2.1 Introduction

The System of National Accounts 1993 (the SNA93) is based on a very explicit treatment of the *gross value added* resulting from the production of *output* and of the distribution of gross value added as *primary income*. There is also an explicit recognition and treatment of the value added tax (VAT) known in some countries (Canada, Australia, New Zealand) as the goods and services tax (GST). (Because of this dual terminology used internationally, value added-type taxes will be referred to under the abbreviation 'VAT/GST'.) This tax has become a major source of government revenue especially in the economies of the European Union whose national accounts are now to be published under the European System of Accounts 1995 (the ESA95).

The first step – and the absolutely basic and extremely important step – in understanding the SNA93/ESA95 is to understand the concept of gross value added. Thence we can understand the concept of gross domestic product. Thence also we can understand the concept and categories of primary income, which are the incomes distributed or taken out of gross value added. Understanding the concept of gross value added also requires an explanation of the concepts of the economic activity of production and the concepts of products and output resulting from production. We need also to understand the concept and categories of final expenditure and the important relationship between gross value added and final expenditure. All this is the task of this chapter and Chapter 3 following.

My method of explanation is to use at first a very simplified arithmetical 'model' of the economy (with easy-to-remember numbers) and then to introduce the real world (UK and Australian) counterparts to the model's (simplified) tables. In this way, the basic concepts, the structure, and the underlying purpose and function of the national accounts tables can all be thoroughly understood.

In these two chapters the model economy has no taxes on products (the word 'products' covers both goods and services); specifically, it has no VAT/GST. This model economy is also an economy without imports. Chapter 4 deals with VAT/GST and its impact on the national accounts, and Chapter 5 deals with imports, but first we have to understand gross value added.

2.2   Enterprises and local kind-of-activity units

One point of terminology needs to be dealt with at the outset of any discussion about the economic activity of production and its resulting income: the difference between the concept of an *enterprise* and the concept of a *local kind-of-activity unit*.

Briefly, the term 'local kind-of-activity unit' is used to denote a *physical* 'facility' at or in which *one* particular type of economic activity is carried out. The definition of 'economic activity' in a strict technical usage is:

> The economic activity of production, hereinafter referred to as 'activity', can be said to take place when resources such as equipment, labour, manufacturing techniques, information networks or products are combined, leading to the creation of specific goods or services. An activity is characterized by an input of products (goods or services), a production process and an output of products. ... Activities are determined by reference to a specific level of NACE Rev. 1 ('Proposal for a Council Regulation (EEC) on the statistical units for the observation and analysis of the production system in the European Community', *Official Journal of the European Communities*, No. C 267, Volume 35, 16 October 1992).

The phrase 'the economic activity of production' or, for short, 'economic activity' is often abbreviated to 'activity', and in what follows the word 'activity' should be so understood – for example, in the term 'local kind-of-activity unit' the word 'activity' means 'economic activity of production' or (synonymously) 'economic activity'. (I shall mainly use the terms 'economic activity' or 'activity' as these are the terms used in the official classifications of economic activities. In a non-technical sense there are economic activities other than production – activities of consumption, engaging in fixed capital formation, acquiring financial assets – but in its technical sense 'economic activity' means the activity of production. The SNA93 uses a synonymous term 'productive activity' – a term I shall not use – and the ESA95 uses only the term 'activity'.)

Note that the word 'product' is used to refer either to a good or to a service or to both.

Any single particular type of economic activity generally involves the production of one type of product (or at the most a few related types of product). Any such physical facility for production will be owned by an *enterprise*, which is a *legal* entity.

The problem of classifying production facilities is complex, because the reality on the ground can be complex. Figure 2.1 is used to illustrate the concepts. Figure 2.1 deals with a single enterprise, called 'Acme Foods plc/ ltd'. In the UK 'plc' means that Acme Foods is incorporated as a public limited [liability] company; in Australia 'ltd' means that Acme Foods is incorporated as a limited liability company. (I use bold typeface to indicate the origin of the abbreviations.)

Acme Foods plc/ltd owns five buildings: going clockwise from the north-east, in one building on North Road bread is manufactured and in a separate production facility within the same building biscuits are manufactured; in a building on East Road biscuits are manufactured; in a building on South Road cheese is manufactured and in a separate production facility within the same building ice cream is manufactured; in a building on West Road bread is manufactured and in a separate production facility within the same building pasta is manufactured; in a building on the corner of North and West Roads, Acme Foods plc/ltd sells the products.

Figure 2.1 identifies each production facility not only by its name but also by its official four-digit economic activity classification number (or 'numerical code'), of which two are given. Additionally, for the sake of the present discussion each production facility is also identified by a roman numeral.

The reason for giving two four-digit classification numbers is that the first four-digit number is from the General Industrial Classification of Economic Activities within the European Communities (referred to as 'NACE Rev. 1') – this is the system used in the United Kingdom for classifying economic activities – and the second four-digit number is from the (matching) Australian and New Zealand Standard Industrial Classification, referred to as the 'ANZSIC' – this is the system used in Australia for classifying economic activities. 'NACE' stands for 'Nomenclature générale des activités économiques dans les Communautés européennes'. The original NACE was compiled in 1970, and 'Rev. 1' stands for the first revised version of NACE established in 1990.

(The relevant publications are: for NACE Rev. 1, *Official Journal of the*

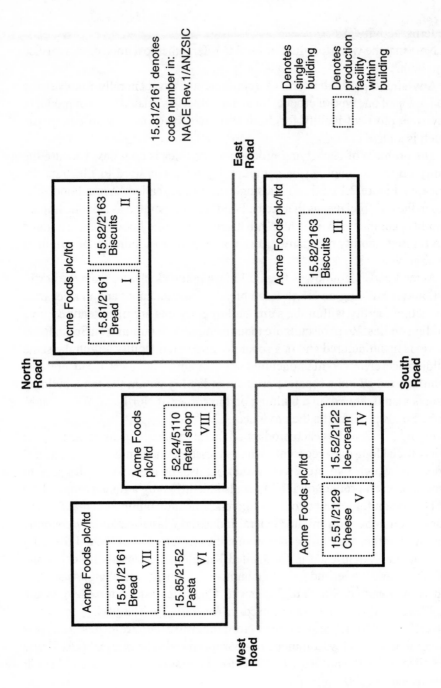

Figure 2.1 Local kind-of-activity units

50

European Communities, No. L 293, Volume 33, 24 October 1990, 'Council Regulation (EEC) No. 3037/90 of 9 October 1990 on the statistical classification of economic activities in the European Community'; and, for ANZSIC, Australian Bureau of Statistics/Department of Statistics [New Zealand], *Australian and New Zealand Standard Industrial Classification 1993 Edition*, ABS Catalogue No. 1292.0/NZ Catalogue No. 19.005.0092.)

Although the following discussion is based partly on the SNA93 and the ESA95, an important explanatory official document on which my explanation is mostly based is the 'Proposal for a Council Regulation (EEC) on the statistical units for the observation and analysis of the production system in the European Community' in the *Official Journal of the European Communities*, No. C 267, Volume 35, 16 October 1992.

The issue of terminology is complicated by the fact that the ESA95 does not use either of the terms 'enterprise' or 'establishment' while each of these terms is used in the SNA93. Making allowance for this, the terms which require explanation are: 'institutional unit'; 'enterprise'; 'kind-of-activity unit'; and 'local kind-of-activity unit' (or, nearly synonymously, 'establishment').

To begin with, the term 'institutional unit' is defined as follows in the ESA95:

> The institutional unit is an elementary economic decision-making centre characterised by uniformity of behaviour and decision-making autonomy in the exercise of its principal function. A resident unit is regarded as constituting an institutional unit if it has decision-making autonomy in respect of its principal function and either keeps a complete set of accounts or it would be possible and meaningful, from both an economic and legal viewpoint, to compile a complete set of accounts if they were required.
>
> In order to be said to have autonomy of decision in respect of its principal function, a unit must:
>
> a) be entitled to own goods or assets in its own right; it will therefore be able to exchange the ownership of goods or assets in transactions with other institutional units;
>
> b) be able to take economic decisions and engage in economic activities for which it is itself held to be directly responsible and accountable at law;
>
> c) be able to incur liabilities on its own behalf, to take on other obligations or further commitments and to enter into contracts (*ESA95*, para. 2.12).

Thus an institutional unit is essentially a concept of a *legal* entity which

can own property, can make contracts, and can sue or be sued. The word
'enterprise' can then be defined as 'an institutional unit engaged in production'
(*SNA93*, para. 5.1).

Note that because government departments are institutional units engaged
in production – for example, an education department and its schools, or the
police force – the term 'enterprise', as used in the national accounts context,
includes these as well as private commercial enterprises.

An enterprise, so defined, may consist of one, or more than one, kind-of-
activity unit, where the term 'kind-of-activity unit' means (1) a *physical*
production facility owned by an enterprise (or more than one such facility
where applicable) and (2) with the physical production facility (or facilities)
being engaged in only *one* type of economic activity, with the type of activity
being specified at the four-digit level in the numbering scheme of the
classification of economic activities.

The term 'kind-of-activity' refers (1) generally to any category of
classification under a classification of economic activities and (2) specifically
to a category of classification at the most disaggregated (smallest) level. Under
the NACE Rev. 1 system which is used in the United Kingdom (and in the
ESA95) and under the ANZSIC system used in Australia, the most
disaggregated level is the four-digit *class* level in the hierarchical system. For
example (with the relevant four-digit numerical code in bold typeface):

NACE Rev. 1	*ANZSIC*
Section D Manufacturing	Division C Manufacturing
Division 15 Manufacture of food products and beverages	Subdivision 21 Food, beverage and tobacco
Group 15.8 Manufacture of other food products	Group 216 Bakery product manufacturing
Class **15.81** Manufacture of bread; manufacture of fresh pastry goods and cakes	Class **2161** Bread manufacturing

Class 15.81 (NACE Rev. 1) or Class 2161 (ANZSIC) is an example of a
kind-of-activity at the most disaggregated level. (Note the hierarachy of the
nested numbering system, common to all such numerical codes, including
that of the SNA93/ESA95. For example, in NACE Rev. 1, 15.8 is part of 15
and 15.81 is part of 15.8; in the ANZSIC, 216 is part of 21 and 2161 is part of
216.)

The technical term 'industry' refers to a grouping of local kind-of-activity units. For example, a grouping, over the economy, of Class 15.81/Class 2161 local kind-of-activity units would constitute the economy's bread manufacturing industry. The concept of an industry also applies to the greater levels of aggregation of local kind-of-activity units.

The classification example quoted above shows kinds of activity at more aggregated levels; for example, Manufacture of food products and beverages (Division 15 (NACE Rev. 1) or Subdivision 21 (ANZSIC – with the addition of tobacco)); this grouping at a two-digit level constitutes an industry at a greater level of aggregation. Aggregation to Manufacturing (Section D (NACE Rev. 1) or Division C (ANZSIC)) also constitutes an industry and this is how the word is most commonly used. National accounts generally report gross value added by industry at the level of Sections (NACE Rev. 1) or Divisions (ANZSIC). Note that at this level of aggregation, the identification code changes to an upper-case letter of the alphabet – an alphabetical code – the purpose of this being to provide the requisite number of categories without having to use very long reference numbers.

A local unit is an enterprise or part thereof situated in a geographically identified place at or from which economic activity is carried out by one or more persons working for the same enterprise.

Combining the criterion of a kind-of-activity unit and the criterion of a local unit gives the concept of a local kind-of-activity unit as that part of a kind-of-activity unit which corresponds to, or is coterminous with, a local unit.

These concepts can now be illustrated with the aid of Figure 2.1 (note that in Figure 2.1 each production facility is given its full and correct numerical code under each of the two systems of classification, but is given only an abbreviated name, not its full and proper NACE Rev. 1 or ANZSIC name).

The concept of an enterprise – an institutional unit which is engaged in production – is illustrated by Acme Foods plc/ltd. Acme Foods plc/ltd is the legal entity which owns all the economic assets, employs all the employees, and engages in economic activities of various sorts. There is only one enterprise in Figure 2.1.

In Figure 2.1, kind-of-activity units are illustrated by:

I and VII	15.81/2161	Bread	
II and III	15.82/2163	Biscuits	
IV	15.52/2122	Ice cream	There are *six* kind-of-activity
V	15.51/2129	Cheese	units in Figure 2.1
VI	15.85/2152	Pasta	
VIII	52.24/5110	Retail shop	

Note that facility I (at North Road) and facility VII (at West Road), despite being at different locations, are treated together as comprising *a single* kind-of-activity unit, because each engages in the same economic activity, namely the manufacture of bread. Likewise facilities II and III are treated together as comprising a single kind-of-activity unit because each manufactures biscuits.

In Figure 2.1, local units are illustrated by:

I and II	(North Road)	
III	(East Road)	
IV and V	(South Road)	There are *five* local units in
VI and VII	(West Road)	Figure 2.1
VIII	(corner North and West Roads)	

Note that two (or more) production facilities at the same address are treated as comprising one single *local* unit regardless of the kind of economic activity involved.

In Figure 2.1, local kind-of-activity units are illustrated by:

I	15.81/2161	Bread (North Road)	
II	15.82/2163	Biscuits (North Road)	
III	15.82/2163	Biscuits (East Road)	
IV	15.52/2122	Ice-cream	There are *eight* local
V	15.51/2129	Cheese	kind-of-activity units in
VI	15.85/2152	Pasta	Figure 2.1
VII	15.81/2161	Bread (West Road)	
VIII	52.24/5110	Retail shop	

Note that the concept of a local kind-of-activity unit applies *both* the locality criterion *and also* the kind-of-activity criterion. Thus the same economic activity at two different addresses counts as two local kind-of-activity units, and the same address which houses two different economic activities also counts as two local kind-of-activity units.

The local kind-of-activity unit corresponds to the concept of an establishment as used in most systems of classification of economic activity, but, as Figure 2.1 makes clear, the term 'establishment' is potentially ambiguous, because it could cover either a local unit or a local kind-of-activity unit. However, if we take 'establishment' to denote the smallest element identified for statistical purposes, then 'establishment' means – and should mean – local kind-of-activity unit. This is the way the term 'establishment' is used in the SNA93:

> The establishment combines both the kind-of-activity dimension and the locality dimension. An establishment is defined as an enterprise, or part of an enterprise, that is situated in a single location and in which only a single (non-ancillary) productive activity is carried out [i.e., only one four-digit level activity] or in which the principal productive activity [at the four-digit level] accounts for most of the value added (*SNA93*, para. 5.21, with my clarifying interpolations in square brackets).

However, a local kind-of-activity unit is one sort of logical concept – a concept of a *physical* facility for production – but an enterprise is an entirely different sort of logical concept – a concept of a *legal* (owning) institutional unit (albeit an institutional unit engaged in production 'in' or 'through' or 'by means of' the local kind-of-activity unit(s) which it owns). On the one hand we have the concept of the enterprise, which is the entity which owns the production facility and which is legally responsible for its activities, transactions, and so on; on the other hand we have the concept of the local kind-of-activity unit, which is the entity which does the producing. We must be very aware of the *conceptual* difference between the two (even if the distinction is often not drawn in practice).

Strictly speaking, all discussion about production should be in terms of local kind-of-activity units because these are the entities in which production involving economic activity of a particular (four-digit) type is physically carried out. However, one problem is that the income resulting from production belongs legally to the enterprise which owns the local kind-of-activity unit. For example, the national accounts data for Figure 2.1 would report the gross operating surplus and the net operating surplus (or profit) for Acme Foods plc/ltd. Furthermore, the payment of wages and salaries is to employees of the enterprise, because the legal employment relationship is between employee and enterprise and is conversely *not* between employee and local kind-of-activity unit.

Another problem is that capital expenditure is legally that of the enterprise. That is, the national accounts data for Figure 2.1 would report gross fixed capital formation for Acme Foods plc/ltd, because the legal entity Acme Foods plc/ltd (that is, its board of directors) is the decision-making locus for capital expenditure in all the production facilities.

A further problem is that the responsibility for remitting VAT/GST to government – a tax arising as a consequence of the production and supply of goods and services – is legally a responsibility of the enterprise and the VAT/ GST arrangements for Acme Foods plc/ltd could be complicated in that it might make one or it might make several VAT/GST returns.

Because we need to deal with the production of output by local kind-of-activity units, with the resulting gross value added, with the distribution of income (by enterprises) from that gross value added, with capital expenditure by enterprises for the purpose of production in a local kind-of-activity unit, and with the payment by enterprises of VAT/GST, in all of what follows throughout this book we simplify by assuming that one enterprise, and one enterprise only, owns the one local kind-of-activity unit under consideration and owns only that one local kind-of-activity unit. We thereby force a one-to-one correspondence between enterprise and local kind-of-activity unit, and we can then make the word 'enterprise' do duty for both. But it should be emphasised that this forced correspondence is only for the purpose of keeping the explanation of national accounts as simple as possible, and is intended to have no application other than this.

2.3   Gross value added and gross domestic product

All production results in a flow of gross value added. But gross value added is a peculiar concept in that it is, as we shall show, a balancing item and so has no quantity units of its own nor, consequently, any prices of its own. (At this point, please refresh your recollection of the classification of flows by looking again at Figure 1.5, p. 20.) Strictly speaking, we should not speak of 'producing gross value added'; rather we should speak of 'producing output which results in gross value added (as a balancing item)'.

We may begin the discussion by using the model economy shown in

Table 2.1. We imagine a simple economy comprising the following local kind-of-activity units: a farm which grows wheat, a mill which buys-in all the wheat and grinds all this wheat into flour, a woodcutter who gathers firewood for fuel, and a bakery which buys-in all the flour and all the firewood, and, using up all these inputs, bakes bread all of which the bakery sells directly to households who, at the final stage, consume the bread. Each of the farm, the mill, the woodcutter and the bakery is a local kind-of-activity unit with its corresponding owning enterprise.

The wheat bought-in and used up by the mill, and the firewood and flour bought-in and used up by the bakery are each technically known as 'intermediate consumption' – that is, the *money value* of transactions on these inputs is known as 'intermediate consumption' – and this term will be further explained later in this section and also in Chapter 3 which deals with final expenditure which is the opposite of intermediate consumption.

The model economy has some households who supply labour services to the enterprises, members of the households being employed for this purpose by the enterprises.

The quantities of each good produced in the model economy relate to a particular accounting period, in this case taken to be one specific year. When each annual quantity is multiplied by its respective price, the result is a flow transaction, measured in money terms, occurring during the particular year. In this model, the euro, €, is taken in Table 2.1 to be the monetary unit for prices and thence the monetary denomination for each flow transaction and thence also the monetary denomination for each balancing item flow.

During the year, the farm's production and sales of wheat amount to the value of €20. To keep matters as simple as posssible, we imagine that the farm buys-in no materials or services from other enterprises for use in production and takes nothing from inventories of goods so we simply ignore the question of seed input. That is, to keep things simple we assume that the farm has zero intermediate consumption. The necessity for this simplification is that it provides us with a convenient starting point for the whole process of production.

In a simple definition, 'gross value added' may be defined and calculated as: Output, sales receipts *minus* Intermediate consumption, purchases. To keep things very simple, initially (and for the purpose of Table 2.1 only) we equate output with sales receipts and we equate intermediate consumption with purchases. This gives us a conveniently simplified equation for gross value added – the equation just given – and we can more readily work with this simple equation in the first stage of explaining the concept of gross value

Table 2.1
Gross value added and primary incomes in a model economy

Economic activity class no. in NACE Rev.1/ ANZSIC	Local kind-of-activity unit, enterprise	€ per annum			Primary incomes	
		Output, sales receipts	Intermediate consumption, purchases	Gross value added	Compensation of employees	Gross operating surplus/gross mixed income
01.11/0121	Farm	20	0	20	15	5 (GMI)
15.61/2151	Mill	30	20	10	5	5 (GOS)
02.01/0302	Woodcutter	5	0	5	0	5 (GMI)
15.81/2161	Bakery	45[a]	35	10	5	5 (GOS)
	Total	100	55	45[b]	25	20

(a) Sale to resident households for consumption; hence this is a final expenditure by resident households, where 'final' means that the product plays no further role in the production process of the specific accounting period recorded in the table.

(b) The total gross value added by all the resident local kind-of-activity units (enterprises) in the economy is known technically as the economy's 'gross domestic product' (but see Chapter 4 for the inclusion of taxes (less subsidies) – not here considered – in the valuation of gross domestic product).

added. I call this equation the 'simplified equation for gross value added'. In the next section we shall explain some complications about output and about intermediate consumption after which we can use the full equation for gross value added, but the full equation can be left for the moment. Consequently the farm's gross value added resulting from the farm's production during the year is (using the simplified equation for gross value added):

$$
\begin{array}{l}
\text{Gross value added} \\
\text{resulting from} \\
\text{farm's production} \\
\text{during the year}
\end{array}
=
\begin{array}{l}
\text{Output, sales} \\
\text{receipts of farm} \\
\text{per annum}
\end{array}
-
\begin{array}{l}
\text{Intermediate} \\
\text{consumption,} \\
\text{purchases by} \\
\text{farm per annum}
\end{array}
$$

$$
= \; €20 \; \text{p.a.} \; - \; €0 \; \text{p.a.}
$$

$$
= \; €20 \; \text{p.a.}
$$

In this calculation, note that the farm's sales receipts are the result of selling an identifiable *quantity* of wheat (for example, 10 kilograms of wheat) multiplied by an identifiable *price* per unit quantity of wheat (for example, €2 per kilogram).

The mill buys-in from the farm the entire quantity of wheat for €20 per annum and during the same year uses up *all* this wheat in production and *only* this wheat in production (in other words, the mill has no changes in inventories of materials (wheat)), so that the farm's sales receipts and the mill's intermediate consumption are identical (see Table 2.1, first row, first column, and second row, second column). The mill grinds all the wheat into flour and during the year sells all this flour to the bakery for €30 per annum. Consequently, the gross value added resulting from the mill's production during the year is (using the simplified equation for gross value added):

$$
\begin{array}{l}
\text{Gross value added} \\
\text{resulting from} \\
\text{mill's production} \\
\text{during the year}
\end{array}
=
\begin{array}{l}
\text{Output, sales} \\
\text{receipts of mill} \\
\text{per annum}
\end{array}
-
\begin{array}{l}
\text{Intermediate} \\
\text{consumption,} \\
\text{purchases by mill} \\
\text{per annum}
\end{array}
$$

$$
= \; €30 \; \text{p.a.} \; - \; €20 \; \text{p.a.}
$$

$$
= \; €10 \; \text{p.a.}
$$

Again, we may note that the mill's sales receipts are the result of selling an identifiable quantity of flour (say, 10 kilograms of flour) multiplied by an identifiable price per unit quantity of flour (say, €3 per kilogram). Likewise, the mill's intermediate consumption is the result of buying-in, for immediate use in production, an identifiable quantity of wheat at an identifiable price per unit quantity.

Accordingly, in the simplified equation for gross value added we can see clearly that the mill's gross value added is a *balancing item* – or the difference between two sets of stand-alone transactions: sales receipts on the one hand and intermediate consumption on the other hand.

Gross value added is thus not an independent, stand-alone, entity – or set of transactions – as is each of sales receipts and intermediate consumption. We cannot point to the mill's gross value added in the same way that we can point to the mill's sales of flour (envisage the sacks of flour leaving the mill and the baker paying the miller) or the mill's purchases of wheat (envisage the sacks of wheat being carried into the mill and the miller paying the farmer). Envisaging these transactions makes it clear that, and how, they are 'independent', 'stand-alone' transactions with 'identifiable' quantity units and prices, and this is important for your proper understanding of the concept of transactions as a type of flow.

By strong contrast, gross value added has no quantity units of its own like sacks of flour or sacks of wheat or transactions relating thereto. Conceptually, gross value added, although a flow for the period, is an entirely different category of flow (balancing item flow) from either sales receipts (transactions flow) or intermediate consumption (transactions flow). This point is most important. We cannot – logically and conceptually cannot – 'envisage' gross value added in the way that we can envisage sales receipts or intermediate consumption. Gross value added is a logically different category of concept: it is an accounting construct for a particular accounting period (such as a specific year), and it is constructed (in the simplified equation for gross value added) as a balancing item arising from the transactions of sales receipts and intermediate consumption (refer to Figure 1.5, p. 20).

Because a balancing item is defined in terms of, and calculated from, transactions flows, any such balancing item must itself be a flow. But, as Figure 1.5 makes clear, such a balancing item flow must be understood as being conceptually distinct from the transactions flows upon which it depends.

The woodcutter gathers firewood as a free supply out of the forest. The woodcutter's intermediate consumption is thus zero, and for €5 per annum the woodcutter sells all the firewood to the bakery for use as fuel. This will be a stand-alone transaction relating to identifiable quantities at an identifiable price per unit quantity; say, 10 bundles of firewood at a price of €0.50 per bundle. By the same method as before, the gross value added resulting from the woodcutter's production during the year is (using the simplified equation for gross value added):

Gross value added resulting from woodcutter's production during the year	=	Output, sales receipts of woodcutter per annum	−	Intermediate consumption, purchases by woodcutter per annum

$$= \ \text{€5 p.a.} - \text{€0 p.a.}$$

$$= \ \text{€5 p.a.}$$

The bakery has intermediate consumption during the year of €35. This comprises the intermediate consumption of flour as ingredient, €30 per annum, plus the intermediate consumption of firewood as fuel, €5 per annum. Note that this intermediate consumption is the result of transactions involving identifiable quantities (of flour and firewood) and identifiable prices (for flour per unit quantity and for firewood per unit quantity).

Using up all the flour (as ingredient) and all the firewood (as fuel) – and conveniently assuming no other inputs apart from (free) water are required – the bakery bakes, say, 45 loaves of bread to be sold at a price of €1 per loaf.

Pause to note that in the bakery's process of production we see two alternative types of intermediate consumption. Intermediate consumption either *transforms* an input or inputs into something else (for example, flour into loaves) or completely *uses up* an input (for example, firewood which is burned as fuel to supply heat). We can thus initially explain intermediate consumption as the value of expenditure on goods and services where those goods and services are transformed or used up in the process of production. (But subsequently we will explain the complications involving goods used in production which may be added to or taken from inventories.)

The 45 loaves of bread are sold by the bakery directly to resident households at a price of €1 per loaf, thus making sales receipts of €45 per annum. By the same method as before, the gross value added resulting from the bakery's production during the year is (using the simplified equation for gross value added):

$$
\begin{array}{rcl}
\text{Gross value added} & & \text{Output, sales} & & \text{Intermediate} \\
\text{resulting from} & = & \text{receipts of} & - & \text{consumption,} \\
\text{bakery's production} & & \text{bakery per} & & \text{purchases by} \\
\text{during the year} & & \text{annum} & & \text{bakery per} \\
& & & & \text{annum}
\end{array}
$$

$$ = \quad €45 \text{ p.a. } - \ €35 \text{ p.a.} $$

$$ = \quad €10 \text{ p.a.} $$

Again, we may note that (in the simplified equation for gross value added) gross value added is a balancing item between two sets of stand-alone transactions, each set comprising identifiable quantities and identifiable prices (on the one hand for sales receipts, 45 loaves of bread at €1 per loaf gives sales receipts, and, on the other hand for intermediate consumption, 10 kilograms of flour at €3 per kilogram and 10 bundles of firewood at €0.50 per bundle – in all of these transactions we can clearly envisage the transactions). However, gross value added is not itself a stand-alone, independent transaction; it must be seen as a concept of a different *logical* category – as an accounting construct in terms of a balancing item.

The advantage of – indeed the necessity for – the concept of gross value added is that it satisfies the following three conditions which are required for measuring the results of production from an economic and from a national income accounting point of view:

1. gross value added is *measurable* for any enterprise or any set of enterprises;
2. gross value added is *comparable* between or among any two or more enterprises;
3. gross value added is *additive* across any two or more enterprises (and this is because gross value added avoids double-counting, as I shall show).

That gross value added is measurable has already been demonstrated in Table 2.1. That it is measurable is a result of the definitional equation (in its simplified version) for gross value added which itself has, on the right-hand side, two measurable sets of transactions: sales receipts and intermediate consumption. In the simplified equation for gross value added, it is important to note that all the variables relating to output and all the variables relating to intermediate consumption are *measurable* variables (and this remains true even after dealing with the complications relating to the technical concepts of output and intermediate consumption – to be discussed in the next section).

Gross value added is also comparable between or among enterprises. This point can be explained as follows, comparing the farm with the mill.

There is a philosophical sense in which gross value added can be seen as measuring 'work done' – usually work done on transforming materials from one state into another (more valuable) state but also covering work done in relation to producing services. Thus the farm has done work by transforming a quantity of wheat seed into 10 kilograms of wheat. The mill has done work by transforming 10 kilograms of wheat into 10 kilograms of flour, where flour is a more valuable product than wheat for the purpose of baking. How can we meaningfully compare the amounts of work done?

From the point of view of physical quantities, the farm and the mill have produced the same physical quantity: 10 kilograms (of wheat and flour respectively). But, when we are concerned with work done, is it economically meaningful to compare 10 kilograms of wheat with 10 kilograms of flour? Surely not, because the two are different products. Producing a given physical quantity of wheat may require a very different amount of work to be done than producing the same physical quantity of flour.

If we should not compare physical quantities, should we compare sales receipts? Looking at sales receipts we can see that the mill's sales receipts are 50 per cent greater than the farm's. But does such a difference in sales receipts correspond to a difference in work done? The farm has to plough, sow, harvest, and thresh; the mill has only to grind the wheat into flour.

Surely we would be right to be dubious about sales receipts being meaningfully comparable when we are concerned with the amount of work done. We could also observe that the bakery's sales receipts are two-and-a-quarter times greater than the farm's, but does such a comparison tell us much about the amount of work done? Surely not.

It would seem that sales receipts are not of much use when comparing or considering the work done by different enterprises. But what happens if we use gross value added to make the comparison?

The mill's gross value added is half that of the farm's: €10 per annum against €20 per annum. Such a comparison appears to be more consonant with regard to a notion of work done. For example, we would not be surprised if the farm had four employees and the mill had only two employees.

As the explanation of gross value added proceeds, the reasonableness of using gross value added to make comparisons between or among enterprises, or groups of enterprises will become obvious.

Gross value added is also additive across enterprises. This means that we can meaningfully sum gross value added across two or more enterprises. This is because gross value added avoids double-counting. This is a most important attribute of gross value added and can be understood as follows.

Take two enterprises such as the farm and the mill where one enterprise sells supplies to the other. The gross value added of the mill can be added to the gross value added of the farm because the deduction of intermediate consumption, in the calculation of the mill's gross value added, means that the sales receipts of the one enterprise to the other enterprise are not double-counted.

To illustrate, first consider the case of sales receipts which does double-count. If we add the sales receipts of the mill to the sales receipts of the farm, the sum of sales receipts is €50 per annum. But the sales receipts of the mill, €30 per annum, includes, and thereby double-counts, the sales receipts of the farm, €20 per annum. Were the farm to do its own milling and sell flour to the bakery, then under this institutional arrangement for production, sales receipts would be only €30 per annum. The aggregate of sales receipts therefore depends upon the institutional arrangements under which production is carried out.

But if we add the gross value added of the mill to the gross value added of the farm, the sum or aggregate of gross value added is €30 per annum. Now consider that if the farm were to mill its own wheat into flour and sell the flour to the bakery, the aggregate of gross value added would still be €30 per annum. The aggregate of gross value added therefore does *not* depend upon the institutional arrangements under which production is carried out. This is because the mill's gross value added is net of the mill's intermediate consumption, and this intermediate consumption is also the farm's sales receipts. So the deduction of intermediate consumption in the calculation of the total gross value added of the two enterprises avoids double-counting and thereby makes it economically meaningful to sum the gross value added of two (or more) enterprises and any such aggregate will not depend upon the institutional arrangements for production. This is what is meant by 'additivity'.

The avoiding of double-counting is a key attribute of gross value added and needs to be thoroughly understood. We can advance our understanding of this issue if we work in terms of physical quantities.

This avoiding double-counting/additivity aspect of gross value added can be illustrated in quantity terms as follows. In the model economy of Table 2.1 the bakery produces and sells 45 loaves of bread per annum. Consider what would happen to Table 2.1 were we to alter the model economy by including a retail shop which buys-in bread wholesale from the bakery for €45 per annum. Suppose that the retail shop buys 45 loaves of bread at a wholesale price of €1 per loaf and sells the 45 loaves of bread to households for a retail price of €1.10 per loaf, thus generating sales receipts for the shop of €49.5 per annum (= 45 loaves per annum × €1.10 per loaf). The retail sales value of the bread includes, and thereby double-counts, the wholesale sales value of the bread (remember that both the bakery and shop sell exactly the same loaves). We can appreciate this point if we are quite explicit about the quantity of loaves involved, as follows:

	Physical quantity of loaves	Price per loaf	Sales receipts, 'output'	Inter-mediate consumption	Gross value added
Bakery	45 p.a.	€1	45	35	10
Retail shop	45 p.a.	€1.10	49.5	45	4.5
Total	90 p.a. (?) or 45 twice p.a.	—	94.5	80	14.5

Double-counting

No double-counting

We can see that the sum of sales receipts is €94.5 per annum. Looking across to the column containing the physical quantity of loaves, we can see that this sum of sales receipts relates to 90 loaves of bread, but there is no sensible way we could say that this economy was producing 90 loaves of bread per annum. The economy is producing 45 loaves of bread per annum, and in the sum of sales receipts (the 'output' of the bakery plus the 'output' of the retail shop) these loaves are counted twice: once in the sales of the bakery and then once again in the sales of the retail shop. In fact, it would seem more appropriate to refer to the total in this column as '45 loaves sold twice per annum'. We can now see that the sum of sales receipts also results from the same loaves being sold twice per annum. This is what is meant by double-counting. The number of 90 loaves of bread per annum very obviously double-counts the loaves. Likewise, sales receipts of €94.5 per annum double-counts, but does this double-counting in (somewhat less obvious) monetary terms.

The next step is the important step. From the point of view of calculating the gross value added balancing item, the double-counting in the sum of sales receipts is counteracted by the deduction of intermediate consumption. This is why the gross value added balancing item is so useful in assessing the results of production.

Accordingly, if we calculate the gross value added of the retail shop as €4.5 per annum (= €49.5 per annum – €45 per annum), the retail shop's intermediate consumption (which is also the bakery's sales receipts) is deducted or netted off, and the retail shop's gross value added of €4.5 per annum can be added to the gross value added of the bakery to give a sum of gross value added of €14.5 per annum. This is an aggregate without double-counting. Gross value added, not sales receipts or quantity of loaves sold, measures the 'contribution' of the retail shop to the economy.

As stated in the SNA93:

> Gross value added is an unduplicated measure [of the results of production] … in which the values of the goods and services used as intermediate inputs are eliminated from the value of output (*SNA93*, para. 6.223, with my clarifying interpolation in square brackets).

Consequently, gross value added can be summed over any number of enterprises to give aggregate gross value added, or gross domestic product for this economy. Any such sum, for the whole of an economy or for any part of an economy, is a measure without double-counting.

Thus gross value added is measurable, comparable, and additive. Consequently, and most importantly, we can, with meaningful result, sum down the gross value added column of Table 2.1 to get the total gross value added of the economy (now not including the hypothetical retail shop) of €45 per annum.

Although each figure in Table 2.1's sales receipts column is an independent, stand-alone transaction, involving identifiable quantities and identifiable prices, aggregating over such data gives an aggregate with double-counting.

Conversely, although the figures in Table 2.1's gross value added column are each an 'artificial' accounting construct in terms of a *balancing item*, aggregating over such numbers gives an aggregate without double-counting.

This is why it is important to understand the conceptual difference between identifiable transactions, on the one hand, and balancing items on the other hand. Generally in economics, balancing items are the significant and meaningful items towards which the economic behaviour of institutional units is directed.

As the SNA93 states:

From an accounting point of view, gross value added is essentially a balancing item. As such, it is not an independent entity. It is defined in the context of a production account, being a function of all the other entries in the account. There is no actual set of goods or services that can be identified with the gross value added of an individual producer, sector or industry. Gross value added is not measured as the sum of any specific set of transactions. As a balancing item it lacks dimensions in the sense that it has no quantity units of its own in which it can be measured, and hence also no prices of its own (*SNA93*, para. 6.224 – the first three figures in the last row of Table 2.1 constitute a production account, as explained in Section 2.5 below).

The total of gross value added over all the resident enterprises (all the local kind-of-activity units) is the economy's *gross domestic product*, abbreviated as GDP and with the SNA93/ESA95 identification code B.1*g – 'B.' is a prefix alphabetical code for a balancing item, '1' is a numerical code (to distinguish it among the balancing items), '*' is a suffix to the numerical code to denote an economy-wide, or 'total economy', aggregate of domestic product with a valuation including D.21 taxes on products (see p. 182), and 'g' is a suffix alphabetical code to denote 'gross of consumption of fixed capital'. As noted by the SNA93:

> GDP is a concept of value added. It is the sum of gross value added of all resident producer units...
>
> The underlying rationale behind the concept of gross domestic product (GDP) for the economy as a whole is that it should measure the total gross values added produced by all institutional units resident in the economy (*SNA93*, paras 2.172 and 6.233).

The gross domestic product of the economy in Table 2.1 is €45 per annum, and in the first instance and in principle we should always understand GDP as comprising the sum (down the third column of Table 2.1) of each of the economy's enterprise's gross value added, this sum being given in Table 2.1's last row. The implication of this statement is that thoroughly understanding the concept of gross value added, both conceptually as a balancing item and practically as to its method of calculation, is an essential prerequisite to understanding the concept of the gross domestic product.

Gross domestic product is basically the sum of all the gross values added, each resulting as balancing item from production during the period, over each and every resident local kind-of-activity unit in the economy.

However, there are many tens of thousands of local kind-of-activity units resident in the economy, and taking a unit-by-unit approach is not a practicable real-world approach to calculating GDP. Accordingly, in the second instance we can understand GDP as follows. If we take the aggregate of sales receipts transactions in an economy and if we take the aggregate of intermediate consumption, then total gross value added for the entire economy, or GDP, can be calculated through the following aggregate approach (but still using the simplified equation for gross value added):

| Total gross value added resulting from production in model economy during the year, GDP per annum | = | Output, total sales receipts in model economy, per annum | − | Total intermediate consumption, purchases, in model economy, per annum |

$$= \text{€}100 \text{ p.a.} - \text{€}55 \text{ p.a.}$$

$$= \text{€}45 \text{ p.a.}$$

The result is necessarily the same as adding down the gross value added column in Table 2.1, but this equation does give us a practical way of calculating and understanding GDP. However, because we have not yet explained the role of taxes on products in the valuation of gross domestic product, this equation is to be taken as a preliminary and provisional definitional equation for gross domestic product. In Chapter 4 (p. 182) we will give the equation for GDP which includes taxes on products.

We need now to complete the explanation of gross value added by considering some technicalities and complications relating to the technical concept of intermediate consumption and the technical concept of output. This takes us from the simplified equation for gross value added to the full equation for gross value added.

2.4   Intermediate consumption and output under accrual accounting

In the discussion so far of gross value added resulting from production by a local kind-of-activity unit (which we can also identify with an enterprise under our simplifying assumption), we have been using a simplified equation for gross value added, which can also be given in a more explicit and annotated version as:

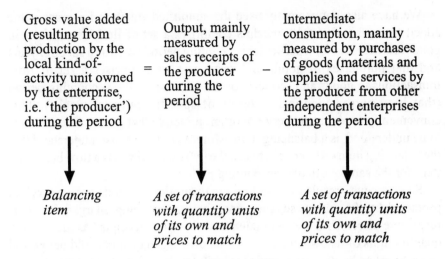

| Gross value added (resulting from production by the local kind-of-activity unit owned by the enterprise, i.e. 'the producer') during the period | = | Output, mainly measured by sales receipts of the producer during the period | − | Intermediate consumption, mainly measured by purchases of goods (materials and supplies) and services by the producer from other independent enterprises during the period |

| *Balancing item* | *A set of transactions with quantity units of its own and prices to match* | *A set of transactions with quantity units of its own and prices to match* |

The full and proper definition of 'gross value added' is simply:

Gross value added is defined as the value of output less the value of intermediate consumption (*SNA93*, para. 6.4; also paras 6.222–6.224).

Accordingly, the full equation for gross value added is (taking the phrase 'value of' as understood):

Gross value added = Output − Intermediate consumption

Understanding this full equation for gross value added requires that we understand more about the technical concepts of output and intermediate consumption, especially with regard to the complications arising from the time at which things are to be recorded but also with regard to types of output other than the type of output which results in sales receipts. It is a reasonable simplification of this definition, for the purpose of initial understanding, to define 'gross value added' as 'Output, sales receipts *minus* Intermediate consumption, purchases' where 'purchases' refers to goods and services bought-in by the enterprise. This is because in the greatly simplified economy of Table 2.1 output can be measured in a simplified way by sales receipts (that is, the products produced during a period are mostly sold during the same period and the cash from sales is received during that same period), and intermediate consumption can be measured in a simplified way by purchases of goods (mostly in the form of materials and supplies) and purchases of services.

We have also conveniently used the simplified equation for gross value added to explain that sales receipts comprises a set of flow transactions in goods and services for a particular accounting period (such as a specific year) and that purchases of goods and services also comprises a set of flow transactions in goods and services for the same particular accounting period (that is, a period identical in terms of specific calendar weeks). This conveniently explains the very important principle that gross value added is to be understood as a balancing item. Moreover, we can also understand that the balancing item difference between the two sets of flows is a flow balancing item for the same particular accounting period.

Sales receipts result from selling the quantities of goods and/or services produced by the enterprise, each good or service being charged for at its respective price. Thus we can understand that sales receipts has identifiable quantity units of its own and prices of its own. Each quantity sold per period and multiplied by its relevant price constitutes the value of a transaction, and total sales receipts for the period is the aggregate of all such transactions for the period.

Likewise we can understand that purchases of goods and services from other independent establishments are the result of transactions involving the buying-in of the quantities of goods and services used by the enterprise, each unit of good or service being paid for at its respective price. Thus intermediate consumption is made up of a set of identifiable quantity units of its own together with a set of identifiable prices of its own.

By contrast we can then understand the important proposition that gross value added, as a balancing item, does not have any quantity units, nor any prices, of its own.

But there is more to output than sales receipts and there is more to intermediate consumption than purchases of goods and services. Specific issues arise in relation to output and intermediate consumption because of what is known as accrual accounting, and these issues, which are fundamental to understanding the basic concepts of output and intermediate consumption, are now explained in turn: first for intermediate consumption; then for output.

Fully explaining the concepts of intermediate consumption and output is a lengthy task which will be spread over part of the rest of this chapter, much of the next chapter, and considerable parts of other chapters. The structure of these concepts is so complex that it is not possible to provide a complete explanation in one go; the reader must be prepared patiently and persistently to accumulate a full understanding only over many stages of explanation. In this section I will explain some initial basic matters which must be understood in relation to these concepts.

Throughout this explanation, I simplify by assuming that all prices are stable. The problems raised by price inflation, although very important, do not need to be dealt with in the present context.

Another important general exclusion is that, until we have discussed taxes on products in Chapter 4, we will not deal with how these taxes affect the valuation of output. In Chapter 4, I will explain output valued at basic prices, output valued at purchaser's prices, and GDP at market prices. But until Chapter 4 these matters will generally be held in abeyance.

First, I deal with the concept of intermediate consumption.

With regard to intermediate consumption in the explicit annotated version of the simplified equation for gross value added, note that 'other independent enterprises' *excludes* the enterprise's own employees; that is, purchases of labour services from own employees is excluded from intermediate consumption. In other words, an employee as such does not constitute an independent enterprise. Note also that intermediate consumption excludes consumption of fixed capital. Consequently value added is gross of, or before deduction of, consumption of fixed capital. Always remember that the technical term 'intermediate consumption' and the term 'purchases of goods and services' *exclude* both the services of own employees and also the services of own fixed capital. Throughout this book, the unqualified word 'services' is without exception to be interpreted as excluding the services of own employees; if we wish to refer to the services of own employees then the term 'employee services' should be used.

Intermediate consumption measures the value of the cost of inputs to the process of production where those inputs are entirely used up during the accounting period but excluding (1) the cost of the input of labour from the enterprise's own employees and (2) the cost of the input of fixed capital owned by the enterprise.

The official definition and explanation of 'intermediate consumption' is:

> Intermediate consumption consists of the value of the goods and services consumed as inputs by a process of production, excluding fixed assets whose consumption is recorded as consumption of fixed capital. The goods or services may be either transformed or used up by the production process. Some inputs re-emerge after having been transformed and incorporated into the outputs; for example, grain may be transformed into flour which in turn may be transformed into bread. Other inputs are completely consumed or used up; for example, electricity and most services (*SNA93*, para. 6.147).

We thus see that intermediate consumption inputs are either transformed in some or other way or are entirely used up by the process of production.

It is a basic and very important principle of the SNA93/ESA95 that transactions should be recorded with reference to the accounting period during which the activity occurs; this is known technically as 'accrual accounting'. Accordingly, the use of materials and supplies from inventories should be recorded for the period during which the use occurs and not for the period during which the inventory was acquired and/or paid for (if the accounting periods for either or both acquisition and payment differ).

The following are three statements about the conventions of the SNA93/ESA95 in regard to accrual accounting for intermediate consumption:

> ... the intermediate consumption of a good or service is recorded *at the time when the good or service enters the process of production*, as distinct from the time it was acquired by the producer (*SNA93*, para. 3.103, italics added).

> Products used for intermediate consumption should be *recorded and valued* at the time they enter the process of production (*ESA95*, para. 3.72, italics added).

> The intermediate consumption of a good or service is recorded at the time when the good or service enters the process of production, as distinct from the time it was acquired by the producer. The two times coincide for inputs of services but not necessarily for goods, which may be acquired some time in advance of their use in production (*UK NACSM*, para. 2.48).

To illustrate, it would be possible to have the following situation:

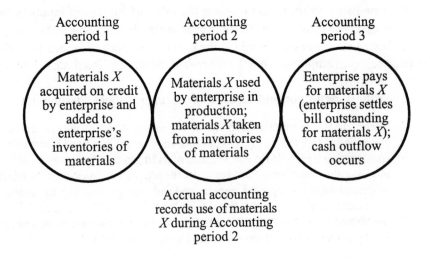

Accounting period 1	Accounting period 2	Accounting period 3
Materials X acquired on credit by enterprise and added to enterprise's inventories of materials	Materials X used by enterprise in production; materials X taken from inventories of materials	Enterprise pays for materials X (enterprise settles bill outstanding for materials X); cash outflow occurs

Accrual accounting records use of materials X during Accounting period 2

With regard to intermediate consumption, the simplified equation for gross value added as 'Output, sales receipts *minus* Intermediate consumption, purchases' simplifies by ignoring these complexities in assuming that all materials (and other supplies) are acquired, paid for, and used during the same accounting period.

As two corollaries of accrual accounting: no materials and supplies are recorded (as intermediate consumption) when materials and supplies are acquired if the accounting period during which acquisition occurs differs from the accounting period during which they are used; and no materials and supplies are recorded (as intermediate consumption) when materials and supplies are paid for (that is, when the cash outflow occurs) if the accounting period during which payment occurs differs from the accounting period during which the materials and supplies are used.

How is intermediate consumption calculated on an accruals basis?

For the purposes of answering this question we may assume that all acquisitions of goods and services for use in production are paid for in cash at the time they are acquired; then we can simply refer to such acquisitions/ payments as 'purchases', where it is understood that purchases are expressed in terms of a monetary value. This leaves the more important question of the accounting period in which purchases may be actually used in production. To discuss this question I will concentrate on goods in the form of materials and supplies. The purchase of services for use in production can be explained quite straightforwardly at the appropriate juncture.

Inventories of materials and supplies, AN.121, are goods that their owners intend to use as intermediate inputs in their own production processes, not to resell (*ESA95*, p. 139). If no inventories of materials and supplies are held, then for any accounting period it must be the case that:

Value of use of materials and supplies = Purchases of materials and supplies

Now suppose that inventories of materials and supplies are held. It is then quite possible, for example, that some materials and supplies could be purchased during an accounting period but not used during that accounting period because these materials and supplies are added, during the period, to inventories of materials and supplies. Using this example we can understand how the use of materials and supplies (during the period) could be less than the purchases of materials and supplies during that accounting period:

$$\begin{matrix} \text{Value of use of} \\ \text{materials and} \\ \text{supplies} \end{matrix} = \begin{matrix} \text{Purchases of} \\ \text{materials} \\ \text{and supplies} \end{matrix} - \begin{matrix} \text{Value of materials and} \\ \text{supplies added to} \\ \text{inventories of materials} \\ \text{and supplies} \end{matrix}$$

A converse example can occur where use of materials and supplies during an accounting period could be greater than the purchases of materials and supplies during that accounting period. Such an example would occur if some materials and supplies used were, during the period, taken from inventories of materials and supplies:

$$\begin{matrix} \text{Value of use of} \\ \text{materials and} \\ \text{supplies} \end{matrix} = \begin{matrix} \text{Purchases of} \\ \text{materials} \\ \text{and supplies} \end{matrix} + \begin{matrix} \text{Value of materials and} \\ \text{supplies taken from} \\ \text{inventories of materials} \\ \text{and supplies} \end{matrix}$$

Of course, materials and supplies can be both added to and taken from inventories of materials and supplies during an accounting period. Consequently we have to put both equations together and write:

$$\begin{matrix} \text{Value of use of} \\ \text{materials and} \\ \text{supplies} \end{matrix} = \begin{matrix} \text{Purchases of} \\ \text{materials} \\ \text{and supplies} \end{matrix} - \begin{matrix} \text{Value of materials and} \\ \text{supplies added to} \\ \text{inventories of materials} \\ \text{and supplies} \end{matrix}$$

$$+ \begin{matrix} \text{Value of materials and} \\ \text{supplies taken from} \\ \text{inventories of materials} \\ \text{and supplies} \end{matrix}$$

Rearranging with the use of brackets and changing signs accordingly:

$$\begin{matrix} \text{Value of use of} \\ \text{materials and} \\ \text{supplies} \end{matrix} = \begin{matrix} \text{Purchases of} \\ \text{materials} \\ \text{and supplies} \end{matrix} - \left[\begin{matrix} \text{Value of materials and} \\ \text{supplies added to} \\ \text{inventories of materials} \\ \text{and supplies} \end{matrix} \right.$$

$$\left. - \begin{matrix} \text{Value of materials and} \\ \text{supplies taken from} \\ \text{inventories of materials} \\ \text{and supplies} \end{matrix} \right]$$

The expression in brackets, the difference between what is added to inventories and what is taken from inventories, is the value of the change in inventories of materials and supplies during the accounting period. That is:

Value of change   Value of materials and   Value of materials and
in inventories   = supplies added to   − supplies taken from
of materials and   inventories of   inventories of
supplies   materials and supplies   materials and supplies

If the value of additions is greater than the value of what is taken, then the value of the change in inventories is positive; if the value of additions is less than the value of what is taken, then the value of the change in inventories is negative.

By substitution:

Value of use   Purchases of   Value of change in
of materials   =   materials and −   inventories of materials
and supplies   supplies   and supplies

In order to ascertain the value of the change in inventories of materials and supplies during a period all that is needed is a stock-take of inventories at the end of each successive period; the end-of-period stock for Accounting period 1 becoming also the beginning-of-period stock for Accounting period 2. Subtracting the begining-of-period stock from the end-of-period stock then gives the value of the change in inventories during accounting period.

Intermediate consumption for an accounting period is the value of the use of materials and supplies for the accounting period *plus* purchases of services for intermediate consumption during the period (by their nature, services must be used, or consumed, as purchased). Accordingly:

                    Purchases of
Intermediate   materials and   Value of change in
consumption   =   supplies and of − inventories of materials
                    services   and supplies

Thus, as stated in the SNA93:

> An estimate of intermediate consumption during a given accounting period
> can … be derived by subtracting the value of changes in inventories of materials
> and supplies from the value of [all] purchases made (*SNA93*, para. 6.151, with
> my clarifying interpolation of 'all' in square brackets to indicate the inclusion
> of services; the same statement occurs in *UK NACSM*, para. 2.49).

Second, I deal with the concept of output.

Output is basically a concept of *all* the goods and services produced in the economy by resident producers during an accounting period, the goods and services having the following two main characteristics: (1) the goods and services are useful and wanted; (2) the goods and services have a market value (or could have a market value estimated or imputed).

The following explanation of output mainly deals with output in the form of finished goods sold in the market at economically significant prices (an economically significant price in the ESA95 definition is a price which results in sales receipts that cover more than 50 per cent of the production costs (*ESA95*, para. 3.19)). Such output is known as 'market output'. In this explanation, I concentrate on finished goods because finished goods can be added to inventories of finished goods. During the explanation a brief explanation will be given on output in the form of work in progress and on output in the form of services, and a brief explanation of non-market output will be given. Thus we will eventually deal with output of all types.

Under the same principle of accrual accounting as applies to intermediate consumption, output for the period should be recorded for the period during which the production of that output occurs and not for the period during which the output was sold and/or paid for (if the accounting periods differ).

The following are two statements about the conventions of the SNA93/ ESA95 in regard to accrual accounting for output:

> The principle of recording on an accrual basis implies that output is recorded *over the period in which the process of production takes place* (*SNA93*, para. 3.102, italics added).

> Output is to be *recorded and valued* when it is generated by the production process (*ESA95*, para. 3.46, italics added).

To illustrate, it would be possible to have the following situation:

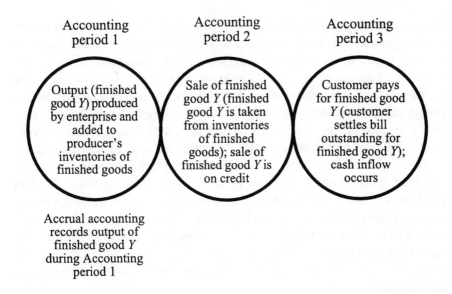

Accounting period 1	Accounting period 2	Accounting period 3
Output (finished good *Y*) produced by enterprise and added to producer's inventories of finished goods	Sale of finished good *Y* (finished good *Y* is taken from inventories of finished goods); sale of finished good *Y* is on credit	Customer pays for finished good *Y* (customer settles bill outstanding for finished good *Y*); cash inflow occurs

Accrual accounting
records output of
finished good *Y*
during Accounting
period 1

With regard to output, the simplified equation for 'gross value added' as 'Output, sales receipts *minus* Intermediate consumption, purchases' simplifies by ignoring these complexities in assuming that all output is produced, sold, and paid for, during the same accounting period.

As two corollaries of accrual accounting: no output is recorded when finished goods produced in a previous accounting period are withdrawn from inventories of finished goods; and no output is recorded when finished goods produced in a previous accounting period are paid for (that is, when the cash inflow occurs) if the period during which payment occurs differs from the period during which production occurred.

Furthermore, and analogously with the problem of changes in inventories of materials and supplies, we must take due account of changes in inventories of finished goods in following the conventions of accrual accounting.

How is output measured on an accruals basis? To answer this question I concentrate upon finished goods; other types of output can then be introduced at an appropriate juncture in the explanation.

For the purposes of answering this question we may assume that all shipments of finished goods by the producer to a customer and all sales of services by the producer to a customer are paid for in cash and in full by the customer at the time they are shipped or sold; then we can simply refer to such shipments/sales as 'sales receipts', where it is understood that sales receipts are expressed in terms of a monetary value. This leaves the question of the accounting period in which the finished goods sold may have been actually produced. (For the output of services, production and sale must, by the very nature of services, occur during the same accounting period – for example, a haircut cannot be produced in one operation during one accounting period and then, in another entirely separate operation in another accounting period, sold to the customer for the haircut.) I also simplify a little by assuming that 'sales receipts' is associated only with sales in the market (which is very largely the case) and is not, for example, associated with barter transactions.

Inventories of finished goods, AN.123, are goods that are ready for sale or shipment by the producer of those finished goods. Very explicitly, finished goods are outputs that their producer does not intend to process further before supplying them to other institutional units. A good is finished when its producer is finished with it, even though it may subsequently be used as an intermediate input by another producer (*SNA93*, para. 10.111; *ESA95*, p. 139). For example, wheat is a finished good for the farm but an intermediate input (materials and supplies) for the mill.

If no inventories of finished goods are held, then for any accounting period it must be the case that:

Value of production of finished goods = Sales receipts for finished goods

Now suppose that inventories of finished goods are held. It is then quite possible, for example, that some finished goods could be sold during an accounting period but not produced during that accounting period because these finished goods are taken from inventories of finished goods. Using this example we can understand that the production of finished goods (during the period) could be less than the sales of finished goods during that accounting period:

$$\begin{matrix} \text{Value of} \\ \text{production of} \\ \text{finished goods} \end{matrix} = \begin{matrix} \text{Sales receipts} \\ \text{for finished} \\ \text{goods} \end{matrix} - \begin{matrix} \text{Value of finished goods} \\ \text{taken from inventories} \\ \text{of finished goods} \end{matrix}$$

Using this equation we can understand the statement in *SNA93* that under accrual accounting 'no output [production] is recorded when [finished] goods produced previously are withdrawn from inventories [of finished goods] and sold' (*SNA93*, para. 6.58, with my clarifying interpolations in square brackets; a similar statement occurs in *UK NACSM*, para. 2.42).

A converse example can occur where production of finished goods during an accounting period could be greater than the sales receipts for finished goods during that accounting period. Such an example would occur if some finished goods used were added to inventories of finished goods:

Value of production of finished goods	=	Sales receipts for finished goods	+	Value of finished goods added to inventories of finished goods

Using this equation we can understand the statement in *SNA93* that under accrual accounting 'output [production] should be recorded at the time it is produced ... whether it is immediately sold ... or entered into inventories [of finished goods] for sale ... later' (*SNA93*, para. 6.58, with my clarifying interpolations in square brackets).

Of course, finished goods can be both taken from and added to inventories of finished goods during an accounting period. Consequently we have to put both equations together and write:

Value of production of finished goods	=	Sales receipts for finished goods	−	Value of finished goods taken from inventories of finished goods

$$+ \text{ Value of finished goods added to inventories of finished goods}$$

Rearranging with the use of brackets:

Value of production of finished goods	=	Sales receipts for finished goods	+	⎡ Value of finished goods added to inventories of finished goods

$$- \begin{array}{l} \text{Value of finished goods} \\ \text{taken from inventories} \\ \text{of finished goods} \end{array} \Bigg]$$

The expression in brackets, the difference between what is added to inventories and what is taken from inventories, is the value of the change in inventories of finished goods during the accounting period. That is:

Value of change in inventories of finished goods	=	Value of finished goods added to inventories of finished goods	−	Value of finished goods taken from inventories of finished goods

If the value of additions is greater than the value of what is taken, then the value of the change in inventories of finished goods is positive; if the value of additions is less than the value of what is taken, then the value of the change in inventories of finished goods is negative. By substitution:

Value of production of = finished goods	Sales receipts for finished + goods	Value of change in inventories of finished goods

In order to ascertain the value of the change in inventories of finished goods during a period all that is needed is a stock-take of inventories of finished goods at the end of each successive period; the end-of-period stock for Accounting period 1 becoming also the beginning-of-period stock for Accounting period 2. Subtracting the begining-of-period stock from the end-of-period stock then gives the value of the change in inventories during an accounting period.

Output also occurs in the form of work in progress. Inventories of work in progress, AN.122, are goods and services that are partially completed but that are not usually turned over to other units without further processing (*SNA93*, para. 10.102; *ESA95*, p. 139). By the nature of work in progress, output produced during a period in the form of work in progress can be recorded only by the value of the change in inventories of work in progress.

Output also occurs in the form of services, both for sale in the market and in other forms, and so all services must be included in the concept of output in the full equation for gross value added.

Furthermore, the technical term 'output' covers more than finished goods and services for sale (or destined for sale) in the market. Output also includes goods and services produced for own-account final use (that is, not for sale to others); for example, when an engineering enterprise builds a piece of equipment for its own use as fixed capital, or when a farmer builds a fence on the farm or when a dairy farm produces milk for the dairy farmer's own final consumption. Output also includes non-market output; that is, output not intended for sale but for provision to others or to the community free of charge; for example when a government school or government hospital produces education services or health services provided to individuals free of charge, or when a police force produces and provides the services of law and order to the community collectively. Such output (which does not generate sales receipts) must be included in the calculation of value added. The concept of output and the different types of output are discussed more fully in Section

2.6 (see Figure 2.3, p. 92) and in Chapter 3. When measuring output for an accounting period, we must take account of all these types of output.

Accordingly, output for an accounting period is the value of the finished goods produced during the accounting period *plus* the value of production of services for sale in the market produced during the accounting period *plus* the value of the change in inventories of work in progress during the accounting period *plus* the production during the accounting period of all the types of output other than output for sale in the market. Accordingly:

$$
\text{Output} =
\begin{matrix}
\text{Sales receipts} \\
\text{for finished} \\
\text{goods and for} \\
\text{services}
\end{matrix}
+
\begin{matrix}
\text{Value of change in} \\
\text{inventories of} \\
\text{finished goods and} \\
\text{of work in progress}
\end{matrix}
+
\begin{matrix}
\text{Value of production} \\
\text{of all other types of} \\
\text{output (goods and} \\
\text{services not sold in} \\
\text{the market)}
\end{matrix}
$$

Thus, as stated in *SNA93* (para. 6.63, with my clarifying interpolations in square brackets):

… the following identity must hold for goods or services produced for sale or other use:

$$
\begin{matrix}
\text{the value} \\
\text{of output}
\end{matrix}
=
\begin{matrix}
\text{the value} \\
\text{of sales}
\end{matrix}
+
\begin{matrix}
\text{other uses} \\[4pt]
\text{[goods and} \\
\text{services not} \\
\text{sold in the} \\
\text{market at} \\
\text{economically} \\
\text{significant} \\
\text{prices]}
\end{matrix}
+
\begin{matrix}
\text{the value of changes} \\
\text{in inventories} \\[4pt]
\text{[of finished goods and} \\
\text{of work in progress]}
\end{matrix}
$$

We can thus see that the full equation for gross value added:

Gross value added = Output − Intermediate consumption

is quite complex with regard to the conceptualisation and the measurement of the variables on the right-hand side. But despite their complexity, these variables remain measurable and retain their characteristic of being independent, stand-alone transactions with their own prices and quantities. Nothing that was said in Section 2.3 about these issues is fundamentally altered in the full equation for gross value added. That is why we can use Table 2.1 as an 'in principle' introduction to the concept of gross value added.

This concludes the discussion of how accrual accounting affects the measurement of intermediate consumption and of output. There will be further discussion of other types of output in Section 2.6 below and in Chapter 3.

Now that we understand more about the concepts of output and intermediate consumption, we can put the concept of gross value added in a better context, as follows:

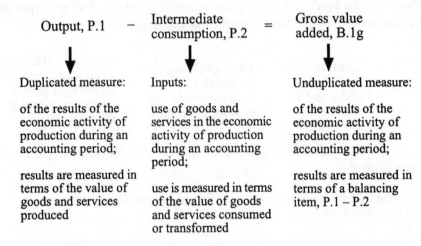

Output, P.1	−	Intermediate consumption, P.2	=	Gross value added, B.1g
Duplicated measure:		Inputs:		Unduplicated measure:
of the results of the economic activity of production during an accounting period;		use of goods and services in the economic activity of production during an accounting period;		of the results of the economic activity of production during an accounting period;
results are measured in terms of the value of goods and services produced		use is measured in terms of the value of goods and services consumed or transformed		results are measured in terms of a balancing item, P.1 − P.2

The SNA93/ESA95 account for the transactions of output and for intermediate consumption, with the balancing item of gross value added, is known as a *production account*. 'The production account ... is designed to emphasize value added as one of the main balancing items in the System' (*SNA93*, para. 2.108). The production account may be given for a sector of the economy and also for the whole economy. In this chapter we are concerned only with the production account for the whole economy.

Out of the gross value added so produced incomes are paid to the employees engaged in that production with the remaining residual (gross) income accruing to the enterprise for the benefit of the owners of the enterprise. Any such income paid out of or taken out of gross value added is known as *primary income* (for a reason subsequently to be explained) and the distribution of primary income is dealt with in what the SNA93/ESA95 calls a 'primary distribution of income account: generation of income account' (see Figure 1.6, pp. 24–5).

The relationship between gross value added and primary income is another reason why gross value added is such an economically significant variable.

We turn now to a consideration of the production account.

2.5   The production account for the whole economy: Account I
Production account

In the SNA93/ESA95 the production account is designed to show how gross value added is produced. This account is new to national accounting and has been introduced for the first time under the SNA93/ESA95. A production account is given for each sector of the economy (so that for the first time the contribution of a sector to the economy can be seen), and is also given for the whole economy. This section considers only the production account for the whole economy.

The economy's production account shows how gross domestic product (total gross value added) has been produced. Accordingly, for the model economy of Table 2.1 we can present in Table 2.2 a model production account. In the SNA93/ESA95 the production account has the identification code Account I.

The SNA93/ESA95 has as headings to the two parts of each current account the terms 'Resources' and 'Uses'. The official definition of the heading 'Resources' is that this term is used for that part of the account containing 'transactions which add to the amount of economic value of a unit or a sector'; the official definition of the heading 'Uses' is that this term is used for that part of the account containing 'transactions that reduce the amount of economic value of a unit or sector' (*SNA93*, para. 2.54).

However, although these SNA93/ESA95 definitions will serve most applications of the terms, they do not properly capture all the applications, and we need to look a bit further into the terms.

The *Oxford English Dictionary* (Second Edition) gives as the relevant meaning of 'resource' (noting its usual use in the plural): 'a means of supplying some want or deficiency; a stock or reserve upon which one can draw when necessary' and gives as the relevant meaning of 'use' 'the act of employing a thing for any (especially a profitable) purpose ... a purpose, object or end, especially of a useful or advantageous nature'.

So resources are broadly a means to an end, and we need to keep this in mind when we see the heading 'Resources' in the SNA93/ESA95. Following on, uses are the ends to which the resources are put and so uses can be broadly understood as the useful or advantageous purposes or objectives or results of the economic transactions listed under the heading 'Resources'. In the preceding sentence, the word 'results' is important, because it applies especially to the balancing item flows, which make their *first* appearance under the

Table 2.2

**Gross domestic product, output approach: production account
for model economy**

SNA93/ESA95 identification code	SNA93/ESA95 name	€ per annum
I	PRODUCTION ACCOUNT	
	Resources	
P.1	Total output	100
Total	Total resources[a]	100
	Uses	
P.2	Intermediate consumption	55
B.1*g	Gross domestic product[b]	45
Total	Total uses	100

(a)   This is a simplified account because we have not yet dealt with the different types of output and with taxes on products (less subsidies on products) which are, as we shall show, included in the full production account.

(b)   Balancing item is calculated as: Total resources *minus* P.2 Intermediate consumption.

Source: Table 2.1; reference: Office for National Statistics, *United Kingdom National Accounts The Blue Book 1999 edition*, tables 1.6.1 and 1.7.1, pp. 40 and 58.

heading 'Uses'. This is because the balancing item is a balance of resources over uses, and thus represents both an addition to economic value and also an ability or potentiality further to use that balance of resources over uses. So in turn these balancing item flows become resources for further uses or ends, and accordingly in the following account in the sequence of SNA93/ESA95 accounts the balancing item flow appears under the heading 'Resources'. These subtleties are not captured by the official SNA93 definitions whereas with the *Oxford English Dictionary* definitions it is perfectly understandable how an advantageous purpose or result of one set of transactions (technically a 'use') can become something on which one can (subsequently) draw (technically a 'resource'). Note also that it is not appropriate to identify a balancing item as a transaction, which is what the official definition does.

The first part of Table 2.2 is concerned with resources. The first row under the heading 'Resources' in Table 2.2's production account gives total output, P.1, as the aggregate of sales receipts in the economy. ('P.' is the prefix alphabetical code for transactions in products (goods and services).) In the P.1 term 'total output', the word 'total' signifies the total of output of all types (these types are fully explained in Figure 2.3, p. 92).

As a resource, total output is thus a means to an end or to various ends. As we have explained, this is a peculiar aggregate because it double-counts sales, for intermediate consumption, from one enterprise to another enterprise. Nevertheless, it is an aggregate of identifiable transactions occurring in the economy and because of its use in calculating gross value added it is an important aggregate.

In the SNA93/ESA95 this aggregate resource may also be referred to as 'total output' for reasons which will be fully explained in the next section, but briefly (and partly), the technical term 'output' includes not only the type of output which results in sales receipts from market transactions ('market output') but also the type of output which is the value of production by an enterprise for its own final use (such as when an engineering enterprise builds a piece of equipment for its own use) and also the type of output which is the value of non-market production by government to be supplied for community or individual use either free of charge or at a price not economically significant. The adjective 'total' in the term 'total output' thus refers to the total output *of all the types* that have been given.

In Table 2.2 which relates to the simplified model economy of Table 2.1 (where there is no type of output other than market output), the first row is concerned only with output measured by sales receipts resulting from market production.

The second part of Table 2.2 is concerned with uses. The first row under the heading 'Uses' gives the intermediate consumption, P.2 – that is, *total* intermediate consumption – in the model economy. This is one of the ends to which output is put. Intermediate consumption is the result of identifiable specific transactions in the economy. To be very explicit, the SNA93/ESA95 term 'intermediate consumption' (classification code P.2) always refers to *total* intermediate consumption, either for the economy as a whole or for the sector, according to whichever is under consideration in the account. In the case of intermediate consumption the adjective 'total' is never needed as there is only one type of intermediate consumption.

The next row gives, by subtraction, the balancing item of the difference between total resources and intermediate consumption. This balancing item

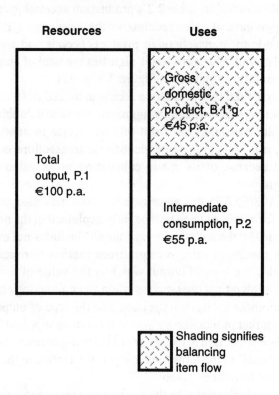

PRODUCTION ACCOUNT

Resources

Uses

Gross domestic product, B.1*g €45 p.a.

Total output, P.1 €100 p.a.

Intermediate consumption, P.2 €55 p.a.

Shading signifies balancing item flow

Figure 2.2   Production account for the whole economy

is total gross value added, which for an economy as a whole is *gross domestic product*, B.1*g. In the production account, the gross value added resulting from production is the balancing item use, or advantageous end, of production – it is one of the purposes or objectives or useful results of producing output.

Effectively, the production account in Table 2.2 simply repeats the first three items in the *last* row of Table 2.1 – the 'Total' row, and this is how you should understand the production account in principle. 'Behind' each production account lies a set of row headings with NACE Rev. 1/ANZSIC headings, as in Table 2.1. The production account is the fundamental starting point of national accounts because it records the economic activity of producing goods and services.

Figure 2.2 illustrates the production account. On the left of Figure 2.2 the height of the vertical bar indicates the value of total resources; in this simplified case resources comprises simply total output as measured by total sales receipts. This, as explained, comprises a set of independent (sales receipts) transactions.

An important principle of the SNA93/ESA95 accounts and Figure 2.2 (and any like diagram) is that total resources *must* equal total uses. That is, there cannot be a use without a resource; and every resource (supplied to the economy) must find a use (of some or other sort including a balancing item use or end).

Accordingly, on the right of Figure 2.2 a vertical bar, of a height equal to the resources bar, shows the (various) uses of these resources with divisions within the vertical bar showing the type of uses. The first use is intermediate consumption. This comprises a set of independent transactions, namely purchases by producers for immediate and actual use in the process of production. The remainder of the vertical bar (which is shaded) then illustrates the balancing item flow of gross value added (output *minus* intermediate consumption), and for the whole economy total gross value added is gross domestic product.

Thus Figure 2.2 provides an illustration of how gross domestic product is produced in the economy. In order to proceed further with the concept of gross domestic product it is timely now to consider some actual real-world data.

2.6 Types of output and the production account for the United Kingdom

Table 2.3 gives the production account for the United Kingdom (a production account has not yet (1999) been published in Australia's SNA93 national accounts). The first thing you will notice about Table 2.3 is that there are three types of output recorded in the table: market output, P.11; output for own final use, P.12; and other non-market output, P.13. Each of these forms a part of total output, P.1 (note the hierarchical numbering system). These types of output need to be explained (and the complete explanation will be spread over this section, Section 3.3 of Chapter 3, and subsequent chapters where specific types of output will be discussed in detail). Taxes on products are to be explained in the Chapter 4 and for the moment taxes on products (less subsidies on products), D.21 – D.31, will simply be mentioned and not explained.

'Products are all goods and services that are created within the production

Table 2.3
Production account for the United Kingdom

SNA93/ESA95 identification code	SNA93/ESA95 name	1997, £ million
I	PRODUCTION ACCOUNT	
	Resources	
P.1	Output	
P.11	Market output	1 309 620
P.12	Output for own final use	50 253
P.13	Other non-market output	166 498
P.1	Total output	1 526 371
D.21 – D.31	Taxes *less* Subsidies on products	90 275
Total	Total resources	1 616 646
	Uses	
P.2	Intermediate consumption	812 757
B.1*g	Gross domestic product	803 889
Total	Total uses	1 616 646

Source: Office for National Statistics, *United Kingdom National Accounts The Blue Book 1999 edition*, table 1.7.1, p. 58.

boundary' (*ESA95*, para. 3.01). The production boundary is discussed fully in Chapter 3, Section 3.3. The official definitions of 'production' and 'output' are in part as follows:

> Production is an activity carried out under the control and responsibility of an institutional unit that uses inputs of labour, capital and goods and services to produce goods and services (*ESA95*, para. 3.07).

> Output consists of the products created [and supplied] during the accounting period (*ESA95*, para. 3.14 with my clarifying interpolation in square brackets, required for Figure 2.3).

In all of what follows we must use the words 'production', 'products' and 'output' carefully in their technical national accounting meaning (it is most important that you not be misled by your familiarity with these words into thinking that you already understand these terms in their technical usage – you must appreciate that these words are, in the SNA93/ESA95 context, highly technical terms the full understanding of which takes considerable effort). For this explanation I shall take the conventions of accrual accounting as always being in force. We have the following simple schema with the relevant SNA93/ESA95 technical concepts in bold typeface:

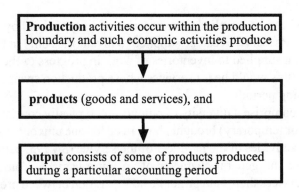

This simple schema will subsequently be elaborated in Chapter 3 (Figure 3.2, p. 122), but for the moment we will take the terms 'production', 'products' and 'output' according to the meaning of the simple schema.

Note carefully that in the SNA93/ESA95, the word 'products' is used to refer either to *goods* or to *services* or to both.

To count as a product, a product must be in demand because it is, or is intended to be, used to meet or fulfil some or other need or want or purpose. (In the SNA93, the name for unwanted 'products' – usually the byproduct of a production process – is 'externalities' (sometimes loosely referred to as 'bads'). Externalities are not recorded in the main accounts of the System because in all cases there are not two *willing* parties to the 'transaction'. Externalities are unsolicited and unilaterally imposed on those affected – the antithesis of a market transaction. Externalities may eventually be recorded in satellite accounts, as attempts are made to quantify the impact of pollution.)

Goods are physical objects (note that this excludes financial assets) with ownership rights which persist through time and which may be transferred from one transactor to another (*SNA93*, para. 6.7). In relation to any good, production and sale are, in principle, separate operations; that is, the production of a good can occur in one operation during one accounting period and in another, quite separate, operation during another accounting period the sale (exchange) of the good can occur. (In regard to any good, the technical term 'sale' refers to the change of ownership of the good.) As stated in *SNA93*:

> The times at which sales are to be recorded are when the receivables and payables are created: that is, when the ownership of the goods passes from the producer to the purchaser or when the services are provided to the purchaser (*SNA93*, para. 6.54).

Any good can be supplied to inventories of all types held by institutional units of all sorts; services can be supplied to inventories only in the restricted sense of being supplied to inventories of work in progress of the producer of the services (this would be for services whose production spanned more than one accounting period).

Services comprise a diversity of outputs and typically consist of a change (permanent or temporary) brought about in or for one unit or a collectivity of units by the activities of the producer of the service (*SNA93*, para. 6.8). Such changes have the general character of an improvement. Consequently, in relation to services there is in principle no separation between production and supply: when an institutional unit produces a service, the production is simultaneous with, and inseparable from, the supply (for example, the service of a haircut). Services cannot be traded separately from their production; there is no sensible notion of a stock of previously-produced haircuts.

The notion of a transferable ownership right, persisting through time, does not apply to a service in the way it applies to a good. For example, the request 'May I borrow your comb?' makes sense; the request 'May I borrow your haircut?' does not make sense. For the word 'comb' we could substitute the name of any good and for the word 'haircut' we could substitute the name of any service; for examples, try 'book' and 'education' or 'vacuum cleaner' and 'vacuuming'.

Production is an activity which uses inputs to produce products. Any process of production produces products, but not all products count as output (note this sentence carefully). Specifically, products produced by an enterprise that are used up during the same accounting period *and* that are used up in the production process within the same producing enterprise (and so which do not leave the producing enterprise) do not count as part of the producing enterprise's output. For example, if a *bakery* were to buy-in wheat and itself grind the wheat into flour for using up by the bakery itself in making bread during the same accounting period, then only the bread would count as part of the bakery's output; conversely the flour, albeit a product, would not count as part of the bakery's output. So the bakery-produced/bakery-used-up flour is a product that is not output. However, if the bakery buys-in wheat and itself grinds that wheat into flour but adds that flour to inventories of flour (and so does not use up that flour in making bread during the current period), then that flour would count as output because the flour, as a product, has been 'supplied' to changes in inventories, in this case classified as work in progress AN.122 – that is, as bread-in-progress (*SNA93*, para. 6.72; *ESA95*, p. 139, definition of AN.1222).

(The reader can now begin to appreciate some of the complexities behind the SNA93/ESA95 words 'product' and 'output' which is why I warned that these words not be taken for granted.)

Output is generally, but not always, produced for supplying to other institutional units. Output is a concept relating to, or dependent upon, the way in which an enterprise's products are supplied and used. (Remember that the term 'enterprise' includes institutional units such as government departments.)

I depict the SNA93/ESA95 concept and classification of output in Figure 2.3. In Figure 2.3, I show in one diagram a classification of supply and uses of output into seven numbered *categories* (which I call 'categories of supply or use') and then, by means of shading, I group these categories into the three SNA93/ESA95 official *types* (called 'types of output' and shown in bold with their SNA93/ESA95 identification codes): *market output*, P.11; *output for own final use*, P.12; and *other non-market output*, P.13. Together these three constitute *output*, P.1. The last two types of output, P.12 and P.13, together constitute non-market output, but this latter concept is only implicitly used in the SNA93/ESA95 which always maintains the distinction between output for own final use (which is non-market output) and other non-market output. Accordingly in Figure 2.3 I put square brackets around the term 'non-market output' to indicate its implicit status (and this is why it does not have an identification code). These types of output, introduced by the SNA93/ESA95, are new to national accounting and these types of output are to be reported in the production account. (Note that in Figure 2.3 shading is only for grouping.)

In order to classify the types of output we must consider the possibilities of what happens to output immediately upon production (that is, during the same accounting period as that in which the production occurred). I call these possibilities the 'supply' of the output. The term 'supply' is used in several senses in the SNA93/ESA95; my use of the term 'supply' in the context of explaining types of output is restricted as follows. Supply includes, but is not

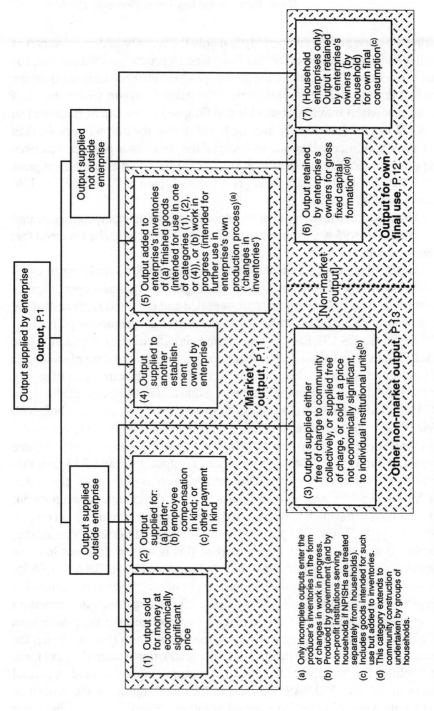

Figure 2.3   The three SNA93/ESA95 types of output

Output supplied by enterprise
Output, P.1

Output supplied outside enterprise

Output supplied not outside enterprise

(1) Output sold for money at economically significant price

(2) Output supplied for:
(a) barter;
(b) employee compensation in kind; or
(c) other payment in kind

(4) Output supplied to another establishment owned by enterprise

(5) Output added to enterprise's inventories of (a) finished goods (intended for use in one of categories (1), (2), or (4)), or (b) work in progress (intended for further use in enterprise's own production process)(a) ('changes in inventories')

Market output, P.11

(3) Output supplied either free of charge to community collectively, or supplied free of charge, or sold at a price not economically significant, to individual institutional units(b)

Other non-market output, P.13

[Non-market output]

(6) Output retained by enterprise's owners for gross fixed capital formation(c)(d)

(7) (Household enterprises only) Output retained by enterprise's owners (by household) for own final consumption(c)

Output for own final use, P.12

(a) Only incomplete outputs enter the producer's inventories in the form of changes in work in progress.
(b) Produced by government (and by non-profit institutions serving households if NPISHs are treated separately from households).
(c) Includes goods intended for such use but added to inventories.
(d) This category extends to community construction undertaken by groups of households.

92

confined to, sale to a customer immediately upon production. Conversely, 'supply' does not extend to any possibility of a use of output which may arise or occur in an accounting period other than the accounting period during production occurred. Explicitly, in what follows we are not concerned with sales of goods which might be made out of goods produced in a previous accounting period. Throughout we observe the conventions of accrual accounting. In the context of explaining types of output, the term 'supply' and its cognates are used in a broad sense, as we shall see.

There are two main possibilities for such supply. First, the output may be supplied to an institutional unit 'outside', or somehow independent of, the enterprise which owns the establishment in which production of the product takes place. Second, the output may be supplied to an institutional unit which is not 'outside', or not independent of, the enterprise either because it is the same enterprise or because it belongs to the same enterprise.

For output supplied outside the enterprise, there are three subsidiary possibilities which give the first three categories of supply or use. (The following bracketed numbers refer to the bracketed numbers in Figure 2.3.)

(1)   The output may be sold in return for money to another institutional unit at an economically significant price. This would be the common case. For example, this sort of supply operates throughout the model economy of Table 2.1. (The meaning of the term 'economically significant price' will be explained shortly.)

(2)   The output may be supplied not in return for money to another institutional unit as a barter transaction, or as compensation in kind to employees, or as some other payment in kind. In this second possibility, a value would have to be estimated for the supply.

(3)   The output may be supplied to another institutional unit either free of charge or at a price which is not economically significant or may be supplied collectively to the community. This form of supply is quite common in any economy: it covers most of the supply of services produced by government either to individuals or to the community collectively. For example, education services or hospital services produced by the government and supplied by the government to an institutional unit either free of charge or at a price not economically significant falls into this category as does the supply of law and order services provided to the community collectively. (The question of estimating a monetary valuation for such supply will be discussed in Chapter 3, Section 3.3.)

For output supplied not outside the enterprise there are four subsidiary possibilities which give the remaining four categories of supply or use (the numbering of the categories will be continued in sequence).

(4)   The output may be supplied to another establishment owned by the same enterprise. The reason for distinguishing this possibility is that there is scope for the enterprise – as the decision-making unit – to determine an 'arbitrary' price for the output. However, for national income accounting purposes, a monetary value for such a transaction should be estimated for the supply at the going market price, regardless of what 'internal accounting' price has been determined by the enterprise for the supply.

(5)   The output may be added to the enterprise's inventories; that is, to the inventories held by the establishment responsible for production. Eventually, of course, these inventories may be sold or otherwise used; but the defining feature is that the disposal of the good to another institutional unit or other use does not take place within the accounting period under consideration, and so this supply must be put in a category by itself.

(6)   The output (good of an appropriate kind only in this case) may be retained by the enterprise (strictly, by the *owners* of the enterprise) for the purpose of gross fixed capital formation in the enterprise. This covers the cases, not uncommon, when a commercial enterprise constructs for its own use a fixed asset or when a household, acting as a producing enterprise, constructs for itself a dwelling or an extension to a dwelling or when communal construction of a community facility occurs.

The seventh and last category of supply or use applies only to household enterprises (that is only to households which are acting as a producing enterprise). This category is especially intended to cover the case of production by own-account subsistence farmers who predominate in less developed economies, but two sorts of production by household enterprises in all economies fall into this category as well. Category (7) is where the output is retained and used by the enterprise's owners (that is, by the household which owns or is the producing enterprise) for the purpose of household consumption. An example of this, mentioned in Chapter 1, is where a dairy farmer supplies to the dairy farmer's household for household consumption some of the dairy farm's milk. Another example would be the production of food (for example, rice, maize, casava) by subsistence food-farmers in a less developed economy. Another example, widespread in all economies, is the production of housing (dwelling-shelter) services by owner-occupier households (the owner-occupier being regarded in the capacity of owner as a producer of housing services which are supplied to itself for consumption in the capacity of occupier). Another example is the production of household services ('domestic services') by paid employees ('domestic servants') of the household where the domestic services are for the household's own use.

These seven categories of supply or use cover, in a mutually exclusive and jointly exhaustive way, all the possibilities for the supply and use of output (*SNA93*, paras. 6.41 and 6.42). The seven categories may now be grouped into three types of output recognised by the SNA93/ESA95 (*SNA93*, paras 6.45–6.51).

First, we may, by the use of shading, put a classification boundary around categories (1), (2), (4) and (5), and this classification boundary delineates the SNA93/ESA95 type *market output*, P.11 (see Figure 2.3). This is because the supply is either directly or indirectly, and immediately or eventually, supplied in a market or market-type transaction.

The official definition of 'market output' is (in part):

> Market output consists of output that is disposed of on the market ... or intended to be disposed of on the market (*ESA95*, para. 3.17).

Market output includes: products sold at economically significant prices; products which are exchanged in a barter transaction; products used for payments in kind; products supplied by one local kind-of-activity unit to another local kind-of-activity unit within the same institutional unit; and products added to the producer's inventories of finished goods or work in progress intended for one or other of the preceding uses. (An example of products supplied between local kind-of-activity units belonging to the same enterprise would occur in Figure 2.1 if the pasta local kind-of-activity unit and the other 15./21 local kind-of-activity units supplied products to the 52.24/ 5110 retail shop local kind-of-activity unit owned by Acme Foods plc/ltd.)

It follows that the remaining categories are non-market output, so that, second, we may put a classification boundary around categories (3), (6) and (7) to delineate non-market output, but this is only an implicit classification because here the SNA93/ESA95 always makes a distinction between, on the one hand, categories (6) and (7) which are grouped into the type *output for own final use*, P.12, and, on the other hand, category (3) which forms by itself the type *other non-market output*, P.13. You can see that category (3) is an important type of its own and is a very different type of output from categories (6) and (7); this is why it is always kept separate.

The official definition of 'output for own final use' is:

> Output produced for own final use consists of goods or services that are retained either for final consumption by the same institutional unit or for gross fixed capital formation by the same institutional unit (*ESA95*, para. 3.20).

The official definition of 'other non-market output' is:

> Other non-market output covers output that is provided free, or at prices that are not economically significant, to other units (*ESA95*, para. 3.23).

Two side issues arise out of this classification. First, for all categories of supply or use other than category (1), a value has to be estimated or imputed for the supply of the output. Matters of valuation will be introduced in Chapter 3 and discussed further in other chapters, so we will not pause to consider such matters here, save to remark that the SNA93/ESA95 recommends the use, whenever possible, of market prices (that is, the prices which would apply for the first category).

Second, in the SNA93, a price is defined as 'economically significant' when it has a significant influence on the amount a producer is willing to supply or on the amounts purchasers wish to buy, presumably meaning in the former case that price is *the* important factor influencing the decision on the producer as to how much to produce and in the latter case that the price 'rations' the quantities bought by purchasers (*SNA93*, para. 6.45).

In the ESA95, the more specific criterion is generally applied that a price is economically significant when it covers more than half the unit cost of production; in other words, when sales receipts at that price would cover more than half the total costs of production (*ESA95*, para. 3.19).

Generally we would of course expect price to be *greater* than the unit total cost of production; in other words, we expect sales receipts at that price to be greater than the total costs of production. The excess of sales receipts over the total costs of production provides for, and is equal to, the net operating surplus – or loosely 'profit' – on production. In other words, the 'mark-up' of price over unit total cost determines what is known as the 'unit net margin' which creates the profit arising from any given volume of production. (For readers unfamiliar with the technical terms in this paragraph, definitions and explanations may be found in Chapter 2 of my book *Profitability, Mechanization, and Economies of Scale.*)

When we defined and explained gross value added in the simplified model economy of Table 2.1, we proceeded, with regard to output, in terms of sales receipts only. In other words, we simplified greatly by identifying output with sales receipts in a market transaction (assuming that production of the output, sale of the output, and receipt of cash all occurred during the same accounting period). The foregoing discussion shows that, when we discuss the production of gross value added in the real world, we must broaden our concept of output to include all seven categories of supply or use of output, or, in SNA93/ESA95 terms, to include all three types of output (and we must also pay heed to the conventions of accrual accounting).

We can now consider the production account in Table 2.3. In the United Kingdom economy during 1997, total output was £1 526 371 million. Of this, £1 309 620 million (85.8 per cent of total output) was market output, £50 253 million (3.3 per cent of total output) was output for own final use, and £166 498 million (10.9 per cent of total output) was other non-market output.

Until Chapter 4 we shall pass over taxes on products (*less* subsidies on products), but we shall simply note that, in the SNA93/ESA95 production account, these, as a resource for government, are added to total output to give what is known as 'total resources' (on the production account). Total resources (on the production account) in the UK economy in 1997 amounted to £1 616 646 million.

We come now to the uses of these total resources on the production account.

The concept of intermediate consumption has already been explained in the context of explaining gross value added. Intermediate consumption consists of the value of goods and services consumed or transformed in the process of production (but excluding the labour services of the enterprise's own employees – so intermediate consumption excludes payment of wages and salaries or other compensation of employees – and excluding the consumption of fixed capital).

Intermediate consumption in the UK economy during 1997 was £812 757 million, and this amounted to 50.3 per cent of total resources.

Total gross value added resulting from production in the UK economy, or gross domestic product, may now be calculated according to the equation:

$$
\begin{array}{l}
\text{Total gross value} \\
\text{added resulting} \\
\text{from production in} \\
\text{the UK economy,} \\
\text{or gross domestic} \\
\text{product, 1997}
\end{array}
=
\begin{array}{l}
\text{Total resources} \\
\text{on the production} \\
\text{account in the} \\
\text{UK economy,} \\
\text{1997}
\end{array}
-
\begin{array}{l}
\text{Intermediate} \\
\text{consumption in} \\
\text{the UK} \\
\text{economy, 1997}
\end{array}
$$

$$= \text{£1 616 646 mn} - \text{£812 757 mn}$$

$$= \text{£803 889 mn}$$

Despite the complexities of the real world (and allowing for taxes on products), this calculation and its result is no different in principle from the calculation of total gross value added for the model economy of Table 2.1 as shown in the production account in Table 2.2.

Gross domestic product is a use of output (more exactly, a use of total resources on the production account) in the sense that gross domestic product is the advantageous 'end' – or purpose or object – of producing output.

We must now consider what happens to the total gross value added, or gross domestic product, so produced. In the next account in the SNA93/ESA95 sequence of accounts – the primary distribution of income account: generation of income account – gross domestic product becomes a resource to serve further ends or purposes.

2.7   Primary incomes and Account II.1.1 Primary distribution of income account: generation of income account

Returning to Table 2.1, the farm's production has resulted in €20 per annum of gross value added, calculated as a balancing item by subtracting intermediate consumption from sales receipts. What happens to this gross value added? In the first instance it is distributed as *primary income*. Primary income is the income paid or taken as a 'primary' distribution out of the gross value added arising as a result of production. The official explanation of primary income is:

> 'Primary income' is the income which resident units [and participating non-resident employees] receive by virtue of their direct participation in the production process, and the income receivable by the owner [resident or non-resident] of a financial asset or a tangible non-produced asset in return for

providing funds to, or putting the tangible non-produced asset at the disposal of, another institutional unit (*ESA95*, para. 8.22, with my amending interpolations in square brackets because the official explanation is incomplete (see Table 5.10, pp. 254–5); see also *SNA93*, paras 7.2 and 7.14).

In addition to the primary incomes paid as compensation to employees out of gross value added, a primary income of gross operating surplus/gross mixed income arises as a balancing item (gross value added *minus* compensation of employees). Property incomes also count as primary income. Property income is explained as follows:

> The primary incomes that accrue by lending or renting financial or tangible non-produced assets, including land, to other units for use in production are described as *property incomes*. Receipts from taxes on production and imports are treated as primary incomes of governments even though not all of them may be recorded as payable out of the value added of enterprises (*SNA93*, para. 7.2, italics added).

Primary incomes are dealt with in two sequential accounts under the general heading of 'Primary distribution of income account' as follows:

Account II Distribution and use of income accounts
    Account II.1 Primary distribution of income account
        Account II.1.1 Generation of income account
        Account II.1.2 Allocation of primary income account

The Primary distribution of income account: generation of income account (Account II.1.1) deals with the distribution of primary incomes out of gross value added in the form of compensation of employees and gross operating surplus/gross mixed incomes (all these terms being explained shortly).

The Primary distribution of income account: allocation of primary income account (Account II.1.2) deals with the further use of gross operating surplus and gross mixed income together with compensation of employees and taxes less subsidies on production as a resource from which to pay property incomes (interest, dividends, rent) but this latter account also includes, as a resource, property incomes and other incomes received by residents from non-residents and, as a use, property incomes and other incomes paid by residents to non-residents. Consequently, Account II.1.2 is a complex account and consideration of these income transactions between residents and non-residents must await an explanation of these transactions in Chapter 5. The present chapter deals only with Account II.1.1 Primary distribution of income account: generation of income account.

The primary distribution of income account: generation of income account may be explained as follows using the model economy of Table 2.1.

Let us suppose that the farm has some employees. These employees have to be paid in return for their work on the farm (so this transaction is a requited transaction). Such remuneration to employees of an enterprise is known in the SNA93/ESA95 as *compensation of employees*, D.1.

Note that compensation of employees has a 'D.' identification code signifiying that it is a distributive transaction. The official definition of 'distributive transactions' is:

> Distributive transactions consist of transactions by means of which the value added generated by production is distributed to labour, capital and government, and of transactions involving the redistribution of income and wealth (*ESA95*, para. 4.01).

The official definition of 'compensation of employees' is:

> Compensation of employees (D.1) is defined as the total remuneration, in cash or in kind, payable by an employer to an employee in return for work done by the latter during the accounting period (*ESA95*, para. 4.02).

In the real world, the make-up of compensation of employees is very complex (it is measured before deduction of income tax payable by the employee and includes contributions by the employer to a pension scheme for the benefit of the employee). The full explanation of compensation of employees as a national accounting item will be deferred to Chapter 6 on the household sector, where we need to consider all the sorts of income received by households.

In Table 2.1 compensation of employees of the farm is €15 per annum. Compensation of employees is one type of primary income.

When compensation of employees has been paid out of the gross value added (that is, deducted from gross value added), the residual balancing item remaining is known in the SNA93/ESA95 either as *gross operating surplus*, B.2g, or as *gross mixed income*, B.3g, and, as explained below, which of the two it is depends upon the type of institutional unit receiving the residual gross income. Each of these is a type of primary income, and each is generally measured gross of consumption of fixed capital, hence the adjective 'gross'. Operating surplus and mixed income can also be measured net of the consumption of fixed capital, when the terms 'net operating surplus', B.2n, or 'net mixed income', B.3n, would apply. Nearly all of the following discussion keeps to the gross measures. (Net operating surplus is an item corresponding approximately to what is commonly called 'profit', but the term 'profit' is not used in the SNA93/ESA95 for a reason shortly to be explained.)

If, and only if, the institutional unit is a household enterprise, owned and operated by a household in which, and for the purpose of production, the owner contributes to the enterprise labour inputs (of a kind similar to those that could be provided by a paid employee), then the residual income balancing item is called 'gross mixed income' (*SNA93*, paras 7.8, 7.81 and 7.85). This is because the gross mixed income implicitly includes an element of remuneration to labour, but it is not possible to separate the remuneration-to-labour element of income, on the one hand, from, on the other hand, the net operating surplus, or 'profit' element of income, arising out of the ownership of the enterprise (after allowing for consumption of fixed capital).

Let us suppose that the farm in Table 2.1 is owned by a farmer (a household) and that the farmer works on the farm alongside the employees. In this case, the balancing item of €5 per annum in the farm's account is gross mixed income.

In any other case, the residual balancing item is called the 'gross operating surplus'. For example, if the institutional unit is an incorporated legal entity, distinct from its owners, then the residual income balancing item is identified as gross operating surplus. For another example, if the institutional unit is an owner-occupied dwelling, in which, for the production of (accommodation) output, the owner does *not* have to contribute labour input of a type that could be provided by a paid employee, the residual income is identified as gross operating surplus.

Turning to the mill, let us suppose that the mill is an incorporated enterprise with an owner who does not work in the mill but simply hires employees to do and to oversee the work. The mill's gross value added is €10 per annum, and compensation of employees is €5 per annum. This leaves a balancing item of residual income of €5 per annum, and this income is classified as gross operating surplus because it is the surplus from the operation of milling which accrues as income (gross) to the owner of the enterprise who does not work in the enterprise.

Let us suppose that the woodcutter works on an own-account, self-employed basis and without employees so that no compensation of employees is required in this case. Then the gross value added of the woodcutter is also the gross mixed income of the woodcutter.

Let us suppose that the bakery is an incorporated enterprise with shareholders who own the enterprise which is run with paid employees to do the work. In this case, the balancing item of residual income is gross operating surplus, and some of the gross operating surplus may be paid as a distribution in the form of dividend income to shareholders – but, as explained, Table 2.1 does not deal with such distributions out of the gross operating surplus; the treatment of these distributions is dealt with separately in Account II.1.2.

The total compensation of employees in the model economy of Table 2.1 is €25 per annum, and the total of gross operating surplus/gross mixed income is €20 per annum. These are the primary incomes in this economy: that is, the incomes paid or taken out of value added, and measured gross of the consumption of fixed capital.

We can see in Table 2.1 that the sum of total compensation of employees and of total gross operating surplus/gross mixed income is equal to the total of gross value added. That is:

Use in Production account (Account I) (balancing item) brought down as a Resource in Primary distribution of income account: Generation of income account (Account II.1.1)

Uses in Primary distribution of income account: Generation of income account (Account II.1.1)

Total gross value added per annum = Total compensation of employees per annum + Total gross operating surplus/gross mixed income per annum

Flow transactions   *Balancing items*

Primary incomes paid or taken out of value added

or:

$$€45 \text{ p.a.} = €25 \text{ p.a.} + €20 \text{ p.a.}$$

This equation holds, of course, because total gross operating surplus/gross mixed income is a balancing item. In other words, the equation should really be written as:

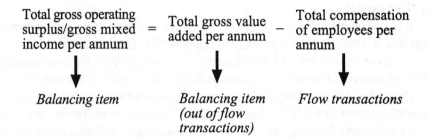

Total gross operating surplus/gross mixed income per annum	=	Total gross value added per annum	−	Total compensation of employees per annum
↓		↓		↓
Balancing item		*Balancing item (out of flow transactions)*		*Flow transactions*

Again, note the logical difference between compensation of employees (as a set of flow transactions) and gross operating surplus/gross mixed income (as balancing item flows). We can envisage the compensation of employees as an identifiable set of transactions (envisage employees queueing up at the end of the week to receive, from their employer, their pay packets). But we cannot, in a like way, 'envisage' the gross operating surplus/gross mixed income.

Net operating surplus/net mixed income is the gross operating surplus/ gross mixed income *minus* consumption of fixed capital. The importance of the *net* balancing item is that it represents 'income proper' or income in the strict sense of the word.

I define 'income' as that which has the potential to *add* to an institutional unit's wealth. In other words, income for an accounting period represents the maximum amount that could be added to wealth during that accounting period providing the income were used for nothing else. Of course, this is a rather hypothetical view because income has to be used for many purposes other than adding to wealth. But it is nevertheless useful to understand the concept of income in terms of its potentiality to add to wealth.

By contrast, provisions set aside for the consumption of fixed capital have no potential to add to an institutional unit's wealth; the only potential which consumption of fixed capital has is to *maintain* wealth constant (or to 'maintain wealth intact' as the phrase goes). This is because consumption of fixed capital during a period is basically the difference between the value of fixed assets at the beginning of the period and the (depreciated) value of fixed assets at the end of the period. Consequently, the only potential of consumption of fixed capital is to 'make up for' the decline in the value of fixed assets. Consumption of fixed capital is therefore not part of income in the strict sense of the word. This is why the *net* operating surplus/*net* mixed income is the significant measure when one is concerned with income (in the strict sense). In its strict sense, the word 'income' is always to be understood as net of the consumption of fixed capital.

It is not incorrect to use the term 'gross income' providing one is aware that this is a broad and loose sense of the word 'income' and providing one knows about the strict meaning of 'income' as a concept net of the consumption of fixed capital. (This will be discussed further in Chapter 6, Section 6.8.)

(Note that net operating surplus corresponds to what is commonly called 'profit', but neither the SNA93 nor the ESA95 uses the word 'profit', because profit, as reported in company 'profit and loss accounts', includes non-trading income, such as interest received, in addition to the net operating surplus. In the SNA93/ESA95, net operating surplus is confined strictly to the profit made as a result of production.)

For the model economy of Table 2.1, the primary distribution of income account: generation of income account is given in Table 2.4.

In the primary distribution of income account: generation of income account, gross domestic product is the resource, and each of the types of primary income is a use of that resource. In Table 2.4, the total resources is the €45 per annum of total gross value added.

This resource is 'used', or apportioned, as the primary income of compensation of employees of €25 per annum, and as the residual primary income of gross operating surplus/gross mixed income of €20 per annum.

This residual income balancing item may be further apportioned according to information on the institutional nature of the enterprise receiving the residual income. As Table 2.1 has been described, €10 per annum of the residual income is gross mixed income (the farm and the woodcutter), and €10 per annum is gross operating surplus (the mill and the bakery).

Now that we have explained the principle of the primary distribution of income account: generation of income account, we can consider some real-world data on primary incomes in the United Kingdom and Australia.

2.8   The primary distribution of income account: generation of income account for the United Kingdom and Australia

Table 2.5 gives the SNA93/ESA95 primary distribution of income account: generation of income account for the United Kingdom and for Australia.

Table 2.4

Primary distribution of income account: generation of income account for model economy

SNA93/ESA95 identification code	SNA93/ESA95 name	€ per annum
II	DISTRIBUTION AND USE OF INCOME ACCOUNTS	
II.1	PRIMARY DISTRIBUTION OF INCOME ACCOUNT	
II.1.1	GENERATION OF INCOME ACCOUNT	
	Resources	
B.1*g	Total resources, gross domestic product	45
	Uses	
D.1	Total compensation of employees	25
B.2g	Gross operating surplus	10
B.3g	Gross mixed income	10
B.1*g	Total uses	45

Sources: Table 2.1; references: Office for National Statistics, *United Kingdom National Accounts The Blue Book 1999 edition*, table 1.7.2, p. 58; Australian Bureau of Statistics, *Australian System of National Accounts 1997–98*, Catalogue No. 5204.0, table 1.8, p. 28 (note that a first printing of the 1997–98 issue of 5204.0 was incorrectly paginated and was replaced by a reprinted and correctly paginated issue and my references are to this latter issue).

In the United Kingdom's Account II.1.1 in 1997, the total resource was gross domestic product of £803 889 million (also see Table 2.3). Out of this gross domestic product, £432 388 million was paid as total compensation of employees; this amounted to 53.8 per cent of GDP.

Residually out of gross domestic product, £222 513 million was taken as gross operating surplus (27.7 per cent of GDP), and £41 665 million was taken as gross mixed income (5.2 per cent of GDP).

Total taxes on production and imports *less* total subsidies on production, D.2 – D.3, amounted to 13 per cent of the UK's gross domestic product in 1997, the greater part of this being value added tax (to be discussed in Chapter 4 – where the difference between taxes on products, D.21, and taxes on production, D.2, will also be explained).

In Australia in 1997–98 (Australian national accounts use as the accounting period the fiscal year which runs from 1 July to 30 June, hence '1997–98' means the period from 1 July 1997 to 30 June 1998), the total resource was gross domestic product of $564 705 million (throughout '$' means the Australian dollar). Out of this gross domestic product, $270 084 million was paid as compensation of employees; this amounted to 47.8 per cent of total GDP (by comparison with the 53.8 per cent in the UK).

Residually out of gross domestic product, $173 878 million was taken as gross operating surplus (30.8 per cent of GDP), and $54 217 million was taken as gross mixed income (9.6 per cent of GDP).

Total taxes on production and imports *less* total subsidies on production amounted to 11.5 per cent of Australia's gross domestic product in 1997–98. Australia did not in this period have a value added tax/goods and services tax, but it did have a wholesale sales tax and an extensive set of other taxes on production. (The statistical discrepancy between income components and GDP, di, allows for any divergence between the total of the income components, as recorded by the national accounts statisticians, and GDP as calculated.)

Subsequently we shall consider how these primary incomes may be supplemented by secondary redistributions of income and how these incomes are used, but we need to explain the concept and categories of final expenditure and this involves further explanation of the concepts of production and output and the production boundary. This is done in the next chapter.

Table 2.5

Primary distribution of income account: generation of income account for the United Kingdom and Australia

SNA93/ESA95 identification code	SNA93/ESA95 name	United Kingdom 1997, £ million	Australia 1997–98, $ million
II	DISTRIBUTION AND USE OF INCOME ACCOUNTS		
II.1	PRIMARY DISTRIBUTION OF INCOME ACCOUNT		
II.1.1	GENERATION OF INCOME ACCOUNT		
	Resources		
B.1*g	Total resources, gross domestic product	803 889	564 705
	Uses		
D.1	Compensation of employees	432 388	270 084
D.2 – D.3	Total taxes on production and imports *less*		
	Total subsidies on production	107 323	64 966
B.2g	Gross operating surplus	222 513	173 878
B.3g	Gross mixed income	41 665	54 217
di	Statistical discrepancy between income components and GDP(a)	—	1 560
B.1*g	Total uses	803 889	564 705

'—' denotes nil.

(a) In the Australian System of National Accounts, this item is called 'statistical discrepancy (I)'.

Sources: Office for National Statistics, *United Kingdom National Accounts The Blue Book 1999 edition*, table 1.7.2, p. 58; Australian Bureau of Statistics, *Australian System of National Accounts 1997–98*, Catalogue No. 5204.0, table 1.8, p. 28.

3 Final Expenditure and Gross Domestic Product

3.1 Introduction

This chapter explains the important concept of final expenditure, the categories of final expenditure, and the relationship of total final expenditure to gross domestic product. This relationship also involves the basic identity of national accounting, and this relationship is explained in this chapter from several different angles.

Final expenditures are aggregates of transactions in products (goods and services). As we shall explain in Figure 3.1, there are three main categories of final expenditure:

P.3   Final consumption expenditure
P.5   Gross capital formation
P.6   Exports of goods and services.

These three categories of final expenditure sum to total final expenditure.

In many of this chapter's explanations we need to use the concept of the production boundary. Understanding the production boundary is necessary for understanding not only final expenditure but also intermediate consumption. The production boundary is also used to explain the national accounts' view of the four related concepts of economic activity, production, products, and output. All this is explained in Sections 3.2 to 3.4 of this chapter.

There is a set of important relationships between final expenditure and gross value added, shown in the following schema (which simplifies by ignoring taxes and subsidies on production, which are to be discussed in Chapter 4):

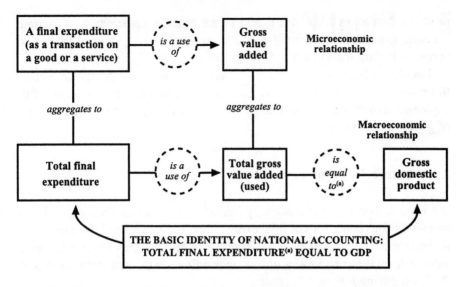

(a)   After deduction of imports of goods and services (non-resident produced gross value added)

As the schema indicates, the relationship between final expenditure and gross value added needs to be understood at two levels. First, the relationship needs to be understood at the microeconomic level of an individual final expenditure transaction. This is fundamental and is explained in Section 3.5. Second, the relationship can then be understood at the macroeconomic level of aggregate, or total, final expenditure, on the one hand, and aggregate, or total, gross value added, on the other hand. The relationship between the aggregates – that is, the equality between total final expenditure, total gross value added, and (allowing for imports) gross domestic product – results in the relationship between total final expenditure and gross domestic product that is rightly described by the SNA93 as 'the basic identity of national accounting' (*SNA93*, para. 6.234).

At this juncture, imports of goods and services become relevant, and so the relationship between the aggregates cannot be fully understood until we have discussed (in Chapter 5) imports of goods and services.

Both intermediate consumption and final expenditure are transactions on goods and services, so once we understand the concepts of intermediate consumption and final expenditure we can explain in Section 3.6 an account of fundamental importance introduced for the first time to national accounting by the SNA93/ESA95: namely, the *goods and services account*, Account 0.

In Section 3.7, I show how the goods and services account relates to the production account (Account I) and to the primary distribution of income account: generation of income account (Account II.1.1), each of these two accounts having been explained in Chapter 2.

Finally, in Section 3.8, I use the production boundary to explain further the basic identity of national accounting but, as already noted, the full explanation of this has to be deferred until after we have considered imports of goods and services.

3.2   Categories of final expenditure

We need to consider the extremely important concept of final expenditure and the various categories of final expenditure. In this section I use Figure 3.1 to explain the categories of final expenditure and then, in Table 3.1, I give some data on these categories of final expenditure in the national accounts of the United Kingdom and Australia.

With each of final expenditure and intermediate consumption we are dealing with transactions in goods and services but final expenditure is the opposite of intermediate consumption. 'Intermediate consumption' is defined as the value of goods and services which are used or consumed as inputs in the process of production during a specific accounting period; this production results in further value adding to the inputs. Conversely, 'final expenditure' can initially be defined, albeit negatively, as expenditure on goods and services which is *not* intermediate consumption.

In plain terms, intermediate consumption is on goods and services that are wanted as *inputs*, during the *current* accounting period, for the production of further goods and services.

Conversely, final expenditure is on goods and services that are wanted *for their own sake* either for *present* purposes of consumption (for example, bread), or for the contribution they can make to production in one or more *future* accounting periods, or for selling to *non*-residents (thereby earning 'foreign exchange' to pay for needed imports). There is a philosophical sense in which fulfilling the final expenditures of various sorts is the ultimate aim or purpose or objective of all production.

Figure 3.1 shows in bold typeface the categories of final expenditure generally reported in national accounts. (Because final expenditure is a type of transaction distinguished from other types of transaction, I call each of the subdivisions among this type of transaction a 'category' – meaning a category or subdivision belonging to that type of transaction.) The SNA93/ESA95

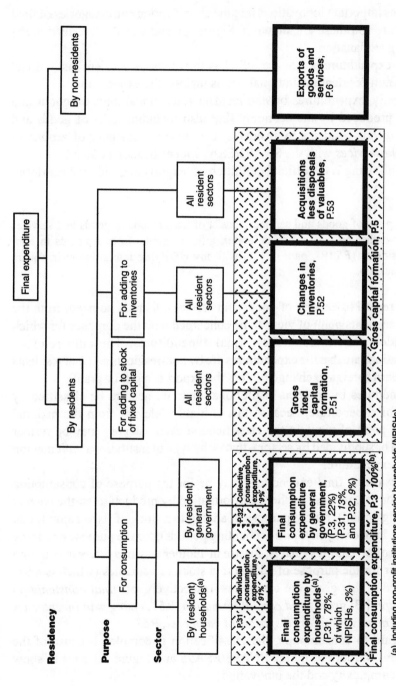

Residency

Final expenditure

By residents — By non-residents

Purpose

For consumption — For adding to stock of fixed capital — For adding to inventories

Sector

By (resident) households[a] — By (resident) general government — All resident sectors — All resident sectors — All resident sectors

Final consumption expenditure by households[a], (P.31; 78%; of which NPISHs, 3%)

Final consumption expenditure by general government, (P.3, 22%) (P.31, 13%, and P.32, 9%)

P.31: Individual consumption expenditure, 91%

P.32: Collective consumption expenditure, 9%

Final consumption expenditure, P.3 *100%*[b]

Gross fixed capital formation, P.51

Changes in inventories, P.52

Acquisitions less disposals of valuables, P.53

Gross capital formation, P.5

Exports of goods and services, P.6

(a) Including non-profit institutions serving households (NPISHs).
(b) Percentages in italics are for the United Kingdom in 1997 (rounded);
source: the *Blue Book 1999 edition*, table 1.6.0, p. 39.

Shading in diagram is only for grouping.

Figure 3.1 The categories of final expenditure

introduces important innovations into the classification and categories of final expenditure and these are shown in Figure 3.1 and will be described in the following explanation.

Final expenditure is first classified as to whether a resident institutional unit or a non-resident institutional unit is making the expenditure.

Basically, expenditures by *non*-resident institutional units on goods and services produced by the economy (but also including gifts of goods and services to non-residents by residents) comprise the category of *exports of goods and services* with the SNA93/ESA95 identification code P.6.

The following is the official definition of 'exports of goods and services', P.6:

> Exports of goods and services consist of transactions in goods and services ([whether by way of] sales, barter, gifts or grants) from residents to non-residents (*ESA95*, para. 3.128, with my clarifying interpolation in square brackets).

With regard to exports of goods and services, there is no need, from the national accounts point of view, to be concerned with the purposes for which *non*-residents are making these final expenditures. The only relevant considerations are that the expenditures are by non-residents and that residents thereby earn foreign exchange (unless the export is a gift or grant).

Expenditures by *resident* institutional units do need to be classified by purpose of expenditure, because this is highly relevant from the national accounts' point of view. In the classification each category may be further classified or subdivided by sector – that is, by type of institutional unit making the final expenditure.

For residents, final expenditure may be for the purpose of consumption (that is, for use, without further transformation by production, in the *current* accounting period), for the purpose of adding to a stock of fixed capital (that is, for use in one way in *future* accounting periods), for the purpose of adding to a stock of inventories (that is, for use in another way in a *future* accounting period), or for the purpose of adding to a stock of valuables (which is a use *sui generis*). This gives the categories, respectively, of: *final consumption expenditure*, P.3; *gross fixed capital formation*, P.51; *changes in inventories*, P.52; and *acquisitions less disposals of valuables*, P.53.

In regard to consumption, the classification is complex because of the innovations introduced by the SNA93/ESA95 and Figure 3.1 tries to show both the complexity and the innovations.

We start with the official definition of 'final consumption expenditure', P.3:

> Final consumption expenditure consists of *expenditure incurred* [directly] by resident institutional units on goods or services that are used for the direct satisfaction of individual needs or wants or the collective needs of members of the community. Final consumption expenditure may take place on the domestic territory or abroad (*ESA95*, para. 3.75, italics added and with my clarifying interpolation in square brackets because in the context of ascribing the expenditure to a sector of the economy the emphasis of 'directly' is helpful as indicating that 'by' means 'directly out of the pocket of ...').

In the System, consumption expenditure is undertaken only by households as households, by non-profit institutions serving households, and by general government. Other institutional units cannot, in principle, make final consumption expenditures.

Figure 3.1 proceeds by subdividing final consumption expenditure according to whether the expenditure is incurred directly by households, giving the category *final consumption expenditure by households* (and Figure 3.1 includes non-profit institutions serving households with households), or whether the expenditure is incurred directly by general government, giving the category *final consumption expenditure by general government*. This is the traditional classification and differs from the innovations introduced in the SNA93/ESA95 classification (that is, items relating to these categories do not appear in the official classification nor in the official template of accounts for the whole economy, although, necessarily, they do appear in the official template of accounts for the household sector and for the general government sector respectively (*SNA93*, pp. 601, 638 and 649; *ESA95*, pp. 304, 333 and 342)). It is pertinent to note that these categories are nevertheless reported in the United Kingdom's ESA95 national accounts for the whole economy (the *Blue Book 1999 edition*, table 1.6.0, p. 39).

In order to help you find your way through this part of Figure 3.1, I use illustrative percentages relating to final consumption expenditure, P.3, in the United Kingdom in 1997. These are the percentages given in italics in the diagram (the actual numbers are available in Table 3.1). This also helps to put the categories in a quantitative perspective relative to each other.

In macroeconomics, the important distinction is between final consumption expenditure by households ('private consumption') and final consumption expenditure by general government ('public consumption').

The problem for national accounting is that final consumption expenditure by general government is a mixture of two very different sorts of expenditure by objective or purpose and it is necessary for the national accounts to take this into consideration. These two sorts of objectives are dealt with in the SNA93/ESA95 as follows.

In the SNA93/ESA95 the subdivision of final consumption expenditure, P.3, is between *individual consumption expenditure*, P.31, and *collective consumption expenditure*, P.32. These categories of final expenditure are new to national accounting and this P.31/P.32 subdivision is an innovation of the SNA93/ESA95. The P.31/P.32 subdivision will be explained further in Chapter 6. For the moment all that is needed is the following brief explanation.

If the purpose of the consumption expenditure is to meet individual needs (explicitly, the needs of individuals who could, in principle, be identified or singled out by name as benefitting from the expenditure), then the final consumption expenditure is identified as being *individual* consumption expenditure, P.31. For example, expenditure incurred directly by households on food is to meet individual needs and so is a P.31 individual consumption expenditure.

If the purpose of the consumption expenditure is to meet collective needs (explicitly, there is, in principle, no sensible way in which the beneficiaries of the expenditure could be identified or singled out by name), then the final consumption expenditure is identified as being *collective* consumption expenditure, P.32. For example, consumption expenditure incurred directly by local government on the electricity used in street lighting is to meet collective needs and so is a P.32 collective consumption expenditure.

But expenditure by general government is not restricted to collective consumption expenditure. General government also makes *individual* consumption expenditure; for example, when the government spends money on providing school education free of charge, the objective of this expenditure is to benefit individuals/households (that is, those schoolchildren who could, in principle, be identified or singled out by name), and so this expenditure is classified as a P.31 individual consumption expenditure *by general government*, and conversely is not classified as a P.32 collective consumption expenditure by general government. Comparing the street lighting example with the school education example (both of which are consumption expenditures incurred *directly* by (that is, out of the pocket of) general government), you can appreciate that street lighting which benefits the community collectively in an unrestricted way is a very different sort of final consumption expenditure from free-of-charge school education which benefits only (identifiable) individuals in the community in a restricted way. You can thus appreciate that total final consumption expenditure by general government is a mixture of these two different sorts of final expenditure.

All final consumption expenditure by households is to meet individual needs (P.31). Accordingly, Figure 3.1 identifies final consumption expenditure by households as being in the P.31 category but puts 'P.31' in brackets because the identification code 'P.31' identifies individual consumption expenditure, and does not identify household consumption expenditure *per se*. It is just that, in this case, final consumption expenditure by households falls entirely within the category of P.31 Individual consumption expenditure.

By convention, all final consumption expenditure by non-profit institutions serving households is classified as consumption expenditure serving individual needs and so is also entirely within the P.31 category (*SNA93*, paras 9.44 and 9.85). I simplify Figure 3.1 by including final consumption expenditure by non-profit institutions serving households with final consumption expenditure by households (for example, expenditure incurred directly by a charity on providing food free of charge from a 'soup kitchen' for the poor). In the United Kingdom in 1997, final consumption expenditure by households (including non-profit institutions serving households) was 78 per cent of total final consumption expenditure. Of this, final consumption expenditure by non-profit institutions serving households was 3 per cent of total final consumption expenditure (conversely and by subtraction, 75 per cent was by households themselves).

Of the final consumption by general government (and as just explained), some is to meet collective needs (P.32) but some is to meet individual needs (P.31). Accordingly, Figure 3.1 identifies final consumption expenditure by general government as being in both the P.31 and the P.32 categories but puts 'P.31 and P.32' in brackets because the identification codes 'P.31' and 'P.32' identify individual consumption expenditure and collective consumption respectively, and do not identify general government consumption expenditure *per se*. Consequently, in Figure 3.1, 'Final consumption expenditure by general government' is shown as crossing the border between individual consumption expenditure and collective consumption expenditure because final consumption by general government falls within both the P.31 category and also the P.32 category.

In the United Kingdom in 1997, general government final consumption expenditure for individual consumption was 13 per cent of total final consumption expenditure and general government final consumption expenditure for collective consumption was 9 per cent of total final consumption expenditure. Looked at another way, of total final consumption expenditure by general government, 59 per cent was for the benefit of individuals, and 41 per cent was for the benefit of the community collectively.

Total final consumption expenditure by general government has to be identified as simply being in the overall P.3 category and in the United Kingdom in 1997 total final consumption expenditure by general government was 22 per cent of total final consumption expenditure.

(The 'missing' item of P.4 *actual final consumption* will be explained in Chapter 6 on general government and the household sector.)

Gross capital formation, P.5, is an opposite to consumption expenditure. The economic nature of consumption is that the goods and services are used in the current accounting period and play no further role in the process of production in that accounting period nor in any future accounting period; the economic nature of capital formation (other than acquisitions less disposals of valuables) is that the goods and services involved in capital formation do play a role in the process of production in one future accounting period or in more than one future accounting period.

In regard to capital formation, the three categories of *gross fixed capital formation*, P.51, *changes in inventories*, P.52, and *acquisitions less disposals of valuables*, P.53, together constitute the final expenditure category of *gross capital formation*, P.5. Each of these can be subdivided by sector and each and every sector in the economy can, and does, engage in these transactions, but (for the sake of keeping the diagram simple) Figure 3.1 does not show these subdivisions.

The official definition of 'gross fixed capital formation', P.51 is (in part):

> Gross fixed capital formation ... consists of resident producers' acquisitions, less disposals, of fixed assets during a given period ... Fixed assets are tangible or intangible assets produced as outputs from processes of production that are themselves used repeatedly, or continuously, in processes of production for more than one year (*ESA95*, para. 3.102).

In the national accounts, gross fixed capital formation may be subdivided according to type of fixed asset acquired (see Figure 1.7, pp. 38–9). There may be national variations in this classification to suit national needs; for example, the Australian System of National Accounts reports gross fixed capital formation in livestock (such as sheep for wool) as a separate category.

Also included in P.51 is the *costs of ownership transfer on non-produced non-financial assets*, P.5132. This is because, for example, the cost of transferring land titles is integrally associated with gross fixed capital formation on new buildings (and the value of the fixed asset in the balance sheet includes the cost of ownership transfer), so that it cannot be classified anywhere else (*SNA93*, paras 10.37 and 10.55-10.61; *ESA95*, para. 3.116).

The official definition of 'changes in inventories', P.52, is (in part):

> Changes in inventories are measured by the value of the entries into inventories *less* the value of withdrawals [from] … goods held in inventories (*ESA95*, para. 3.117, italics added and with my clarifying interpolation in square brackets).

If withdrawals from inventories is greater in value than entries into inventories, then changes in inventories can be negative.

The official definition of 'valuables' in the term 'acquisitions less disposals of valuables', P.53, is:

> Valuables are non-financial goods that are not used primarily for production or consumption, do not deteriorate (physically) over time under normal conditions and that are acquired and held primarily as stores of value (*ESA95*, para. 3.125).

In this context, valuables are such things as precious stones and metals (diamonds and so on, non-monetary gold, silver, and so on), jewellery made out of precious stones and metals, works of art, antiques, and so on.

In order to count as a valuable, an item has to be of 'recognised' 'high value or artistic significance', and this excludes 'ordinary' jewellery, paintings and so on 'whose purchase should be included in households' final consumption expenditure' (*UK NACSM*, paras 8.7 and 3.66).

Acquisitions less disposals of valuables is an awkwardly mixed category of final expenditure, capable of simultaneously being somewhat like consumption *and* somewhat like 'investment'. To illustrate, valuable jewellery is bought to accompany clothing (a consumption item) and valuable paintings are bought to decorate homes, but these valuables are also acquired in the expectation that they will retain their value and perhaps appreciate in value. In order to prevent expenditure on valuables being shifted between classifications, this P.53 category also applies, by an agreed convention of the ESA95, to acquisitions of valuables by museums and public art galleries, despite the fact that in such institutions valuables are used like fixed assets in the process of production (*ESA95*, para. 3.126; *UK NACSM*, para. 3.66).

Accordingly this P.53 category of expenditure has to be treated as a kind of its own.

The various categories of final expenditure generally used in national accounts are shown in bold typeface in Figure 3.1. Of these, the category of acquisitions less disposals of valuables is, as we shall see, exceedingly small relative to the other categories. The discussion that follows in this chapter is mostly confined to the other categories.

We may now consider the reporting of final expenditures in the System's national accounts. Table 3.1 gives the final expenditure by category for the United Kingdom economy in 1997 and for the Australian economy in 1997–98. Total final expenditure in the United Kingdom in 1997 was £1 032 711 million; total final expenditure in Australia in 1997–98 was $684 438 million.

It is interesting to compare the structure of each of these totals by percentages. In the United Kingdom in 1997, 64.4 per cent of total final expenditure was final consumption expenditure; in Australia in 1997–98 this percentage was 63.7 per cent, almost no different from that in the UK. The percentages of household final consumption expenditure and general government final consumption expenditure were also very similar in the United Kingdom and Australia: for households, 50.1 per cent and 48.6 per cent respectively, and for general government, 14.3 per cent and 15.1 per cent respectively.

Of general government final consumption expenditure (and taken as a percentage of total final expenditure), individual consumption expenditure was 8.5 per cent in the United Kingdom and 7.6 per cent in Australia, while collective consumption expenditure was 5.8 per cent in the United Kingdom and 7.5 per cent in Australia.

There are differences in the other categories of final expenditure. In the United Kingdom in 1997, 13.4 per cent of total final expenditure was gross capital formation; in Australia in 1997–98 this percentage was 19.6 per cent, a considerable difference.

Of gross capital formation (and taken as a percentage of total final expenditure), gross fixed capital formation was 13 per cent in the United Kingdom and 19.3 per cent in Australia, and changes in inventories was 0.4 per cent in the United Kingdom and 0.4 per cent in Australia.

We may note that for the United Kingdom in 1997 the P.53 category, acquisitions less disposals of valuables, was a very small proportion of total final expenditure: 0.004 per cent. Note that for some years this P.53 item can be negative which indicates net disposals by residents to non-residents (*UK NACSM*, para. 12.61).

In the United Kingdom in 1997, 22.2 per cent of total final expenditure was exports of goods and services; in Australia in 1997–98 this percentage

Table 3.1
Final expenditure in the United Kingdom and Australia

SNA93/ ESA95 identification code	SNA93/ESA95 name	United Kingdom 1997, £ million	Australia 1997–98, $ million	Percentage of total United Kingdom 1997	Australia 1997–98
P.3	Final consumption expenditure				
P.31	By households[a]	517 032	332 311	50.1	48.6
P.3	By general government				
P.31	For individual consumption	87 721	51 878	8.5	7.6
P.32	For collective consumption	60 052	51 703	5.8	7.5
P.3	Total by general government	147 773	103 581	14.3	15.1
P.3	Total final consumption expenditure	664 805	435 892	64.4	63.7
P.5	Gross capital formation				
P.51	Gross fixed capital formation	134 153	131 930	13.0	19.3
P.52	Changes in inventories	4 388	2 413	0.4	0.4
P.53	Acquisitions less disposals of valuables[b]	39	—	0.004	—
P.5	Total gross capital formation	138 580	134 343	13.4	19.6
P.6	Exports of goods and services	229 326	114 203	22.2	16.7
Total	Total final expenditure	1 032 711	684 438	100	100

(a) Including non-profit institutions serving households (which in the United Kingdom spent £18 725 million on individual consumption expenditure).
(b) Category not reported in the Australian System of National Accounts.

Sources: Office for National Statistics, *United Kingdom National Accounts The Blue Book 1999 edition*, table 1.6.0, p. 39; Australian Bureau of Statistics, *Australian System of National Accounts 1997–98*, Catalogue No. 5204.0, tables 1.8, 2.15 and 2.21, pp. 28, 55 and 61.

was 16.7 per cent, so the percentage is considerably lower in Australia.

Having initially defined final expenditure as expenditure on goods and services that is not intermediate consumption and having considered the categories of final expenditure, we can define final expenditure in terms of the production boundary and thence begin to discuss the economic difference between intermediate consumption and final expenditure. All this is key to understanding the economic nature of final expenditure.

What is the production boundary?

3.3   The production boundary

The production boundary as used in both the SNA93 and the ESA95 is a boundary between activities that count as production (economic activities) and activities that do not count as production.

Because products are the result of economic activity and because output consists of products, the production boundary determines what counts as output in the System and what does not count as output. Gross value added is Output *minus* Intermediate consumption, and primary incomes are the incomes distributed out of gross value added, so, by determining what counts as output, the production boundary determines the amount of gross value added recorded by the System and thence the amount of primary incomes recorded by the System.

The production boundary is thus a fundamental concept in the SNA93/ESA95. Furthermore, the production boundary can be used to explain, and to define positively, the concepts of output, intermediate consumption and final expenditure. I call these positive definitions (to be given in Section 3.4) the 'production boundary definitions', and the production boundary definitions are essential to a proper understanding of these concepts.

The production boundary is used in other important definitions as well. For example, as we shall see, the definition of 'employment' uses the production boundary.

We have quoted in Chapter 2 (Section 2.6) the official definition of 'production' as an activity carried out under the control and responsibility of an institutional unit that uses inputs of labour, capital [as well as land] and goods and services to produce goods and services. This means that production does not cover natural processes that occur without any human involvement. For example, the unmanaged growth of fish stocks in international waters does not count as production, but fish farming, because of its human involvement, does count as production.

Figure 3.2 shows how we can understand the production boundary. Figure 3.2 is intended to explain both the production boundary and also the relation between the activities of production and the related classifications of the categories of supply and uses of output and of the types of output given in Figure 2.3 of Chapter 2 (so the reader should look back at Figure 2.3, p. 92, during the following explanation).

The organisation of the explanation of Figure 3.2 is complex but this should cause no difficulty providing my basic method of explanation is made clear at the outset.

Starting at the top of Figure 3.2, I proceed from left to right and downwards ending up in turn with each of the boxes at the bottom of Figure 3.2. The first box to be explained is in the bottom left-hand corner, and so on. In all but two cases, these boxes contain a sort of output (where 'sort' refers to the special characteristics of output in that box and to the Figure 2.3 type of output). The two exceptions are: an activity (economic) inside the production boundary which results in products but not in output; and an activity (not counted as economic) outside the production boundary (the last box on the right).

For each sort of output as it occurs I give a brief explanation of the consequences for national accounting of that sort of output. This explanation comprises explanations of: the valuation of the relevant sort of output; the constituents of the relevant intermediate consumption; the relevant types of primary income arising; and, where relevant, the category of final expenditure involved. All this is required for a proper understanding of the production boundary.

Gross value added can be understood in all cases as Output *minus* Intermediate consumption and needs no further discussion.

The explanations of valuations of own-account output for own final use are more lengthy than the other explanations; this is because own-account output for own final use is not the subject of an exchange or transaction in the market and this necessitates the use of imputed values, and these imputations need explanation. In explaining these valuations I simplify by using the terms 'prices' and 'market prices' without further elaboration, but in the next chapter we will discuss the exact meaning of 'market prices'. The imputations also have implications for the primary incomes arising out of the resulting gross value added.

Figure 3.2 starts at the top with *any* activity by an institutional unit using inputs to produce goods and services.

As we will explain, some of the activities with which we start in Figure 3.2 are classified as being within the production boundary while others are

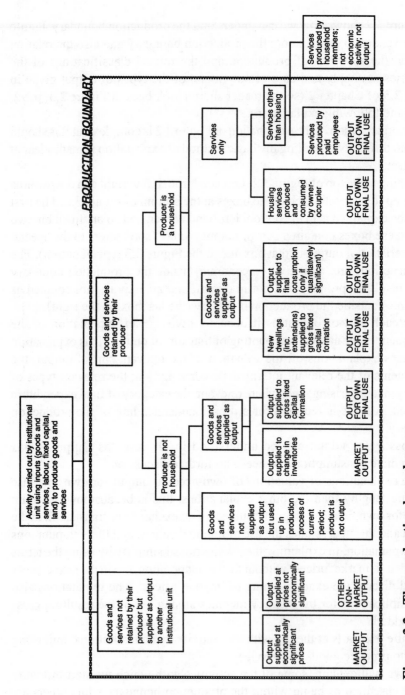

Figure 3.2 The production boundary

The diagram, titled **PRODUCTION BOUNDARY**, shows:

Activity carried out by institutional unit using inputs (goods and services, labour, fixed capital, land) to produce goods and services

This branches into:

Goods and services not retained by their producer but supplied as output to another institutional unit
- Output supplied at economically significant prices → MARKET OUTPUT
- Output supplied at prices not economically significant → OTHER NON-MARKET OUTPUT

Goods and services retained by their producer

Producer is not a household
- Goods and services not supplied as output but used up in production process of current period; product is not output
- Goods and services supplied as output
  - Output supplied to change in inventories → MARKET OUTPUT
  - Output supplied to gross fixed capital formation → OUTPUT FOR OWN FINAL USE

Producer is a household
- Goods and services supplied as output
  - New dwellings (inc. extensions) supplied to gross fixed capital formation → OUTPUT FOR OWN FINAL USE
  - Output supplied to final consumption (only if quantitatively significant) → OUTPUT FOR OWN FINAL USE
- Services only
  - Housing services produced and consumed by owner-occupier → OUTPUT FOR OWN FINAL USE
  - Services other than housing
    - Services produced by paid employees → OUTPUT FOR OWN FINAL USE
    - Services produced by household members; not economic activity; not output

122

classified as not being within the production boundary; the production boundary can thus be understood in terms of those activities which are classified as being within the production boundary and which thereby count as *economic* activity.

Figure 3.2 shows that there are two main possibilities in relation to goods and services produced by using inputs. The first main possibility is that the goods and services are *not* retained by their producer but are instead supplied to an institutional unit other than their producer. The second main possibility is that the goods and services *are* retained by their producer.

In the first main possibility, where the goods and services are not retained by their producer but are supplied to other institutional units, the activity of producing those goods and services qualifies, by that fact of supply alone, as an economic activity of production. Consequently, the goods and services so produced count as products; and furthermore, because the product is supplied, the product counts as output.

There are two resulting sorts of output from this sort of economic activity: market output, which is output supplied at economically significant prices, and other non-market output, which is output supplied free of charge or at prices not economically significant (Figure 2.3).

Output supplied in market transactions at economically significant prices is simply valued in terms of those market prices. This sort of economic activity can be undertaken by any type of institutional unit acting as a producer: non-financial corporations, financial corporations, general government and households (including non-profit institutions serving households, such as charity shops).

Intermediate consumption for this sort of production is likewise valued at market prices and simply covers the range of usual intermediate inputs.

Primary incomes of compensation of employees and gross operating surplus/gross mixed income arise in the way described in Chapter 2, Section 2.7, for Table 2.1.

Table 2.1 dealt entirely with this sort of output, which is the dominant sort of output in the economy: when discussing Table 2.3 we saw that in the United Kingdom in 1997 this sort of output accounted for 85.8 per cent of the United Kingdom's total output in that year (but note that in this there is a further part of market output in Figure 3.2 which we have not yet discussed).

Because such output is valued at market prices, a net operating surplus/net mixed income will arise. That is, sales receipts, as the valuation of output, will be greater than the sum of the costs of production. (This was not dealt with in Table 2.1 because in Chapter 2 we did not extend the discussion to a consideration of the consumption of fixed capital as a cost of production, important though it is as a cost of production. Table 2.1 did not consider consumption of fixed capital because it was concerned only with *gross* value added and consequent gross operating surplus/gross mixed income.)

Output supplied in non-market transactions either free of charge or at prices not economically significant is known as other non-market output (Figure 2.3). This sort of economic activity is undertaken by only two types of institutional units acting as producers: general government and non-profit institutions serving households. When discussing Table 2.3 we saw that in the United Kingdom in 1997 other non-market output accounted for 10.9 per cent of the United Kingdom's total output in that year (and of this, 89 per cent was produced by general government and 11 per cent by non-profit institutions serving households – the *Blue Book 1999 edition*, table 1.7.1, pp. 58–9).

Valuing output supplied at prices not economically significant is a complex issue. The basic principle of the SNA93/ESA95 is that the concept of opportunity cost is employed in valuations. In other words, value of output is to be measured by 'the amount of the benefits that could have been secured by using the asset or good in alternative ways' (*SNA93*, para. 1.60). In practical terms this means that market prices are used for valuations wherever possible. If this is not possible, then the value of output is to be be measured at the sum of its costs of production (*ESA95*, para. 1.52).

These costs of production comprise (*SNA93*, para. 6.91):

Intermediate consumption;
Compensation of employees;
Consumption of fixed capital; and
Other taxes, less subsidies, on production.

Other non-market output produced by general government or by non-profit institutions serving households is valued at the sum of its costs of production. The consequence of valuing output at the sum of the costs of production is that the gross operating surplus for this type of output is equal to consumption of fixed capital (because gross operating surplus is calculated as output *minus* intermediate consumption *minus* compensation of employees *minus* other taxes, less subsidies, on production). Consequently also, by this accounting convention, the net operating surplus arising for this sort of output is zero (net operating surplus being gross operating surplus *minus* consumption of fixed capital). That is, there is no allowance for any mark-up over and above the sum of the costs of production including consumption of fixed capital. This result accords with commonsense, because we do not consider that the government or a non-profit institution serving households makes a 'profit' (a net operating surplus) on its production of other non-market output.

(Taxes on production and so on will be explained in Chapter 4 so for the moment this item will be held over.)

This concludes the discussion of the first main possibility with its two different sorts of output.

In the second main possibility, the goods and services are retained by their producer. This is own-account production for own-account use and, with one exception, this own-account use is a final use; that is, involves a final expenditure by the producer. This sort of economic activity can be undertaken by any sort of institutional unit acting as producer, but most of this economic activity is undertaken by households as producers: in 1997, 90 per cent of the UK's output for own final use, P.12, was produced by households including non-profit institutions serving households (the *Blue Book 1999 edition*, table 1.7.1, pp. 58–9).

This second main possibility can be divided in the first instance between those cases where the producer is not a household unit and those cases where the producer is a household unit.

For the case where the producer is *not* a household unit there are in turn two subsidiary possibilities.

The first subsidiary possibility is where the goods and services are not supplied as output but are instead used up in producing the current accounting period's output. In this first subsidiary possibility, the goods and services produced do not count as output (because they are not 'supplied') although they do count as products which are the result of economic activity within the production boundary.

In Section 2.6 of Chapter 2, we discussed hypothetically the example of a *bakery* buying-in wheat and itself grinding the wheat into flour for use by itself in making bread during the same accounting period. This example of bakery-produced/bakery-used-up flour would exemplify the first subsidiary possibility – the flour is a product which is the result of economic activity but the flour, not being 'supplied' (instead being used up by its producer in the same accounting period), does not count as output in the technical sense of the word 'output'.

This production which is not output is the one exception where retention of a product by a producer does not involve or imply a final expenditure. This is by the nature of the product being used as an intermediate input during the same accounting period in which it was produced. (However, if the bakery-produced flour is *not* used as an intermediate input in the same accounting period, but is added to inventories of work in progress (a final expenditure), then the bakery-produced flour becomes output by virtue of being so supplied to inventories.)

The second subsidiary possibility is where the goods and services are retained by their non-household producer but are nevertheless 'supplied' as output. This second possibility has two subdivisions.

The first subdivision applies to output in both forms (goods and services) and occurs where the goods or services are 'supplied' in the sense of being added to the producer's inventories of finished goods or of work in progress (inventories of work in progress include services-in-progress as well as goods-in-progress; work in progress is especially important in industries where some considerable time is needed to produce the finished good (for example, shipbuilding and large structures)).

This sort of supply of output is known as changes in inventories, and this output is classified as market output because the goods or services in the inventories could or will eventually be sold on the market or because the goods and services are to be used further in the enterprise's production process (see Figure 2.3). An illustrative example of this first subdivision would occur if the mill added some flour to its inventories of flour (a finished good from the mill's point of view).

(Finished goods are, by their very nature as finished goods, intended for sale, but it is possible in exceptional circumstances (such as the sale of the enterprise) to transfer the ownership of (that is, 'sell') items classified as work in progress.)

This sort of output supplied to inventories of finished goods or work in progress is in principle valued at the market price which would have been realised had the output been immediately sold. For finished goods, the full market price can be applied. For work in progress the valuation is obtained by multiplying the relevant price by the share of the (eventual) total production costs incurred during that accounting period. For example, if, for an item added to inventories of work in progress, three-quarters of the (eventual) total production cost had been incurred during the accounting period, then the valuation should be at three-quarters of the relevant price.

For this sort of output, intermediate consumption arises in the usual way, and the primary incomes of compensation of employees and gross operating surplus/gross mixed income arise in the usual way. Because market prices are used and because these prices include a mark-up for net operating surplus/net mixed income, a net operating surplus or net mixed income will arise for this sort of output.

Such production of output which ends up being added to the inventories of finished goods or work in progress of the producer implies a corresponding final expenditure – a P.52 expenditure – by the producer (*ESA95*, paras 3.18 and 3.122). Note that although such inventories may be used *in a subsequent accounting period*, this is not relevant for the classification of changes in inventories as a final expenditure *of the current accounting period*.

The second subdivision applies to output only in the form of goods and occurs where the goods (which must be of an appropriate sort) are 'supplied' in the sense of being added to the producer's stock of fixed capital; this sort of supply of output is known as own-account gross fixed capital formation, and this output is classified as output for own final use (see Figure 2.3). An illustrative example of this first subdivision would occur if the bakery itself constructed an oven (fixed capital) for its own use in baking bread. Enterprises in farming and mining are especially prone to this sort of production. For example, farmers often construct for themselves fences, ditches, and so on, on the farm; mining enterprises construct their own mine shafts and associated works. General government may also produce computer software (an intangible fixed asset) for its own use.

This sort of output from own-account production supplied to own-account gross fixed capital formation is in principle to be valued at the market price which would have been realised had the output been offered for sale in the market or, equivalently, had the output been bought from an independent supplier. This depends on the existence of markets for such goods so that reliable prices could be obtained for the purpose of valuation. If such prices cannot be obtained, then 'a second best procedure must be used in which the value of the output of the goods or services produced for own use is deemed to be equal to the sum of their costs of production' (*SNA93*, para. 6.85).

For producing this sort of output, intermediate consumption arises in the usual way as does compensation of employees. If the valuation is at market prices then there will arise both a gross operating surplus and a net operating surplus (or, depending on the type of producer, a gross mixed income and a net mixed income) – this is because the market price will include a mark-up which allows for a net operating surplus or a net mixed income. However, if the valuation is at the sum of the costs of production only a gross operating surplus or a gross mixed income (equal to consumption of fixed capital) will arise – this is because there is in the sum of the costs of production (by definition of those costs) no allowance for a mark-up which would determine a net operating surplus or a net mixed income.

Such own-account production of output in the form of fixed capital assets for own-account gross fixed capital formation implies a corresponding final expenditure – a P.51 expenditure – by the producer (*SNA93*, para. 10.35 (*d*); *ESA95*, para. 3.103).

In addition to functioning as *consuming* institutional units, households can also function as *producing* institutional units (*SNA93*, paras 4.138–4.150). The role of households as producers will be explained in stages throughout this section, and in the following paragraphs we will see some of the ways in which households function as producers of output for own final use. In the United Kingdom in 1997, households (including non-profit institutions serving households) produced 12.6 per cent of the United Kingdom's total output, and of households' total output, 24 per cent was output for own final use (the *Blue Book 1999 edition*, table 1.7.1, pp. 58–9).

For the case where the producer *is* a household unit there are in turn two subsidiary possibilities, each with subdivisions. The first subsidiary possibility is where goods only are produced and supplied as output. The second subsidiary possibility is where services only are produced (and note that, as will be explained, not all of these services count as output from the national accounting point of view).

The first subsidiary possibility concerns *goods* produced and retained by households and this first subsidiary possibility has two subdivisions.

The first subdivision applies only to the own-account construction of a dwelling (or an extension to a dwelling) – the dwelling being for the use of the producing household itself. This first subdivision may be extended to cover voluntary community construction of a building – such as would occur when the members of a church, volunteering their labour free of charge, construct a church or church hall. Such own-account construction is gross fixed capital formation and is classified as output for own final use, and this output classification is deemed to cover the case of work in progress (that is, where the dwelling and so on is not completed within the accounting period). Conversely, work in progress intended for this own-account capital formation is excluded from the definition of inventories of work in progress (*ESA95*, p. 139, definition of 'work in progress', AN.122; *UK NACSM*, 'own-account construction', p. 106).

The valuation of household own-account construction of dwellings and so on is either at the market prices of similar fixed assets or, if such prices are not available, at the sum of the costs of production, including in these costs an estimated valuation at market wage rates for the time of voluntary free labour used in the construction. If the valuation is at market prices, the mark-up in those prices leads to both a gross mixed income and a net mixed income

(*ESA95*, para. 3.113). If the valuation is at the sum of the costs of production, a net mixed income does not arise.

Such own-account production of output in the form of new dwellings and so on for own-account use implies a corresponding final expenditure – a P.51 expenditure – by the producer.

The second subdivision applies only to the production of goods for the household's own consumption, such as occurs in the example of subsistence farmers in less developed economies who grow and eat their own food, or such as the carrying of water to supply the household (an activity that may be considered analogous to extracting oil). Such production is recorded in national accounts only 'if this type of production is significant, i.e. if it is believed to be quantitatively important in relation to the total supply of that good in a country' (*ESA95*, para. 3.08). In the ESA95, own-account production, storage and processing of goods in the form of agricultural products is in principle to be recorded, but in the United Kingdom such production is generally not recorded: 'in practice produce from gardens or allotments has proved impossible to estimate in the United Kingdom so far' (the *Blue Book 1999 edition*, p. 13). However, when such output is recorded or estimated, such own-account production of goods for final consumption is classified as output for own final use (see Figure 2.3).

The valuation of goods produced by households for own final consumption is at the market prices for which the goods could be sold if offered for sale on the market.

Intermediate consumption for this type of output may be recorded in the usual way, and if the producing household employs employees in such own-account production then compensation of employees will arise with the residual primary income being gross mixed income. Because market prices are used, which include a mark-up on production costs, net mixed income will also arise from this type of production.

Such own-account production of output in the form of consumption goods for own-account use implies a corresponding final expenditure – a P.31 expenditure – by the producer (*ESA95*, para. 3.76).

The second subsidiary possibility concerns *services* produced and retained by households. This second subsidiary possibility has two subdivisions and the second subdivision has in turn two sub-subdivisions.

The first subdivision applies only to those households known as 'owner-occupier households' (or 'owner-occupiers' for short). In this first subdivision, a household which owns and lives in ('occupies') its own dwelling (hence 'owner-occupier') must be treated in two roles. As owner, the household has the role of a producer who, using a very substantial fixed asset (the dwelling), produces housing services (that is, dwelling-shelter services); these services are supplied to itself in its other role as occupier; this supply counts as final consumption by the occupier (just as payment of rental by a tenant of a dwelling to a landlord counts as final consumption expenditure by the tenant). Such output of housing services by the owner is classified as output for own final (consumption) use. The important feature of this first subdivision is that the production depends upon a fixed asset which is important in the wealth of many households, and the total value of these fixed assets is also important in the economy's stock of fixed assets. To illustrate, in Australia's national balance sheet for 30 June 1998, dwellings (both owner-occupied and rented-out) accounted for 34 per cent of Australia's total fixed assets, and dwellings (again of both sorts) accounted for 26 per cent of households' total wealth (*Australian System of National Accounts 1997–98*, tables 1.15 and 2.24, pp. 35 and 64).

Housing services produced and supplied by owner-occupiers are included within the production boundary because of their quantitative significance in most economies. The value of output from any owner-occupied dwelling is measured as being equal in value to the rental that would be paid on the market for accommodation of the same size, quality and type (*SNA93*, para. 9.58). It is also obvious that it would be anomalous to include landlord–tenant output/rentals in output/final expenditure but not do the same for owner-occupied dwellings.

Expenditure by owner-occupiers on decoration, maintenance and repairs of their dwellings counts as intermediate consumption (and is conversely excluded from household final consumption expenditure). The treatment of owner-occupiers and landlords in regard to such expenditure is exactly the same, as it has to be for the sake of consistency. This intermediate consumption by owner-occupiers is deducted from the output of owner-occupied dwellings to give gross value added resulting from production by owner-occupiers.

Housing services produced by owner-occupiers is a unique sort of output in that this is the only sort of production that, of itself, requires no labour input: the dwelling has merely to be lived in in order to produce its output (*ESA95*, para. 11.16). Consequently and in principle, there arises in the case of such production no compensation of employees. As a consequence of this, all the gross value added resulting from production by an owner-occupier is classified as gross operating surplus. This (imputed) gross operating surplus accrues as primary income to the owner-occupier. Deducting consumption of fixed capital from this gross operating surplus gives a net operating surplus accruing as imputed primary income to the owner-occupier.

Note that we accept as an obvious proposition that the net operating surplus received by a landlord out of the rental on a dwelling should be subject to income tax (after allowing for interest paid on any finance borrowed to acquire the dwelling). It used to be the case in the United Kingdom (between 1803 to 1816 and then again between 1842 to 1963) that the imputed net operating surplus primary income of owner-occupiers was (after allowing for interest) subject to income tax under Schedule A.

Such own-account production of output in the form of housing services for own-account use implies a corresponding final expenditure – a P.31 expenditure – by the owner-occupier (*SNA93*, para. 9.58; *ESA95*, para. 3.76). Note that final consumption expenditure also arises when a tenant pays a rental to a landlord; this case is covered by the bottom left-hand sort of output.

In the United Kingdom in 1997, households paid £20.7 billion in 'actual rentals for housing' (actual cash outflow), and 'paid' £41 billion in 'imputed rentals for housing' (not a cash outflow), so the latter is almost twice as great as the former. In Australia in 1997–98, households paid \$14.8 billion in 'actual rent for housing' and 'paid' \$44.2 billion in 'imputed rent for owner-occupiers', so the latter is nearly three times greater than the former. This demonstrates the magnitude, and importance, of owner-occupation in relation to dwellings (the *Blue Book 1999 edition*, table 6.4, p. 218; *Australian System of National Accounts 1997–98*, table 2.25, p. 65).

We now consider the second subdivision of services other than the housing services of owner-occupiers. This second subdivision has two sub-subdivisions. The first sub-subdivision applies to services ('domestic services') produced by paid employees of the household ('domestic servants') for the household's own final consumption. Domestic services produced by domestic servants count as an economic activity of own-account production, with the output being supplied to the household which employs the domestic servants. Paid domestic servants are by convention of national accounting treated as separate from the employer's household and do not count as part of the employer's household even if they live on the same premises (*SNA93*, para. 4.135).

How is this output valued? By a convention of national accounting any intermediate consumption incurred in such production is ignored and 'the value of the output produced is deemed to be equal to the compensation of employees paid, including any compensation in kind such as food or accommodation' (*SNA93*, para. 6.88). By the same convention, gross value added is equal to the compensation of employees. Because of this, no gross operating surplus arises for this sort of output.

One important feature of the production of domestic services is that a primary income of compensation of employees is earned (by the domestic servant) as a result of the production (and is properly subject to income tax and social security contributions). Therefore this sort of activity must be classified within the production boundary. Because there is no gross operating surplus and hence no net operating surplus, no further income tax is levied against this sort of economic activity (that is, no income tax arises other than the income tax on the wages of the domestic servants).

Such own-account production of output by domestic servants implies a corresponding final expenditure – a P.31 expenditure – by the household employing the domestic servants (*ESA95*, para. 3.76).

The second sub-subdivision applies to services (of the domestic service type) produced by members of the household for the household's own consumption. As shown in Figure 3.2 the convention of the SNA93/ESA95 is to draw the production boundary around all and only the economic activities so far considered; conversely, the production boundary excludes services produced by household members for household own consumption.

Economic activities are those activities which occur within the production boundary so that, under the conventions of the SNA93/ESA95, production of services by household members for the use of the household itself is excluded from the production boundary and so does not count as economic activity.

This exclusion is considered by some to be unjustified. However, the logical consequences of including such own-account production for own-account use within the production boundary are unacceptable in at least three respects.

First, if such activities were to be included within the production boundary, then a net mixed income would arise, and such income should properly be subject to income tax (as in the case of the income of owner-occupiers). However, while everybody accepts that whenever a domestic servant is paid to sweep one's kitchen floor the income tax inspector has a right to demand income tax on the employee compensation (primary income) arising from this production, nobody would accept that the income tax inspector has a right to demand income tax on the net mixed income (primary income) that would arise were sweeping one's own kitchen floor to be included within the production boundary. Yet this is the logical consequence of putting sweeping one's own kitchen floor on the same footing as having one's kitchen floor swept by a paid domestic servant!

Second, once these activities are included within the production boundary, the very important terms 'employment' and 'unemployment' become meaningless. A key feature of those activities which are counted as being within the production boundary is that any person engaged in any one of these economic activities within the production boundary is classified as being *employed* (either in an employee job or in a self-employed job) in the two basic senses that such a person is able, literally, to put food on the table for the sustenance of that person's family and that the person derives from this activity a primary income which is, or could reasonably be, subject to income tax.

The official definition of 'employment' is:

> Employment covers all persons – both employees and self-employed – engaged in some productive activity that falls *within the production boundary* of the system (*ESA95*, para. 11.11, italics added).

Conversely, any person not engaged in an activity that falls within the production boundary can be described as being unoccupied. Unoccupied persons without work but available for work and seeking work (that is, able and willing and wishing to be employed) are classified as *unemployed*; the remainder of unoccupied persons are classified as being *not in the labour force* (*SNA93*, p. 408; also *ESA95*, para. 11.20).

Those classified as unemployed are unemployed in the two basic senses of not being able by their own activities to put food on the table and of not having a primary income that could be subject to income tax.

However, if own-account production of services for the household produced by members of the household were to be included within the production boundary, then nearly every able-bodied adult would become 'employed' and, conversely, almost nobody would be 'unemployed'. This logical consequence is not acceptable because we do need the terms 'employment' and 'unemployment' to have their current, well understood and widely accepted, meanings.

Third, the consequences of including the relatively large magnitude of the activity of own-account production of household services for the household by members of the household are unacceptable in terms of what would happen to the gross domestic product. If the imputed output of this non-market production were to be included in the gross domestic product, the estimates of the gross domestic product would be very considerably changed and many of the purposes served by estimates of GDP would be vitiated. For example, it would then not be clear what labour productivity figures (the greatly enlarged GDP divided by number employed – the denominator including nearly all the adult population) would mean.

All these logical consequences being generally unacceptable, it is necessary to count services produced by household members for household use as being outside the production boundary.

Figure 3.2 defines the production boundary in terms of those activities which are included within the production boundary – those activities that count as economic activities in the national accounting sense of the term. But the production boundary is more than this. The production boundary is not only a boundary around activities that count as production and activities that do not count as production; it is also a boundary around the production of the output for the current accounting period. Under the conventions of accrual accounting, all output must be reckoned as output for a particular, or current, accounting period *and for that period only*. The production boundary is thus also a *temporal* boundary around the current accounting period.

Related to this temporal aspect of the production boundary is the fact that the production boundary can also be seen as a boundary between, on the one hand, resident institutional units – of whatever sort – acting as producers, called by me 'producers-as-producers', and, on the other hand, resident institutional units not acting as producers and all non-resident institutional units.

Once we understand the production boundary, we can define 'output' as the goods and services produced within the production boundary and supplied during an accounting period. This is the production boundary definition of 'output'. Obviously, in order to understand this definition one must first understand the production boundary, this is one reason why it is necessary to explain the production boundary so thoroughly.

The production boundary is also important because we can use the production boundary to define 'final expenditure' positively and also to define 'intermediate consumption'. Thence we can explain the economic nature of final expenditure and thence also its relation to gross value added, thus laying the foundations for understanding the basic identity of national accounting.

3.4   Final expenditure crosses the production boundary going outwards

If we restrict our consideration to purchases of goods and services produced by resident producers during the current accounting period, then 'final expenditure' can be positively defined as expenditure on those goods and services which cross the production boundary going outwards. This I call the production boundary definition of 'final expenditure'.

In most cases the final expenditure is by an institutional unit different from the producer, as when a household buys bread from the bakery, and so is an actual transaction. In some cases the final expenditure is by the same institutional unit as the producer, and so is an imputed transaction. For example, the imputed transaction by an occupier on the housing services produced by itself as owner, or the imputed transaction by a producer-as-investor acquiring a fixed asset produced on own-account.

From its production boundary definition, any final expenditure can be understood as a transaction between a producer-as-producer and either any resident institutional unit acting in a capacity other than that of producer or any non-resident institutional unit, noting that in the case of imputed transactions we have to consider the same institutional unit acting in two roles.

'Intermediate consumption' can then be defined as expenditure on those goods and services, produced during the current period, that do not cross the production boundary going outwards or as expenditure on those goods and services which cross the production boundary coming inwards from inventories. This is the production boundary definition of 'intermediate consumption'.

The common case of intermediate consumption is when the expenditure is on a good or service produced during the same production period; this is the case which applies throughout Table 2.1. However, if the intermediate consumption is not out of current production, but is out of inventories of goods (previously produced and accumulated inventories), then intermediate consumption has to be represented as coming into the production boundary from these inventories. Accordingly, intermediate consumption also includes any transaction coming inwards across the production boundary.

These definitions and this explanation are all illustrated in Figure 3.3. Figure 3.3 draws three boundaries: the production boundary; a boundary around resident institutional units, with the production boundary being within this residents' boundary; and a separate boundary around non-resident institutional units. Within the production boundary are located institutional units acting as producers, or what I call 'producers-as-producers'.

Outside the production boundary but within the residents' boundary are located resident institutional units who are not acting as producers. These may be households or government departments acting as consumers or any resident institutional unit including any producer acting as an investor in fixed capital or as an investor in inventories or as an investor in valuables.

In the common case, intermediate consumption comprises expenditure on goods and services that remain within the production boundary and these

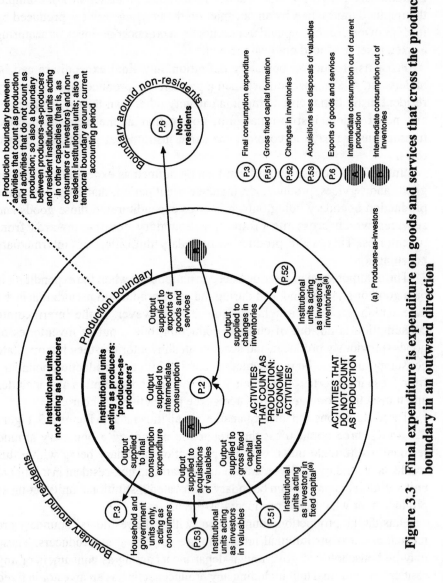

Figure 3.3   Final expenditure is expenditure on goods and services that cross the production boundary in an outward direction

Within the figure:

Boundary around residents

Production boundary

Production boundary between activities that count as production and activities that do not count as production; so also a boundary between producers-as-producers and resident institutional units acting in other capacities (that is, as consumers or investors) and non-resident institutional units; also a temporal boundary around current accounting period

Boundary around non-residents

(P.6) Non-residents

Institutional units not acting as producers

Institutional units acting as producers: 'producers-as-producers'

Output supplied to exports of goods and services

Output supplied to intermediate consumption

Output supplied to changes in inventories

(P.2)

ACTIVITIES THAT COUNT AS PRODUCTION: 'ECONOMIC ACTIVITIES'

ACTIVITIES THAT DO NOT COUNT AS PRODUCTION

(P.52) Institutional units acting as investors in inventories[a]

Output supplied to final consumption expenditure

Output supplied to acquisitions of valuables

Output supplied to gross fixed capital formation

(P.3) Household and government units only, acting as consumers

(P.53) Institutional units acting as investors in valuables

(P.51) Institutional units acting as investors in fixed capital[a]

(P.3) Final consumption expenditure
(P.51) Gross fixed capital formation
(P.52) Changes in inventories
(P.53) Acquisitions less disposals of valuables
(P.6) Exports of goods and services
(A) Intermediate consumption out of current production
(B) Intermediate consumption out of inventories

(a)   Producers-as-investors

products are subject to a further process of value adding during the current accounting period. Intermediate consumption in the common case can thus be shown by the arrow labelled 'A' which remains within the production boundary. This 'A' arrow represents those goods and services produced during the current period by one producer and sold to another producer for use as an input during the same period. This output does not cross the production boundary and is simply used in producing the current period's output. This 'A' arrow is thus shown as going 'internally' to the P.2 transaction of intermediate consumption.

In the less common case (in relative terms), intermediate consumption can be shown by an arrow coming inwards across the production boundary. This arrow is labelled 'B'. This 'B' arrow represents those goods, produced during a previous accounting period and held in inventories, which cross the production boundary coming inwards to be used in producing the current period's output. This 'B' arrow is also shown as going to the P.2 transaction of intermediate consumption.

This 'B' arrow represents a *reduction* in inventories. The following argument is restricted to inventories of materials and supplies held by the producer. (It is also possible for intermediate consumption to be supplied out of inventories of finished goods held by an institutional unit other than the producer intending to use those goods as inputs.) We have the equation for intermediate consumption derived in Section 2.4:

$$\begin{array}{l}\text{Intermediate}\\\text{consumption}\end{array} = \begin{array}{l}\text{Purchases of}\\\text{materials and supplies}\\\text{and of services}\end{array} - \left[\begin{array}{l}\text{Value of change in}\\\text{inventories of}\\\text{materials and supplies}\end{array}\right]$$

For the sake of being clear about the resulting algebra I have inserted brackets in this equation. The negative change in inventories has, in this equation, a negative in front of the brackets, so accordingly a negative change in inventories of materials and supplies becomes a positive for intermediate consumption.

If we restrict our consideration to purchases of goods and services produced by resident producers during the current accounting period, then final expenditure can be explained and understood as any expenditure on goods and services that crosses the production boundary going outwards. Final expenditure can thus be shown in Figure 3.3 by any arrow (representing goods and services) which does cross the production boundary going outwards. There are various arrows, each representing a different category of final expenditure, and each pointed towards a circle labelled according to its respective P. identification code (see Figure 3.1, p. 111).

Note that, under our restriction, each of the P.3, P.51, P.53 and P.6 outward going arrows represents purchases of finished goods and services produced during the current accounting period, or represents the value of the production during the current accounting period of all other types of output (goods and services not sold in the market).

However, it is also possible for some final expenditure to be met out of inventories of previously produced finished goods; this results in a negative change in inventories of finished goods. Such negative inventory changes for final expenditure are not shown in Figure 3.3, simply because this would clutter up an already-crowded diagram. However, it should be noted that each of the P.3, P.53 and P.51 circles can also be supplied (from without the production boundary) by negative changes in inventories of previously produced finished goods or by imports (as explained in Chapter 5).

We need to see how a negative change in inventories fits into the national accounts. I consider two illustrative cases. The first case is where the bakery makes sales from inventories of finished goods (this illustrates the case for final expenditure). The second case is where the bakery has intermediate consumption from its own inventories of materials and supplies (this illustrates the case for intermediate consumption and shows how the 'B' arrow in the diagram works).

For the first case, we know from Section 2.4's equation for output that:

$$
\text{Output} =
\begin{array}{c}
\text{Sales receipts} \\
\text{for finished} \\
\text{goods and} \\
\text{for services}
\end{array}
+
\begin{array}{c}
\text{Value of change} \\
\text{in inventories of} \\
\text{finished goods} \\
\text{and of work in} \\
\text{progress}
\end{array}
+
\begin{array}{c}
\text{Value of} \\
\text{production of} \\
\text{all other types of} \\
\text{output (goods and} \\
\text{services not sold} \\
\text{in the market)}
\end{array}
$$

Suppose that in the economy of Table 2.1, the bakery holds inventories of bread (a finished good). Suppose that production for the accounting period and the sales receipts for bread to households remain as Table 2.1 shows. The bakery's output is therefore €45 per annum. Suppose that, out of the inventories of bread (a finished good) the bakery makes export sales of, say, €15 per annum. The bakery's sales receipts thus rise to €60 per annum (= €45 per annum (to households) + €15 per annum (to non-residents)). But the bakery's inventories of finished goods changes by – €15 per annum (because this is the source of the export sales). The equation above shows that the bakery's *output* remains at €45 per annum, as follows:

$$\text{Output} = \begin{matrix} \text{Sales receipts} \\ \text{for finished} \\ \text{goods and} \\ \text{for services} \end{matrix} + \begin{matrix} \text{Value of change} \\ \text{in inventories of} \\ \text{finished goods} \\ \text{and of work in} \\ \text{progress} \end{matrix} + \begin{matrix} \text{Value of} \\ \text{production of} \\ \text{all other types of} \\ \text{output (goods and} \\ \text{services not sold} \\ \text{in the market)} \end{matrix}$$

$$= \text{€60 per annum} + [-\text{€15 per annum}] + \text{€0 per annum}$$

Because the bakery's output remains at €45 per annum, Table 2.1 is unaltered.

If we put the final sales to/final consumption expenditure by households, P.3, together with the final sales to/final expenditure by non-residents, P.6, the total of these final sales/final expenditures is €60 per annum. But the aggregate of all final expenditures in this economy must also include changes in inventories. So total final expenditure in the economy is as follows:

P.3	Final consumption expenditure	€45 per annum
P.6	Exports of goods and services	€15 per annum
P.52	Changes in inventories	– €15 per annum
	Total final expenditure	€45 per annum

So the equality between total final expenditure and gross domestic product is still preserved in this first case for the model economy.

For the second case, we know from Section 2.4's equation for intermediate consumption that:

$$\begin{matrix} \text{Intermediate} \\ \text{consumption} \end{matrix} = \begin{matrix} \text{Purchases of} \\ \text{materials and supplies} \\ \text{and of services} \end{matrix} - \begin{bmatrix} \text{Value of change in} \\ \text{inventories of} \\ \text{materials and supplies} \end{bmatrix}$$

Suppose that in the economy of Table 2.1, the bakery holds inventories of firewood (fuel); these are inventories of materials and supplies, AN.121. Suppose that the bakery's production for the accounting period and the sales receipts for bread to households remain as Table 2.1 shows. The bakery's output is therefore €45 per annum. Suppose that, instead of buying firewood (fuel) from the woodcutter during the period, the bakery uses an equivalent amount of firewood from its inventories of materials and supplies; the bakery's inventories of materials and supplies thus change by – €5 per annum, so the P.52 final expenditure is – €5 per annum (this illustrates the 'B' arrow in the

Figure 3.3). The bakery still buys in €30 per annum of flour from the mill (this illustrates the 'A' arrow in Figure 3.3).

The bakery's intermediate consumption is thus:

$$\text{Intermediate consumption} = \begin{array}{c}\text{Purchases of}\\ \text{materials and supplies}\\ \text{and of services}\end{array} - \left[\begin{array}{l}\text{Value of change in}\\ \text{inventories of}\\ \text{materials and supplies}\end{array}\right]$$

$$= \quad \text{€30 per annum} \quad - \quad [-\text{€5 per annum}]$$

$$= \quad \text{€35 per annum}$$

Suppose, just to complete the explanation, that the woodcutter produces no output during the period. Table 2.1 is then altered as follows:

	Output	Intermediate consumption	Gross value added
	€ per annum		
Farm	20	0	20
Mill	30	20	10
Woodcutter	0	0	0
Bakery	45	35	10
Total	95	55	40

Because the woodcutter has not produced any output during the accounting period, total gross value added – gross domestic product – has changed to €40 per annum.

Final consumption expenditure on bread is still €45 per annum. But the changes in inventories in this second case is – €5 per annum. The total final expenditure in this economy is:

P.3	Final consumption expenditure	€45 per annum
P.52	Changes in inventories	– €5 per annum
	Total final expenditure	€40 per annum

So the equality between total final expenditure and gross domestic product is still preserved in this second case for the (altered) model economy.

Having shown in these two contrasting cases how changes in inventories fit in, I shall assume for the rest of the explanation that all final expenditures are made on current production by resident producers. This keeps the explanation as simple as possible.

As per Figure 3.1, exports of goods and services, P.6, consists of output that is supplied to non-residents; thus this supply results in a final expenditure on output that crosses both the production boundary and the residents' boundary.

The other final expenditures are on output that crosses the production boundary going outwards but does not cross the residents' boundary. In accordance with Figure 3.1 these final expenditures are categorised among: final consumption expenditure, P.3 (note that Figure 3.3 does not divide this between final consumption expenditure by households (including non-profit institutions serving households) and final consumption expenditure by general government, nor between individual consumption expenditure and collective consumption expenditure); gross fixed capital formation, P.51; changes in inventories, P.52; and acquisitions less disposals of valuables, P.53.

Output supplied to final consumption 'disappears' so to speak from the production process altogether and is simply consumed or deemed to be consumed during the accounting period.

Output (goods) supplied to gross fixed capital formation is supplied to institutional units acting in their capacity as investors in fixed capital. The essential feature distinguishing goods supplied to gross fixed capital formation is that they are supplied across the *temporal* boundary of production to play an on-going role in production in *future* accounting periods. The picture we should have in mind of such fixed assets is as follows:

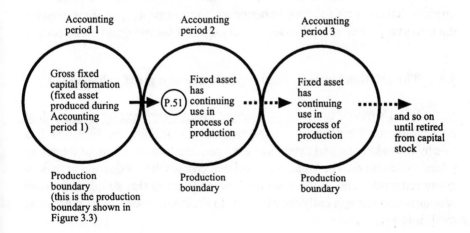

Because such goods (fixed assets) cross the temporal production boundary, expenditure on such goods is a final expenditure, recorded as such for Accounting period 1. (Under accrual accounting, the production is also recorded for Accounting period 1.)

The use of goods as a supply to changes in inventories means that, by definition, the goods play no further role in the production of the current accounting period's output. These too are goods which cross the *temporal* production boundary (for use in a subsequent accounting period).

Such products (items for inventories) are used for intermediate consumption in a subsequent period but the significant feature is that they cross the production boundary of their period of production, and so count as final expenditure for that period.

Output supplied to acquisitions of valuables is difficult to categorise because it partakes both of consumption and investment. Households and other institutional units buy valuable jewellery and valuable paintings and so on partly as consumption and partly as an investment (because the valuable is expected to retain its value and possibly to appreciate in value). However, these complexities do not affect the status of acquisitions less disposals of valuables as a final expenditure.

Figure 3.3 thus helps positively to explain the concept of final expenditure and gives a picture of the difference between economic activities that count as production and other activities such as consuming, investing, or exporting. These latter activities are to be understood as taking place outside the production boundary (explicitly, in these activities the institutional units are acting in a capacity other than that of producer-as-producer).

Now that we understand final expenditure as expenditure on goods and services that cross the production boundary going outwards, we may consider the important relationship between final expenditure and gross value added.

3.5   The relation between final expenditure and gross value added

In Table 2.1's model economy, the sale of bread by the bakery is to resident households for the purpose of consumption. Accordingly, in Table 2.1 this sale by the bakery to, and expenditure by, resident households is annotated as a final expenditure. The bread is a good that crosses the production boundary going outwards. This is the only final expenditure in this simplified model economy and consequently we can refer to the final expenditure on bread as total final expenditure.

It is then an important feature of Table 2.1 that total final expenditure, €45 per annum, is equal to gross domestic product, €45 per annum. This is an example and illustration of the basic identity of national accounting (*SNA93*, para. 6.234).

Why does this equality between gross domestic product and total final expenditure occur? What is the economic meaning of this equality? What lies behind this basic identity of national accounting?

One answer may be given by considering what may be called the algebra behind Table 2.1 (and hence behind any like table for gross value added) in the economy as a whole. When we calculate total gross value added over all the rows in Table 2.1, the numbers in the first column appear with a plus sign and the numbers in the second column appear with a minus sign. With one significant exception, all the numbers in the first column are repeated in the second column. Accordingly in the calculation of gross total value added the pluses and minuses cancel out, and there is left only the one exception: the final sales of bread by the bakery. Consequently subtracting the sum of the numbers in the second column from the sum of the numbers in the first column will leave only final sales of, or final expenditure on, bread. This is the algebraic reason why in this and in any like table total final expenditure will equal total gross value added, or, in an economy without imports, gross domestic product. However, the algebraic answer, while true, is superficial and does not deal with the fundamental economics of the basic identity of national accounting.

A better answer may be given if we go beyond the algebra and examine the economic meaning of the equality between any final expenditure and gross value added. This equality arises because of the important relationship between final expenditure and gross value added. This relationship needs to be understood at a fundamental 'microeconomic' level of *an individual* final expenditure transaction (such as the purchase of a loaf of bread). Failure to understand this microeconomic relationship leads to an inability to understand the macroeconomic relationship between the aggregates and thence to an inability to understand the basic national accounting identity (and thence to an inability to understand basic macroeconomics). The following explanation lays the foundation for the initial explanation in Section 3.8 of the macroeconomics of the basic identity of national accounting between total final expenditure and gross domestic product.

The microeconomic explanation is illustrated in Figure 3.4 showing what I call the 'chain of production' for the model economy of Table 2.1. The chain of production is a metaphor to express the truth that enterprises are connected

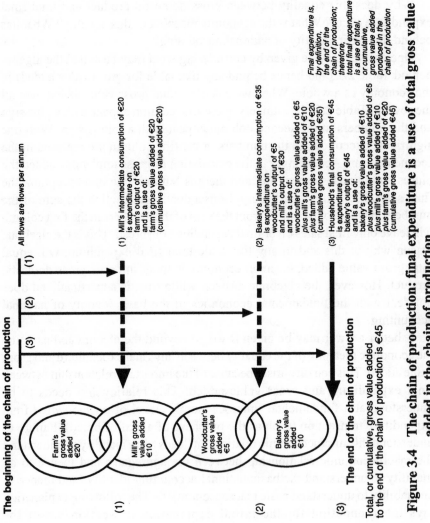

The beginning of the chain of production

All flows are flows per annum

(1) Mill's intermediate consumption of €20
is expenditure on
farm's output of €20
and is a use of:
farm's gross value added of €20
(cumulative gross value added €20)

(2) Bakery's intermediate consumption of €35
is expenditure on
woodcutter's output of €5
and mill's output of €30
and is a use of:
woodcutter's gross value added of €5
plus mill's gross value added of €10
plus farm's gross value added of €20
(cumulative gross value added €35)

(3) Household's final consumption of €45
is expenditure on
bakery's output of €45
and is a use of:
bakery's gross value added of €10
plus woodcutter's gross value added of €5
plus mill's gross value added of €10
plus farm's gross value added of €20
(cumulative gross value added €45)

*Final expenditure is,
by definition,
the end of the
chain of production;
therefore,
total final expenditure
is a use of total,
or cumulative,
gross value added
produced in the
chain of production*

Farm's gross value added €20

Mill's gross value added €10

Woodcutter's gross value added €5

Bakery's gross value added €10

The end of the chain of production

Total, or cumulative, gross value added
to the end of the chain of production is €45

Figure 3.4   The chain of production: final expenditure is a use of total gross value added in the chain of production

to each other and to the eventual customer making a final expenditure. The argument behind the chain of production metaphor is as follows.

Enterprises are connected to each other because one enterprise produces output which it supplies to another for use as intermediate consumption. That is, and looking forward in the chain of production, one enterprise's output can become another enterprise's intermediate input.

The process of production adds value (gross) to intermediate inputs. Accordingly, the 'links' in the chain connecting enterprises are links of gross value added: that is, enterprises are linked according to the value which each adds to all its intermediate inputs. To show this, the links in the chain of production are labelled in Figure 3.4 according to gross value added.

Looking backward in the chain of production, intermediate consumption by one enterprise should be understood not only as being a use of the output of other enterprises, to which the enterprise is immediately connected in the chain of production (in the sense of purchasing the output(s) of the enterprise(s)), but should also be understood as being a use of gross value added of all the preceding enterprises in the chain of production.

While it is easy to understand that intermediate consumption is a use of output supplied – we can see very clearly that the mill uses the farm's wheat or that the bakery uses the mill's flour – it is less obvious that each intermediate consumption transaction is a use of all the preceding gross value added in the chain of production, so in due course this argument will be explained further using Figure 3.4.

Eventually, at the end of the chain of production, an enterprise's output is sold to final expenditure. Final expenditure, by definition of crossing the production boundary going outwards, is the end of the chain of production; that is, the chain of production, with respect to that particular transaction, is completed for that current accounting period and the good or service which is the object of the final expenditure is subject to no more value adding during that current accounting period.

But, just as with intermediate consumption, final expenditure should be understood not only as being a use of output (for example, bread), but should also be understood as being a use of all the gross value added in the chain of production. The latter argument needs further explanation which is given below using Figure 3.4.

Although I use a metaphor of the chain of production, it is not the case that each enterprise has to be connected in strict sequence to each preceding enterprise in the chain of production and to only one enterprise in the chain of production, so we must not take the metaphor too literally, although its basic truth – that some enterprises are connected to other enterprises – obviously holds.

While it is reasonably obvious that each of intermediate consumption and final expenditure is a use of *output*, the abstract proposition that each is also a use of *gross value added* is less obvious, and this argument needs more explanation as follows.

From the equation for gross value added (and setting aside issues related to accrual accounting which are not germane to the present explanation):

Gross value added (resulting from production by the local kind-of-activity unit owned by the enterprise, that is, 'the producer') during the period = Output, mainly measured by sales receipts of the producer during the period − Intermediate consumption, mainly measured by purchases of goods (materials and supplies) and services by the producer from other independent enterprises during the period

we have by rearrangement:

Output, mainly measured by sales receipts of the producer during the period = Intermediate consumption, mainly measured by purchases of goods (materials and supplies) and services by the producer from other independent enterprises during the period + Gross value added (resulting from production by the local kind-of-activity unit owned by the enterprise, that is, 'the producer') during the period

This equation I call the 'output equation'. This important equation says that the producer's output is measured by the value of the producer's intermediate consumption *plus* the value which the producer has added to those intermediate inputs (the producer's gross value added).

The output equation explains why the links in the chain of production are links of gross value added.

We may now use the illustrative data from Table 2.1 as given in Figure 3.4 to explain matters further. In the following explanation, all flows are flows per annum taken from Table 2.1. The explanation in the text follows the (repeated) bracketed numbers in Figure 3.4.

(1) The farm's output becomes the mill's intermediate consumption. The farm has no intermediate consumption so, conveniently, we do not need to consider this and the farm's output is also conveniently the farm's

gross value added. We thus have a definite starting point with the farm's output (the farm's sales receipts) which becomes the mill's intermediate consumption.

In Figure 3.4 the mill's intermediate consumption of €20 is expenditure on the farm's output which is also the farm's gross value added (the farm having no intermediate consumption of its own – see the output equation). So here we see quite clearly that mill's intermediate consumption is a *use* of the farm's gross value added. In the chain of production the mill is linked to the farm through the farm's gross value added.

In this context I mean by the word 'use' that the mill's intermediate consumption depends upon and is not possible without the farm's output, *and hence* depends upon and is not possible without the farm's gross value added. The difficulty with this proposition is that while the proposition is very obvious with regard to output, especially when that output is seen in *physical* terms – we know as an exceedingly obvious fact that the mill cannot produce flour without wheat – the proposition becomes conceptually complex with regard to the *balancing item* of gross value added. However, we shall appreciate this complex proposition as we proceed with the explanation of Figure 3.4.

(2) The mill's output becomes the bakery's intermediate consumption. Furthermore, the woodcutter's output also becomes the bakery's intermediate consumption

The bakery's intermediate consumption, €35, is on the woodcutter's output, €5, which is also the woodcutter's gross value added (the woodcutter having no intermediate consumption – see the output equation) and on the mill's output, €30. But the mill's output comprises the mill's gross value added, €10, and the mill's intermediate consumption, €20 (see the output equation). Furthermore, we have just shown that the mill's intermediate consumption is also the farm's gross value added. Consequently by substitution for the mill's intermediate consumption, the bakery's intermediate consumption is a use of the woodcutter's gross value added, the mill's gross value added and the farm's gross value added. Again, we see that intermediate consumption is a use of gross value added. In the chain of production the bakery is linked to the woodcutter, to the mill, and to the farm through the woodcutter's gross value added, the mill's gross value added and the farm's gross value added.

(3)   The bakery's output becomes households' final expenditure. Households' final expenditure of €45 is thus on the bakery's output of €45. But the bakery's output comprises the bakery's gross value added, €10, and the bakery's intermediate consumption, €35. Furthermore, we have just shown that the bakery's intermediate consumption is a use of the woodcutter's gross value added, the mill's gross value added and the farm's gross value added. Consequently by substitution for the bakery's intermediate consumption, households' final expenditure is a use of the bakery's gross value added, the woodcutter's gross value added, the mill's gross value added and the farm's gross value added. At the end of the chain of production (because we are now at a *final* expenditure which has crossed the production boundary going outwards), the household is linked to the bakery, to the woodcutter, to the mill, and to the farm through the bakery's gross value added, the woodcutter's gross value added, the mill's gross value added and the farm's gross value added.

Households' final expenditure is the last transaction in the chain of production for the specific current accounting period; in other words, there is no more value adding after households' final expenditure – the chain of production ends here. By virtue of crossing the production boundary going outwards, final expenditure ends the process of production for the current accounting period. Consequently households' final expenditure, being the only final expenditure in this chain of production, is, and must be, equal to the total of gross value added in this economy (without imports and taxes on production), and, because gross domestic product is the total of gross value added resulting from production by resident producers, households' final expenditure is equal to gross domestic product (in the model economy with no imports and no taxes on production).

Thus what you are doing, in economic terms, when you consume (a loaf of) bread is to 'consume' all the gross value added in the chain of production which led to the bread being produced. You are, so to speak, 'linked' to all the enterprises in the chain of production. Unfortunately, many of us simply take bread for granted as a commonplace of our everyday lives and therefore we never think deeply about the conceptually complex economics underlying bread as a product which is the subject of final expenditure. We know of course that when we consume bread, we consume a product. We know that this product somehow 'involves' wheat, flour and firewood (fuel). What we do not see, because it is a complex and abstract proposition, is that when we consume bread, we consume or use the gross value added in the entire chain of production which led to that output as an object of a final expenditure.

Once we have Table 2.1 in front of us, it is immediately obvious that we could not consume bread without the farmer having grown the wheat, without the miller having ground the wheat into flour, without the woodcutter having supplied the fuel, and without the bakery having baked the flour with fuel to produce the bread. This much, in terms of physical products, is quite obvious. But how can we measure the contribution of each enterprise in the chain of production?

The only way we can sensibly measure each enterprise's contribution to our consumption of bread, valued at its final expenditure, is to take the gross value added resulting from production by each enterprise involved in the chain of production, because in that way we avoid double-counting. Remember that avoiding double-counting is an essential feature of the gross value added concept.

The problem of understanding what consumption of a loaf of bread means can be put in the following schema:

When you consume a loaf of bread, you consume the items (in bold typeface):

In terms of goods and services (physical products), but this involves double-counting	In terms of balancing items (gross value added), this avoids double-counting
the **wheat** which went into the **flour** and the **firewood (fuel)** both of which went into the **bread**	the farm's **gross value added** the mill's **gross value added** the woodcutter's **gross value added** the bakery's **gross value added**

So your consumption, *without double-counting*, is total **gross value added**

Accordingly, there is a very real economic sense in which the final expenditure on a loaf of bread is a use of – or depends upon and is not possible without – the farm's gross value added, the mill's gross value added, the woodcutter's gross value added, and the bakery's gross value added – the links in the chain of production.

This is what is shown diagrammatically in the chain of production in Figure 3.4. Figure 3.4 shows the conceptually complex underlying microeconomic reality which lies behind final expenditure on bread. The fundamental microeconomic truth is that final expenditure on the bread consumes or uses, without double-counting, the gross value added resulting from production by all the enterprises contributing to the production of the ingredients and fuel in the bread and resulting from production of the bread itself using those inputs. Without this chain of production and its resulting links of gross value added no consumption of bread (final expenditure) is possible. Consequently, *what we are doing when we consume bread is to consume or use the gross value added resulting from production by all the enterprises in the chain of production.*

Clearly, the *use* of gross value added in purchasing the bread for consumption (€45) must be matched by an equal *supply* of gross value added from all the contributing enterprises (€45): every use must have a matching supply.

Once we understand the microeconomic reality of an individual final expenditure being a use of gross value added in that particular chain of production, it is a simple matter to proceed to the macroeconomic reality of *total* final expenditure.

What is true for one instance of final expenditure must be true for all instances of final expenditure. If one individual final expenditure is a use of gross value added in its particular chain of production, then total final expenditure must be a use of all the gross value added in all the chains of production. That is, total final expenditure must use total gross value added.

This is why (in an economy without imports and without taxes on production) the total final expenditure in the economy is equal to the total gross value added arising in the economy. But the total supply of gross value added by all the resident producers in the economy is gross domestic product. Accordingly (in an economy without imports) total final expenditure is equal to gross domestic product. This is the basic identity of national accounting. This basic identity is affected by taxes on products and by imports and these matters will be explained in Chapters 4 and 5 respectively.

A further important consequence follows from this way of looking at products which are the subject of final expenditure. Gross value added is distributed in the form of primary incomes as compensation to employees and as gross operating surplus/gross mixed income. Thus, when you buy a loaf of bread (make a final expenditure), you are not only benefitting from and using the aggregate of gross values added resulting from production by all the contributing enterprises, you are also paying the compensation of employees engaged in those enterprises *and* paying the gross operating surplus/gross mixed income of the owners of enterprises. Without the final sales/final expenditure on bread all these primary incomes would cease. There is thus, in economics, a very important connection:

Final expenditure ⟶ Gross value added ⟶ Primary incomes

In order to take the explanation of the basic identity of national accounting a stage further, we need first to explain both the goods and services account and second the relation of the goods and services account to the production account. We turn to these tasks in Sections 3.6 and 3.7 respectively.

3.6   Account 0: Goods and services account

The goods and services account is an important SNA93/ESA95 account (new to the system of national accounts) which we have not so far considered. The purpose of the goods and services account is, on the one hand, to show the goods and services becoming available in the economy and, on the other hand, to show how those goods and services were used in the economy. The goods and services becoming available are given under the heading 'Resources'; the uses of those goods and services are given under the heading 'Uses'. As its name implies, the goods and services account is an account which is comprehensively about products (goods and services), and is basically about products only. More exactly and specifically, the goods and services account is an account for all and only *transactions* in products, with the exception that the closely related transactions of taxes on products (and subsidies on products) are also included in the goods and services account.

The goods and services account is an account which can be compiled only for the whole economy (it cannot be compiled for sectors of the economy, unlike the other accounts so far considered), and so it contains only economy-wide aggregates. It is, as we shall show, a very different sort of account from those so far considered. It thus stands outside the sequence of accounts shown in Figure 1.6, and for that reason is identified as Account 0; that is, with a number distinct from that in the System's sequence.

A simplified version of Account 0: Goods and services account can be given for the model economy. (This is necessarily a simplified version because we have not yet discussed many of the items in the goods and services account: on the resources side of the account, we have not yet discussed taxes on products, nor have we discussed imports; on the uses side of the account, we have illustrated in Table 2.1 only final consumption expenditure by households.)

In this section, I shall explain the goods and services account for the model economy of Table 2.1 in two steps. The first step (Figure 3.5) looks at a pictorial version of the goods and services account using depictions of physical products only. The purpose of the pictorial version is firmly to establish in your mind the rationale of the goods and services account. The second step (Table 3.2) looks at a simplified table which gives the goods and services account using the numbers of Table 2.1 in monetary units. The purpose of this table is to pave the way for a consideration, in a later chapter, of the real-world goods and services account in its full detail.

Figure 3.5 shows the pictorial version of the goods and services account for the model economy of Table 2.1. The account is about goods and services; that is, products in the form of output. Under the heading 'Resources' on the left-hand side of the picture are shown the products (output) becoming available to the economy. Under the heading 'Uses' on the right-hand side of the picture are shown the uses to which those products are put. There are two sorts of annotations in the picture. In square brackets, but only as an aid, are given the institutional units creating and using the products. The square brackets indicate that these annotations do not occur in the goods and services account. Figure 3.5 also gives in bold the SNA93/ESA95 identification codes and names of the items which do occur in the goods and services account; these refer to the value of the products enclosed by the relevant broken line.

The first important purpose of the goods and services account is to show the products becoming available to the economy as a whole. In the model economy, the products that become available, during the accounting period, are: wheat, flour, firewood (fuel) and bread. These are the *resources*, or products that 'add to the economic value' of the economy. In the model economy, this total supply is the SNA93/ESA95 item P.1 Total output.

The other important purpose of the goods and services account is to show how these products are used by the economy as a whole.

In the first instance, Figure 3.5 shows that the wheat is used by the mill and the flour and firewood (fuel) are used by the bakery, in each case as intermediate consumption. Accordingly, we may put a broken line around these products and label that as the SNA93/ESA95 item P.2 Intermediate consumption.

In the second instance, Figure 3.5 shows that the bread is used by households for consumption. Accordingly, we may put a broken line around the bread and label that as the SNA93/ESA95 item P.3 Final consumption expenditure.

We come now to an important feature of the goods and services account. This is the feature that for the economy as a whole, it must necessarily be the case that:

Goods and services account

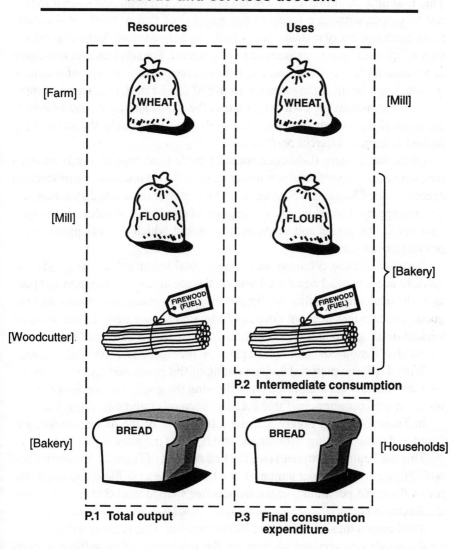

Figure 3.5   A picture, for the model economy, of SNA93/ESA95
Account 0: Goods and services account

> Total resources on the   Total uses on the
> goods and services account   =   goods and services account

This is simply commonsense. On the one hand, the economy cannot have a use of output without a resource (or 'supply' of that output); on the other hand, each and every resource (or 'supply' of output) must find a use, even if only a 'left over' use as an increase in inventories. For services every resource is necessarily a use – one cannot, for example, have a supply of a haircut without there being at the same time a use of that haircut. In the case of own-account production for own-account use, the use is simply the other side of the coin of the output (the resource) – the two are simply the same thing looked at from a different perspective.

(Note that a sharp distinction must be made (and kept in mind) between total resources on goods and services account and total resources on production account – see Chapter 2's Section 2.5. The importance of this distinction will become apparent when we discuss imports of goods and services, which are a resource in the goods and services account but which do not appear in the production account.)

Because, for the economy as a whole, total resources on the goods and services account must equal total uses on the goods and services account (due to a physical impossibility of things being otherwise), this means that the goods and services account does not have a balancing item. In the pictorial version of the goods and services account, the products listed on the left-hand side under 'Resources' must find a place on the right-hand side under 'Uses'.

With this basic pictorial understanding of the goods and services account we may consider the simplified table showing the goods and services account for the model economy of Table 2.1. The account is given in Table 3.2.

In Table 3.2, as in Figure 3.5, the total output of the model economy is listed under the heading 'Resources' and is €100 per annum (see Table 2.1).

This total output comprises (see the first column of Table 2.1 in conjunction with Figure 3.5): €20 per annum of the farm's wheat; €30 per annum of the mill's flour; €5 per annum of the woodcutter's wood; and €45 per annum of the bakery's bread.

Total output thus amounts to €100 per annum. This is also total resources on the goods and services account for the model economy without imports and taxes on products.

In Table 3.2, as in Figure 3.5, the uses of total resources are listed under the heading 'Uses'. There are in the model economy of Table 2.1 two uses of output: intermediate consumption of €55 per annum (see the total in the second

Table 3.2
Goods and services account for model economy

SNA93/ESA95 identification code	SNA93/ESA95 name	€ per annum
0	GOODS AND SERVICES ACCOUNT	
	Resources	
P.1	Total output	100
Total	Total resources	100
	Uses	
P.2	Intermediate consumption	55
P.3	Final consumption expenditure by households[a]	45
Total	Total uses	100

(*a*)   This is the only type of final expenditure in the model economy.

Source: Table 2.1; reference: Office for National Statistics, *United Kingdom National Accounts The Blue Book 1999 edition*, table 1.6.0, p. 39.

column of Table 2.1, and the relevant part of the right-hand side of Figure 3.5); and final consumption expenditure of €45 per annum (see, from the other side of this transaction, the bakery's sales receipts in the first column of Table 2.1 and the relevant part of the right-hand side of Figure 3.5).

Total uses on the goods and services account thus amounts to €100 per annum.

We can now see in Table 3.2 the important feature of any goods and services account that it balances globally: total resources on the goods and services account must equal, and be equalled by, total uses on the goods and services account. Conversely, there is in the goods and services account no balancing item; that is, there is *in principle* no place for a balancing item in the goods and services account.

The goods and services account for the model economy of Table 2.1 is a simplified account but further consideration of the goods and services account in national income accounts will have to wait until after we have considered both the role of imports of goods and services in the economy and also the role of taxes on products less subsidies.

Meanwhile it is necessary to explain where the goods and services account fits into the general scheme of national accounts. This is done in the next section.

3.7   The economy-wide resources and uses diagram

What we have learnt in Chapter 2 and this chapter may be summed up in Figure 3.6 which presents an integrated diagram showing the economy's 'resources' and the 'uses' of those resources. I call this economy-wide diagram an 'integrated diagram' because it integrates into an interrelated whole the three accounts so far considered: Account 0 Goods and services account; Account I Production account; and Account II.1.1 Primary distribution of income account: generation of income account.

In an economy without imports resources are simply the total of the economy's output. The uses are intermediate consumption and the final expenditures. Accordingly, the resources and uses diagram of Figure 3.6 (which is not to scale) starts with the production of total output as a resource in Account 0 Goods and services account – but remember that this is an economy without imports. The total resources on goods and services account (in this case only total output) is represented by a bar (second from left), the height of which indicates the money value of total annual output (and we can also, as per Figure 2.3, note in the bar that total output is made up of market output, output for own final use, and other non-market output).

In Account 0 the uses are intermediate consumption and final expenditure, in this case final consumption expenditure. This is represented by the bar on the left, the height of which indicates the money value of total uses on the goods and services account, equal to total resources on the goods and services account as must necessarily be the case. The uses are final consumption expenditure by households (the only final expenditure in the model economy), and intermediate consumption. As already explained, the goods and services account has no balancing item.

Next we deal with the production account. In the SNA93/ESA95 Account I Production account (shown in Tables 2.2 and 2.3), total output is a resource and in this economy without taxes on products or subsidies on products, total

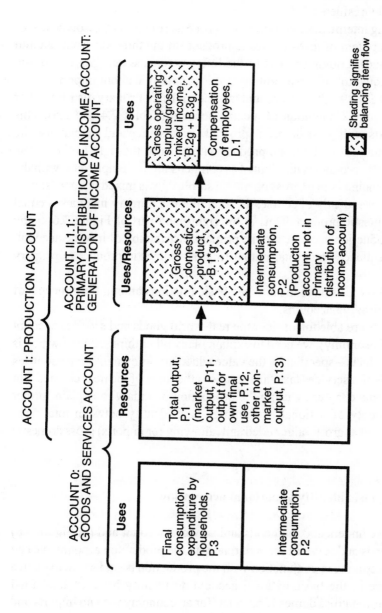

Figure 3.6 Resources and uses diagram (economy with no imports)

ACCOUNT I: PRODUCTION ACCOUNT

ACCOUNT II.1.1:
PRIMARY DISTRIBUTION OF INCOME ACCOUNT:
GENERATION OF INCOME ACCOUNT

ACCOUNT 0:
GOODS AND SERVICES ACCOUNT

Uses

Final consumption expenditure by households, P.3

Intermediate consumption, P.2

Resources

Total output, P.1 (market output, P11; output for own final use, P.12; other non-market output, P.13)

Uses/Resources

Gross domestic product, $B.1^*g$,

Intermediate consumption, P.2 (Production account; not in Primary distribution of income account)

Uses

Gross operating surplus/gross mixed income, $B.2g + B.3g$,

Compensation of employees, D.1

Shading signifies balancing item flow

157

output is the only resource. Note that imports of goods and services never enters the production account because this account is concerned only with production by residents.

Deducting intermediate consumption as one use of this total resource leaves the balancing item of gross domestic product (in the third bar from left and shown shaded). Looking across to the left, we can see that gross domestic product is equal to final expenditure in this economy without imports.

The next SNA93/ESA95 account is Account II.1.1 Primary distribution of income account: Generation of income account (Tables 2.4 and 2.5). This account starts with gross domestic product as a resource and we may use the bar comprising gross domestic product with a bar to the right to show how gross domestic product is distributed as compensation of employees, with the residual balancing item of gross operating surplus/gross mixed income (shown shaded). Consequently of course, the total of these primary incomes is equal to gross domestic product. Thus in the right-hand part of Figure 3.6, using both the production account and the primary distribution of income account, we go in sequence from total output to gross domestic product to primary incomes.

Figure 3.6 thus serves to show the basic relations among the concepts of the SNA93/ESA95 accounts.

Before we are able to consider the real-world goods and services account (for the UK economy), we need to explain many other things, one of which is taxes on products – specifically the value added tax, known in some countries as the goods and services tax – and so this is the topic of the next chapter. But I conclude this chapter by using the production boundary to explain further the basic identy of national accounting – the identity between total final expenditure, total gross value added and (allowing for imports) gross domestic product.

3.8   The basic identity of national accounting

Now that we understand the goods and services account and (in Figure 3.6) how the goods and services account relates to the production account, we can use these accounts, in conjunction with the production boundary, to explain a further stage in the basic national accounting identity between total final expenditure and gross domestic product (for an economy with no imports and with no taxes on production).

Figure 3.7 illustrates the argument. Figure 3.7 starts with the production

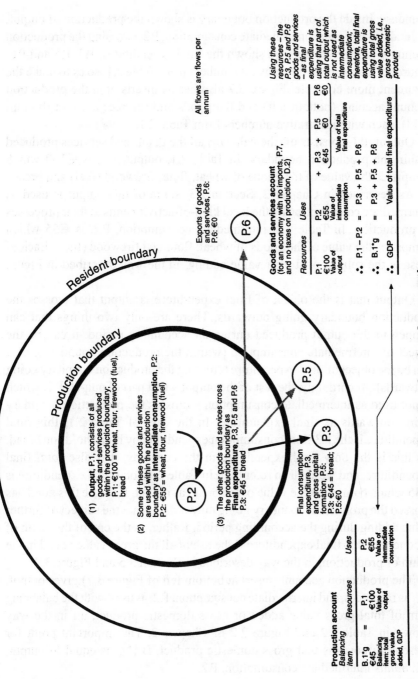

Figure 3.7 To illustrate the basic identity of national accounting

boundary. Inside the production boundary is shown the production of output, P.1, and the associated intermediate consumption, P.2. Crossing the production boundary going outwards are shown the final expenditures, P.3, P.5 and P.6. Figure 3.7 contains all the relevant numbers from Table 2.1, so as to make the argument more concrete. Figure 3.7 also has as inserts both the production account account (bottom left) and the goods and services account (bottom right), each with illustrative numbers from Table 2.1.

Output, P.1, consists of (the value of) all the goods and services produced within the production boundary. In Table 2.1, output, P.1, is €100 which comprises the value of the goods of wheat, flour, firewood (fuel) and bread.

As described in Chapter 2, Section 2.3, some of this output is used as intermediate consumption by the local kind-of-activity units in their processes of production. In Table 2.1, intermediate consumption, P.2, is €55 which comprises the value of the goods of wheat, flour and firewood (fuel). Each of these is the subject of further value adding, in the way described in Figure 3.4.

Output that is the object of final expenditure is output that crosses the production boundary going outwards. There are only two things that can happen to the output produced during an accounting period: it can be the object of intermediate consumption (within the production boundary); or it can be the object of final expenditure (crossing the production boundary going outwards). Accordingly, the rest of the output – that part of output, P.1, which is not used as intermediate consumption – crosses the production boundary going outwards as final expenditure. In the case of Table 2.1, this final expenditure is the P.3 final consumption expenditure by households on bread. As this is the only final expenditure in the economy, it is also *total* final expenditure, and we shall so refer to it. In Table 2.1, total final expenditure is €45 which comprises the value of the bread as output. Because this good has crossed the production boundary going outwards it is not the subject of further value adding during the accounting period. Rather, as the end of the chain of production, this final expenditure is the use of all the gross value added in the chain of production, in the way described in Section 3.5 and Figure 3.4.

The production account (insert at bottom left of Figure 3.7) gives output, P.1, as resources, and intermediate consumption, P.2, as uses, with the balancing item of total gross value added or gross domestic product, all in the way shown in Table 2.2 and Figure 2.2 of Chapter 2. The important point for present purposes is that gross domestic product, B.1*g, is equal to output, P.1, *minus* intermediate consumption, P.2.

The goods and services account (insert at bottom right of Figure 3.7) gives the total resources becoming available to an economy during an accounting period; that is, it gives the total goods and services becoming available. In Table 2.1's economy without imports (and without taxes on production), the total resources are simply output, P.1. The other part of the goods and services account is to give the various and total uses of those resources (that is, all the uses of the goods and services which become available during an accounting period). One of these uses is intermediate consumption, P.2. The other uses are, and can only be, final expenditures of various sorts. In Table 2.1's economy, the only, and therefore the total, final expenditure is final expenditure on bread.

The equation of the goods and services account, resources *equals* uses, is shown in the top row of the insert at the bottom right:

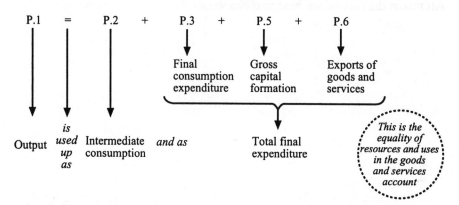

In the economy of Table 2.1, P.3 = €45 per annum, and P.5 = P.6 = €0.

In Figure 3.7 the goods and services account is annotated fully with respect to the monetary values from Table 2.1. We can manipulate the resources and uses equation of the goods and services account to show that the value of total final expenditure must be equal to the value of output, P.1, *minus* the value of intermediate consumption, P.2:

$$\underbrace{\text{P.1} - \text{P.2}}_{\substack{\text{Gross domestic product}\\ \text{(balancing item on}\\ \text{the production account)}}} = \underbrace{\text{P.3} + \text{P.5} + \text{P.6}}_{\substack{\text{Total final}\\ \text{expenditure}}}$$

This is the basic identity of national accounting (for an economy with no imports and no taxes on products)

As shown by the double-headed arrow at the bottom of Figure 3.7, the right-hand side of this equation means that the value of total final expenditure is equal to the balancing item from the production account; that is, the value of total final expenditure is equal to gross domestic product.

Again however, the economic reality of this basic identity of national accounting is that each and every final expenditure represents a use of gross value added in the completed chain of production, and therefore (in an economy without imports) total final expenditure represents, and must represent, a use of total gross value added, or gross domestic product.

This completes the initial stage of explaining the basic identity of national accounting. A complete explanation of this basic identity requires that we understand the role of taxes on production (less subsidies on production), especially taxes on products (less subsidies on products) and the role of imports. All this is the task of the next two chapters.

4   Taxes on Products and the Valuation of Gross Domestic Product

4.1   Introduction

This chapter explains the way in which taxes on products affect the valuation of gross domestic product. The main point to be explained in the chapter is that because the valuation of total final expenditure must include taxes on products, so consequently the valuation of gross domestic product must likewise include taxes on products. As well as understanding gross domestic product as the sum of gross values added (Chapter 2), we must now understand that the SNA93/ESA95 valuation of gross domestic product also includes, as an additional element, taxes on products. This very important point is explained from several different angles.

The two main concepts which we need to understand are the concept of basic prices and the concept of purchasers' prices. In order to understand these price concepts we need to understand all about taxes on production, which are divided between taxes on products (such as value added tax or excise duties) and other taxes on production (such as payroll taxes or property rates levied on business premises). Consequently, the first thing needed is an explanation of the classification system for the various taxes on production. This is explained in Section 4.2 with the aid of Figure 4.1.

The most important tax on products is the value added tax (VAT), also known in some countries (Canada, Australia, New Zealand) as the goods and services tax (GST), referred to by the SNA93/ESA95 as 'value added type taxes (VAT)', but which I shall call 'VAT/GST' because this is a brief term which covers both of the names used internationally. In the United Kingdom in 1997, VAT accounted for 57 per cent of total taxes on products (the *Blue Book 1999 edition*, table 10.1, p. 252; this includes taxes paid to the European Union).

Section 4.3 explains, very briefly, the main features of VAT/GST, adapting for this purpose the model economy of Table 2.1.

Following that, Section 4.4 explains and illustrates the way in which VAT/GST affects the valuation of final expenditures and we show how VAT/GST consequently fits into the goods and services account.

Section 4.5 then explains the consequences of the goods and services account treatment of taxes on products for the production account. Using this account we can explain and understand the valuation of gross domestic product in the SNA93/ESA95 and the complexity of the concept of market prices.

Section 4.6 explains how taxes on products other than VAT/GST affect valuations and gross domestic product, further adapting for this purpose the model economy of Table 2.1 (already adapted to show the impact of VAT/GST).

Section 4.7 explains how taxes on production other than taxes on products affect the primary distribution of income account: generation of income account, again adapting the model economy.

Finally, Section 4.8 uses data from the United Kingdom and Australia to show how all the taxes on production fit into the national accounts and to introduce subsidies on production which are explained with the aid of Figure 4.2.

4.2   Taxes on production

With respect to government revenue from taxation, the SNA93/ESA95 distinguishes between *taxes on production and imports*, D.2, and *current taxes on income, wealth, etc.*, D.5. In addition to these two sources of revenue from taxation, governments may derive revenue from assets which it owns and government social security funds may receive revenue from 'social contributions' to those funds. In this chapter we are concerned only with taxes on production and imports, D.2, and not with any other government revenue. These other sources of revenue will be discussed in Chapter 6 but in this chapter we must examine taxes on production and imports because some of these taxes directly affect the prices of goods and services and hence they affect the valuation of output and intermediate consumption. This has implications for the measurement of gross value added and final expenditure as we shall see.

Figure 4.1 gives the SNA93/ESA95 classification scheme for the various taxes on production. The SNA93/ESA95 identification codes are given for the specific items in the SNA93/ESA95 accounts, and the diagram also gives some examples of taxes falling under each coded item, but these examples do not have an identification code in the SNA93/ESA95 (there is a separate system for all taxes in the Government Finance Statistics classification of the International Monetary Fund). In Figure 4.1, the listing of the coded items is comprehensive and exhaustive of all the various types of taxes on production and imports classified in the System but the list of uncoded examples of taxes is not to be taken as exhaustive.

In this chapter I explain three types of taxes on production and imports: value added type taxes (as the most important of the taxes on products); taxes on products except VAT (where I shall use the example of a fuel excise duty); and other taxes on production (where I shall use the example of property taxes levied on an enterprise's business premises).

Taxes are payments (in cash or in kind, but nearly always the former), compulsory by law, made by institutional units to a government or to institutions of the European Union (in the case of member states). Payments of contributions to an international organisation, such as the United Nations, are separately treated as D.74 current international cooperation (*ESA95*, para. 4.122).

Tax payments are *unrequited* payments, because in return for the tax payment by an institutional unit the government provides nothing in return specifically to that particular institutional unit. Rather, in return the government either provides generally for the community collectively (for example, law and order, roads) or provides services or transfers which usually benefit other institutional units individually (for example, education, age pensions).

(This chapter is concerned only with taxes on production and my method of explaining is to proceed one step at a time. Consequently, this chapter is not the appropriate place to explain the government outlays financed by these taxes; some government outlays are considered in Chapter 6.)

Taxes on production and imports, D.2, are taxes levied in respect of:

1. either the production or the importation of goods and services; and/or
2. the employment of labour; and/or
3. the ownership or use of land, buildings or other assets used in production;

and these taxes are payable whether or not profits are made (this clause distinguishes taxes on production from taxes on income such as profit, because payment of taxes on profits requires that a profit has actually been made).

Taxes on products, D.21, are taxes that are payable per unit of some good or service produced, imported, or transacted. The tax may be levied as an

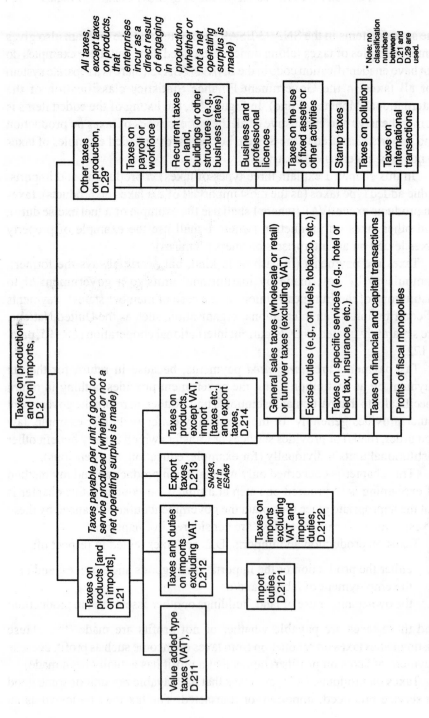

Figure 4.1 The classification of taxes on production and on imports

amount of money per specified unit by quantity of the good or service, or it may be levied as a proportion of the price per unit or as a proportion of the value of the transaction.

The payment of D.21 taxes on products requires that production has actually occurred; for example, if an enterprise's production is halted for a period because of a strike by employees, then D.21 taxes on products will not accrue for that period because no products will have been produced.

Other taxes on production, D.29, are taxes, other than taxes on products, that enterprises incur as a result of engaging in production. Generally, these other taxes on production accrue whether or not products have been produced during the period. For example, property taxes paid by enterprises to government have to be paid whether or not products have been produced during the period; to continue our illustration using the impact of a strike, most D.29 other taxes on production will accrue and will be levied even for a period when the enterprise's production had been interrupted by a strike.

4.3   VAT/GST and gross value added at basic prices

Unless there is a specific alternative convention for valuing output (such as valuing non-market production at the sum of the costs of production), the SNA93/ESA95 stipulates that 'output is to be valued at basic prices' (*ESA95*, para. 3.47; *SNA93*, para. 6.37). The following is the definition of 'basic price' (in part):

> The *basic price* is the amount receivable by the producer from the purchaser for a unit of a good or service produced as output minus any tax payable [that is, minus any D.21 tax on products], and plus any subsidy receivable [that is, D.31 subsidy on products], on that unit as a consequence of its production or sale (*SNA93*, para. 6.205, italics in original and with my clarifying interpolations in square brackets; see also *ESA95*, para. 3.48).

The important point of this definition is that the basic price *excludes* taxes on products. This means that any valuation at basic prices excludes taxes on products. Note carefully that this statement refers only to the valuation of the output of the producer whose products are being taxed; it has no reference to the valuation of the output of producers further up the chain of production (not subject to the tax), the valuation of whose output, *at basic prices*, may be affected by a 'knock-on' effect of taxes on the products of producers lower down the chain of production (this point will be illustrated later when we discuss Table 4.4).

As will be explained in Section 4.8, subsidies on products can be regarded as negative taxes on products, and so subsidies have exactly the opposite, or converse, treatment from taxes. However, until Section 4.8 we will discuss only taxes on production.

(The SNA93, but not the ESA95, permits an alternative valuation of output at producers' prices 'when valuation at basic prices is not feasible' (*SNA93*, para. 6.218; *ESA95*, para. 1.25; *UK NACSM*, para. 5.19). Producers' prices exclude value added type taxes, D.211, but not the other taxes on products. This alternative valuation, which is unlikely to be commonly used, is not discussed in this book.)

I shall illustrate the meaning of 'basic price' first by considering only VAT/GST, D.211, and then by considering VAT/GST together with a D.214 tax on products in the form of a fuel excise duty. For this we shall adapt the model economy of Table 2.1. (Note that the example of a D.214 tax serves also to illustrate what would occur were a D.212 or a D.213 tax to be levied.)

The value added tax/goods and services tax, VAT/GST, can be briefly explained as follows.

Any legislation for VAT/GST must impose at least the following four requirements.

1. Every enterprise making a taxable supply of goods or services must by law be registered for the purposes of VAT/GST.
2. Each registered enterprise is required by law to charge, to any purchaser, VAT/GST at the appropriate rate on the amount of any taxable supply of goods or services.
3. Each registered enterprise is required by law to pay the tax so charged to the government *except that* the registered enterprise is entitled, against this payment of tax, to a credit for any VAT/GST paid by the registered enterprise on the inputs required to produce that taxable supply.
4. The appropriate rate of VAT/GST for exports of goods and services is zero, meaning that exports are free of VAT/GST. The Australian GST legislation applies 'GST-free' status as the equivalent of zero-rating, and exports (as well as specified other products) have 'GST-free' status. This fourth requirement is the fundamental economic reason for the entire system of VAT/GST. This chapter is concerned only with the first three requirements.

In all of what follows 'the government' is shorthand for the authority, or government agency, responsible for administering and collecting VAT/GST;

in the United Kingdom the administering authority is HM Customs and Excise.

In the legislation of the United Kingdom (the Value Added Tax Act 1994, section 24), the tax charged by a registered enterprise is called the 'output tax' and the tax paid by a registered enterprise on inputs is called the 'input tax'. In the Australian legislation (A New Tax System (Goods and Services Tax) Act 1999, Division 7), the corresponding terms are, respectively, 'GST' and 'input tax credit'. In the SNA93 the synonymous terms are 'invoiced VAT' and 'deductible VAT' respectively, where 'invoiced' is to be understood as 'invoiced *out*' by the registered enterprise/producer making the taxable supply, and 'deductible' is to be understood as 'deductible *by*' the registered enterprise/producer from its obligation to pay output tax to the government (*SNA93*, para. 6.209). In what follows, the word 'producer' should be understood as referring to a registered enterprise making taxable supplies – generally such a producer is referred to in the legislation by the wider designation of 'taxable person' (Value Added Tax Act 1994, section 3). (Explicitly, this excludes enterprises who are not registered because their annual supply is below the legal threshold and enterprises who are engaged wholly in making exempt supplies.)

I shall use mainly the SNA93 terms, 'invoiced VAT' and 'deductible VAT', but occasionally I also mention the UK terms, because the UK terms 'output tax' and 'input tax' are helpful in understanding the method whereby VAT/GST is levied. (When I use the SNA93 terms 'invoiced VAT' and 'deductible VAT', I omit the reference to GST, which should be taken as read.) Some of my other terminology is taken from the United Kingdom and European Community legislation but there will be analogous terms in any other country's VAT/GST legislation. It is also helpful in what follows to be specific about distinctly identifying invoices *out*, which are invoices issued to a purchaser by the producer, and distinctly identifying invoices *in*, which are invoices received by the purchaser.

The working of VAT/GST can be illustrated if we suppose that a VAT/GST rate of 0.10, or 10 per cent, is applied in the model economy of Table 2.1 (this means that we suppose, for the sake of the example, that food is subject to VAT/GST – in the real world food is often kept outside the scope of VAT/GST). Table 4.1 gives the relevant data.

Row (1) of Table 4.1 repeats the first column of Table 2.1, p. 58. These values are at the prices before, or excluding, all taxes on products, D.21, and so this row represents output valued at basic prices. In the absence of any other taxes on products, this row also represents the taxable base, known in the European Union as the 'taxable amount', to which the VAT/GST rate of 0.10 (or 10 per cent) is to be applied.

In row (2) of Table 4.1 the VAT/GST rate of 10 per cent is applied to each enterprise's taxable amount to determine that enterprise's invoiced VAT or

Table 4.1

Value added tax/goods and services tax, VAT/GST, levied at rate 0.10 (10 per cent) in the model economy of Table 2.1

		€ per annum			
	Farm	Mill	Wood-cutter	Bakery	Total
Invoices out					
(1) At prices excluding all D.21 taxes on products, or at **basic prices**; 'taxable amount' or VAT/GST base	20	30	5	45	100
(2) Invoiced VAT, or 'output tax': $0.10 \times (1)$	2	3	0.5	4.5	10
(3) At tax inclusive price: $(1) + (2)$	22	33	5.5	49.5	110
Invoices in					
(4) At VAT/GST exclusive prices; if row (5) taxes are deductible by purchaser then this is at **purchasers' prices**	0	20	0	35	55
(5) Deductible VAT [a], or 'input tax': $0.10 \times (4)$	0	2	0	3.5	5.5
(6) At tax inclusive prices: $(4) + (5)$	0	22	0	38.5	60.5
Gross value added and VAT/GST					
(7) Value added tax [or GST], D.211: $(2) - (5)$	2	1	0.5	1.0	4.5
(8) Gross value added at basic prices; B.1g: $(1) - (4)$	20	10	5	10	45

(a) Deductible only if enterprise is a registered enterprise and purchases are used wholly within the business in furtherance of the business.

Source: For rows (1) and (4) of this table, Table 2.1; for other rows, explanation in text.

output tax. Accordingly, row (2) gives the amount of tax which each producer has by law to invoice out. Note that the producer has generally to give this as a *separate* item in the tax invoice out, thus charging this amount of tax to the purchaser of the good at the appropriate rate, whomsoever that purchaser be ('Sixth Council Directive of 17 May 1977 on the harmonization of the laws of the Member States relating to turnover taxes–Common system of value added tax: uniform basis of assessment (77/388/EEC)', *Official Journal of the European Communities*, No. L 145, Volume 20, 13 June 1977, *Article 22*, hereinafter cited as the Sixth Directive; my explanation of VAT is drawn from the United Kingdom's Value Added Tax Act 1994, from Australia's A New Tax System (Goods and Services Tax) Act 1999, from the Sixth Directive, and from *De Voil Indirect Tax Service* (Butterworths, 1999) which is the most comprehensive and authoritative reference on VAT; the history and origin of the value added tax is given in *De Voil Indirect Tax Service*, Part V1, especially Division V1.3).

Row (3) of Table 4.1 may now be calculated as output at basic prices *plus* the invoiced VAT; this is output at tax inclusive prices and each figure in this row represents what the producer receives from the purchaser, whomsoever that purchaser be.

Each producer is required, under the VAT/GST legislation, to remit to the government the amount of row (2) invoiced VAT, or output tax, *except that* each producer is, under the VAT/GST legislation, entitled to a credit for any tax paid on the supplies used in the production of a taxable supply. This credit entitlement works as follows.

For purchases of inputs (including fixed assets) to be used 'for the purpose of the business', each registered enterprise will have invoices *in* stating the taxable amount (at VAT/GST exclusive prices), row (4), with the separately itemised amount of VAT/GST, row (5).

(Table 4.1 is an economy with no imports, but in the case of imports VAT/GST is charged to and collected from the importer on the value of the import (in the UK this is done by HM Customs and Excise), and the VAT/GST charged and collected on imports is thereafter treated in the same way. For reasons of space, I do not discuss the special arrangements which obtain in the European Community under the Single Market for 'acquisitions' – no longer referred to as 'imports' – by a taxable person in one member state from a supplier in another member state, except to remark that the taxable person making such an acquisition (previously 'import') has to declare and pay (to his government) VAT on the acquisition (because there are no border controls within the

European Community); these special arrangements are described and explained in *De Voil Indirect Tax Service*, V3.3.)

The method of VAT/GST collection now proceeds as follows: 'In so far as the goods and services [purchased by a registered enterprise] are used for the purposes of ... [making the enterprise's] taxable transactions [taxable supplies]' the registered enterprise is entitled to deduct VAT invoiced in (or paid on imports or acquisitions) from the obligation to pay to the government the VAT invoiced out (Sixth Directive, *Article 17*; Value Added Tax Act 1994, section 26; A New Tax System (Goods and Services Tax) Act 1999, section 7-5).

In Table 4.1 all the purchases are of *intermediate* inputs for use in making taxable supplies, and we will continue with this illustration, but the entitlement to a credit is not restricted to inputs for intermediate consumption and if a registered enterprise buys a *fixed asset* for business purposes the entitlement to a credit extends to the invoiced VAT or GST on such gross fixed capital formation as well. The same entitlement applies to goods bought for resale.

In Table 4.1, row (5) gives the amount of the VAT/GST invoiced in to each registered enterprise, which the UK legislation calls the 'input tax', which the Australian legislation calls the 'input tax credit', and which the SNA93/ESA95 calls the 'deductible VAT'. For a registered enterprise buying inputs for use in the business, these row (5) amounts of input tax are, under the VAT/GST legislation, a deductible credit (hence the term 'input tax credit') against its obligation to remit to the government the amount of row (2) invoiced VAT or output tax.

Row (6) simply gives the total amount which each producer has to pay to the supplier; that is, the amount at the tax inclusive price.

Each registered enterprise must calculate the amount of tax required by law to be remitted to the government as follows:

Registered enterprise		Invoiced VAT, or		Deductible VAT, or
has to remit	=	output tax,	−	input tax,
to government		invoiced out		invoiced in

If the right-hand side of this equation results in a positive number, the registered enterprise makes a remittance of the positive amount to the government; if the right-hand side of this equation results in a negative number, the registered enterprise claims a refund of the negative amount from the government. (For example, a negative amount may result if the enterprise has bought fixed assets during the period.) In the real world, each registered enterprise makes a VAT/GST return to the government at periodic intervals, generally three monthly, adding up all the VAT/GST invoiced out during the period, all the VAT/GST invoiced in during the period, subtracting the latter from the former, and remitting a payment or claiming a refund according to the result. (Because a registered enterprise is entitled to claim from the government a refund of any negative amount, the legislation relating to, and the administration of, registration is very carefully specified and controlled to prevent institutional units who are not entitled to be registered from becoming or remaining registered.) In row (7) of Table 4.1 each amount is positive, indicating payment to the government.

Accordingly, row (7) of Table 4.1 gives the amount of tax which each registered enterprise has by law to remit to the government, and the last figure in row (7) is the total so remitted. These amounts can be identified as the D.211 value added type taxes (VAT). The total of €4.5 per annum is the total amount of VAT/GST which the government will receive. (Pause to note that the terms 'value added tax' or 'goods and services tax' can be confusing because each can be, and is, applied to the amounts in row (2), to the amounts in row (5), and to the amounts in row (7). Because of this multiple application, it may be helpful to think of the name 'value added tax' or 'goods and services tax' not as the name of a tax as such (that is, not as the name of an amount in any of the aforementioned rows) but rather as the name of a *method* of taxing; then when you use the term 'value added tax' or 'goods and services tax' you will look at the method of levying the tax (that is, the method described in Table 4.1's rows (2), (5) and (7) as (7) = (2) − (5)) rather than thinking that there must be some specific numbers (that is, numbers specific to only one row of Table 4.1) which can be identified as 'the' tax.)

Note that, although the row (7) tax is by law remitted by each registered enterprise to the government, no registered enterprise bears the burden of the tax because each registered enterprise simply passes along the invoiced VAT which it has received from the purchaser.

For example, although the farm remits €2 per annum of tax to the government, the farm receives €2 per annum of tax from the mill, so the farm simply passes this amount along; although the mill remits €1 per annum of tax to the government and pays €2 per annum of tax to the farm, the mill receives €3 per annum of tax from the bakery, so the mill simply passes this amount along – one part to the mill's suppliers and one part to the government. And so on for each producer.

The institutional units who bear the burden of the tax are the households who purchase bread for €49.5 per annum, an increase of €4.5 per annum on what had to be paid for bread in the model economy in Table 2.1 without

VAT/GST. Households, as such, are not registered enterprises making a taxable supply, so there is no possibility for households as such to claim a refund of the VAT/GST invoiced in to the household. (This is why the registration process is very carefully controlled both in legislation and in administration.)

The final expenditure by households (which is also the total final expenditure in this model economy) is thus €49.5 per annum.

That final consumption expenditure by households is at prices which include VAT/GST is a key, and most important, feature of Table 4.1. This valuation, which includes *non*-deductible VAT/GST, is the appropriate valuation for household final consumption expenditure because it is the amount by which households are 'out of pocket' for bread.

Pause to examine Table 4.1 in order thoroughly to understand that, from the point of view of households, €49.5 per annum is the only sensible valuation for their final consumption expenditure. It is true that, of this amount, only €45 per annum ends up being retained by the bakery (so the bakery has a different valuation, from its point of view, for the sale of bread), but from the point of view of households we must understand that the burden of the tax on products is being borne by them, and so we must value their final expenditure accordingly (*SNA93*, para. 9.66).

However, in Chapter 3 (Section 3.5 and Figure 3.4, p. 144) I explained that total final expenditure is equal to total gross value added produced in the chain of production. As we shall see, this remains the case, but now we have to take account of the additional element of taxes on products. Effectively, total final expenditure must now be understood as comprising two elements: (1) total gross value added in the chain of production; and (2) taxes on products.

A value added type tax is thus a tax on goods or services which is collected in stages by enterprises, but which is not borne by enterprises, and which is ultimately charged in full to the household purchaser of the good or service. The following official explanation is explicit:

> Value added tax (VAT) is a percentage tax on products which is collected by enterprises. 'Invoiced VAT' is shown separately on the seller's invoice but the full amount of this is not paid over to the government as producers are allowed to withold the amount ('deductible VAT') that they themselves have paid in VAT on goods and services purchased for their own internal consumption, gross fixed capital formation or resale. VAT paid by households for purposes of final consumption or fixed capital formation in dwellings is not deductible (*UK NACSM*, para. 2.55).

How does all this affect the measurement of gross value added and the gross domestic product?

Gross value added is defined as output *minus* intermediate consumption. We have already noted that the SNA93/ESA95 requires output to be measured at basic prices which exclude any D.21 taxes on products.

Again, pause to examine Table 4.1 in order thoroughly to understand that, from the point of view of the bakery, €45 per annum is a sensible valuation for its output, because although the bakery receives €49.5 per annum from its customers, €4.5 per annum of this is invoiced VAT and of the invoiced VAT €3.5 per annum is paid to the bakery's suppliers (the mill and the woodcutter) and €1 per annum is remitted to government. 'The basic price measures the amount [per unit of output] *retained* by the producer [to pay all costs of production and to make a net operating surplus/net mixed income] and is, therefore, the price most relevant for the producer's decision-taking' (*SNA93*, para. 6.206, italics added and with my clarifying interpolations in square brackets). Accordingly in Table 4.1 output, for the purposes of national accounts, is to be measured as in row (1).

The SNA93/ESA95 requires that intermediate consumption be valued at purchasers' prices (*SNA93*, para. 6.220; *ESA95*, para. 3.72). The official definition of 'purchaser's price' is (in part):

> ... the purchaser's price is the price the purchaser actually pays for the products; including any [D.212, D.213, or D.214] taxes ... on products (*but excluding* [D.211] **deductible** *taxes like VAT* on the products) ... (*ESA95,* para. 3.06, italics added and with my clarifying interpolations in square brackets; note the special emphasis in bold typeface on 'deductible').

To be very explicit about this definition:

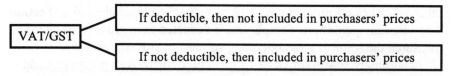

The reason that deductible VAT/GST is not included in the purchaser's price is that this deductible VAT/GST is recouped directly out of the invoiced VAT/GST. For example, if the producer does not have to levy invoiced VAT/GST because the supply is a zero-rated (or GST-free) export, then the producer receives a refund of the deductible VAT/GST directly from the government.

Accordingly the valuations at purchasers' prices for intermediate consumption in Table 4.1 are the valuations given in row (4).

By contrast, for households-as-households, VAT/GST is *non*-deductible, so for household final consumption expenditure the valuation *at purchasers' prices* (which prices exclude only *deductible* VAT/GST) is the valuation given in the second-last figure in row (3).

(A household such as the woodcutter's may also, as a business, be a registered enterprise; if so, it is only the purchases for the strictly business purposes of making taxable supplies on which VAT/GST is deductible, and such a household enterprise must maintain a strict separation between its purchases for use by the business and its purchases for use by the household and must be able to demonstrate this to the VAT/GST administering authority when its accounts are inspected by that authority.)

We may now define 'gross value added at basic prices' as output valued at basic prices *minus* intermediate consumption valued at purchasers' prices. This definition is the appropriate one and the SNA93 explains the reason for this:

> From the point of view of the producer, purchasers' prices for [intermediate consumption] inputs and basic prices for outputs represent the prices actually paid [for inputs] and received [for output]. Their use [these prices] leads to a measure of gross value added which is particularly relevant for the producer ... [but] there is no named aggregate in the System which corresponds to the sum of the gross values added of all the enterprises measured at basic prices (*SNA93*, para. 6.226, with my clarifying interpolations in square brackets).

The reason why gross value added measured in this way at these prices is 'particularly relevant for the producer' is that (setting aside other taxes on production, D.29, which are to be explained in Section 4.7, and setting aside other subsidies on production, D.39, which are to be explained in Section 4.8) when compensation of employees is deducted from gross value added so measured the result is gross operating surplus/gross mixed income.

Accordingly, row (8) of Table 4.1 gives each enterprise's gross value added at basic prices, calculated as the enterprise's output at basic prices in row (1) *minus* the enterprise's intermediate consumption at purchasers' prices in row (4). Each of these row (8) numbers may properly be identified by the SNA93/ESA95 identification code B.1g (without the asterisk).

The aggregate of these B.1g gross values added is €45 per annum, but, as noted at the end of the explanation just quoted, this aggregate is not named in the System. Explicitly, for any economy with D.21 taxes on products, this total is *not* gross domestic product. This important statement is explained in Section 4.5, and is the reason why I said in Chapter 2 that the definition/explanation of gross domestic product given in Chapter 2 was an initial and provisional definition/explanation.

Note explicitly that total final expenditure (in the model economy with no imports) is equal to total gross value added *at basic prices* plus taxes on products:

Model economy (with no imports) with VAT/GST at 10 per cent (Table 4.1), € per annum

Total final expenditure at purchasers' prices	Total gross value added at basic prices	Total taxes on products
49.5	45	4.5

We must now consider the valuation of gross domestic product when there are D.211 value added type taxes in the economy. This involves first considering the goods and services account, because this account shows the reason why, in the production account, the SNA93/ESA95 values gross domestic product in the way it does; namely, including taxes on products.

4.4 The goods and services account and the valuation of final expenditure

We saw in Chapter 3, Section 3.6, that the goods and services account, Account 0, gives (1) the resources becoming available to the economy and (2) the uses of those resources for intermediate consumption and for final expenditure.

For our explanation of the goods and services account and the eventual impact of this on the production account and hence on the valuation of gross domestic product, it is necessary in the goods and services account to start with the *uses* on that account. The uses on the goods and services account are intermediate consumption and the various categories of final expenditure. These uses are valued at purchasers' prices, and this means, as previously explained, that household final consumption expenditure *includes* taxes on products such as VAT/GST.

Table 4.2 gives the goods and services account and the first column gives the goods and services account for the model economy of Table 4.1, which is the model economy of Table 2.1 adapted to include VAT/GST at rate 0.10.

(The second column of Table 4.2 is for use later in Section 4.6.)

The key feature of Table 4.2 is that final consumption expenditure by households, P.3, is valued at purchasers' prices *including* VAT/GST (because in this final expenditure VAT/GST is non-deductible). Consequently the amount reported here is €49.5 per annum, the amount by which households are 'out of pocket' for bread.

(In the official SNA93/ESA95 accounts, the term 'at purchasers' prices' is not included and so does not appear in the published accounts. Accordingly,

Table 4.2

Goods and services account for model economy when there are taxes on products, D.21

		€per annum; model economy of Table 2.1 with:	
SNA93/ ESA95 identification code	SNA93/ESA95 name	VAT/GST at rate 0.10	VAT/GST at rate 0.10 and fuel excise duty at rate 0.40
0	GOODS AND SERVICES ACCOUNT		
	Resources		
P.1	Total output [at basic prices]	100	102
D.21	Taxes on products	4.5	6.7
Total	Total resources	104.5	108.7
	Uses		
P.2	Intermediate consumption [at purchasers' prices]	55	57
P.3	Final consumption expenditure by households [at purchasers' prices]	49.5	51.7
Total	Total uses	104.5	108.7

Sources: Tables 4.1 and 4.4.

in Table 4.2, I put the term 'at purchasers' prices' in square brackets to indicate that it is my unofficial clarifying interpolation which the reader should not expect to see in the official national accounts. Likewise for other interpolations in square brackets in this chapter's tables which represent the SNA93/ESA95 tables.)

This valuation is most important because it means that the total of VAT/GST collected by (remitted to) the government is included in this valuation of final expenditure uses. This valuation should be understood by contrast with the valuation of final consumption expenditure by households of €45 per annum which appeared in Table 3.2's goods and services account for the model economy of Table 2.1 with no taxes on products (p. 155).

The other use of resources on the goods and services account is intermediate consumption. Intermediate consumption is valued at purchasers' prices, but in the case of intermediate consumption by registered enterprises VAT/GST is deductible and so is *not* included in the purchasers' prices valuation. Consequently, the valuation for intermediate consumption in Table 4.2 is €55 per annum (and this is the same as the valuation in Table 3.2, p. 155).

This valuation for intermediate consumption means that there is no double-counting of VAT/GST (as would occur were the valuation of intermediate consumption to be taken at the valuation in row (6) of Table 4.1). In other words, we can now understand the SNA93/ESA95 definition of 'purchasers' prices' as 'excluding deductible taxes like VAT'.

Consequently the total uses on goods and services account for the model economy of Table 4.1 is €104.5 per annum. This is a most important valuation because it has consequences for all the other entries, not only in the goods and services account but also, as we shall see, in the production account.

On the resources side of the goods and services account, output, P.1, is the main resource for this model economy (with no imports), and output is valued at basic prices excluding all taxes on products for the reason explained by the SNA93 and quoted above. This means that output is valued for the model economy of Table 4.1 at €100 per annum (see Table 4.1, row (1) total).

Now, because (as just explained) total uses on the goods and services account includes taxes on products, and because the valuation of output excludes taxes on products, and because total resources on goods and services account must equal total uses on goods and services account, it is necessary for the list of resources on the goods and services account to include, as a separate item, taxes on products which is thus to be added in the sum of total resources. This is the way in which total resources is made equal to total uses, given the way in which the other items in the goods and services account are valued.

As stated in the ESA95 with reference to the goods and services account:

> Given the way in which output is valued at basic prices and uses at purchaser's prices, taxes less subsidies on products must be included [as a separate item] in the resources section [of the goods and services account] (*ESA95*, para. 8.80, with my clarifying interpolations in square brackets).

Accordingly, in the first column of Table 4.2 we show, as a separate, or 'line', item, the D.21 taxes on products as a resource. The total VAT/GST D.21 taxes on products in the model economy of Table 4.1 is €4.5 per annum and this is the amount of tax 'actually payable' by households (even if households are not themselves responsible for remitting the tax to the government – the remitting of the tax being done in the staged way by enterprises as described).

The sum of total output at basic prices and taxes on products is total resources of €104.5 per annum, so total resources is equal to total uses. The goods and services account thus balances globally, as is required. (As explained in Chapter 3's Section 3.6, the goods and services account has no balancing item.)

The goods and services account in the real world deals also with imports of goods and services, and imports have not yet been discussed so we cannot proceed to an example of a real-world goods and services account (the goods and services account for the UK economy in 1997 is given in Table 5.7, p. 225).

We now consider the consequences of all this for the production account and the valuation of gross domestic product.

4.5   The production account and the valuation of gross domestic product

The production account explains the valuation of gross domestic product. The production account for the model economy of Table 4.1 is given in the first column of Table 4.3.

As the two resources on the production account, Account I gives total output, P.1, and (total) taxes on products, D.21.

Importantly, we note in Table 4.3 that total output is at basic prices and this means that it excludes taxes on products. Following the convention of measuring resources on the goods and services account, taxes on products

Table 4.3
Production account for model economy when there are taxes
on products, D.21

SNA93/ ESA95 identifi- cation code	SNA93/ESA95 name	€ per annum; model economy of Table 2.1 with:	
		VAT/GST at rate 0.10	VAT/GST at rate 0.10 and fuel excise duty at rate 0.40
I	PRODUCTION ACCOUNT		
	Resources		
P.1	Total output [at basic prices]	100	102
D.21	Taxes on products	4.5[a]	6.7[b]
Total	Total resources	104.5	108.7
	Uses		
P.2	Intermediate consumption [at purchasers' prices]	55	57
B.1*g	Gross domestic product [at market prices]	49.5	51.7
Total	Total uses	104.5	108.7

(a) Total value added tax/goods and services tax received by general government.
(b) Comprises: total value added tax/goods and services tax of €4.7 per annum (see Table 4.4, total in row (9)); and total fuel excise duty of €2 per annum (see Table 4.4, total in row (2)).
Sources: Tables 4.1 and 4.4.

needs to be included as a separate or line item on the resources side of the production account.

The totals of output [at basic prices] and taxes on products are, respectively, €100 per annum (Table 4.1, row (1) total), and €4.5 per annum (Table 4.1, row (7) total). The consequences of including taxes on products as a line item among resources is that the total resources on production account in the model economy is €104.5 per annum. It is most important to note that, and how, this total includes taxes on products because a great deal follows from this.

As the two uses on the production account, Account I gives intermediate consumption [at purchasers' prices], P.2, and gross domestic product, B.1*g, where gross domestic product is derived as a balancing item; that is, as the difference between total resources on production account and intermediate consumption [at purchasers' prices].

Importantly (and by contrast with Table 2.2, p. 84), we specifically note in Table 4.3 that intermediate consumption is at purchasers' prices. This means, for intermediate consumption by registered enterprises engaged in production, that deductible VAT/GST is excluded from the valuation (see Table 4.1, row (4) total). Intermediate consumption valued thus is, for the model economy of Table 4.1, €55 per annum.

'Gross domestic product' may now be defined and calculated as total resources on production account for the whole economy *minus* intermediate consumption on production account for the whole economy. By contrast with the provisional equation defining gross domestic product given in Chapter 2 (p. 68), we can now give and apply the full definitional equation for gross domestic product:

$$
\begin{array}{l}
\text{Gross} \\
\text{domestic} \\
\text{product,} \\
\text{B.1*g}
\end{array}
=
\begin{array}{l}
\text{Total resources on the} \\
\text{production account for} \\
\text{whole economy (includes} \\
\text{taxes on products)}
\end{array}
-
\begin{array}{l}
\text{Intermediate consumption, P.2,} \\
\text{on the production account for} \\
\text{whole economy (excludes} \\
\text{deductible VAT/GST)}
\end{array}
$$

$$
= \ \text{€}104.5 \text{ p.a.} - \text{€}55 \text{ p.a.}
$$

$$
= \ \text{€}49.5 \text{ p.a.}
$$

As this definitional equation and its application makes clear, the valuation of gross domestic product, B.1*g, includes taxes on products, D.21, because total resources on the production account for the whole economy includes taxes on products (that is, the asterisk in 'B.1*g' denotes not only an economy-wide total but also a valuation which includes D.21 taxes on products).

What is the rationale for including taxes on products (received by government) in the valuation of gross domestic product?

In brief, the answer is in three steps: (1) the valuation of final expenditure includes – that is, must include – non-deductible taxes on products; (2) the basic identity of national accounting is that gross domestic product is equal to total final expenditure (after deduction of imports of goods and services); (3) therefore, to conform with (1) and (2) – that is, to preserve the basic identity of national accounting – the valuation of gross domestic product must include taxes on products.

In synoptic form:

Basic identity of national accounting

↓

Gross domestic product　=　Total final expenditure (allowing for deduction of
　　　　　　　　　　　　　　　　　　　　　　　　imports if economy has
　　　　　　　　　　　　　　　　　　　　　　　　imports)

↓

Final expenditure is valued
including non-deductible taxes on
products (that is, at purchasers' prices)

Therefore, gross domestic product must be valued
*including total taxes on products (collected **and***
retained by government); this preserves the basic
identity of national accounting

This answer and synopsis may be elaborated as follows.

First, note that the term 'market prices' used in Chapter 3, Section 3.3, in connection with making valuations has the following meanings (and note the plural). When *output* is being valued, 'market prices' means *basic prices*; when *intermediate consumption* or *final expenditure* is being valued, 'market prices' means *purchasers' prices*.

Generally, we are rightly uncomfortable when a single term has a very different meaning depending on the context in which it is used, but in this case there is effectively no escape from this dilemma because 'market prices' is a very complex concept. Hence the ESA95 generally avoids the term and hence the wary attitude of the SNA93 to the term 'market prices', the SNA93 acknowledging that when there are taxes on products 'the traditional concept of the "market" price becomes somewhat blurred' because for the same transaction the price from the buyer's point of view can be different from that of the seller's (*SNA93*, para. 6.214; see also *UK NACSM*, para. 2.56).

Thus when the SNA93 states that 'Market prices are ... the basic reference for valuation in the System' (*SNA93*, para. 2.68; *ESA95*, para. 1.51), we must be careful in our understanding of the term 'market prices' because, as the SNA93 explains:

The preferred method of valuation of output is at *basic prices* ... [and] all transactions on the uses of goods and services (like final consumption, intermediate consumption, capital formation) are valued at *purchasers'prices* (*SNA93*, paras 2.72 and 2.73, italics added and with my joining interpolation in square brackets).

The ESA95 differs from the SNA93 in making 'a clear [mandatory] choice in favour of valuing output at basic prices' (*ESA95*, para. 1.25, with my interpolation in square brackets to indicate that EU member states are bound by this).

As explained, for final consumption (and for gross fixed capital formation by households), the valuation of the final expenditure includes taxes on products.

The basic identity of national accounting is that gross domestic product is equal to the total of final expenditure (after allowing for imports). It is this identity that dictates the valuation of gross domestic product in the SNA93/ESA95 and this valuation must be at market prices including taxes on products. But the concept of market prices is complex. We now understand the following synopsis of 'market price':

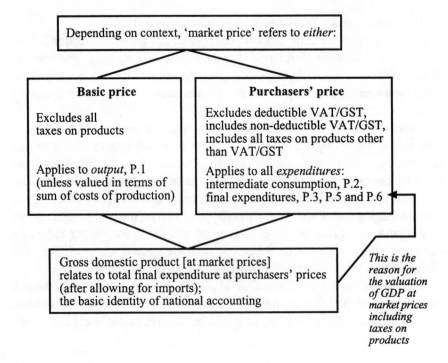

Depending on context, 'market price' refers to *either*:

Basic price

Excludes all taxes on products

Applies to *output*, P.1 (unless valued in terms of sum of costs of production)

Purchasers' price

Excludes deductible VAT/GST, includes non-deductible VAT/GST, includes all taxes on products other than VAT/GST

Applies to all *expenditures*: intermediate consumption, P.2, final expenditures, P.3, P.5 and P.6

Gross domestic product [at market prices] relates to total final expenditure at purchasers' prices (after allowing for imports); the basic identity of national accounting

This is the reason for the valuation of GDP at market prices including taxes on products

Table 4.3 states that the valuation of gross domestic product is at market prices because this valuation of gross domestic product is equal to the total of final expenditures (in an economy with no imports) at the prices which purchasers pay for their final expenditures. This is the basic identity of national accounting explained in Chapter 3.

The term 'at market prices' is not officially used in the template accounts of the SNA93/ESA95, but it is used in the United Kingdom national accounts (the *Blue Book 1999 edition*, tables 1.1, 1.2, 1.4 and 1.5, pp. 30–38; *UK NACSM*, para. 4.53). This is relevant to the basic identity of national accounting, so it is useful always to bear in mind that the unqualified SNA93/ESA95 term 'gross domestic product' is at market prices. In Table 4.3 I give the term in square brackets.

Subsidies on products, D.31, can simply be treated like negative D.21 taxes on products, and from an aggregate point of view, all that is relevant in the production account is the combined 'Taxes on products *less* Subsidies on products', D.21 – D.31. Accordingly in real-world production accounts, this is the item that generally appears in the place of Table 4.3's simplified illustration of D.21 taxes on products.

Consequently, Table 4.3 puts us in a position better to understand the production account for the United Kingdom in 1997, given in Chapter 2's Table 2.3 (p. 88).

We now need to consider other taxes on products.

4.6   Taxes on products other than VAT/GST

In order to consider taxes on products other than VAT/GST, let us suppose that (as a fuel conservation measure, say) the government introduces a fuel excise duty to be levied at a rate of 0.40, or 40 per cent, on sales of fuel. This means that the woodcutter has to remit to the government the fuel excise duty, levied at this rate on the tax exclusive sales of fuel. The fuel excise duty is levied in addition to VAT/GST (we keep VAT/GST for a reason which will be explained). The relevant figures are given in Table 4.4.

The figures for the farm and the mill remain as before.

The output of the woodcutter is valued at basic prices excluding *all* taxes on products. Accordingly, the valuation of the woodcutter's output at basic prices is €5 per annum as given in row (1) of Table 4.4. This is the amount the woodcutter retains in consequence of selling firewood (fuel) and so this is the appropriate valuation of output from the woodcutter's point of view.

Table 4.4

Value added tax, VAT/GST, levied at rate 0.10 (10 per cent) and fuel excise duty levied at rate 0.40 (40 per cent) in the model economy of Table 2.1

	€ per annum				
	Farm	Mill	Woodcutter	Bakery	Total
Invoices out					
(1) At prices excluding all D.21 taxes on products, or at **basic prices**	20	30	5	47	102
(2) Fuel excise duty: 0.40 × (1) where applicable on supply of fuel	n.a.	n.a.	2	n.a.	2
(3) 'Taxable amount', or VAT/GST base: (1) + (2)	20	30	7	47	104
(4) Invoiced VAT, or 'output tax': 0.10 × (3)	2	3	0.7	4.7	10.4
(5) At tax inclusive prices: (3) + (4)	22	33	7.7	51.7	114.4
Invoices in					
(6) At VAT exclusive prices; if row (7) taxes are deductible by purchaser then this is at **purchasers' prices**	0	20	0	37	57
(7) Deductible VAT (a) , or 'input tax': 0.10 × (6)	0	2	0	3.7	5.7
(8) At tax inclusive prices: (6) + (7)	0	22	0	40.7	62.7
Gross value added and VAT/GST					
(9) Value added tax [or GST], D.211: (4) − (7)	2	1	0.7	1	4.7
(10) Gross value added at basic prices: (1) − (6)	20	10	5	10	45

(a) Deductible only if enterprise is a registered enterprise and purchases are used wholly within the business in furtherance of the business.

Source: Table 4.1 and text; 'n.a.' means 'not applicable'.

In accordance with the various taxes levied in this economy, the woodcutter has to do two things.

First, the woodcutter has to pay a fuel excise duty at a rate of 0.40 on this supply at tax exclusive prices of €5 per annum. Accordingly, the woodcutter has to pay €2 per annum (= 0.40 × €5 per annum) of fuel excise duty to the government. The amount of this tax is given in row (2) of Table 4.4. The fuel excise duty does not apply to any other enterprise and so is not applicable in those cases.

The likelihood is that the woodcutter will pass this €2 per annum excise duty on to the bakery. If so, although the woodcutter is responsible for remitting the tax to the government, the woodcutter does not bear the burden of the tax because the tax is simply 'passed along' to the purchaser of fuel (in this case the bakery). However, the *structure* of the SNA93/ESA95 accounts does not depend on this assumption (of the tax being passed along) holding in the real world; I make the assumption because it leads to the simplest possible illustration.

Note carefully that this tax passed along to the bakery by the woodcutter is *not* deductible by the bakery from its obligation to remit output tax to the government. (There is no legal obligation on the woodcutter to show this amount of fuel excise duty of €2 per annum as a separate item on the woodcutter's invoice out.)

Second, the woodcutter has to charge VAT/GST at a rate of 0.10 on the taxable amount which *includes* the fuel excise duty. This needs explaining.

For the purposes of VAT/GST, the taxable amount – the base upon which VAT/GST is to be levied – is the value of the taxable supply *including* any such excise duty (Sixth Directive, *Article 11*, A 2 (a); see also HM Customs and Excise, *The VAT Guide A guide to the main VAT rules and procedures*, Notice 700, March 1996, para. 3.1 (g); for a commentary see *De Voil Indirect Tax Service*, V3.154; A New Tax System (Goods and Services Tax) Act 1999, section 108-5). In effect, under the rules for VAT/GST the excise duty is also taxed! Illustrating this VAT/GST principle of 'taxing the tax' is the reason for keeping VAT/GST in the model economy.

Consequently, the woodcutter's taxable amount (including the fuel excise duty) is €7 per annum (row (3) of Table 4.4) and VAT/GST has to be charged on this at rate 0.10. Accordingly, the woodcutter has to invoice €0.7 per annum of invoiced VAT or output tax (row (4) of Table 4.4).

Note carefully that this tax *is* deductible by the bakery from its obligation to remit output tax to the government.

As a consequence of all the taxes on products, the bakery has to pay the woodcutter €7.7 per annum for firewood (fuel).

The bakery's purchases for intermediate consumption are at purchasers' prices, and this valuation excludes *deductible* VAT/GST but includes any other taxes on products; specifically, in this case the fuel excise duty. The bakery's intermediate consumption at purchasers' prices is thus €37 per annum (row (6) of Table 4.4) and this comprises €30 per annum for flour and €7 per annum for firewood (fuel).

The purchasers' prices are the prices most 'relevant for the producer's decision-taking'. Deductible VAT/GST is not relevant for the producer's decision-making (because deductible VAT/GST simply comes out of the bakery's VAT/GST invoiced out) but the non-deductible fuel excise duty passed on to the bakery by the woodcutter *is* relevant to the bakery's decision-making because there is nothing other than output at basic prices from which the fuel excise duty can be recouped. Consequently, for example, we could reasonably imagine the bakery trying to economise on the now more expensive fuel – the fuel excise duty included in the purchase of fuel is treated by the bakery just as any other cost of production.

Assume that the bakery wishes to continue making the same gross operating surplus as in Table 2.1 (namely, €5 per annum) and we know that the bakery has to pay employee compensation of €5 per annum (as in Table 2.1). This means that the bakery has to achieve a gross value added of €10 per annum (because in this model economy gross operating surplus is gross value added at basic prices *minus* compensation of employees).

Consequently, given intermediate consumption at purchasers' prices of €37 per annum, the bakery has to charge a basic price for bread which will result in sales receipts at basic prices of €47 per annum to be received and retained by the producer. The basic price charge of €47 per annum arises because gross value added at basic prices must be €10 per annum, and this is to be calculated as:

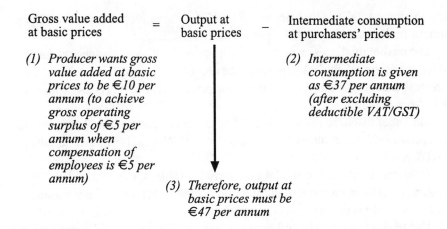

Gross value added = Output at − Intermediate consumption
at basic prices   basic prices   at purchasers' prices

(1) Producer wants gross value added at basic prices to be €10 per annum (to achieve gross operating surplus of €5 per annum when compensation of employees is €5 per annum)

(2) Intermediate consumption is given as €37 per annum (after excluding deductible VAT/GST)

(3) Therefore, output at basic prices must be €47 per annum

The bakery is the one enterprise to increase its output at basic prices (row (1); compare row (1) of Table 4.1) and this increase reflects the impact of the fuel excise duty as a sort of 'knock-on' effect. Note, however, that this knock-on effect is not relevant to the definition of 'basic prices' as excluding taxes on products because that definition applies to the valuation of the *woodcutter's* output, and has no reference to any knock-on effect higher up the chain of production.

The consequence of this is that total output at basic prices in this economy is €102 per annum; see the total in row (1) in Table 4.4.

The bakery has by law to invoice VAT/GST at rate 0.10 on its taxable amount of €47 per annum. This means that the bakery has to invoice VAT/GST of €4.7 per annum (row (4) of Table 4.4). This amount of VAT/GST is charged to, and received from, household consumers by the bakery.

In the model economy of Table 4.4 the government receives two types of taxes on products. First, the government receives €2 per annum of fuel excise duty (row (2) total in Table 4.4). Second, the government receives €4.7 per annum of VAT/GST (Table 4.4, row (9) total; note that by comparison with Table 4.1 the total VAT/GST has increased by €0.2 per annum because VAT/GST is levied at 10 per cent on the fuel excise duty itself of €2 per annum). This amount of €4.7 per annum can be seen in one way as the €4.7 per annum of invoiced VAT/GST by the bakery to households, for whom the VAT/GST is non-deductible. Alternatively, the amount of VAT/GST may be calculated as the difference between total VAT invoiced out and total deductible VAT: €10.4 per annum (row (4) total) *minus* €5.7 per annum (row (7) total).

Consequently, the government in the model economy of Table 4.4 receives and retains a total of €6.7 per annum of D.21 taxes on products (= €2 per annum fuel excise duty + €4.7 per annum VAT/GST).

The upshot of all this can be seen in the goods and services account for the model economy of Table 4.4, given in the second column of Table 4.2 (p. 178). One resource is total output valued at basic prices, P.1, and this is, as explained, €102 per annum.

The other resource is the total D.21 taxes on products of €6.7 per annum, comprising €2 per annum of fuel excise duty, D.214, and €4.7 per annum of VAT/GST, D.211.

Total resources in the model economy of Table 4.4 is thus €108.7 per annum (= €102 per annum of output at basic prices, P.1 + € 6.7 per annum of D.21 taxes on products).

The uses in the goods and services account for the model economy of Table 4.4 are intermediate consumption and final expenditure.

Intermediate consumption is valued at purchases' prices. This valuation excludes deductible VAT but includes any taxes on products, such as the fuel excise duty, which is not deductible. This affects the bakery's intermediate consumption. Consequently, the bakery's intermediate consumption at purchasers' prices is €37 per annum, comprising purchases of €30 per annum for flour from the mill (see row (3) for the mill in Table 4.4) and €7 per annum for fuel from the woodcutter (see row (3) for the woodcutter in Table 4.4). To be very explicit, this latter purchase by the bakery includes the non-deductible fuel excise duty of €2 per annum and excludes both the deductible VAT/GST of €0.7 per annum on purchases of fuel and also the deductible VAT/GST of €3 per annum on purchases of flour.

Accordingly, total intermediate consumption at purchasers' prices in the model economy is €57 per annum (row (6) total in Table 4.4) and this is the figure given in the goods and services account in the second column of Table 4.2.

Final consumption expenditure by households (the only final expenditure in this economy) is at purchasers' prices. Purchasers' prices exclude only deductible VAT/GST, and for households as households VAT/GST is non-deductible, so final consumption expenditure by households is valued at €51.7 per annum (row (5) for bakery's sales at tax inclusive prices in Table 4.4).

By comparison with Table 2.1, the economy with no taxes on products, where final consumption expenditure was €45 per annum, households are now additionally 'out of pocket' by the full amount of all taxes on products, €6.7 per annum, so their final consumption expenditure is most appropriately valued, from their point of view, as €51.7 per annum. Accordingly, this is the valuation of final consumption expenditure by households reported in the goods and services account for the model economy of Table 4.4 (second column of Table 4.2).

We can see that the goods and services account balances globally: total resources, €108.7 per annum, equals total uses, €108.7 per annum.

We may now consider the consequences of all this for the valuation of gross domestic product in the model economy of Table 4.4. This is explained through the production account.

The production account for the model economy of Table 4.4 is given in the second column of Table 4.3 (p. 181). As just explained, total output at basic prices is €102 per annum (total for row (1) in Table 4.4), and total taxes on products is €6.7 per annum. Accordingly, total resources on production account in the model economy of Table 4.4 is €108.7 per annum.

The first use of these resources on production account is intermediate consumption of €57 per annum. As just explained, the bakery's intermediate consumption at purchasers' prices has increased by comparison with the model economy of Table 4.1 because of the fuel excise duty.

Gross domestic product, B.1*g, is calculated as the balancing item in the production account, and according to the equation for gross domestic product given in Section 4.5:

Gross domestic product, B.1*g	=	Total resources on the production account for whole economy (includes taxes on products)	−	Intermediate consumption, P.2, on the production account for whole economy (excludes deductible VAT/GST)

$$= \quad €108.7 \text{ p.a.} \quad - \quad €57 \text{ p.a.}$$

$$= \quad €51.7 \text{ p.a.}$$

Comparing this with the final expenditure in the goods and services account we can see that in this model economy (with no imports) the basic identity of national accounting holds good: Gross domestic product *equals* Total final expenditure (after allowing for imports which are zero in this economy).

In both illustrations (only VAT at 10 per cent and VAT at 10 per cent together with a fuel excise duty at 40 per cent) the sum of gross values added at basic prices remains at €45 per annum (see totals in: row (8) of Table 4.1; and row (10) of Table 4.4 and compare these with the total in the third column of Table 2.1).

We may now demonstrate the connection between the sum of gross values added at basic prices and gross domestic product. We have the following table of the valuation of gross domestic product and the basic identity of national accounting:

€ per annum

			Basic identity of national accounting	
	Total gross value added at basic	*plus*	*equals* Gross domestic product,	Total final expen-
Model economy	prices	Taxes on products	B.1*g	diture[a]
Without VAT	45	0	45	45
With only VAT at 10 per cent	45	4.5	49.5	49.5
With VAT at 10 per cent and fuel excise duty at 40 per cent	45	6.7	51.7	51.7

(*a*) Economy with no imports.

This synoptic table illustrates and demonstrates the basic argument of this chapter on the SNA93/ESA95 valuation of gross domestic product: namely, (1) that the valuation of gross domestic product includes taxes on products, and (2) that this is done to preserve the basic identity of national accounting.

We can now finalise the explanation of the relation between the valuation of total final expenditure (in an economy with no imports) and the valuation of gross domestic product.

The valuation of final expenditure must necessarily include taxes on products. But final expenditure is also a use of gross value added (Chapter 3's Section 3.5), and we may now add the clause that this is a use of gross value added *at basic prices* (which excludes taxes on products). Consequently, we must now understand final expenditure as consisting of two elements: a use of gross value added at basic prices (this part of final expenditure goes to the producers in the chain of production), and taxes on products (this part of final expenditure goes to the general government).

If the basic identity of national accounting is to be preserved, then the valuation of gross domestic product must likewise include taxes on products.

We can express this in a summary synopsis which relates the argument of this chapter to the argument of Chapters 2 and 3:

The basic identity
of national accounting
(economy with no imports)

↓

Total final expenditure   =   **Gross domestic product**

Is a use of total gross value added at basic prices	*Is essentially a concept of total gross value added at basic prices*
But final expenditure also and additionally includes taxes on products (because non-deductible taxes on products fall ultimately on purchasers making final expenditures)	*To preserve the basic identity of national accounting, the valuation of gross domestic product, B.1*g, must include taxes on products*

We have thus explained why and how taxes on products affect the valuation of gross domestic product, B.1*g, as officially defined and measured, by being added on to the sum of the B.1g gross values added at basic prices.

This addition, or inclusion of taxes on products in the valuation of gross domestic product, partly explains the asterisk in 'B.1*g'; the other part of the asterisk being explained by the fact that 'B.1*g' refers only to an economy-wide total, whereas 'B.1g' can refer to gross value added for a part of the economy. The following may be helpful in remembering the significance of the asterisk:

B.1g   Gross value added at   **basic prices**   for   **part**   of the economy

↑ ↑

B.1*g   Gross value added at   **market prices** for the **whole** economy

What holds for the model economies' national accounts also holds for real-world national accounts.

We now need to consider how taxes on production other than taxes on products fit into the national accounts and to consider subsidies on production.

4.7   Other taxes on production and the primary distribution of income account: generation of income account

So far we have seen that the two types of D.21 taxes on products, value added type taxes, D.211, and excise duties, D.214 (which also does duty in showing what would happen if D.212 or D.213 taxes on products were to be levied), have an impact on the valuation of gross domestic product.

We need now to consider the other taxes on production, D.29, which do not have a direct impact on the valuation of gross domestic product because these D.29 taxes are not levied per unit of product and so do not *directly* affect the prices for products. To illustrate these D.29 other taxes on production, suppose that, in the economy of Table 4.4, property taxes ('rates') are levied at a rate of €1 per annum per enterprise (this assumes that each enterprise owns and occupies only one piece of real estate – premises – for its business, and that the rate is a flat-rate money amount of €1 per annum per business premises). This D.29 other tax on production is levied whether or not products are produced, and this differentiates these taxes from all the D.21 taxes on products.

To illustrate the impact of D.29 other taxes on production, I take the simplest possible illustration based on the assumption that gross value added at basic prices remains the same as in Tables 2.1, 4.1 and 4.4. In the real world, this assumption is unlikely to hold, but this does not make any difference to the *principle* by which D.29 other taxes on production are treated and does not make any difference to the *structure* of the resulting Account II.1.1 Primary distribution of income account: generation of income account. A more realistic assumption about the response of producers to D.29 taxes on production (that is, that producers will increase their basic prices) will alter the numbers in Account II.1.1, but will not alter the structure of that account.

Accordingly, Table 4.5 gives gross value added at basic prices for each of the enterprises as these occur in Tables 2.1, 4.1 and 4.4.

Compensation of employees is also the same for each enterprise as in Table 2.1 and total compensation of employees remains at €25 per annum (Table 2.1, total in fourth column of data).

By contrast with Table 2.1, Table 4.5 requires a column for other taxes on production, D.29. Under the illustration, each enterprise has to pay to the government a tax on its business premises of €1 per annum, and this is shown in Table 4.5 with the total of these D.29 taxes being €4 per annum.

Gross operating surplus/gross mixed income accruing to enterprises must now be calculated as:

$$
\begin{array}{l}
\text{Gross operating} \\
\text{surplus/gross} \\
\text{mixed income,} \\
\text{B.2g/B.3g}
\end{array}
=
\begin{array}{l}
\text{Gross value} \\
\text{added at} \\
\text{basic prices,} \\
\text{B.1g}
\end{array}
-
\begin{array}{l}
\text{Compensation} \\
\text{of employees,} \\
\text{D.1}
\end{array}
-
\begin{array}{l}
\text{Other} \\
\text{taxes on} \\
\text{production,} \\
\text{D.29}
\end{array}
$$

Accordingly, as shown in the last column of Table 4.5 each enterprise makes a gross operating surplus/gross mixed income of €4 per annum; as in Table 2.1, Table 4.5 distinguishes between gross operating surplus and gross mixed income and we can see that the total of gross operating surplus is €8 per annum and the total of gross mixed income is €8 per annum, making a total gross operating surplus/gross mixed income of €16 per annum.

By comparison with Table 2.1's total of gross operating surplus/gross mixed income of €20 per annum, the total gross operating surplus/gross mixed income has been reduced by €4 per annum, or by the amount of the D.29 other taxes on production.

Other taxes on production, D.29, do not have to be included in the goods and services account, nor in the production account because D.29 taxes do not directly affect the valuation of final expenditure nor the valuation of gross domestic product. Consequently the structure of each of these accounts is not affected by D.29 other taxes on production.

But D.29 other taxes on production do have to be included in Account II.1.1 Primary distribution of income account: generation of income account, because the primary incomes of gross operating surplus/gross mixed income are affected by D.29 other taxes on production.

The primary distribution of income account: generation of income account, Account II.1.1, is given in Table 4.6.

The total resources on Account II.1.1 is gross domestic product. For the model economy of Table 4.4, gross domestic product is €51.7 per annum

Table 4.5
Other taxes on production (local government property taxes) levied at
rate €1 per annum per enterprise in model economy of Table 4.4

Enterprise	Gross value added at basic prices, B.1g	Compensation of employees, D.1	Other taxes on production, D.29	Gross operating surplus/gross mixed income, B.2g/B.3g	
Farm	20	15	1	4	(GMI)
Mill	10	5	1	4	(GOS)
Woodcutter	5	0	1	4	(GMI)
Bakery	10	5	1	4	(GOS)
Total	45	25	4	16	

(€ per annum across all value columns)

Source: Tables 2.1 and 4.4, and text.

(see the second column of Table 4.3). As previously explained, this valuation includes D.21 taxes on products.

For the model economy, there are five types of uses of the resource of gross domestic product on Account II.1.1: (1) compensation of employees, D.1, of €25 per annum; (2) taxes on products, D.21, of €6.7 per annum (because these are included in the valuation of gross domestic product – see Table 4.3); (3) other taxes on production, D.29, of €4 per annum (because these have consequences for gross operating surplus/gross mixed income); and the residual balancing items, (4) gross operating surplus, B.2g, of €8 per annum, and (5) gross mixed income, B.3g, of €8 per annum.

The total uses on Account II.1.1 thus equal total resources of gross domestic product at market prices.

As noted, this is the simplest form of illustration of other taxes on production that could be devised. However, suppose that each enterprise recouped its D.29 other tax on production of €1 per annum by increasing the basic price charged for its products. This would increase, in row (1) of Table 4.4, each enterprise's output at basic prices. The increase in output is made sufficient to provide each enterprise with a gross value added at basic prices increased by €1 per annum (and the numbers in row (10) of Table 4.4 would be altered

Table 4.6
Primary distribution of income account:
generation of income account for model economy with taxes on
products and other taxes on production

SNA93/ ESA95 identifi- cation code	SNA93/ESA95 name	€ per annum
II	DISTRIBUTION AND USE OF INCOME ACCOUNTS	
II.1	PRIMARY DISTRIBUTION OF INCOME ACCOUNT	
II.1.1	GENERATION OF INCOME ACCOUNT	
	Resources	
B.1*g	Total resources, gross domestic product[a]	51.7
	Uses	
D.1	Total compensation of employees	25
D.21	Taxes on products	6.7
D.29	Other taxes on production	4
B.2g	Gross operating surplus	8
B.3g	Gross mixed income	8
Total	Total uses	51.7

(*a*)   Valuation includes D.21 taxes on products.
Source: Tables 4.3 and 4.5.

accordingly). From this increased output at basic prices and consequently increased gross value added at basic prices, each enterprise could pay the D.29 other taxes on production of €1 per annum while maintaining its gross operating surplus/gross mixed income as it was in Table 2.1. Although all the numbers (other than the zeroes) in Table 4.4 (and Tables 4.2 and 4.3) and in Table 4.6 would change, there is no need to change the *structure* (that is, the row headings) of Table 4.6. As an exercise to show that the structure of these accounts copes with the different illustration, the reader can redo Tables 4.4, 4.2, 4.3 and 4.6 (in that order) under the assumption that each enterprise recoups its D.29 other taxes on production of €1 per annum by increasing its basic price by an amount sufficient to increase its gross value added at basic prices by €1 per annum. (To check your answer: gross domestic product under this illustration becomes €56.54 per annum and the total of D.21 taxes on products becomes €7.54 per annum.)

It is useful to summarise the treatment of the various types of D.2 taxes on production and imports in the relevant accounts of the SNA93/ESA95:

SNA93/ESA95 account	Includes	Reason
As a resources item		
Goods and services account	Taxes on products, D.21	Valuation of final expenditure
Production account	Taxes on products, D.21	Valuation of GDP for purpose of preserving basic identity of national accounting
As uses items		
Primary distribution of income account: generation of income account	Taxes on products, D.21	Included in valuation of GDP as a resource, so must be taken account of as a use
	Other taxes on production, D.29	Affects balancing items of gross operating surplus/gross mixed income, B.2g/B.3g
	Taxes on production and imports, D.2	Total of D.21 and D.29

4.8 Taxes on production, subsidies, and the generation of income account in the United Kingdom and Australia

To conclude this chapter, we consider in Table 4.7 the primary distribution of income account: generation of income account, Account II.1.1, for the United Kingdom in 1997 and for Australia in 1997–98. In Table 4.7 we give extra details not given in Table 2.5 (p. 107). The purpose of Table 4.7 is to show explicitly how D.21 and D.29 taxes fit into the national accounts and also to introduce subsidies on production which are explained with the aid of Figure 4.2.

The United Kingdom's gross domestic product [at market prices] in 1997 was £803 889 million (see Table 2.3, p. 88) and Australia's gross domestic product [at market prices] was $564 705 million. Gross domestic product is the total resource on Account II.1.1 (see Tables 2.4 and 2.5, pp. 105 and 107).

The uses of total resources are as follows, given both in monetary amounts and (for purposes of comparison between the two economies) in percentages of gross domestic product. Total compensation of employees in the United Kingdom was £432 388 million or 53.8 per cent, and in Australia was $270 084 million or 47.8 per cent.

In the United Kingdom, D.21 taxes on products and imports were, in total, £98 319 million or 12.2 per cent of gross domestic product. (Footnote (*a*) gives the breakdown of this total among the various D.21 types of taxes and by the recipient 'government' – the UK government and the institutions of the European Union. The purpose of this footnote and of the other footnotes is simply to indicate the sort of interesting details which can be extracted from the national accounts.)

For Australia, matching data on D.21, taxes on products, as a separate item are not available.

The next entry in Table 4.7 is D.31, subsidies on products, and so we need now to consider subsidies, not so far discussed in this chapter. The most important thing to understand about subsidies is that they can be simply treated as negative taxes on production, that is, as taxes on production with a minus sign, and this is the way they occur in the accounts so far considered.

The classification of subsidies is given in Figure 4.2.

The ESA95 official definition of 'subsidies' is (in part):

> Subsidies (D.3) are current unrequited payments which general government or the Institutions of the European Union make to resident producers, with the objective of influencing their *levels* of production, their *prices* or the

Table 4.7

Primary distribution of income account: generation of income account for the United Kingdom and Australia

SNA93/ESA95 identification code	SNA93/ESA95 name	United Kingdom 1997, £ million	Australia 1997–98, $ million	Percentage of GDP United Kingdom 1997	Australia 1997–98
II	DISTRIBUTION AND USE OF INCOME ACCOUNTS				
II.1	PRIMARY DISTRIBUTION OF INCOME ACCOUNT				
II.1.1	GENERATION OF INCOME ACCOUNT				
	Resources				
B.1*g	Total resources, gross domestic product	803 889	564 705	100	100
	Uses				
D.1	Total compensation of employees	432 388	270 084	53.8	47.8
D.21	Taxes on products and imports	98 319 [a]	n.a.	12.2	n.a.
– D.31	*less* Subsidies on products	–8 044 [b]	n.a.	–1.0	n.a.
D.21 – D.31	Taxes *less* Subsidies on products	90 275	41 294	11.2	7.3
D.29	Production taxes other than on products	17 048 [c]	n.a.	2.1	n.a.
D.39	*less* Production subsidies other than on products	—	n.a.	—	n.a.
D.29 – D.39	Production taxes *less* Subsidies other than on products	17 048	23 672	2.1	4.2
B.2g	Gross operating surplus	222 513	173 878	27.7	30.8
B.3g	Gross mixed income	41 665	54 217	5.2	9.6
di	Statistical discrepancy between income components and GDP	—	1 560	—	0.3
B.1*g	Total uses	803 889	564 705	100	100

'n.a.' means not available; '—' means nil (or less than £0.5 million).

(a) Of which: £52 257 million was D.211 value added tax received by the United Kingdom general government; £3397 million was D.211 value added tax received by the European Union; £40 290 million was D.214 taxes on products excluding VAT and import duties received by the United Kingdom general government; £1999 million was D.2121 import duties received by the European Union; and £376 million was D.214 taxes on products excluding VAT and import duties received by the European Union.

(b) Of which: £4870 million was D.31 subsidies on products paid by the United Kingdom general government; and £3174 million was D.31 subsidies on products paid by the European Union.

(c) Of which: £16 924 million was received by the United Kingdom central government; and £124 million was received by United Kingdom local government.

Sources: Office for National Statistics, *United Kingdom National Accounts The Blue Book 1999 edition*, tables 1.7.2, 5.1.3, 5.2.3, 5.3.3 and 7.1.2, pp. 58, 176, 185, 195 and 226; Australian Bureau of Statistics, *Australian System of National Accounts 1997–98*, Catalogue No. 5204.0, tables 1.8, 3.1 and 3.2, pp. 28 and 72–73; D.29 – D.39 other taxes on production *less* subsidies on production calculated as the difference between gross domestic product at basic prices (table 3.2) and total factor incomes (table 3.1); D.21 – D.31 taxes *less* subsidies on products calculated as the difference between D.2 – D.3 taxes *less* subsidies on production and imports (table 1.8) and D.29 – D.39 other taxes *less* subsidies on production and imports.

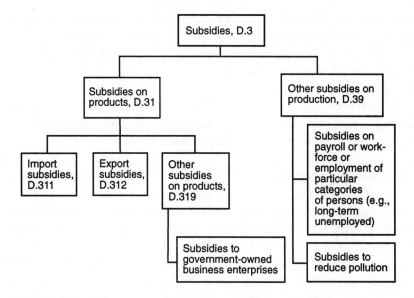

Figure 4.2   Classification of subsidies

remuneration of the factors of production [labour and capital] (*ESA95*, para. 4.30, italics added and with my clarifying interpolation in square brackets).

The SNA93 official definition of 'subsidies' is:

> Subsidies are current unrequited payments that government units, including non-resident government units, make to enterprises on the basis of the levels of their production activities or the quantities or values of the goods or services which they produce, sell or import. They [the subsidies] are receivable by resident producers or importers. In the case of resident producers they [the subsidies] may be designed to influence their [the producers'] *levels* of production, the *prices* at which their outputs are sold or the *remuneration* of the institutional units engaged in production. Subsidies are equivalent to negative taxes on production in so far as their [the subsidies'] impact on the operating surplus is in the opposite direction to that of taxes on production (*SNA93*, para. 7.71, italics added with my clarifying interpolations in square brackets).

Subsidies, D.3, are divided between subsidies on products, D.31, and other subsidies on production, D.39.

Subsidies on products, D.31, cover any subsidy 'payable per unit of a good or service produced or imported' (*ESA95*, para. 4.33).

Subsidies on imports, D.311, are those subsidies which are payable when the goods cross the frontier coming in or when the imported service is delivered to the resident institutional unit.

Subsidies on exports, D.312, are classified in the SNA93 but not in the ESA95. Subsidies on exports are those subsidies which 'become payable when the goods leave the economic territory or when the services are delivered to non-resident units' (*SNA93*, para. 7.76). Generally, subsidies on exports are not permitted under agreements relating to the World Trade Organisation and thus do not play an important role in most countries' national accounts.

Other subsidies on products, D.319, are subsidies on products used domestically and are 'payable to resident enterprises in respect of their outputs which are used or consumed within the economic territory' (*SNA93*, para. 7.78). One important example of such D.319 subsidies is the subsidy paid to government-owned enterprises 'intended to compensate for persistent losses – i.e., negative operating surpluses – which they incur on their productive activities as a result of charging prices which are lower than their average costs of production as a matter of deliberate government economic and social policy [to have 'low' prices]' (*SNA93*, para. 7.78, with my clarifying interpolation in square brackets).

From the national accounts point of view the important point is that, in the accounts so far considered, subsidies on products can be treated as negative taxes on products.

The official definition of 'other subsidies on production', D.39, is (in part):

> Other subsidies on production (D.39) consist of subsidies except subsidies on products which resident producer units may receive as a consequence of engaging in production (*ESA95*, para. 4.36).

Examples of these D.39 other subsidies on production are given in Figure 4.2. Governments may, as a matter of economic and social policy, subsidise producers in their employment of particular categories of persons, such as physically handicapped persons, persons who have been unemployed for a long time, or trainees entering the labour market. Governments may subsidise the costs of pollution control or abatement, thus reducing these costs to producers. This list is not exhaustive of such D. 39 subsidies (and a fuller treatment of these is given in *ESA95*, paras 4.36 to 4.38).

From the national accounts point of view the important point is that, in the accounts so far considered, other subsidies on production can be treated as negative other taxes on production.

Returning to our consideration of Table 4.7, we have now explained that subsidies can be entered as a negative item among the uses in the generation of income account for the whole economy (*ESA95*, para. 4.40). This is because 'their impact on the operating surplus [and mixed income] is in the opposite direction to that of taxes on production' (*SNA93*, para. 7.71, with my clarifying interpolation in square brackets).

Accordingly in Table 4.7, from D.21 taxes on products and imports we need to subtract D.31 subsidies on products. In the United Kingdom in 1997, D.31 subsidies on products totalled £8044 million or 1.0 per cent of gross domestic product (and footnote (*b*) gives the breakdown by governmental source of these subsidies, so that we can see the extent of subsidies from the European Union to UK producers).

For Australia, matching data on D.31 subsidies as a separate item are not available.

Table 4.7 gives the combined total of D.21 – D.31 taxes less subsidies on products in the United Kingdom of £90 275 million (and note in Table 4.7 how this total has been calculated), or 11.2 per cent of gross domestic product, and in Australia of $41 294 million, or 7.3 per cent of gross domestic product, so that this combined item in Table 2.3 (p. 88) can be better understood.

In the United Kingdom, D.29 production taxes other than on products (wording used in the *Blue Book 1999 edition*) or other taxes on production (official SNA93/ESA95 wording) totalled £17 048 million or 2.1 per cent of gross domestic product (and footnote (*c*) gives the breakdown by level of United Kingdom general government which received these D.29 taxes).

The United Kingdom national accounts for 1997 reported D.39 production subsidies other than subsidies on products as nil (or less than £0.5 million) and this applies for all years between 1990 and 1997 inclusive (the *Blue Book 1999 edition*, table 5.1.3, p. 176). Consequently, D.29 – D.39 other taxes on production *less* subsidies on production for the UK in 1997 was £17 048 million or 2.1 per cent of gross domestic product.

In Australia, D.29 – D.39 other taxes on production *less* subsidies on production totalled $23 672 million or 4.2 per cent of gross domestic product.

Finally as balancing items, B.2g gross operating surplus in the United Kingdom was £222 513 million or 27.7 per cent of gross domestic product and in Australia was $173 878 million or 30.8 per cent of gross domestic product.

B.3g gross mixed income in the United Kingdom was £41 665 million or

5.2 per cent of gross domestic product and in Australia was $54 217 million or 9.6 per cent of gross domestic product.

In each country's national accounts there is an item for the statistical discrepancy between gross domestic product and the sum of the income etc. components; for the United Kingdom economy in 1997 this was reported as nil or less than £0.5 million, and for the Australian economy in 1997–98 this was reported as $1560 million or 0.3 per cent of GDP.

In both accounts, total uses equals total resources because of the balancing items B.2g and B.3g (and because of the statistical discrepancy).

In this chapter we have explained the (rather complicated) methods whereby VAT/GST is levied. The reader may well ask: Why raise VAT/GST in stages from *all* the registered enterprises in the economy (requiring registration for this purpose)? Why not raise the tax simply by levying a retail sales tax on the bread as it leaves the bakery? This would raise the same amount of tax without all the complications of collection in stages. The answer to these questions is that the fundamental economic purpose, or rationale, of VAT/GST is that exports of goods and services are *not* subject to VAT/GST, and because goods or services may be exported at any stage of the chain of production it is necessary to use the VAT/GST method of taxation so that whatever is exported may be free of VAT/GST.

Now that we understand final expenditures (Chapter 3) and how taxes on products and other taxes on production fit into the SNA93/ESA95 (this chapter), we need to consider the role of imports of goods and services and especially how imports of goods and services, P.7, affects the basic identity of national accounting.

5 External Transactions, the Balance of Primary Incomes and Gross National Income

5.1 Introduction

An external transaction is any transaction between a resident institutional unit and a non-resident institutional unit. An external transaction can be of nearly any type but this chapter is concerned with only two main types of external transactions: requited transactions on goods and services; and requited transactions on property income – the concept and classification of the types of property income being introduced and explained in Section 5.5. We also consider one quantitatively minor type of external transaction: compensation of employees.

The purpose of this chapter is twofold. First, Sections 5.2 to 5.4 show how external transactions in *goods and services* affect the national accounts, especially the basic identity of national accounting concerning the relationship between gross domestic product and final expenditure. (The reader will have become aware of the number of times the qualifying clause 'in an economy with no imports' has been appended to various explanations, tables and diagrams throughout the book so far, and the time has come to dispense with this qualifying clause by introducing imports of goods and services into the analysis.)

Second, Sections 5.5 and 5.6 explain and illustrate the allocation of primary income account, Account II.1.2 – an SNA93/ESA95 account new to national accounting – which records, as its end-result, a balance of primary incomes for each resident sector in the economy, for the economy as a whole (that is, all the resident sectors) and for the rest of the world (that is, non-residents). The concept of primary income is fully explained, including property income (Figure 5.2).

The concept of gross national income is explained via two routes: first, as the sum of the resident sectors' balances of primary incomes; and second, by deducting the balance of primary incomes of the rest of the world (non-residents) from gross domestic product.

The concept of a resident as an institutional unit which has 'a centre of economic interest' in the territory of the economy was explained in Chapter 1, Section 1.3. The concepts of a resident and its opposite, a non-resident, are fundamental to this chapter and an understanding of these concepts is here taken as given.

The explanation proceeds one step at a time. First, I explain a model economy which has imports but no exports. Once this is understood, I explain a model economy which has both imports and exports. Then we examine data for the United Kingdom (using the goods and services account) and for Australia. Thus we can understand the basic identity of national accounting in an economy with imports and exports.

We then switch to considering external transactions relating to primary income. I introduce and explain the various types of property income which occur both for external transactions and also for transactions between residents, and thence explain the allocation of primary income account for a model economy, with the resulting balances of primary incomes, so that we can understand the difference between gross national income and gross domestic product.

Finally, we consider in Tables 5.10 and 5.11 the allocation of primary income account for the United Kingdom economy in 1997 and for the Australian economy in 1997–98.

5.2   Imports of goods and services

Imports of goods and services, P.7, consists of transactions in goods and services (whether by way of purchases, barter, gifts or grants – but mostly by way of purchases) from non-residents to residents (*ESA95*, para. 3.129).

Generally, an import or an export of a *good* occurs when there is a change of ownership of the good from a non-resident to a resident. But there are exceptions to this change of ownership principle. In this context, the technical term 'goods' covers the following five items: *general merchandise; goods for processing; repairs on goods; goods procured in ports by carriers; and non-monetary gold* (*BPM5*, para. 195). These categories are used in balance of payments statistics, and are not required by the SNA93/ESA95 national accounts which record only imports as a whole and exports as a whole.

The technical term 'general merchandise' refers to moveable goods for which changes in ownership occur between residents and non-residents (*BPM5*, para. 196). Most imports and exports of goods are of general merchandise. 'Goods for processing' refers to goods that are exported or imported across frontiers for processing (without a change of ownership), such as when a petroleum company imports crude oil for refining in one of its own refineries (*BPM5*, para. 197). 'Repairs on goods' covers repair activity that involves work performed by residents on moveable goods owned by non-residents or vice versa. 'Goods procured in ports by carriers' refers to goods (such as fuels or provisions) procured by resident carriers abroad (import) or by non-resident carriers in the economy compiling the data (export). 'Non-monetary gold' refers to exports and imports of all gold not held as reserve assets (monetary gold) by the authorities.

In relation to external transactions in goods, the SNA93/ESA95 convention is that goods are valued at their market value at the customs frontier of the country in which they have been produced and from which they are being exported (*SNA93*, paras 14.36–14.38; *ESA95*, para. 3.138; *BPM5*, para. 222). I shall refer to this frontier as the 'producing country's frontier'. Note also that in what follows, the word 'customer' is to be understood as referring to a customer resident in a country other than the one where the good was produced; a customer can be any type of institutional unit: enterprise, household, or government.

This valuation convention is referred to as valuation 'free on board' – abbreviated 'f.o.b.'. Thus the value of the goods f.o.b. includes the cost of transport *within* the producing country from the place of production to the producing country's frontier but valuation f.o.b. does *not* include the cost of transport from the producing country's frontier to the customer. Also note that valuation f.o.b. excludes any VAT/GST and customs duties which may be levied by the *importing* country. This means that imports are valued at basic prices (*ESA95*, para. 3.138).

If the valuation is done at the frontier of the customer's country, the valuation is referred to as valuation including 'cost, insurance, freight' – abbreviated 'c.i.f.' – between the exporting country's frontier and the importing country's frontier.

The use of f.o.b. values for both imports of goods and exports of goods means that each is valued consistently, at the producing country's frontier, and the cost of transport from each producing country's frontier to the customer is treated as a separate service to the customer provided by a carrier. If the carrier service is an external transaction (that is, a service provided by a non-resident carrier to the customer), then that carrier service is treated separately as an import of a service by the customer's country. If the carrier service is not an external transaction (that is, a service provided by a carrier resident in the same country as the customer), then there is no import of a service.

Imports of *services* consist of all services rendered by non-residents to residents (*BPM5*, chapters XI, XII and XIII), but note that this does *not* include the services rendered by a non-resident *employee* (such as a border worker) to a resident employer (such employee services are recorded in another account as compensation of employees, so you must understand clearly that the technical term 'imports' *excludes* such compensation of employees; likewise for 'exports').

Services relate to such services as *transportation* (passenger, freight and other transportation), *travel services* (primarily the goods and services purchased in an economy by travellers, where 'traveller' is defined as an individual staying for less than one year in an economy of which he/she is not a resident, but the one-year rule does not apply to students and to medical patients who remain residents of their economies of origin even if the length of their stay in another economy is one year or more and all expenditures by students and medical patients are recorded under *travel* and separately identified if possible (*BPM5*, para. 244)), *communications services* (such as telecommunications and postal and courier services), *construction services* (work performed on construction projects and installations by employees of an enterprise in locations outside the economic territory of the enterprise), *insurance services* (the provision of various types of insurance to residents by non-resident enterprises or vice versa), *financial services* (conducted between residents and non-residents), *computer and information services* (computer data and news-related service transactions between residents and non-residents including software implementation), *royalties and licence fees* (the exchange of payments and receipts between residents and non-residents for the authorised use of intangible, non-produced, non-financial assets and proprietary rights such as patents, copyrights, trademarks, franchises, and so on), *other business services* (legal, accounting, management consultancy services, and so on), *personal, cultural and recreational services* (such as fees for distribution rights, for correspondence courses, and so on), and *government services* (a residual category covering government service transactions such as transactions in services with embassies or with United Nations agencies, and so on).

Imports of services, and exports of services, are valued at the actual prices agreed.

In order to explain how imports fit into, and affect, the national accounts, I shall adapt the economy of Table 2.1 (p. 58). This means that we have a familiar starting point. In order to keep things as simple as possible, I revert to an economy with no taxes or subsidies on production; this permits a straightforward comparison with the economy of Table 2.1. (Taxes on products and other taxes on production can be straightforwardly introduced at a subsequent stage when we consider the real-world national accounts.)

In order to introduce imports into the model economy, suppose that the bakery, in addition to buying €30 per annum of flour from the mill and €5 per annum of firewood (fuel) from the woodcutter, buys €3 per annum of yeast from a non-resident – that is, the bakery imports €3 worth of yeast per annum.

This import transaction is valued f.o.b., but to keep the analysis as simple as possible we omit any detail on the transport of yeast from the producing country's frontier to the bakery (this could be either an import of a service or not an import of a service, depending upon the country of residence of the carrier).

The relevant figures are given in Table 5.1.

The figures for the farm, the mill and the woodcutter are unchanged from Table 2.1.

With the import of yeast, the bakery has intermediate consumption of €38 per annum, comprising €30 per annum of flour, purchased from the (resident) mill, €5 per annum of firewood (fuel), purchased from the (resident) woodcutter, and the imported €3 per annum of yeast, purchased from a non-resident. Because of the import, the bakery's intermediate consumption has increased by comparison with Table 2.1. Assume that the bakery wishes to continue making the same €5 per annum gross operating surplus as before, and with compensation of employees unchanged at €5 per annum, this means that the bakery must achieve a gross value added of €10 per annum, and in turn this means that the bakery must sell its bread for €48 per annum (we could argue that the bakery is able to increase the price for bread, now improved by the use of the imported yeast). However, these assumptions are made only for the sake of keeping the illustration as simple as possible and, as I shall show, nothing about the principle of the argument or the structure of the resulting accounts depends on these assumptions being fulfilled. Other scenarios for imports will also be discussed, but this is a useful starting point.

Table 5.1
Production in a model economy with imports (but no exports)

			€ per annum		
				Primary incomes	
Enterprise	Output	Intermediate consumption	Gross value added	Compen- sation of employees	Gross operating surplus/gross mixed income
Farm	20	0	20	15	5 (GMI)
Mill	30	20	10	5	5 (GOS)
Woodcutter	5	0	5	0	5 (GMI)
Bakery	48	38 (a)	10	5	5 (GOS)
Total	103	58	45	25	20

(a) Of which, €3 per annum is purchases from non-residents (imports).

Source: Adaptation in text of Table 2.1.

Note two important features of Table 5.1. First, final consumption expenditure by households on bread is €48 per annum and, by comparison with Table 2.1, this has increased by €3 per annum. Because final consumption expenditure by households is the only final expenditure in the model economy, final consumption expenditure is here also doing duty for *total* final expenditure (in what follows our concern is fundamentally with total final expenditure, rather than with any particular component of final expenditure).

Second, total gross value added is €45 per annum, and this is unchanged from Table 2.1. In this simplified economy with no taxes on products, total gross value added is equal to gross domestic product, so gross domestic product is €45 per annum.

In Chapters 3 and 4 we explained that, in an economy with no imports, total final expenditure is *equal* to gross domestic product at market prices. We can now explain an important proposition relating to imports of goods and services: *in an economy with imports of goods and services, total final expenditure **exceeds** gross domestic product by the amount of the imports of goods and services*. (In real-world national accounts, an allowance may also have to be made for a statistical discrepancy between gross domestic product and the expenditure components of gross domestic product, de.)

To illustrate this proposition with data from the model economy of Table 5.1:

Total final expenditure	*exceeds*	Gross domestic product	*by*	Imports of goods and services
↓		↓		↓
€48 per annum		€45 per annum		€3 per annum

Why does this proposition hold?

In Chapter 3 (Figure 3.4, p. 144), I explained that (in an economy with no taxes or subsidies on products) final expenditure was ultimately reducible to the total of gross value added in the chain of production. This explanation still holds, but with the introduction of imports the chain of production involved in final expenditure also includes gross value added produced by non-residents – that is, imports.

In Chapter 2, I explained that gross domestic product is the sum of gross values added resulting from production by *resident* producers. (In Chapter 4 we had to extend this statement to include taxes on products less subsidies on products, but for the time being we omit this as a matter not relevant to the principle here being discussed.) Consequently, gross domestic product cannot, in principle, include any gross value added resulting from production by *non-resident* producers. In other words, gross domestic product must *exclude* the value of imports.

In summary form:

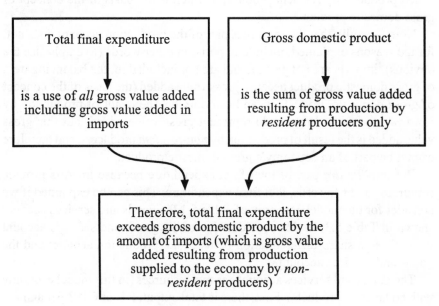

We can analyse this further if we consider for the model economy of Table 5.1 the production account shown in Table 5.2.

In the production account we see the first three figures of the last row of Table 5.1. Total resources on production account (for this economy with no taxes or subsidies on products) is the total output, P.1, of €103 per annum.

Note carefully that total resources on the *production* account, Account I, is confined to production of output by *resident* producers. The purpose of the production account is to deal only with production occurring domestically within the economy. This means that imports are excluded from the production account, and this exclusion is an 'in principle' exclusion.

Coming to the uses on the production account, one use of these resources is intermediate consumption of €58 per annum. Again, this is intermediate consumption by *resident* producers; perhaps this is an obvious point, but it needs to be mentioned explicitly because (to repeat) the production account deals only with production occurring within the economy; that is, with production by resident producers. But this intermediate consumption by resident producers does include the value of any imports used in intermediate consumption.

The other use is the balancing item of gross domestic product, B.1*g, of €45 per annum (= €103 per annum – €58 per annum). As we can see by considering the third column of Table 5.1, this is the total of gross values added produced by resident producers, which is the basis of the concept of gross domestic product.

Note carefully that the resources part of the production account does not, for the reasons explained, include imports; in other words (to emphasise the obvious), imports are not part of, and are not included in, the balancing item of gross domestic product because gross value added (the basis of the concept of gross domestic product) is, and can only be, the result of production by *resident* producers. Imports do represent gross value added, but this gross value added is the result of production by *non-resident* producers, and therefore cannot be part of an economy's gross domestic product.

But imports *are* part of total final expenditure because imports provide resources for, or towards, that final expenditure. This can be explained if we consider for the model economy of Table 5.1 the goods and services account shown in Table 5.3. In this consideration of the goods and services account we will see a sharp differentiation between the production account and the goods and services account.

The goods and services account has two resources (in this model economy with no taxes on products). First, there is total output, P.1, of €103 per annum.

Table 5.2
Production account for model economy with imports
(but no exports)

SNA93/ESA95 identification code	SNA93/ESA95 name	€ per annum
I	PRODUCTION ACCOUNT	
	Resources	
P.1	Total output	103
Total	Total resources	103
	Uses	
P.2	Intermediate consumption	58
B.1*g	Gross domestic product	45
Total	Total uses	103

Source: Table 5.1.

It is important again to note that this resource refers to the production of products by *resident* producers.

Second, there are imports of goods and services, P.7, of €3 per annum. It is important explicitly to note the obvious: this resource refers to production of products by *non-resident* producers whose products are supplied to the economy.

Consequently total resources on goods and services account (in this model economy with no taxes on products) is €106 per annum. This total measures the total value of products becoming available to the economy, whether becoming available by way of production by resident producers (total output) or whether becoming available by way of imports (production and supply by non-resident producers, that is, imports).

The uses on the goods and services account are first, intermediate consumption, P.2, of €58 per annum and, second, final consumption expenditure by households, P.3 (also the total of final expenditure in this model economy), of €48 per annum. The goods and services account, with no

Table 5.3

Goods and services account for model economy with imports (but no exports)

SNA93/ESA95 identification code	SNA93/ESA95 name	€ per annum
0	GOODS AND SERVICES ACCOUNT	
	Resources	
P.1	Total output	103
P.7	Imports of goods and services	3
Total	Total resources	106
	Uses	
P.2	Intermediate consumption	58
P.3	Final consumption expenditure by households[a]	48
Total	Total uses	106

(*a*)   The only, and therefore total, final expenditure in this model economy.

Source: Table 5.1.

balancing item, balances globally, so total resources of €106 per annum is equal to total uses of €106 per annum.

Thus we can see that the goods and services account is concerned not only with the products produced by resident producers (as is the production account) but also with the products becoming available to the economy through imports (which do not appear in the production account), and that the goods and services account then shows the total uses of these products.

This point is so important that it may be helpful to reinforce it by considering the picture of the goods and services account shown in Figure 5.1. The important new feature of this diagram is that it is annotated, on the resources side, with respect to whether the producer of the resource is a resident or a non-resident. The purpose of these annotations is to make it clear that *non-resident* producers can, and do, contribute to the resources of the economy on the goods and services account.

Goods and services account

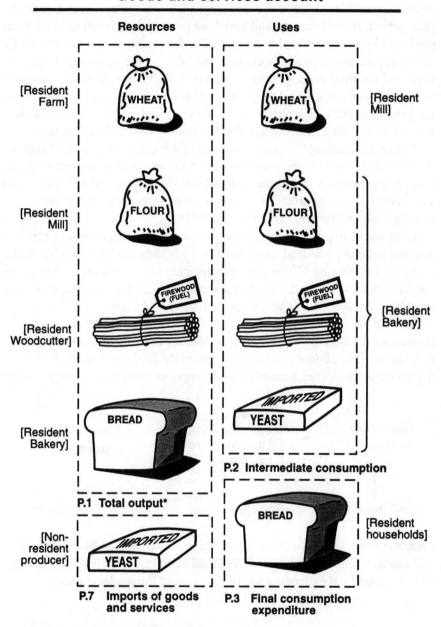

Figure 5.1   The goods and services account with imports

Under the heading 'Resources', we can see the resources in terms of the physical quantities of goods becoming available to the economy during the year: wheat, flour, firewood and bread, all produced by *residents*; and yeast produced by a *non-resident* and supplied to the economy (that is, imported). These are all the products becoming available in the economy during the year, and the total value of these products is €106. In this model economy with no taxes (or subsidies) on products, this is also the total of resources on the goods and services account. (In an economy with taxes on products these have to be included as a resource for the reason explained in Chapter 4.)

Under the heading 'Uses', we can see in the goods and services account depicted in Figure 5.1 the uses in terms of the physical quantities of goods used in the economy during the year: wheat, flour, firewood and (imported) yeast used by resident producers as intermediate consumption; and bread used as a final expenditure by resident households.

Looking at Figure 5.1 we can understand why the goods and services account balances – indeed, must balance – globally (and with no balancing item): this is because all the products depicted on the resources side of the diagram must again be depicted on the uses side of the diagram: every use must have a resource, and every resource must find a use.

We can now use the goods and services account in conjunction with the production account to explain the basic identity of national accounting when there are imports of goods and services. From the production account of Table 5.2 we know that, in this simplified model economy with no taxes on products:

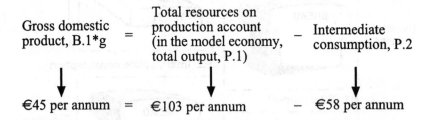

From the goods and services account of Table 5.3 we have, as the basic equation of Account 0 (remember, however, that final consumption expenditure is doing duty for total final expenditure in this version of the model economy):

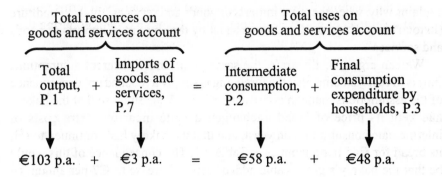

This equation can be rearranged as follows:

| Total output, P.1 | – | Intermediate consumption, P.2 | = | Final consumption expenditure by households, P.3 | – | Imports of goods and services, P.7 |

| €103 p.a. | – | €58 p.a. | = | €48 p.a. | – | €3 p.a. |

But, for the model economy, the left-hand side of this equation is the balancing item gross domestic product, B.1*g. Therefore, substituting gross domestic product on the left-hand side we obtain the basic identity of national accounting for the model economy with only imports:

Total final expenditure

| Gross domestic product, B.1*g | = | Final consumption, expenditure by households, P.3 | – | Imports of goods and services, P.7 |

| €45 p.a. | = | €48 p.a. | – | €3 p.a. |

This equation is (for the simplified model economy) the basic identity of national accounting. The basic identity of national accounting equation explains why, when there are imports of goods and services, final expenditure (in total) exceeds gross domestic product by the amount of imports of goods and services.

We can argue, or illustrate, the same point under different assumptions (this is in case you think that the foregoing is simply a 'cooked up' consequence of the assumptions made in constructing Table 5.1). Suppose that the bakery had kept its price of bread unchanged despite incurring extra costs of intermediate consumption on yeast, and that the bakery had continued to sell its bread for €45 per annum as in Table 2.1. The consequence of this would be that the bakery's gross value added would decrease to €7 per annum (= €45 per annum – €38 per annum), and also that, if compensation of employees remained at €5 per annum, the bakery's gross operating surplus would decrease to €2 per annum.

Under this alternative assumption about the bakery's pricing behaviour, total final (consumption) expenditure in the economy would be €45 per annum, but total gross value added in the economy would be €42 per annum (= €20 per annum + €10 per annum + €5 per annum + €7 per annum). The same €3 per annum *difference* between total final expenditure and total gross value added (gross domestic product) would still obtain under this alternative assumption. Moreover, this difference would obtain regardless of the assumptions made about the bakery's pricing behaviour (for example, suppose that the bakery raises prices only slightly so that final expenditure on bread were to be €46 per annum, or suppose that the bakery raises prices greatly so that final expenditure on bread were to be €50 per annum – in either of these cases you can, by reworking Table 5.1, verify that the same €3 per annum difference obtains between total final expenditure and total gross value added (which is also gross domestic product)).

We may now note that imports have two routes into final expenditure: a direct route and an indirect route. No matter which route imports take, imports are part of, and are included in, final expenditure, and imports constitute the difference between total final expenditure and gross domestic product.

The indirect route for imports into final expenditure is the route illustrated by Table 5.1. This indirect route is where the import is for intermediate consumption, but (and this is the important point), final expenditure covers or includes the cost of all intermediate consumption in the chain of production, and so the imports are also included in final expenditure, albeit by the indirect route of imports going first into intermediate consumption.

An example of the direct route for imports into final expenditure would occur if yeast were to be purchased directly by households as part of household final expenditure (for use, say, in making home-made bread). Such 'direct' final expenditure imports commonly occur (for example, quite regularly I buy books directly from a bookseller overseas; for another example, much of gross fixed capital formation final expenditure is directly on imports – when an airline in a country other than the USA buys a Boeing 747 'jumbo' jet, then that is a direct final expenditure on an import).

This direct route has not been discussed in this chapter but it is a simple matter to construct a production account and a goods and services account for the case where households directly buy €3 worth of yeast imports per annum for final consumption; the production account is unchanged from that given in Table 2.2 (p. 84), and the goods and services account is simply that given in Table 3.2 (p. 155) with the addition of €3 of imports to resources, making total resources €103 per annum, and, on the uses side, the addition of €3 per annum to final consumption expenditure by households.

We have the following synopsis:

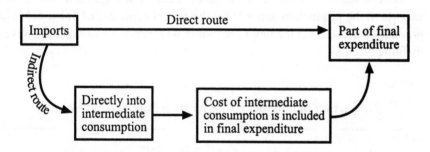

In either route, or in both routes (if both occur together), imports still constitute the difference between total final expenditure and gross domestic product (at market prices) as we shall see in the national accounts for the United Kingdom and Australia.

But before that we need to consider exports of goods and services.

5.3 Exports of goods and services

In order to introduce exports into the model economy (with imports), suppose that in the economy of Table 5.1, the farm, in addition to producing and supplying €20 of wheat per annum to the mill, produces and supplies wheat worth €4 per annum to a non-resident – that is, the farm exports €4 of wheat per annum.

The relevant figures are given in Table 5.4. With exports, the farm's output is €24 per annum and, still assuming zero intermediate consumption by the farm, the farm's gross value added is €24 per annum. Assuming unchanged compensation of employees at €15 per annum the farm's gross mixed income increases to €9 per annum. The figures for each of the other enterprises are unchanged from Table 5.1.

Total output in the economy is €107 per annum, in consequence of the increase in the farm's output. Intermediate consumption is €58 per annum. Total gross value added in the economy is €49 per annum, an increase of €4 per annum by comparison with Table 5.1, because of the farm's additional gross value added.

The important point here is that exports are part of gross value added resulting from production by *residents*, and (because gross domestic product is the total of gross values added from production by residents) exports are thus part of gross domestic product.

We can see how gross domestic product has been affected by the farm's exports in the production account for the model economy of Table 5.4. The production account for the model economy with imports and exports is given in Table 5.5.

Table 5.4
Production in a model economy with imports and exports

	€ per annum				
				Primary incomes	
Enterprise	Output	Intermediate consumption	Gross value added	Compen-sation of employees	Gross operating surplus/gross mixed income
Farm	24 (a)	0	24	15	9 (GMI)
Mill	30	20	10	5	5 (GOS)
Woodcutter	5	0	5	0	5 (GMI)
Bakery	48	38 (b)	10	5	5 (GOS)
Total	107	58	49	25	24

(a) Of which, €4 per annum is sales to non-residents (exports).

(b) Of which, €3 per annum is purchases from non-residents (imports).

Source: Adaptation in text of Table 5.1.

The total resources on the production account is total output of €107 per annum. Intermediate consumption is €58 per annum, so the balancing item of gross domestic product is €49 per annum. The important point here is that exports are part of gross domestic product.

We may now consider the goods and services account for the model economy with imports and exports; Account 0 is given in Table 5.6.

The resources of the economy on the goods and services account are twofold: first, total output of €107 per annum; and second, imports of goods and services of €3 per annum. Total resources are thus €110 per annum.

The uses of these resources are threefold: first, intermediate consumption of €58 per annum; second, final consumption expenditure by households of €48 per annum; and third, exports of goods and services of €4 per annum. Total uses are thus €110 per annum. Note that the goods and services account, with no balancing item, balances globally.

Using the production account and the goods and services account, we can see how the basic identity of national accounting works. As before (in this economy with no taxes on products):

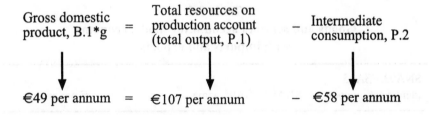

But from the goods and services account:

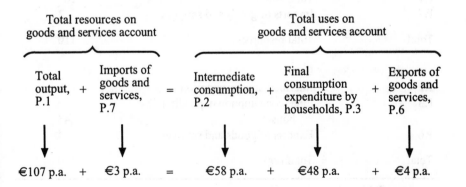

Table 5.5
Production account for model economy with imports and exports

SNA93/ESA95 identification code	SNA93/ESA95 name	€ per annum
I	PRODUCTION ACCOUNT	
	Resources	
P.1	Total output	107
Total	Total resources	107
	Uses	
P.2	Intermediate consumption	58
B.1*g	Gross domestic product	49
Total	Total uses	107

Source: Table 5.4.

Table 5.6
Goods and services account for model economy
with imports and exports

SNA93/ESA95 identification code	SNA93/ESA95 name	€ per annum
0	GOODS AND SERVICES ACCOUNT	
	Resources	
P.1	Total output	107
P.7	Imports of goods and services	3
Total	Total resources	110
	Uses	
P.2	Intermediate consumption	58
P.3	Final consumption expenditure by households	48
P.6	Exports of goods and services	4
Total	Total uses	110

Source: Table 5.4.

This equation can be rearranged as follows:

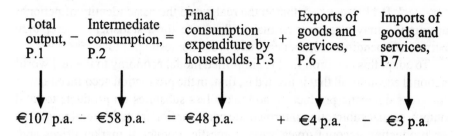

Total output, P.1	−	Intermediate consumption, P.2	=	Final consumption expenditure by households, P.3	+	Exports of goods and services, P.6	−	Imports of goods and services, P.7
€107 p.a.	−	€58 p.a.	=	€48 p.a.	+	€4 p.a.	−	€3 p.a.

But, for the model economy, the left-hand side of this equation is the balancing item gross domestic product, B.1*g. Therefore, substituting gross domestic product on the left-hand side we obtain the basic identity of national accounting for the model economy with imports and exports:

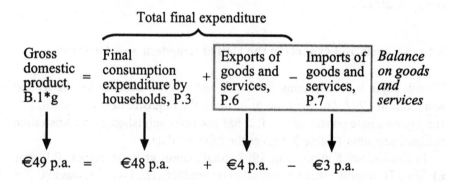

Total final expenditure

Gross domestic product, B.1*g	=	Final consumption expenditure by households, P.3	+	Exports of goods and services, P.6	−	Imports of goods and services, P.7	*Balance on goods and services*
€49 p.a.	=	€48 p.a.	+	€4 p.a.	−	€3 p.a.	

Again, we see that, when there are imports, total final expenditure exceeds gross domestic product by the amount of the imports of goods and services, and this is the basic identity of national accounting. As stated in the SNA93:

> ... the sum of gross values added must be identical with the sum of final expenditures on consumption, gross capital formation and exports less imports. This is ... the basic identity of national accounting (*SNA93*, para. 6.234).

Note that the difference calculated as exports of goods and services *minus* imports of goods and services, P.6 − P.7, is known technically in the balance of payments accounts as the *balance on goods and services*; for reasons to be explained in Chapter 7, the balance on goods and services is the *negative* of what is known in the national accounts as the 'external balance of goods and services', B.11. Note, too, that in the real world the basic identity of national accounting may also have to make allowance for a statistical discrepancy between expenditure components and gross domestic product.

To adapt this equation for the simplified model economy to the real world national accounts all that is needed is, first, in the production account equation for gross domestic product, to add taxes less subsidies on products to total output, so that subtracting intermediate consumption from this total resources on production account gives gross domestic product at market prices and, second, in the goods and services account equation to include on the right-hand side all final expenditures other than final consumption expenditure by households and exports of goods and services. This then gives us the full equation for the basic identity of national accounting. We can now consider this full equation as it occurs in the national accounts of the United Kingdom and of Australia.

5.4   Imports and exports in the United Kingdom and Australia

We can begin by considering the goods and services account for the United Kingdom in 1997. (At the time of writing, the requisite data on output, P.1, and intermediate consumption, P.2, has not been published in the Australian national accounts.) Table 5.7 gives the relevant data.

In the United Kingdom in 1997, total output at basic prices, P.1, was £1 526 371 million; taxes *less* subsidies on products, D.21 – D.31, was £90 275 million, and imports of goods and services, P.7, was £228 822 million. Consequently, the total resources on goods and services account was £1 845 468 million. This total is the analogue of the total of €110 per annum for the model economy of Table 5.6 (but with the inclusion in the UK total of taxes less subsidies on products, for the reason explained in Chapter 4 and we can now see that taxes less subsidies on products can be quite straightforwardly incorporated into the analysis).

In the United Kingdom in 1997, the uses on the goods and services account were: intermediate consumption, P.2, of £812 757 million; final consumption expenditure by households (including NPISHs), P.31, of £517 032 million; final consumption expenditure by government, P.3, of £147 773 million; total gross capital formation, P.5, of £138 580 million; and exports of goods and services, P.6, of £229 326 million.

Table 5.7
Goods and services account for the United Kingdom

SNA93/ESA95 identification code	SNA93/ESA95 name	1997, £ million
0	GOODS AND SERVICES ACCOUNT	
	Resources	
P.1	Total output	1 526 371
D.21 – D.31	Taxes *less* Subsidies on products [a]	90 275
P.7	Imports of goods and services	228 822
Total	Total resources	1 845 468
	Uses	
P.2	Intermediate consumption	812 757
P.31	Final consumption expenditure by households[b]	517 032
P.3	Final consumption expenditure by government	147 773
P.5	Total gross capital formation	138 580
P.6	Exports of goods and services	229 326
de	Statistical discrepancy between expenditure components and GDP	—
Total	Total uses	1 845 468

'—' means nil.
(a) Taxes and subsidies to and from both UK general government and institutions of the European Union.
(b) Including final consumption expenditure of £18 725 million by non-profit institutions serving households (NPISHs).
Source: Office for National Statistics, *United Kingdom National Accounts The Blue Book 1999 edition*, table 1.6.0, p. 39 (correcting for misprint in total).

In the real-world national accounts there is at this point an item to allow for any discrepancy in measurement/recording between the expenditure components (after allowing for imports) and gross domestic product, but for the United Kingdom in 1997 this statistical discrepancy item, de, was reported as nil (or less than £0.5 million).

Consequently, in the United Kingdom in 1997 the total uses on goods and services account was £1 845 468 million and this equals the total resources on the goods and services account.

We can now see how the basic identity of national accounting applies to the United Kingdom economy in 1997. Using the production account for the United Kingdom (Table 2.3, p. 88), gross domestic product [at market prices], $B.1^*g$, is:

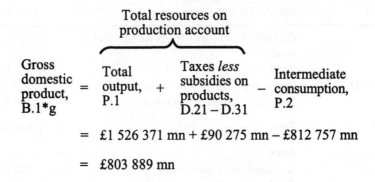

$$\begin{array}{l}
\text{Gross} \\
\text{domestic} \quad = \quad \begin{array}{l}\text{Total}\\ \text{output,}\\ \text{P.1}\end{array} \quad + \quad \begin{array}{l}\text{Taxes } less\\ \text{subsidies on}\\ \text{products,}\\ \text{D.21}-\text{D.31}\end{array} \quad - \quad \begin{array}{l}\text{Intermediate}\\ \text{consumption,}\\ \text{P.2}\end{array} \\
\text{product,}\\
B.1^*g
\end{array}$$

$$= \quad £1\ 526\ 371\ mn + £90\ 275\ mn - £812\ 757\ mn$$

$$= \quad £803\ 889\ mn$$

From the goods and services account (Table 5.7), we have:

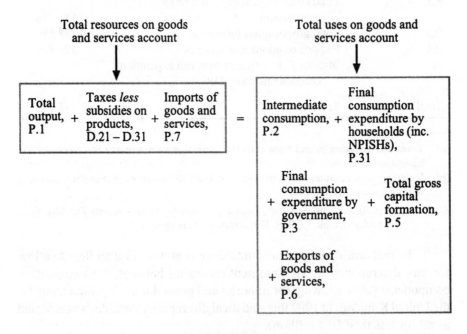

By rearrangement, and inserting the relevant figures for the United Kingdom in 1997 (but omitting the negligible statistical discrepancy item, de), we obtain for the United Kingdom economy in 1997 the basic identity of national accounting:

$$
\begin{array}{ccccc}
\text{Total} & & \text{Taxes } less & & \text{Intermediate} \\
\text{output,} & + & \text{subsidies on} & - & \text{consumption,} \\
\text{P.1} & & \text{products,} & & \text{P.2} \\
& & \text{D.21 - D.31} & &
\end{array}
$$

$$= \text{£1 526 371 mn} + \text{£90 275 mn} - \text{£812 757 mn}$$

Total final expenditure

$$
\begin{array}{ccccccccc}
& \text{Final} & & \text{Final} & & & & & \\
& \text{consumption} & & \text{consumption} & & \text{Total} & & \text{Exports} & \text{Imports} \\
& \text{expenditure by} & + & \text{expenditure} & + & \text{gross} & + & \text{of goods} & \text{of goods} \\
= & \text{household} & & \text{by} & & \text{capital} & & \text{and} & - \text{and} \\
& \text{(inc. NPISHs),} & & \text{government,} & & \text{formation,} & & \text{services,} & \text{services,} \\
& \text{P.31} & & \text{P.3} & & \text{P.5} & & \text{P.6} & \text{P.7}
\end{array}
$$

= £517 032 mn + £147 773 mn + £138 580 mn + £229 326 mn

   − £228 822 mn

= £803 889 mn

= Gross domestic product, B.1*g, for 1997

Because of the lack of data on total output and intermediate consumption in the Australian System of National Accounts at the time of writing, it is not possible to give the comparable goods and services account in full. However, we may present data for the right-hand side of the basic identity of national accounting for the Australian economy in 1997–98 using data from Tables 2.5 and 3.1 (pp. 107 and 119), together with the supplementary information that in 1997–98 imports of goods and services in the Australian economy amounted to $118 510 million and that in 1997–98 the statistical discrepancy between expenditure components and gross domestic product (called the 'statistical discrepancy (E)' in the Australian System of National Accounts) was –$1 223 million (Australian Bureau of Statistics, *Australian System of National Accounts 1997–98*, Catalogue No. 5204.0, table 1.8, p. 28):

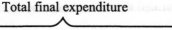

Total final expenditure

Final consumption expenditure by households (inc. NPISHs), P.31		Final consumption expenditure by government, P.3	Total gross capital formation, P.5	Exports of goods and services, P.6	Imports of goods and services, P.7
	+		+	+	−

$$+ \quad \text{Statistical discrepancy (E), de}$$

$= \quad \$332\,311 \text{ mn} + \$103\,581 \text{ mn} + \$134\,343 \text{ mn} + \$114\,203 \text{ mn}$

$\quad\quad - \$118\,510 \text{ mn} + (-\$1223 \text{ mn})$

$= \quad \$564\,705 \text{ mn}$

$= \quad$ Gross domestic product, B.1*g, for 1997–98

The reason for this basic identity of national accounting is that total final expenditure is a use of all gross value added at basic prices becoming available to the economy *plus* taxes on products (less subsidies on products). But some of this gross value added results from production by non-residents and supplied to the economy in the form of imports of goods and services. Consequently, if we deduct from the total use of gross value added the gross value added produced by non-residents we must be left with the use of gross value added produced by residents, and the gross value added produced by residents is gross domestic product (also making allowance for taxes less subsidies on products included in the valuation of final expenditure and included in the valuation of gross domestic product at market prices).

The basic identity of national accounting is important in media discussion of changes in gross domestic product, which you will regularly see when quarterly data on gross domestic product is released. Such discussion usually focusses on the final expenditure components of gross domestic product, including the balance on goods and services or 'net exports'.

5.5 Property income, the allocation of primary income account and gross national income

So far in this book the focus has been mostly on the production of *output*, on the resulting balancing item of gross value added and on the associated gross domestic product. The focus of the discussion is now going to change considerably as we switch to considering the primary *incomes* derived from production, the allocation of those primary incomes, the resulting balancing item of the balance of primary incomes, gross, and the associated gross national income (sometimes abbreviated as 'GNI').

In this section I explain the allocation of primary income account, Account II.1.2 and the resulting *balance of primary incomes, gross*, B.5g. Primary incomes are the incomes that accrue to institutional units (resident and non-resident) as a consequence of their involvement in production or ownership of assets, real and financial. For the government, primary income includes taxes on production and imports (but subsidies are netted off). Primary incomes thus comprise: gross operating surplus, gross mixed income, compensation of employees, property income (such as interest or dividends) and, for the government, taxes less subsidies on production. All of these except property income have been previously explained and discussed, so this section introduces and explains property income. The key feature of property income is that it may have to be *paid by* an institutional unit as well as being received by an institutional unit.

The concept of primary income is quite complex and the following synopsis may be useful in understanding the composition of primary income:

Primary income		
Compensation of employees, D.1 Operating surplus, B.2 Mixed income, B.3 *Primary income for labour and for owners of produced assets, all generated by production*	Property income, D.4 *Primary income for owners of financial assets and non-produced tangible (or 'natural') assets*	Taxes on production and imports (less subsidies), D.2 – D.3 *Primary income for government (levied on products and production but measured net of subsidies)*

The way to understand the concept of primary income is as follows. Gross operating surplus and gross mixed income have each to be considered as a sort of 'partitioned' or 'two tier' primary income. The first tier of primary income is that, in the first instance and as a result of production, gross operating surplus/gross mixed income accrue, each as a balancing item in its entirety, to the producer as owner of the produced 'physical' assets (fixed capital and so on) used in that production. But the acquisition of these produced assets may have involved finance provided by institutional units other than the producer. Consequently, there arises a partition of gross operating surplus/gross mixed income into a portion, called 'property income', that has, in the second instance, to be paid, as a transaction, to the owners of the financial assets by the owner of the produced assets (the producer who owes a liability to the holders of the financial assets). This property income is then the partitioned second tier of primary income. In other words, the gross operating surplus/gross mixed income may have to be shared by the owner of the produced asset (the producer) with the owners of the financial assets. In schematic form, the partitioned two-tier primary income should be understood as follows:

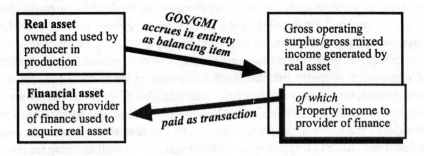

Compensation of employees is a straightforward primary income transaction as a return to labour for its contribution to production, but note that some interest, such as consumer debt interest (a form of property income), may have to be paid out of primary income received by way of compensation of employees.

Taxes on production and imports (less subsidies) is a primary income transaction which is a kind of its own, and represents the government's (primary) income from levies against production (net of subsidies).

As noted by the SNA93:

> The allocation of primary income account focuses on resident institutional units or sectors in their capacity as *recipients* of primary incomes rather than as producers whose activities generate primary incomes. It includes the amounts of property incomes *receivable* *and payable* by institutional units or sectors. ... the aggregate value of the *gross balances of primary incomes* for all [resident] sectors is defined as *gross national income* (GNI). ... GNI is obtained by summing the balance of primary incomes of the ... resident institutional units

(*SNA93*, paras 7.12, 7.16 and 7.17, italics added with special emphasis in bold typeface and with my explanatory interpolation in square brackets).

Although the term 'balance of primary incomes, gross' may appear complex at first sight, the concept is in principle very straightforward when applied to a single institutional unit: it is the institutional unit's overall primary income including, for example, interest income received *and* interest paid and it is measured gross of, or before deduction of, the consumption of fixed capital in those cases where such a deduction would be relevant. The word 'balance' arises because, for example, interest *paid by* the institutional unit is *deducted* in calculating the institutional unit's *balance* of primary incomes. For example, it is easy to understand the following three very commonplace things in regard to a single household: first, the household receives, as primary income, compensation of employees (in return for a member of the household participating in production as an employee); second, the household receives, as primary income, an amount of dividends (because it owns some shares); and, third, the household pays, as primary income, an amount of interest (because it owes money to a consumer credit financial institution). The balance of primary incomes, or overall primary income, for this household is (and note especially the minus sign):

$$\begin{matrix} \text{Balance of} \\ \text{primary} \\ \text{incomes} \end{matrix} = \begin{matrix} \text{Compensation} \\ \text{of employees} \end{matrix} + \begin{matrix} \text{Dividends} \\ \text{received from} \\ \text{company} \end{matrix} - \begin{matrix} \text{Interest paid to} \\ \text{consumer credit} \\ \text{financial institution} \end{matrix}$$

For another example of the balance of primary incomes, a non-financial corporation makes a gross operating surplus, earns interest on some financial assets that it owns and pays dividends to its shareholders. This corporation's balance of primary incomes is:

$$\begin{matrix} \text{Balance of} \\ \text{primary} \\ \text{incomes, gross} \end{matrix} = \begin{matrix} \text{Gross operating} \\ \text{surplus} \end{matrix} + \begin{matrix} \text{Interest} \\ \text{received} \end{matrix} - \text{Dividends paid}$$

The balance of primary incomes is an important concept because it is the amount of before-tax primary income (gross) which an institutional unit has available to pay taxes on income and so on, and otherwise to spend and/or to save. In the case of households (and non-profit institutions serving households) the balance of primary incomes may be supplemented by 'secondary' income transfers received from general government (for example, social security received), but this is a matter for discussion in Chapter 6 on general government and households.

We need to consider fully the concept of property income. The SNA93/ESA95 classification of the distinct types of property income is given in Figure 5.2. We start with the official definition of 'property income' as:

> Property income (D.4) is the income receivable by the owner of a financial asset or a tangible non-produced asset in return for providing funds to, or putting the tangible non-produced asset [e.g., 'natural' assets such as land] at the disposal of, another institutional unit (*ESA95*, para. 4.41, with my explanatory interpolation in square brackets; *SNA93*, para. 7.88).

This is a definition from the point of view of the institutional unit *receiving* the property income, but property income can also be considered from the point of view of the institutional unit *paying* the property income and is also thus treated in the SNA93/ESA95 accounts.

Note that, with two exceptions, the concept of property income applies both to transactions between residents and also to transactions between

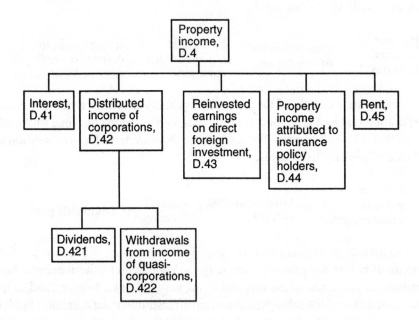

Figure 5.2   The SNA93/ESA95 classification of property income

residents and non-residents (external transactions). Consequently when we consider property income we will see both non-external transactions and external transactions; however, the *external* transaction property incomes are of especial interest, as we shall see. There are five main types of property income (one of which has two sub-categories) and we need to understand each of these types as shown in Figure 5.2.

Interest, D.41, arises when one institutional unit, known as a creditor, lends funds to another institutional unit, known as a debtor. Such loans create financial assets for the creditor (conversely a financial liability for the debtor) in the forms of deposits, AF.2, securities other than shares, AF.3, loans, AF.4, and other accounts receivable, AF.7. Interest is the property income arising for the creditor from one of these types of financial assets, and 'interest' is defined as follows:

> Under the terms of the financial instrument [AF.2, AF.3, AF.4, AF.7] agreed between them [the debtor and the creditor], interest (D.41) is the amount that the debtor becomes liable to pay to the creditor over a given period of time without reducing the amount of the principal [the debt] outstanding (*ESA95*, para. 4.42, with my clarifying interpolations in square brackets; also *SNA93*, para. 7.93).

The amount of interest per period is generally determined by applying the agreed rate of interest per period (for example, per cent per annum) to the debt (or 'principal') outstanding. But the amount of interest may also be determined as the positive difference between the amount for which the security is redeemed and the (lesser) amount initially loaned or subscribed.

The *distributed income of corporations*, D.42, is income distributed out of gross operating surplus in return for finance supplied. There are two sub-categories of distributed income. First, there are *dividends*, D.421. The official definition of the term 'dividends' is (in part):

> Dividends (D.421) are a form of property income received by owners of shares (AF.5) to which they become entitled as a result of placing funds at the disposal of corporations [through subscribing to shares] (*ESA95*, para. 4.53, with my clarifying interpolation in square brackets).

Dividend property income may be explained as follows. There are two main ways for a corporation to obtain finance. First, the corporation may accept loan finance from creditors who lend and who thereby become entitled to a payment of interest, whether or not a net operating surplus, or 'profit', is made and to whom the corporation has a liability (to make repayment) fixed in monetary terms. This gives rise to the property income of interest. Second, the corporation may issue shares to institutional units who become shareholders through subscribing to the shares and who may be entitled to a dividend only if a net operating surplus, or 'profit', has been made and only if the directors, at their own discretion, declare a dividend, while the liability of a corporation to its shareholders is not fixed in monetary terms. This second form of finance gives rise to the property income of dividends. In other words, property income in the form of dividends should be understood in contradistinction to, or as a sort of 'opposite' of, property income in the form of interest.

The second sub-category relates to what are called quasi-corporations. Quasi-corporations are unincorporated enterprises, like partnerships or subsidiaries (operating in the economy) of a non-resident institutional unit, which function as if they were corporations, with accounts separate from the accounts of the institutional units, such as the partners, who own the quasi-corporations. Withdrawals of income by owners from such quasi-corporations are like dividends but because there is no formal share capital such property income is classified separately from dividends in a class of its own. This property income sub-category is *withdrawals from income of quasi-corporations*, D.422. The official definition of 'withdrawals from the income of quasi-corporations' is:

> Withdrawals from the income of quasi-corporations (D.422) consist of the amounts which entepreneurs actually withdraw for their own use from the profits earned by the quasi-corporations which belong to them (*ESA95*, para. 4.56).

Reinvested earnings on direct foreign investment, D.43, is a special type of property income which refers only to external transactions. This is one of the two exceptions to the rule that property income transactions can cover both external and non-external transactions. Direct foreign investment occurs where a resident institutional unit – a 'direct investor' – in one economy has an investment 'involving a long-term relationship reflecting a lasting interest' in an institutional unit resident in an economy other than that of the investor – a 'direct [foreign] investment enterprise'; the purpose of the investment being 'to exert a significant degree of influence on the management' of the direct foreign investment enterprise (*ESA95*, para. 5.132; *BPM5*, chapter XVIII). To count as such, the direct investor must own 10 per cent or more of the ordinary shares or voting power of the direct foreign investment enterprise. Where more than 50 per cent is owned, the direct foreign investment enterprise is called a 'subsidiary', and where the direct foreign investment enterprise is wholly owned it is called a 'branch' (*ESA95*, para. 4.65; *BPM5*, paras 362–4).

A direct investor may benefit from two types of property income arising from ownership of a direct foreign investment enterprise. First, the direct investor may receive dividends or withdrawals from income of quasi-corporations; these are treated under the items D.421 and D.422.

Second, the direct investor benefits from income retained by the direct foreign investment enterprise (because this increases the direct investor's equity, or 'stake', in the enterprise). The national accounting convention is to treat such 'retained earnings ... as if they were distributed and remitted to foreign direct investors' (*ESA95*, para. 4.66). For this purpose, the retained earnings are ascribed to the direct investors in proportion to their ownership of the equity of the enterprise. The converse convention is that the national accounts then assume that, matchingly, the direct investor remits the retained earnings back into the enterprise. The purpose of this set of conventions is so that the national accounts and the balance of payments can keep track of the extent of the liabilities of the foreign direct investment enterprises to their non-resident owners or part-owners.

Another form of primary income is *property income attributed to insurance policy holders*, D.44. Insurance enterprises and pension funds invest the funds of their policy holders, and retain the income generated by these investments for the benefit of the policy holders. However, because this income accrues to the benefit of the policy holders, who are the ultimate beneficiaries of the income, the convention is to ascribe the income to the policy holders and then, matchingly, to deem that the income is reinvested in the funds. This means that the national accounts can keep track of the liabilities of the funds to the policy holders.

The SNA93/ESA95 makes a distinction between *rent* which is a type of property income paid on tangible *non-produced*, or 'natural', assets such as land and sub-soil assets and *rental* which is an amount payable by the user of a fixed asset to its owner under an operating lease; a rental is treated as a purchase of a service from the owner of a *produced* asset. For example, a *rent* is paid for the use of land, while a *rental* is paid for the use of a building. A rental is thus not a property income under the definitions and conventions of the SNA93/ESA95 (*SNA93*, paras 7.90–7.92).

Rent, D.45, thus comprises the income derived from land and from sub-soil assets, both of which are non-produced tangible assets, or 'natural assets'. Rent on land is the property income that landowners receive from tenants of the land. This includes rent payable to owners of inland waters and rivers for the right to use those facilities. As explained, this *rent* income does not include *rental* of buildings or of dwellings (produced assets); such rentals are shown in the accounts as intermediate consumption of enterprises or as final consumption of households or government. Rent income can only be paid by a resident to a resident; if a non-resident buys land in a country, then the non-resident is deemed to become a resident institutional unit owning that land. This is the other of the two exceptions to the rule that property income transactions can cover both external and non-external transactions.

There is provision in the SNA93/ESA95 for a subdivision of primary income into *entrepreneurial income*, B.4, where 'entrepreneurial income' is defined as: gross operating surplus (or gross mixed income) *plus* property income receivable *minus* interest and rent payable (*SNA93*, para. 7.18). The concept of entrepreneurial income corresponds as closely as possible to the concept of *profit* as found in business accounting. However, this subdivision is not applied in the United Kingdom national accounts and is not further discussed here (*UK NACSM*, p. 75).

With this understanding of property income, we can explain the allocation of primary incomes in the economy as given in the SNA93/ESA95 allocation of primary income account.

It is useful to have a broad idea of the allocation of primary income account and of gross national income before we get into the details. Figure 5.3 shows a simplified scheme for the balance of primary incomes which is the balancing item in, or end result of, the allocation of primary income account. Part of the simplification relates to compensation of employees and for this diagram we assume no compensation of employees transactions between residents and non-residents. This simplification means, for non-residents, that the balance of their property income is also the balance of their primary incomes. (In due course, we deal with compensation of employees received by, and paid by, non-residents.) The other part of the simplification relates to omitting taxes less subsidies on production (a simplification maintained until the next section). Figure 5.3 takes a consistent *recipient view* of the balance of primary incomes.

There are two routes to understanding gross national income: a route via the resident sectors of the economy, which I call the 'resident sectors route', and which is the route used in the SNA93/ESA95, and a route via aggregates for the whole economy, which I call the 'aggregate route'.

The resident sectors route to gross national income proceeds in five steps. First, for a resident sector of the economy we can start, on the left side of Figure 5.3, with the primary incomes of compensation of employees, gross operating surplus, or gross mixed income received by that sector.

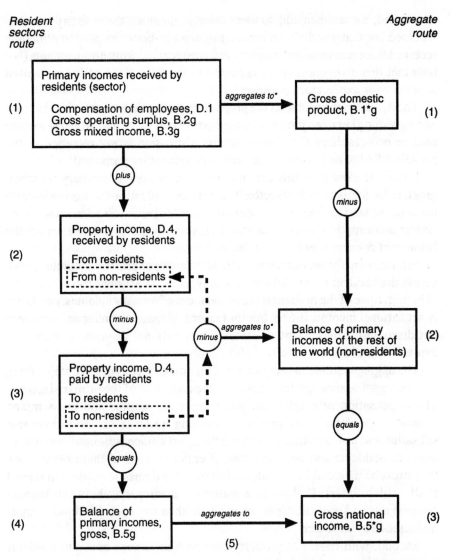

Figure 5.3 Simplified scheme for balance of primary incomes and gross national income

Second, we can then add, to these primary incomes, the property incomes received by that resident sector, distinguishing between property income received from residents and property income received from non-residents (but note that this distinction is *not* recorded in the SNA93/ESA95, and is used here only for explanatory purposes).

Third, we can then subtract the property income paid by that resident sector, distinguishing between property income paid to residents and property income paid to non-residents (but note that this distinction is *not* recorded in the SNA93/ESA95, and is used here only for explanatory purposes).

Fourth, the result of this calculation is the balance of primary incomes, gross, B.5g, for that resident sector. This balance is identified as a *gross* balance because we started from *gross* operating surplus/*gross* mixed income; if we deduct consumption of fixed capital, K.1, from the gross balance we get the balance of primary incomes, net, B.5n.

Fifth and finally, the aggregate of these balances of primary incomes, gross, across the resident sectors of the economy, is gross national income, B.5*g. (The aggregate of the resident sectors' balances of primary incomes, net, B.5n, is net national income, B.5*n, but for reasons of space, net national income is not discussed in this chapter; however, net national disposable income is explained in Chapter 6, Section 6.8.)

The aggregate route to gross national income proceeds in three steps. First, the aggregate, across resident sectors of the economy, of the primary incomes of compensation of employees, gross operating surplus and gross mixed income is gross domestic product (assuming no taxes on production less subsidies and also assuming no transactions on compensation of employees between residents and non-residents; if either or both of these occur, then they must be included in the calculation of gross domestic product in ways I shall explain later). If there is a statistical discrepancy between income components and gross domestic product, di, then any such discrepancy must be included at this stage.

Second, with regard to property income transactions between residents and non-residents in Figure 5.3 we take a *recipient view* (that is a non-resident view) of these transactions. (The reason for taking this viewpoint will be explained in Chapter 7.) Accordingly, we calculate property income paid by residents to non-residents *minus* property income received by residents from non-residents and then aggregate the results of this calculation across the resident sectors of the economy. Under the assumption of no compensation of employee transactions between residents and non-residents, this is also the balance of primary incomes for the rest of the world (non-residents). Note that the balance of primary incomes for the rest of the world (non-residents) can be negative as well as positive. (For the balance of primary incomes for the rest of the world we do not have to use the adjectives 'gross' or 'net' because, in principle, neither gross operating surplus/gross mixed income nor consumption of fixed capital is applicable to the rest of the world.)

Note that the aggregate, across resident sectors of the economy, of property income received by residents from residents *minus* property income paid by residents to residents must necessarily be zero, because the former equals the latter, each being the same aggregate looked at from a different point of view. (This zero aggregate is not indicated in Figure 5.3.)

Third, if we subtract from gross domestic product the balance of primary incomes for the rest of the world (non-residents) we get gross national income (allowing, if necessary, for any statistical discrepancy between income components of gross domestic product and gross domestic product itself depending on the conventions used to report gross national income).

We can now describe and analyse gross national income in detail using first the resident sectors route and then the aggregate route.

For this purpose, we extend the model economy of Table 5.4 by supposing the property income payments shown in Table 5.8 (and described in the following paragraphs). I also introduce into the analysis transactions in compensation of employees between residents and non-residents by supposing that the farm employs some non-resident border workers (workers who cross the border each working day to work and so who count as non-resident of the

Table 5.8
Property incomes in the model economy

	€ per annum		
	Payment by resident enterprise to:		
Resident enterprise	Resident households	Non-resident	Received by resident from non-resident
Farm	1ᵃ (rent, D.45)	6ᵇ (interest, D.41)	—
Mill	1ᶜ (interest, D.41)	—	—
Bakery	2ᵈ (dividends, D.421)	—	1ᵉ (dividends, D.421)

a,b,c,d,e Annotations for identification in Table 5.9 and text.

economy in which they work and from which they derive their employee compensation primary income). Employee compensation between residents and non-residents is a feature of the real world, although the amounts involved tend to be relatively very small.

The suppositions regarding property income shown in Table 5.8 are the following (and each property income is annotated by a superscript letter to enable us to track that particular item of income both as property income received and as property income paid). For the sake of the explanation, Table 5.8 mostly shows property income by the institutional unit *paying* the property income (not by the institutional unit receiving the income) except for dividends paid by a non-resident enterprise to the resident bakery.

The farm pays, to a resident landowner (a household) who owns the farming land, a rent, D.45, of €1[a] per annum. Conversely, this is property income for the landowning resident household. The farm has borrowed from a non-resident bank, and so has to pay interest, D.41, of €6[b] per annum to the non-resident bank. Conversely, this is property income for a non-resident. The mill has borrowed from a resident household and has to pay interest of €1[c] per annum to the resident household. Conversely, this is property income for the resident household holding the mill's IOU. The bakery, which is an incorporated enterprise with shareholders who are all members of households, pays €2[d] per annum of dividends, D.421, to the resident shareholders. Conversely, this is property income for these share-owning resident households. The bakery is assumed to own shares in a non-resident enterprise, and this non-resident enterprise pays €1[e] per annum of dividends (property income) to the bakery. Conversely, this is property income, from a non-resident, for the share-owning resident bakery. These are all the property incomes paid and received in the model economy.

The supposition regarding the employment of non-resident border workers is the following. The farm pays to its non-resident employees €2 per annum and pays to its resident employees €13 per annum. The farm's total compensation of employees is unchanged from Table 5.4 at €15 per annum. Note that while this leaves the economy's total compensation of employees in Table 5.4 unaltered at €25 per annum, *resident* households now receive only €23 per annum as compensation of employees, the remaining €2 per annum of compensation of employees going to non-residents. (In real world national accounts this is one of two reasons why total compensation of employees in the generation of income account differs from total compensation of employees for households in the allocation of primary income account; the other reason being the receipt by residents of employee compensation from non-residents, as we shall show.)

We can now use this data to present, for the model economy, the very important Account II.1.2: Allocation of primary income account. This account is presented in Table 5.9 in detail for each of the enterprises, and takes resident households as a group or sector of the economy, and also takes non-residents as a sector. The real-world SNA93/ESA95 accounts present Account II.1.2 in the same format, but have each sector of the economy in the column headings, so effectively, the example of the farm, the mill, and so on, is each a surrogate for a sector of the economy. Table 5.9 also gives a column containing the total for all residents, and separately a column for non-residents. Table 5.9 is important because it models, but with a modification of layout used in the *Blue Book 1999 edition*, the official SNA93/ESA95 template for the allocation of primary income account (*SNA93*, table 7.2, p. 159; *ESA95*, table 8.4, p. 156).

In Table 5.9, the resources on the allocation of primary income account are, on the one hand, the receipts of primary incomes of gross operating surplus, gross mixed income, and compensation of employees and, on the other hand, the receipts of property income.

The receipts of primary incomes are: €5 per annum of gross operating surplus, B.2g, for each of the mill and the bakery (see last column of Table 5.4); €9 per annum of gross mixed income, B.3g, for the farm (ditto); €5 per annum of gross mixed income for the woodcutter (ditto); and €23 per annum of compensation of employees for households as a sector (we have already explained how the €25 per annum total compensation of employees in Table 5.4 is divided between payment of €23 per annum to employees who are members of resident households and payment of €2 per annum to employees who are non-residents (border workers)). In the rest of the world (non-residents) column we show the €2 per annum of compensation of employees which non-resident border worker employees receive.

So far, we have dealt with the primary incomes shown in Table 5.4.

Now we consider recording in Table 5.9 the property incomes shown in Table 5.8. In the first instance (and following Figure 5.3) these property incomes are treated as resources, meaning property income *received*. Accordingly, Table 5.8's primary incomes are first recorded in Table 5.9 for the *recipients* of the property income before being recorded for the institutional units paying the property income.

Households receive the following property incomes: €1[c] per annum of interest (from the mill); €2[d] per annum of dividends (from the bakery); and

Table 5.9
Allocation of primary income account and balances of primary incomes, gross, in model economy

SNA93/ESA95 identification code	SNA93/ESA95 name	€ per annum						
		Residents					Total residents	Rest of the world (non-residents)
		Farm	Mill	Wood-cutter	Bakery	House-holds		
II	DISTRIBUTION AND USE OF INCOME ACCOUNTS							
II.1	PRIMARY DISTRIBUTION OF INCOME ACCOUNT							
II.1.2	ALLOCATION OF PRIMARY INCOME ACCOUNT							
	Resources							
B.2g	Gross operating surplus	—	5	—	5	—	10	...
B.3g	Gross mixed income	9	—	5	—	—	14	...
D.1	Compensation of employees	...	...	...	...	23	23	2
D.4	Property income, received							
D.41	Interest	—	—	—	—	1 [c]	1	6 [b]
D.421	Dividends	—	—	—	1 [e]	2 [d]	3	—
D.45	Rent	—	—	—	—	1 [a]	1	...
D.4	Total property income	0	0	0	1	4	5	6
Total	Total resources	9	5	5	6	27	52	8

Gross domestic product, B.1*g

Uses								
	Property income, paid							
D.4								
D.41	Interest	6[b]	1[c]	—	2[d]	—	7	1[c]
D.421	Dividends	—	—	—	—	—	2	—
D.45	Rent	1[a]	—	—	—	—	1	—
.D.4	Total property income	7	1	0	2	0	10	1
B.5g	Balance of primary incomes, gross	2	4	5	4	27	*Gross national income,* B.5*g 42	7
Total	Total uses	9	5	5	6	27	52	8

a, b, c, d, e Annotations for identification as receipt (resource) and as payment (use).

... signifies: not applicable in principle (by definition of item).

— signifies: not occurring in the model economy.

B.5*g identifies gross national income for model economy.

Source: Tables 5.4 and 5.8 and text.

243

€1ᵃ per annum of rent (from the farm). Total property income received by households is thus €4 per annum, and together with €23 per annum of compensation of employees, households have €27 per annum of total resources on the allocation of primary income account.

The bakery receives €1ᵉ per annum of dividends from the non-resident enterprise in which the bakery owns shares, and together with €5 per annum of gross operating surplus the bakery has €6 per annum of total resources on the allocation of primary income account. The farm, the mill and the woodcutter receive no property incomes so their total resources on allocation of primary income account are simply gross operating surplus or gross mixed income received.

Non-residents receive interest of €6ᵇ per annum (from the farm to the non-resident bank), and together with €2 per annum of compensation of employees (from the farm to its non-resident employees), total resources for non-residents on the allocation of income account is €8 per annum.

As a result of all of this we have the following row for total resources on the allocation of primary income account: farm, €9 per annum; mill, €5 per annum; woodcutter, €5 per annum; bakery, €6 per annum; households, €27 per annum; all residents, €52 per annum; and non-residents, €8 per annum.

Also as a result of all this we have the following primary incomes as resources for total residents: gross operating surplus, €10 per annum; gross mixed income, €14 per annum; compensation of employees, €23 per annum; interest, €1 per annum; dividends, €3 per annum; rent, €1 per annum; and total property income, €5 per annum.

The allocation of primary income account then shows, as uses, the *payments* of property income by sector. In the model economy, each enterprise's payment of property incomes is shown. The reason for this will be explained shortly. The farm pays €6ᵇ per annum as interest to the non-resident bank and €1ᵃ per annum as rent on the land to a resident household. The farm's total property income payments are thus €7 per annum. The mill pays €1ᶜ per annum of interest to a resident household, and this is also the total property income payment which the mill makes. The woodcutter has no property income payments. The bakery pays €2ᵈ per annum dividends to resident households, and this is also the total property income payment which the bakery makes. Non-residents pay €1ᵉ per annum of dividends to the bakery, and this is also the total property income payment made by non-residents.

As a result of all of this we have the following row for total property income payments on the allocation of primary income account: farm, €7 per annum; mill, €1 per annum; woodcutter, €0 per annum; bakery, €2 per annum;

households, €0 per annum; all residents, €10 per annum; and non-residents, €1 per annum.

Also as a result of all this we have the following property incomes paid by total residents: interest, €7 per annum; dividends, €2 per annum; rent, €1 per annum; and total property income, €10 per annum.

If, for any sector, we deduct the total property income payments from the total resources on the allocation of primary income account (that is, the total of primary incomes, including property incomes, received), then we arrive at the balancing item called the *balance of primary incomes, gross*, B.5g.

As a result of this calculation we have the following row for the balances of primary incomes, gross, as the balancing item on the allocation of primary income account for each enterprise or sector: farm, €2 per annum; mill, €4 per annum; woodcutter, €5 per annum; bakery, €4 per annum; households, €27 per annum; and non-residents, €7 per annum. Note especially that the balance of primary incomes for the rest of the world (non-residents) is positive, indicating payment (net) by residents to non-residents. It is also possible for this balance of primary incomes to be negative, indicating payment (net) by non-residents to residents. In the next section we shall see an example of a positive balance of primary incomes for the rest of the world for the Australian economy in 1997–98, and an example of a negative balance of primary incomes for the rest of the world for the United Kingdom economy in 1997.

Note also that in Table 5.9, the balance of primary incomes for the rest of the world (non-residents) includes their receipt of the primary income of compensation of employees. This will be discussed further below.

The balance of primary incomes is thus a measure of the primary income derived by the institutional unit, or sector, as a result of production and/or ownership of assets/liabilities.

Note the following features of Table 5.9, which reflect features of the real world. The balance of primary incomes gross for the farm is less than its total resources of primary income (and this is typical for a non-financial enterprise: for example as we shall see, in the United Kingdom in 1997 the balance of primary incomes for the sector of non-financial corporations was only about one-half of its total resources of primary income, the other half being distributed as property income paid). The farm has €9 per annum of gross mixed income, but only €2 per annum of a balance of primary income for itself after payment of interest and rent.

The balance of primary incomes gross for households is much greater than simply compensation of employees because households receive a substantial amount of property income (net). For example as we shall see, in the United Kingdom in 1997, the balance of primary incomes for households was more than one-third greater than total compensation of employees.

Note also that for any category of property income and for property income as a whole, the following relationship applies for 'Total residents' and for 'Rest of the world (non-residents)':

Property income [category] received by total residents	−	Property income [category] paid by total residents	=	Property income [category] paid by rest of the world (non-residents)	−	Property income [category] received by rest of the world (non-residents)

To illustrate from Table 5.9 for interest:

Interest received by total residents, €1 p.a.	−	Interest paid by total residents, €7 p.a.	=	Interest paid by rest of the world (non-residents), €0 p.a.	−	Interest received by rest of the world (non-residents), €6 p.a.

And for total property income:

Total property income received by total residents, €5 p.a.	−	Total property income paid by total residents, €10 p.a.	=	Total property income paid by rest of the world (non-residents), €1 p.a.	−	Total property income received by rest of the world (non-residents), €6 p.a.

Any such equation I call a 'total economy–rest of the world net property income equation'. Each of the total economy–rest of the world net property income equations is important because each indicates, for the total economy, what type of property income is being paid (net) to the rest of the world or is being received (net) from the rest of the world and each also checks the consistency of the allocation of primary income account.

The resident sectors route to gross national income concludes (at the fifth step in Figure 5.3) by summing the balances of primary incomes of the resident sectors:

	Balance of primary incomes, gross, B.5g, € per annum
Farm	2
Mill	4
Woodcutter	5
Bakery	4
Households	27
Total economy: gross national income, B.5*g	42

Note that, by comparison with Tables 5.4 and 5.5, gross national income is less than gross domestic product. This is because we have modelled an economy where non-residents receive primary income from residents in excess of the primary income paid by non-residents to residents. In order to appreciate this it is necessary to consider the aggregate route to gross national income from gross domestic product (Figure 5.3).

In Table 5.9, gross domestic product may, as indicated by the boxed area at the top right, be calculated as the sum of the total gross operating surplus, total gross mixed income (both of which, in the column for 'Total residents' are each the total generated domestically) and that amount of total compensation of employees which is generated domestically regardless of to whom paid. In the case of total compensation of employees generated domestically, we must consider two things.

First, some of total compensation of employees generated domestically is paid to non-residents and is accordingly entered, not in the 'Total residents' column but in the 'Rest of the world (non-residents)' column. Consequently, this amount of compensation of employees (€2 per annum in the model economy) must be *added to* the amount of compensation of employees entered in the 'Total residents' column.

Second, some of the total compensation of employees included in compensation of employees received by residents may be paid by non-residents and is, conversely, not compensation of employees generated domestically. Consequently, the amount of any such compensation of employees paid by non-residents to residents must be *subtracted from* the amount of compensation of employees entered in the 'Total residents' column. In the case of the model economy this amount does not occur and so we may note it as €0 per annum.

The issue of compensation of employees between residents and non-residents may be resolved by entering in this D.1 row in Table 5.9 the *net amount* calculated as: compensation of employees paid by residents to non-residents *minus* compensation of employees paid by non-residents to residents. I shall call this net amount the 'net receipts of compensation of employees by the rest of the world (non-residents)'. This is the solution we shall adopt in the next section when we consider the allocation of primary income accounts for the United Kingdom and for Australia (but it should be noted that this is not a solution of the SNA93/ESA95). For the model economy the *net amount* of employee compensation between residents and non-residents, or net receipts of compensation of employees by the rest of the world (non-residents) is: €2 per annum – €0 per annum = €2 per annum.

To summarise the general solution (remember that this is for an economy with no taxes and subsidies on production) and to apply it to the model economy:

$$
\begin{array}{l}
\text{Gross} \qquad\quad \text{Gross} \qquad \text{Gross} \qquad \text{Compensation of} \\
\text{domestic} \;=\; \text{operating} + \text{mixed} + \text{employees generated} \\
\text{product} \qquad\quad \text{surplus} \qquad \text{income} \quad \text{domestically}
\end{array}
$$

$$
\begin{array}{l}
\qquad\quad \text{Gross} \qquad\quad \text{Gross} \qquad \text{Compensation of} \\
\;=\; \text{operating} + \text{mixed} + \text{employees in 'Total} \\
\qquad\quad \text{surplus} \qquad \text{income} \quad \text{residents' column}
\end{array}
$$

$$
+ \begin{bmatrix} \text{Compensation of} & & \text{Compensation of} \\ \text{employees paid by} & - & \text{employees paid by} \\ \text{residents to non-} & & \text{non-residents to} \\ \text{residents} & & \text{residents} \end{bmatrix}
$$

$$
\begin{array}{l}
\qquad\quad \text{Gross} \qquad\quad \text{Gross} \qquad \text{Compensation of} \\
\;=\; \text{operating} + \text{mixed} + \text{employees in 'Total} \\
\qquad\quad \text{surplus} \qquad \text{income} \quad \text{residents' column}
\end{array}
$$

$$
+ \begin{bmatrix} \text{Net receipts of} \\ \text{compensation of} \\ \text{employees by non-} \\ \text{residents} \end{bmatrix}
$$

$$
= \text{€}10 \text{ p.a.} + \text{€}14 \text{ p.a.} + \text{€}23 \text{ p.a.}
$$

$$
+ [\text{€}2 \text{ p.a.} - \text{€}0 \text{ p.a.}]
$$

$$
= \text{€}49 \text{ p.a.}
$$

Given this way of calculating gross domestic product, the aggregate route to gross national income proceeds by subtracting from gross domestic product the balance of primary incomes of the rest of the world (non-residents). (In Figure 5.3, this balance was simplified to net property incomes received by non-residents, but we now have to take account of the net receipts of compensation of employees by non-residents.)

The concept of the rest of the world's balance of primary incomes is: property income received by non-residents from residents *minus* property income paid by non-residents to residents *plus* the net *receipts* of compensation of employees by non-residents. With the application of the definition to the model economy, the net property income received by non-residents is defined as:

Net property income received by non-residents	=	Property income received by non-residents	−	Property income paid by non-residents
	=	€6 p.a.	−	€1 p.a.
	=	€5 p.a.		

But, in addition to net property income received by non-residents, we have also to consider the external transactions in compensation of employees, because:

Balance of primary incomes of the rest of the world (non-residents)	=	Net property income received by non-residents	+	Net receipts of compensation employees received by non-residents

Accordingly, for the model economy:

Balance of primary incomes of the rest of the world (non-residents)	=	€5 p.a.	+	€2 p.a.
	=	€7 p.a.		

The aggregate route to gross national income starts from gross domestic product and subtracts from that the balance of primary incomes of the rest of the world (non-residents). Accordingly, for the model economy the aggregate route to gross national income is expressed in, and applied by, the following equation:

$$
\begin{array}{ccccc}
\text{Gross national} & & \text{Gross domestic} & & \text{Balance of primary} \\
\text{income, B.5*g} & = & \text{product, B.1*g} & - & \text{incomes of the rest of the} \\
& & & & \text{world (non-residents)}
\end{array}
$$

$$
= \quad \text{€49 p.a.} \quad - \quad \text{€7 p.a.}
$$

$$
= \quad \text{€42 p.a.}
$$

Another way of looking at this equation is to give the details for the balance of primary incomes of the rest of the world (non-residents):

$$
\begin{array}{ccccc}
\begin{array}{l}\text{Gross} \\ \text{national} \\ \text{income,} \\ \text{B.5*g}\end{array} & = & \begin{array}{l}\text{Gross} \\ \text{domestic} \\ \text{product,} \\ \text{B.1*g}\end{array} & - & \left[\begin{array}{l}\text{Primary incomes} \\ \text{payable to the} \\ \text{rest of the world} \\ \text{(non-residents)}\end{array} - \begin{array}{l}\text{Primary incomes} \\ \text{receivable from the} \\ \text{rest of the world} \\ \text{(non-residents)}\end{array}\right]
\end{array}
$$

$$
\begin{array}{ccccc}
& = & \begin{array}{l}\text{Gross} \\ \text{domestic} \\ \text{product,} \\ \text{B.1*g}\end{array} & - & \begin{array}{l}\text{Primary incomes} \\ \text{payable to the} \\ \text{rest of the world} \\ \text{(non-residents)}\end{array} + \begin{array}{l}\text{Primary incomes} \\ \text{receivable from the} \\ \text{rest of the world} \\ \text{(non-residents)}\end{array}
\end{array}
$$

$$
= \quad \text{€49 p.a.} \quad - \quad \text{€8 p.a.} \quad + \quad \text{€1 p.a.}
$$

$$
= \quad \text{€42 p.a.}
$$

As stated in the SNA93: 'GNI is equal to GDP less primary incomes payable to non-resident units plus primary incomes receivable from non-resident units' (*SNA93*, para. 2.181; also *UK NACSM*, para. 11.33).

We can thus see that the difference between gross domestic product and gross national income is the amount of the balance of primary incomes for the rest of the world (non-residents). This is important in understanding the difference between gross domestic product and gross national income.

Comparing gross domestic product of €49 per annum with gross national income of €42 per annum, we could ask: What is the significance of the two figures? What is economic meaning of the difference between the two? Equivalently, what is the economic significance of the balance of primary incomes of the rest of the world (non-residents) of €7 per annum?

The answer to these questions needs to be given, not in monetary terms, but in terms of physical products. For the purpose of this answer, let us concentrate on physical products required for sustenance through consumption, and let us ignore physical products required for gross fixed capital formation, exports, and so on. In other words, let us for a moment imagine that gross domestic product can be simply represented (as in Table 2.1) by a loaf of bread. We can thus think of the gross domestic product of the model economy as consisting of a loaf of bread divided into seven slices (choosing seven because both 49 and 42 in the preceding equation are divisible by seven). In other words, the physical end-result of production by residents has been to produce seven slices of bread. This is the 'real', or 'physical products for sustenance', view of gross domestic product which it is necessary to imagine in order to understand the *principle* of the difference between gross domestic product and gross national income.

The seven slices of bread (gross domestic product) can be used for sustenance, but whose sustenance exactly? This is the question which is answered by the concept of gross national income.

If positive, the balance of primary incomes for the rest of the world (non-residents), represents the claims of non-residents on the 'physical products for sustenance' which constitute the gross domestic product. Accordingly, in the model economy, we must imagine the non-residents (the rest of the world) claiming one slice of bread (or one-seventh of €49 per annum) to be used for their own sustenance, leaving only six slices of bread for the sustenance of residents (or six-sevenths of gross domestic product). So the €42 per annum of gross national income (= six-sevenths of €49 per annum of gross domestic product) represents the benefits, in terms of end-result physical products, which residents of the economy derive from their production. Because the residents have obtained finance (net) from non-residents and because there has been a contribution to domestic production from non-resident border workers, residents have to share some of the slices of bread they have produced (gross domestic product) with non-residents. The amount of this sharing is represented by the *positive* balance of primary incomes for the rest of the world (non-residents).

Conversely, if the balance of primary incomes of the rest of the world (non-residents) is *negative*, then the rest of the world has to share with residents some of their (non-resident produced) slices of bread, and consequently gross national income is greater than gross domestic product. The economic significance of this is that the quantity of 'physical products for sustenance' of the gross domestic product is, for residents, *supplemented* by what non-residents have to share (out of their production) with residents.

There is one outstandingly important consequence of all this which must be well understood. If one wants to measure the standard of living of the population of an economy (a measure which is quite often wanted), then the appropriate measure is *gross national income* per head of population; *not* gross domestic product per head of population. To illustrate, in the model economy, it is clear that the standard of sustenance ('living') per head of population in the model economy is *six* slices of bread divided by the resident population, and conversely is most emphatically not seven slices of bread divided by the resident population. (There is a further discussion, not entered into here (but see Chapter 6, Section 6.8), as to whether *net* national income would be the more appropriate numerator for measuring the standard of living; but whether net or gross it should be clear that *national income*, not domestic product, is the appropriate numerator in any measure of the standard of living.)

5.6   The allocation of primary income account and gross national income in the United Kingdom and Australia

Finally in this chapter, I consider briefly the allocation of primary income account in the United Kingdom and in Australia in order to show how all the concepts and the allocation of primary income account we have learnt about in Section 5.5 apply in the real world.

The sectors of the economy have been introduced and briefly explained in Chapter 1, and that explanation is here taken as given.

The official SNA93/ESA95 template for the allocation of primary income account (*SNA93*, table 7.2, p. 159; *ESA95*, table 8.4, p. 156) is here presented in the modified layout used in the *Blue Book 1999 edition*, table 1.7.3, pp. 60–61.

Table 5.10 gives Account II.1.2 Allocation of primary income account for the United Kingdom economy in 1997.

At first sight, Table 5.10 looks daunting, but it is no more complex in principle and in structure than Table 5.9, which has been fully explained and discussed and is thus an essential stepping stone to understanding Table 5.10 which is a very important account in the SNA93/ESA95. The complexity of Table 5.10 is only in the detail: the column headings give all the resident sectors of the economy (Figure 1.2, p. 9) together with the total for the UK economy and the rest of the world (non-resident) sector, and the row headings give all the various types of primary income, especially property income

(Figure 5.2, p. 232). The benefit from this complexity of detail is that Table 5.10 is a rich source of information on the working of the macroeconomy. It is not possible in the space limitations of this book fully to discuss all the economic information in Table 5.10, but a few significant features will be mentioned in passing.

The reader should understand that Table 5.10 is a learning tool and, like any tool, it must be used if it is to be understood. How should the reader 'use' Table 5.10? First, as a means of familiarising yourself with the table it is essential that, using a calculator, you should check all the arithmetic in the table (checking all the sub-totals, totals and balancing items calculations for each and every column and row, practising your understanding of row headings and column headings as you go). This establishes your understanding of the structure of the table. Second, check that the total economy–rest of the world net property income equations apply. This establishes your understanding of the consistency of the table. Third and without fail, check for yourself any calculation which I may mention in the following explanation.

The first key feature of Table 5.10 is the calculation for resident sectors of each sector's balance of primary incomes, gross, B.5g. Using your calculator and noting carefully the row headings in which quantitatively significant items occur, work out each sector's balance of primary incomes, gross.

For example, observe, as you go, that most of the primary income received by the sector of non-financial corporations is gross operating surplus (because you will not remember the numbers involved, and in any case these change from year to year, ascertain for this sector the *percentage* contribution of gross operating surplus to total resources on the allocation of primary income account; this percentage is likely to be stable from year to year and is a useful figure to remember; the percentage in Table 5.10 is 77 per cent, and this can usefully be rounded to 'about three-quarters' for ease of remembering; continue to work out percentages to illustrate the ensuing discussion). This is not surprising: institutional units in this sector operate to achieve a gross operating surplus from their gross value added, so the figure of £173 983 million tells us about their achievements in 1997.

Observe that the sector of non-financial corporations does not receive a great deal of property income; their holdings of financial assets are generally incidental to their production operations (which necessitate the holding of real assets). By contrast, observe that this sector does pay out a great deal of property income; this sector finances its holdings of real assets by borrowing and by issuing shares and these financial liabilities lead to the property income payments. We may observe that total property income payments by this sector

Table 5.10

Allocation of primary income account and balances of primary incomes, gross, in the United Kingdom economy, 1997

£ million

SNA93/ESA95 identification code	SNA93/ESA95 name	Non-financial corporations, S.11	Financial corporations, S.12	General government, S.13	Households and NPISHs, S.14 + S.15	Not sectorised, S.N	UK total economy, S.1	Rest of the world, S.2
II	DISTRIBUTION AND USE OF INCOME ACCOUNTS							
II.1	PRIMARY DISTRIBUTION OF INCOME ACCOUNT							
II.1.2	ALLOCATION OF PRIMARY INCOME ACCOUNT							
	Resources							
B.2g	Gross operating surplus	173 983	18 151	11 840	44 217	-25 678	222 513	...
B.3g	Gross mixed income				41 665		41 665	...
D.1	Total compensation of employees				432 471		432 471	-83 [a]
D.21	Taxes on products			92 547			92 547	5 772
D.29	Other taxes on production			17 048			17 048	—
-D.31	less Subsidies on products [b]			-4 870			-4 870	-3 174
D.4	Property income, received							
D.41	Interest	10 468	184 628	8 317	26 043		229 456	70 858
D.42	Distributed income of corporations [c]	29 223	39 855	1 620	38 467		109 165	18 697
D.43	Reinvested earnings on direct foreign investment	11 366	4 394	—			15 760	5 562
D.44	Property income attributed to insurance policy holders	878	75	33	51 800		52 786	694
D.45	Rent	120	28	717	104		969	...
D.4	Total property income	52 055	228 980	10 687	116 414		408 136	95 811
-P.119	Adjustment to property income for financial services (FISIM)		-25 678			25 678	0	...
Total	Total resources	226 038	221 453	127 252	634 767	0	1 209 510	98 326

Uses

D.4	Property income, paid						
D.41	Interest	27 983	127 403	33 939	42 045	...	231 370	68 944
D.42	Distributed income of corporations	82 215	23 453	...	...	...	105 668	22 194
D.43	Reinvested earnings on direct foreign investment	4 369	1 193	...	...	...	5 562	15 760
D.44	Property income attributed to insurance policy holders	...	53 480	...	...	...	53 480	—
D.45	Rent	752	—	—	217	...	969	...
D.4	Total property income	115 319	205 529	33 939	42 262	...	397 049	106 898
B.5g	Balance of primary incomes, gross	110 719	15 924	93 313	592 505	...	812 461	−8 572
Total	Total uses	226 038	221 453	127 252	634 767	...	1 209 510	98 326

NPISHs = Non-profit institutions serving households; FISIM = Financial intermediation services indirectly measured;
... = Not applicable in principle (by definition of item); — = Nil, or less than £0.5 million and not recorded; boxed figures sum to GDP.

(a) This item is the net compensation of employees received by the rest of the world (non-residents) and is calculated as: £924 million compensation of employees received by the rest of the world (non-residents) minus £1007 million compensation of employees paid by the rest of the world (non-residents). In reporting this as a net item, I depart from the SNA93/ESA95 presentation in the *Blue Book 1999 edition*. In the *Blue Book 1999 edition* for the purpose of calculating the balance of primary incomes for the rest of the world of −£8572 million (a figure not recorded in the *Blue Book 1999 edition*, although this balance is required for the aggregate route to gross national income).

(b) Note that nil (or less than £0.5 million) D.39 other subsidies on production were recorded for 1997.

(c) The division: Dividends, D.421, and Withdrawals from income of quasi-corporations, D.422, was not reported in the *Blue Book 1999 edition*.

Source: Office for National Statistics, *United Kingdom National Accounts The Blue Book 1999 edition*, tables 1.7.3 and 7.1.2 (for employee compensation between residents and non-residents), pp. 60–61 and 226–7.

amount to one-half of total primary incomes received and two-thirds of gross operating surplus. This tells us a considerable amount about how this sector 'works' economically and leads on to other interesting investigations. For example, we can ascertain from the SNA93/ESA95 Account IV.3 Closing balance sheet that, at the end of 1997, this sector of the UK economy owned £642.9 billion of financial assets but owed £1930.8 billion of financial liabilities, so the total of their financial liabilities was three times greater than the total of their financial assets (the *Blue Book 1999 edition*, table 3.1.9, pp. 120–21).

Turning to the sector of financial corporations, observe the amount of interest received by this sector and compare this with the amount of interest paid by this sector. Unlike the sector of non-financial corporations this sector holds most of its assets as financial assets (loans, and so on), but it obtains those financial assets by accepting deposits or otherwise borrowing for on-lending.

Turning to households (including non-profit institutions serving households), observe the relatively large amount of property income received by households. Consequently and in conjunction with its receipt of compensation of employees, observe that this sector has the largest single balance of primary incomes, gross, among the resident sectors (73 per cent of the UK economy total balance of primary incomes, gross).

Following the first key macroeconomic feature of Table 5.10 – the calculation of the balances of primary incomes – when we aggregate across the resident sectors' balances of primary incomes, gross, B.5g, we obtain gross national income, B.5*g, as follows for the United Kingdom economy:

	Balance of primary incomes, gross, B.5g, 1997, £ million,
Non-financial corporations, S.11	110 719
Financial corporations, S.12	15 924
General government, S.13	93 313
Households and NPISHs, S.14 + S.15	592 505
UK total economy, S.1: gross national income, B.5*g	812 461

This illustrates the resident sectors route to gross national income.

The second key macroeconomic feature of Table 5.10 is the aggregate route from gross domestic product to gross national income. The boxed items in the block at the top right of the table aggregate to gross domestic product, which for the United Kingdom in 1997 was £803 889 million. Observe that in the real world, taxes on products and other taxes on production less subsidies on products constitute primary income for the general government and this means that gross domestic product is measured at market prices, and consequently gross national income is also measured at market prices.

Note that for the member states of the European Union taxes on products are also received, and subsidies on products are paid, by the European Union whose institutions count as a non-resident governmental authority, hence the relevant entries for these rows in the 'Rest of the world' column.

Note that net receipts of employee compensation by non-residents was negative for the rest of the world (Table 5.10's footnote (*a*)).

The total primary incomes payable to the rest of the world (total resources on allocation of primary income account for the rest of the world) in 1997 was £98 326 million, and total primary income (in this case property income) paid by the rest of the world (in other words, total primary income receivable from the rest of the world) was £106 898 million. Accordingly, we have for the United Kingdom in 1997:

Balance of primary incomes of the rest of the world = Primary incomes payable to the rest of the world − Primary incomes receivable from the rest of the world

= £98 326 mn − £106 898 mn

= −£8 572 mn

The negative sign indicates that, in 1997, non-residents had to pay primary incomes to residents in excess of the primary incomes non-residents received from residents.

The aggregate route to the United Kingdom's gross national income in 1997 is now as follows:

Gross national income, B.5*g = Gross domestic product, B.1*g − Balance of primary incomes of the rest of the world (non-residents)

= £803 889 mn − (−£8 572 mn)

= £812 461 mn

This means that the total of the United Kingdom's domestically generated incomes was, in 1997, supplemented for residents by the primary incomes which the rest of the world paid (net) to the residents of the United Kingdom. The amount of this supplementation was 1.1 per cent of gross domestic product.

Table 5.11 presents the allocation of primary income account for the Australian economy in 1997–98. The same general features as can be seen in the United Kingdom's account can also be seen in Australia's account. The aggregate of the resident sectors' balances of primary incomes, gross, B.5g, is gross national income, B.5*g, as follows for the Australian economy:

	Balance of primary incomes, gross, B.5g, 1997–98, $ million
Non-financial corporations, S.11	67 029
Financial corporations, S.12	13 887
General government, S.13	73 428
Households and NPISHs, S.14 + S.15	390 007
Australian total economy, S.1: gross national income, B.5*g	544 351

For the aggregate route to gross national income the boxed figures in the top right aggregate to gross domestic product of $564 705 million (after adding in the statistical discrepancy between income components and gross domestic product, or the 'statistical discrepancy (I)', of $1 560 million (Table 2.5, p. 107)).

Note that Australia does not have taxes on production going to a non-resident governmental institution; nor does it receive subsidies from any such non-resident governmental institution.

A major difference between Australia and the United Kingdom is the balance of primary incomes for the rest of the world.

The total primary incomes payable to the rest of the world (total resources on allocation of primary income account for the rest of the world) in 1997–98 was $28 230 million, and total primary income (in this case property income) paid by the rest of the world (in other words, total primary income receivable from the rest of the world) was $9344 million. Accordingly, we have for Australia in 1997–98:

Balance of primary incomes of the rest of the world = Primary incomes payable to the rest of the world − Primary incomes receivable from the rest of the world

= $28 138 mn − $9 344 mn

= $18 794 mn

The (silent) positive sign indicates that, in 1997–98, non-residents received primary incomes from residents in excess of the primary incomes non-residents paid to residents.

The aggregate route to Australia's gross national income in 1997–98 is now as follows (making the converse allowance for the statistical discrepancy (I) according to the conventions used in the Australian System of National Accounts for reporting gross national income):

Gross national income, B.5*g = Gross domestic product, B.1*g − Balance of primary incomes of the rest of the world (non-residents) − Statistical discrepancy (I)

= $564 705 mn − $18 794 mn − $1 560 mn

= $544 351 mn

This means that the total of Australia's domestically generated incomes was, in 1997–98, diminished for residents by the primary incomes which the rest of the world received (net) from the residents of Australia. The amount of this diminution was about 3.3 per cent of gross domestic product, and this is a consequence of Australia's relatively large 'foreign debt'.

At 30 June 1998, Australian residents owned $260.3 billion of claims on the rest of the world (non-residents), but Australian residents owed $582.0 billion of liabilities to the rest of the world. Accordingly, Australia's liabilities to the rest of the world net was $321.7 billion (Table 7.12, pp. 398–400). In relative terms Australia's liabilities net amounted to over half of annual gross domestic product. This explains why the rest of the world had, *vis-à-vis* Australia, a large positive balance of primary incomes and why Australia's gross national income is smaller than gross domestic product.

Table 5.11
Allocation of primary income account and balances of primary incomes, gross, in the Australian economy, 1997–98

SNA93 identification code (ascribed)	Australian System of National Accounts name	$ million					
		Non-financial corporations, S.11	Financial corporations, S.12	General government, S.13	Households and NPISHs, S.14+S.15	Australian total economy, S.1	Rest of the world, S.2
	Income						
	Primary income receivable						
B.2g	Gross operating surplus	106 373	10 122	10 932	46 451	173 878	...
B.3g	Gross mixed income	...	...	...	54 217	54 217	...
D.1	Compensation of employees	...	...	...	270 176	270 176	−92 (a)
D.2 – D.3	Taxes less Subsidies on production and imports	...	...	64 966	...	64 966	—
D.4	Property income receivable						
D.41 + D.44	Interest and property income attributed to insurance policy holders	6 249	53 590	4 252	36 964	101 055	14 370
D.42	Dividends	3 776	7 402	7 837	7 867	26 882	8 815
D.43	Reinvested earnings on direct foreign investment	2 116	1 305	...	...	3 421	5 045
D.45	Rent on natural assets	—	—	1 420	18	1 438	...
D.4	Total property income receivable	12 141	62 297	13 509	44 849	132 796	28 230
Total	Total primary income receivable	118 514	72 419	89 407	415 693	696 033	28 138

Use of income

	Primary income payable						
D.4	Property income payable						
D.41 + D.44	Interest and property income attributed to insurance policy holders	21 457	49 344	15 979	25 593	112 373	3 052
D.42	Dividends	24 156	8 670	...	...	32 826	2 871
D.43	Reinvested earnings on direct foreign investment	4 527	518	...	...	5 045	3 421
D.45	Rent on natural assets	1 345	—	—	93	1 438	...
D.4	Total property income payable	51 485	58 532	15 979	25 686	151 682	9 344
Total	Total primary income payable	51 485	58 532	15 979	25 686	151 682	9 344
B.5g	Balance of primary incomes, gross	67 029	13 887	73 428	390 007	544 351	18 794 (b)
Total	Total use of income	118 514	72 419	89 407	415 693	696 033	28 138

NPISHs = Non-profit institutions serving households; ... = Not applicable in principle (by definition of item); — = Nil, or less than $0.5 million and not recorded.
(a) Calculated as: $659 mn compensation of employees receivable *minus* $751 mn compensation of employees payable. For GDP, include statistical discrepancy (I) of $1560 mn with boxed figures.
(b) Entered in the *Australian System of National Accounts 1997–98*, table 1.12, p. 32, with negative sign as 'Net primary income from non-residents'.

Source: Australian Bureau of Statistics, *Australian System of National Accounts 1997–98*, Catalogue No. 5204.0, tables 2.1, 2.9, 2.14, 2.20, 2.27, pp. 41, 49, 54, 60, 67; I have ascribed the SNA93 identification codes as these are not used in the published accounts.

6   General Government, Households and Disposable Income

6.1   Introduction

This chapter is basically about social welfare and the redistribution of income in the economy through taxes on income, social contributions and social welfare benefits. We explain the various types of benefits received under social welfare schemes and the contributions to those schemes and the taxation of income. We also consider some other similar transactions such as insurance premiums and claims. The chapter explains the SNA93/ESA95 accounts which deal with the *redistribution* of income, both in cash and in kind, where such redistribution is largely, but not entirely, carried out by means of transfers between the general government and the household sectors of the economy.

In the preceding chapters we explained the SNA93/ESA95 accounts which deal with production and with the distribution of income arising out of that production. Specifically, we have seen how, through production of output and the earning of incomes, sectors of the economy obtain a balance of primary incomes. But primary incomes are not the only flows into and out of the accounts of institutional units. Institutional units also receive and pay flows of current transfers (such as unemployment benefits or taxes on income) and capital transfers. The current transfers in cash are dealt with in what the SNA93/ESA95 calls the 'secondary distribution of income account'. Accordingly, in this chapter, we consider how each sector's balance of primary incomes is affected by the secondary distribution of incomes, resulting in a balancing item for each sector known in the SNA93/ESA95 as *disposable income, gross*, B.6g. For the economy as a whole, the sum of the sectors' balances of gross disposable income is gross national disposable income, B.6*g.

We also have to consider how disposable income is affected by current transfers in kind so as to result in *adjusted disposable income, gross*, B.7g. This is recorded in the SNA93/ESA95 Account II.3: Redistribution of income in kind account.

Finally in this chapter, we explain briefly the concept of income in relation to the consumption of fixed capital.

In order to understand the accounts dealing with the redistribution of income, we have first to understand the complex concept of current transfers.

6.2   Current transfers

Institutional units receive primary incomes by producing goods and services. These incomes are *requited* transactions, as described in Chapter 1 (see Figure 1.4, p. 16). Requited transactions are transactions with a counterpart; they are 'two-way' transactions; the income is in return for contributing to the process of production; these are the incomes which arise out of the process of production; in a metaphorical description they can be thought of as 'new' incomes arising out of the production of 'new' goods and services. But institutional units may also receive 'second-hand incomes' called transfers: transfers are *unrequited* transactions which are distributed out of 'new' incomes and out of the goods and services produced. The meaning of 'unrequited' is that the transaction is a transaction without a counterpart; the transaction is a 'one-way' transaction: nothing specific is provided, as part of the *same* transaction, in return for the transfer. A transfer may be in cash or in kind.

The following is the official definition of 'transfer':

> A transfer is a transaction in which one institutional unit provides a good, service or asset [including cash] to another unit without receiving from the latter any good, service or asset in return as counterpart. ... A unit making [paying out] a transfer receives no specific quantifiable benefit in return *that can be recorded as part of the same transaction* (*SNA93*, paras 8.3 and 8.28, with my clarifying interpolations in square brackets and with italics added because, for example, payment of contributions to a social security fund or payment of premiums to an insurance policy entitles the paying unit to certain benefits, but not *as part of the same transaction*, and consequently such contributions or premiums are classified as transfers).

The classification of transfers is shown in Figure 6.1. It is important to understand the distinction between current transfers and capital transfers, because current transfers can be easily defined negatively as transfers which are not capital transfers. Current transfers are difficult to define positively other than by way of enumeration (this is because current transfers encompass so many different types of transactions, as we shall see).

A transfer involving cash is a capital transfer if the transfer is purposefully intended to assist with or be involved in the acquisition of an asset (other than inventories) by the institutional unit to whom the cash is transferred, and a transfer in kind is a capital transfer if it transfers the ownership of an asset (other than inventories). The asset may be either a fixed asset or a financial asset. Transfers involving inventories come under current transfers, because in this case goods (for consumption) are being transferred. Capital transfers tend not to occur at regular periods; they are 'episodic' rather than 'periodic', but some non-capital, or current, transfers may also be 'episodic' such as transfers under insurance claims or transfers from government in compensation for natural disasters. Capital transfers often involve relatively large amounts. The most important point is that capital transfers are not intended, *as their main purpose*, directly to affect the disposable income of the institutional unit receiving the transfer; their main purpose is a purpose other than this and is generally a purpose connected with the acquiring or holding of assets.

Current transfers are all transfers other than capital transfers. Many current transfers occur at regular periods (such as payment of a retirement pension), and so may be described as 'periodic', but some current transfers may be irregular and episodic (for example, the payment of a 'one-off' social security maternity benefit, or the payment of an insurance claim, or compensation from the government for flood damage). Current transfers usually involve relatively small amounts. The most important point is that current transfers are intended, *as their main purpose*, directly to affect the disposable income of the institutional unit receiving the transfer.

There are many types of current transfers, and so it is difficult to proceed to a single, all-encompassing definition of 'current transfer'; consequently, it is useful to define 'current transfer' by enumeration of the different types, and this is done in Figure 6.1.

It is necessary to make a distinction between current transfers in cash and current transfers in kind, because each type is recorded in a different account: current transfers in cash are recorded in Account II.2: Secondary distribution of income account; current transfers in kind are recorded in Account II.3: Redistribution of income in kind account.

Current transfers in cash are those transfers where cash is transferred between the two institutional units involved in the transfer (unless the transfer

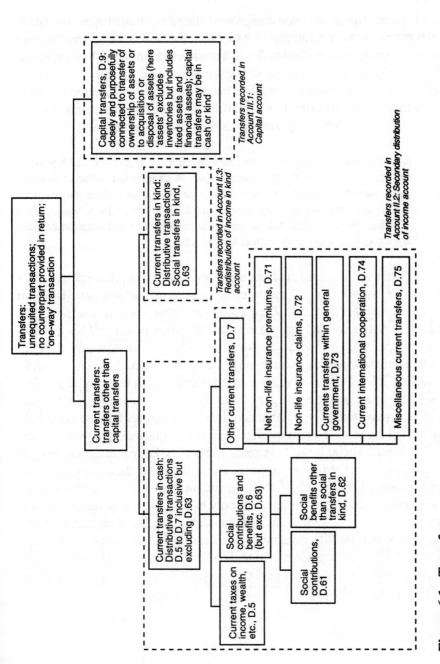

Figure 6.1 Transfers

265

in cash is specifically intended to reimburse the acquisition of approved goods and services by the institutional unit to whom the cash is transferred because any such reimbursement is classified as a transfer in kind – as will be explained later in this chapter). Current transfers in kind are those transfers where goods and services are provided to resident household units by government units (including social security funds) and by non-profit institutions serving households. The SNA93 explains the difference as follows:

> A cash transfer consists of the payment of currency or transferable deposit by one unit to another without any counterpart. A transfer in kind consists either of the transfer of ownership of a good or asset, other than cash, or the provision of a service, again without any counterpart (*SNA93*, para. 8.27; however, when studying this definition bear in mind the reimbursement exception because this exception is not dealt with in the definition).

As shown in Figure 6.1, current transfers in cash comprise: *current taxes on income, wealth, etc.,* D.5; *social contributions and benefits,* D.6 (but excluding *social transfers in kind,* D.63), and *other current transfers,* D.7. Current transfers in kind comprise *social transfers in kind,* D.63. Each of these will be explained in the course of this chapter. Consequently, the term 'current transfers' has to be understood by enumeration of the SNA93/ESA95 categories D.5 to D.7 inclusive, with special treatment for D.63 social transfers in kind (because it is this category which is recorded separately in Account II.3). It is only when we understand all these categories that we shall fully understand the term 'current transfer', and it is to this task that we now turn. We begin with social benefits in cash, technically known as *social benefits other than social transfers in kind,* D.62; we shall then explain *social contributions,* D.61. Each of these including their sub-categories will be explained in full. I then explain, but only briefly, current taxes on income, wealth, etc., D.5, and other current transfers, D.7, but with some special attention to net non-life insurance premiums, D.71, and non-life insurance claims, D.72. Social transfers in kind, D.63, is explained in the course of this chapter, but the explanation is given in several stages in order to fit in with the unfolding explanation of social welfare.

6.3 Social benefits in cash

In order to understand the secondary distribution of income account as it relates to households we have first to understand the related concepts of social benefits and social contributions. This section explains the concept of social benefits in general (in cash and in kind), and then explains in detail social benefits in cash. Social benefits in kind will be explained in detail in the next section; we treat social benefits in kind separately because of their link (to be explained) with final consumption expenditure by general government and by non-profit institutions serving households and because they are separately reported in Account II.3.

The classification of social contributions and benefits, D.6, is shown in Figure 6.2. Figure 6.2 has to be read in conjunction with Figure 6.3 (which closely follows) and vice versa. Additionally, parts of Figure 6.2 have to be understood in the light of Figure 6.4, which is given in Section 6.4, and in the light of Figure 6.5, which is given in Section 6.5.

Social contributions, D.61, will be explained fully in Section 6.5. For the moment we need only note that social contributions are payments made by employers (actual payments and imputed payments, each made on behalf of employees), payments made by employees (actual payments on behalf of themselves), payments made by self-employed persons (ditto), and (occasionally) payments made by non-employed persons (ditto). These social contributions are made in order to secure an entitlement to social benefits, but, as will be explained in Section 6.5, the route taken by the first group of these payments (rerouted through compensation of employees) needs to be carefully understood.

Social benefits are (unrequited) current transfers to households, either periodic (regular) payments or lump-sum payments, in cash or in kind, mostly intended to relieve households from the financial burden of one or more of twelve specified sorts of risks or needs (which are listed in Figure 6.3 below according to *ESA95*, para. 4.84; see also *ESA95*, paras 4.83 and 4.85 and *SNA93*, paras 8.7 and 8.75–8.83).

Social transfers in kind are mostly intended to cover the twelve specified sorts of risk or need, but a few social transfers in kind go beyond the scope of the twelve specified sorts of risk or need; these latter social transfers are classified with social benefits because, as will be explained in Section 6.4, these social transfers *in kind* along with other social benefits *in kind* constitute individual consumption expenditure by general government and individual consumption expenditure by non-profit institutions serving households. This

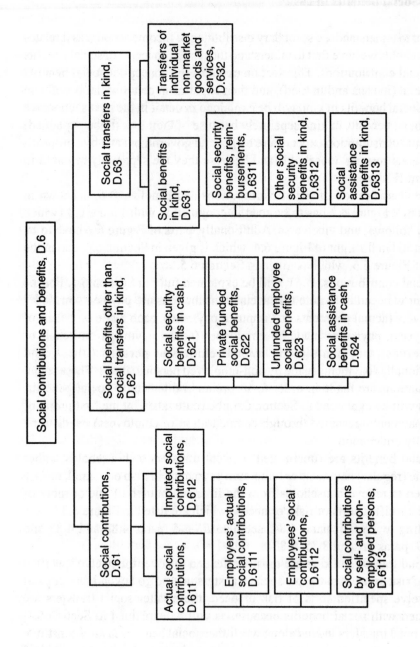

Figure 6.2   The SNA93/ESA95 classification of social contributions and social benefits

Social contributions and benefits, D.6

Social contributions, D.61

Actual social contributions, D.611

Imputed social contributions, D.612

Employers' actual social contributions, D.6111

Employees' social contributions, D.6112

Social contributions by self- and non-employed persons, D.6113

Social benefits other than social transfers in kind, D.62

Social security benefits in cash, D.621

Private funded social benefits, D.622

Unfunded employee social benefits, D.623

Social assistance benefits in cash, D.624

Social transfers in kind, D.63

Social benefits in kind, D.631

Transfers of individual non-market goods and services, D.632

Social security benefits, reimbursements, D.6311

Other social security benefits in kind, D.6312

Social assistance benefits in kind, D.6313

being said, the concept of social benefits can be understood (mainly) in terms of the twelve specified risks or needs (or, more exactly, in terms of responding to contingencies arising from any one or more of the twelve specified risks or needs).

The list of the twelve specified risks or needs is shown in the row headings on the left side of Figure 6.3. Figure 6.3 has a complex double role. First, it is intended as an analysis of the SNA93/ESA95 *concept* of social benefit. Second, having explicated the concept of social benefit, Figure 6.3 can be used to explain the SNA93/ESA95 *classification* of both social benefits and social contributions. This is why the SNA93/ESA95 identification codes for categories of social benefits and social contributions (given in Figure 6.2) are included in Figure 6.3, and these categories will all be explained in due course. But first we need to have some understanding of the concept and purposes of social benefits, and this is where the specified risks or needs covered or met by social benefits comes in.

The first eight specified risks or needs, from unemployment to family (that is, number of dependants) cover what may broadly be described as social security. The ninth risk or need, general neediness, is a miscellaneous category to deal with miscellaneous risks and needs – or causes of poverty – not elsewhere classified. The last three risks or needs – housing, promotion of employment and education – are more difficult to describe generally, and could be called social welfare (but note that social security is also social welfare). All twelve specified risks or needs share the common feature that, if the contingency involved in the risk or need comes to bear upon a household, then the contingency adversely affects the welfare the household either by reducing its income and/or by imposing additional demands upon the household's resources. In this way the contingencies involved in the risks or needs can be causes of the complex phenomenon identified generally as poverty (for a further discussion of the concept of poverty, the reader may consult my book, *Poverty* (Macmillan, 1972)).

There are two main types of social benefits as shown at the top of Figure 6.3: social *insurance* benefits; and social *assistance* benefits.

By definition, entitlement to social *insurance* benefits depends upon social contributions having been paid or being paid into an organised social insurance scheme (*SNA93*, paras 8.7 and 8.55). Social contributions can be paid by parties other than the beneficiaries, but social contributions will usually also have been made by the beneficiaries themselves.

By contrast and also by definition, the payment of social *assistance* benefits to any individual requires no prior social contributions by or on behalf of that

	Social benefits						
	Social insurance benefits (requires social contributions)					Social assistance benefits (does not require social contributions)	
SNA93/ESA95 social contributions (D.61)	D.6111, D.6112, D.6113 — Government units (social security schemes, plus)		Private funded schemes		D.612 — Private[a] unfunded schemes	Government units and non-profit institutions serving households	
			D.6111, D.6112, D.6113 — Third parties (insurance enterprises, autonomous pension funds)	D.6111, D.6112 — Employer's special reserves			
SNA93/ESA95 social benefits (D.62 and D.63)	In cash	In kind	In cash or kind	In cash or kind	In cash or kind	In cash	In kind
Risk or need covered or met	D.621 [1]	D.6311 D.6312 [2]	D.622 [3]	D.622 [4]	D.623 [5]	D.624 [6]	D.6313 D.632 [7]
① Unemployment							
② Sickness							
③ Invalidity or disability							
④ Occupational accident or disease							
⑤ Old age (e.g., retirement pension, retirement homes)							
⑥ Survivors (e.g., death benefits, pensions to widows, orphans)							
⑦ Maternity							
⑧ Family (i.e., number of dependants)							
⑨ General neediness							
⑩ Housing							
⑪ Promotion of employment							
⑫ Education							

(a) Including government schemes for government's own employees which fall under this rubric.

Figure 6.3 The social welfare matrix concept of social benefit

individual; in other words, social assistance benefits comprise any form of social security or social welfare which is outside a social insurance scheme.

A social insurance scheme is any scheme in which employees, other workers or non-employed persons are obliged or encouraged by general government or by employers (in the case of employees) to participate, through contributions, in a scheme of insurance against one or more of the twelve risks or needs specified at the left of Figure 6.3 (*ESA95*, para. 4.88). Social insurance schemes may be organised and run by government units or by private units. By contrast, social assistance schemes are organised and run only by government units or by non-profit institutions serving households.

When an individual person takes out an insurance policy in his or her own name, on his or her own initiative independently of a requirement by an employer or by the government, then the policy does not count as *social insurance* but is called an 'individual policy'. Individual policies may also be taken out, subject to the same definitional conditions, by institutional units other than persons. The payment of premiums under, and the claims made upon, such individual policies will be discussed subsequently: non-life insurance individual policies will be discussed in this chapter; life insurance individual policies will be mentioned in Chapter 7.

As shown in the column headings of Figure 6.3 there are three main types of social insurance schemes, and one of these (private funded schemes) has two sub-categories of social insurance schemes, all dependent upon social contributions, and there is a fourth category of social assistance schemes, which is the category not dependent upon social contributions.

First, a social insurance scheme may be organised by government units to cover either the entire community or large sections of the community. Any such government-organised scheme is called a *social security scheme* and one of its features is that the social 'benefits paid to individuals, or households, are not necessarily determined by the amounts previously paid in contributions, while the levels of the benefits paid out to the community as a whole may be varied in accordance with the requirements of the government's overall economic policy' (*SNA93*, para. 8.64). Generally, the social security funds established by social security schemes are managed separately from other government funds by separate government units but such funds remain the property of the government and are not the property of the beneficiaries of the scheme (*ESA95*, Annex III, para. 4, p. 267).

Second, a social insurance scheme may be organised by a private institutional unit on a funded basis with contributions (overall) intended to cover payouts (overall). However, note that in this context a scheme organised by a government institutional unit for its own employees only is included under the rubric 'private scheme' because of its similarity to other such schemes. There are two sub-categories of such private funded schemes. In the first sub-category, the social contributions are paid to a 'third party' such as an insurance enterprise or an autonomous pension fund, where the third party is a separate institutional unit from both the employers and the employees. In the second sub-category, the employer maintains a special reserve, segregated from the employer's other reserves, but the separate fund does not constitute a separate institutional unit. Such a fund is referred to as a 'non-autonomous pension fund'.

Third, a social insurance scheme may be organised by a private unit (including a government unit for its own employees only) in an unfunded way. The term 'unfunded' means that the employer pays social benefits to employees, former employees, or dependants of employees or former employees out of the employer's own resources, without creating a special reserve for that purpose. Note that an employer who runs a funded scheme (say, in respect of retirement) may also have an unfunded scheme in respect of other needs or risks (say, in respect of sickness or maternity pay).

The fourth and last type of scheme in Figure 6.3 is the type of scheme called by the SNA93/ESA95 'social assistance' and this type of scheme involves only government units or non-profit institutions serving households. Social assistance leads to social benefits payable outside any social insurance scheme and to social transfers in kind, and each of these will be explained shortly.

Social benefits are benefits which may be paid, under any scheme, in cash or in kind in response to any of the twelve specified needs or risks. An example of a social benefit in cash would be the payment of an age or retirement pension; an example of a social benefit in kind would be the provision of free housing for the elderly. Other examples would be sickness pay (social benefit in cash), provision of medical treatment without charge (social benefit in kind). Note that reimbursement, by a social insurance scheme or under a social assistance scheme, of approved expenditure by the household (such as medical expenses) is classified as the provision of a benefit in kind (*SNA93*, para. 8.101).

The distinction between benefits in cash and benefits in kind is important, because (as shown in Figure 6.1) only benefits in cash are recorded in Account II.2: Secondary distribution of income account (and Account II.2 also records all other current transfers in cash). Benefits in kind are recorded in Account II.3: Redistribution of income in kind account. For social security schemes and for social assistance schemes the SNA93/ESA95 makes and maintains a rigorous distinction between social benefits paid in cash (recorded in Account II.2) and social benefits paid in kind (recorded in Account II.3). For private funded schemes and for private unfunded schemes, the SNA93/ESA95 makes no distinction between social benefits in cash and social benefits in kind (if any) and these social benefits are all recorded in Account II.2 (*SNA93*, paras 8.79 and 8.80). The convention is that private funded benefits cannot be social transfers in kind and the same convention is then applied to private unfunded benefits (even though, very occasionally, these may occur in kind – for example, the provision of retirement homes).

Social benefits (whether in cash or in kind) become payable when a contingency related to any of the specified risks or needs occurs in a way that would adversely affect the welfare of households either by reducing income or by imposing additional demands on their resources or both.

In Figure 6.3, there are five types and sub-categories of scheme as shown in the column headings and in the case of social security schemes and social assistance schemes a distinction is made and maintained between social benefits in cash and social benefits in kind. Thus Figure 6.3 has in all seven columns, numbered by the numbers in squares. There are twelve specified types of risk or need as given in the row headings, numbered by the numbers in circles. With its seven columns and twelve rows, Figure 6.3 forms a matrix which I call the 'social welfare matrix'. In the social welfare matrix there are $7 \times 12 = 84$ boxes or compartments, each of which I shall call a 'social welfare possibility'. (The magnitude of the number 84 indicates why social welfare is a complex subject!) As indicated, a scheme does not have to cover *all* the social welfare possibilities in its column; many schemes focus upon social welfare possibilities involving only old age (that is, retirement) and survivors (social benefits for surviving dependants), but some schemes may cover other social welfare possibilities, and social security schemes and social assistance schemes generally cover all social welfare possibilities.

The concept of a social benefit is thus of a benefit intended to cover any one of the eighty-four social welfare possibilities in Figure 6.3 and the concept of a social benefit must thus be understood in terms of the social welfare matrix's two dimensions of (1) the type of risk or need covered (as per the specified list), and (2) the type of scheme under which the social benefit is paid (with, where applicable, a distinction being made between a social benefit in cash and a social benefit in kind). Additionally, the classification categories of social benefit are extended to cover a few items of transfers in kind which are not related to the twelve specified risks or needs, but which are most conveniently classified here because they also (along with social benefits in kind in the strict sense of 'social benefits') form part of final consumption expenditure by general government and by non-profit institutions serving households (as will be explained in Section 6.4).

Given this understanding through the social welfare matrix of the complex concept of a social benefit, we can consider the classification of the categories of social benefit used in the SNA93/ESA95. In theory, it would be possible to have an eighty-four-fold classification system but this would produce an unmanageable number of items to be reported in the context of national accounts (although, of course, in the context of a publication dealing separately with social welfare statistics such a detailed classification system might be more appropriate). The SNA93/ESA95 adopts a more manageable classification system of two main categories of social benefits – namely, social benefits in cash and social benefits in kind – with, under each, a relatively small number of different sub-categories, all of which are given in Figure 6.2.

The remainder of this section deals with social benefits in cash; social benefits in kind are discussed in Section 6.4.

As shown in Figure 6.2, social benefits in cash are officially called *social benefits other than social transfers in kind*, D.62. This category has to be understood as an aggregate of its four main sub-categories.

Social security benefits in cash, D.621, comprises social insurance benefits payable in cash to households by social security schemes. Using Figure 6.3, this is simply the aggregate of any and all social benefits paid in the first column of Figure 6.3. The main benefits would relate to the first eight rows of Figure 6.3 (*SNA93*, para. 8.78).

Private funded social benefits, D.622, comprises social insurance benefits payable to households by insurance enterprises or other institutional units administering private funded social insurance schemes (including funded government schemes for government's own employees). Using Figure 6.3, and noting that in this sub-category no distinction is made between social benefits in cash and social benefits in kind (if any), D.622 is simply the aggregate of any and all social benefits paid in the third and fourth columns of Figure 6.3. One could speculate that the main benefits covered under such schemes would in all likelihood relate to the second to sixth rows inclusive – sickness through survivors – of Figure 6.3, and would relate especially to old age and survivors in the case of autonomous pension funds.

Unfunded employee social benefits, D.623, comprises benefits payable by employers administering unfunded social insurance schemes. Typically these benefits would include: payment of normal or reduced wages during periods of absence from work as a result of ill health, accidents, or maternity; payment of education allowances in respect of dependants; payment of retirement or survivors' pensions; payment of redundancy payments in the event of termination of employment. Because, in these schemes no distinction is made between benefits in cash and benefits in kind, D.623 benefits also includes such items as general medical services not related to the employee's work or the provision of convalescent or retirement homes (*SNA93*, para. 8.80). D.623 is simply the aggregate of any and all social benefits paid in the fifth column of Figure 6.3.

Social assistance benefits in cash, D.624, comprises current transfers payable in cash to households by government units or non-profit institutions serving households which payments meet any of the twelve specified risks or needs but which are differentiated by being outside the scope of any social insurance scheme with social contributions. Social *assistance* benefits, by definition, do not depend upon social contributions; and the other way round: any social benefit paid without social contributions is classified as social assistance. For example, the schemes of social welfare run in Australia by the government have never had any element of social contribution (apart from 'workers' compensation' for injuries at work), and so, apart from workers' compensation, all Australian social benefits from the government are classified as social *assistance* benefits. (In Australia, the provision of medical care does have a contribution under the 'medicare' scheme, but the 'medicare' benefits are provided in kind.) D.624 is simply the aggregate of any and all social benefits paid in the sixth column of Figure 6.3.

Note that, because of the restriction to the twelve specified risks or needs, transfers in cash or in kind made to households because of natural disasters (such as floods or earthquakes) are not recorded as social benefits but are recorded under other current transfers (*SNA93*, para. 8.83), specifically under *miscellaneous current transfers*, D.75.

All these social benefits in cash – technically, *social benefits other than social transfers in kind*, D.62 – are kept separate from social benefits in kind because the D.62 benefits are recorded in Account II.2: Secondary distribution of income account. The D.62 benefits paid by general government and by non-profit institutions serving households are outlays in cash by general government and non-profit institutions serving households, but these D.62 benefits are transfers and so do *not* form part of final consumption expenditure by general government and non-profit institutions serving households. By contrast, the social benefits in kind – technically, *social transfers in kind*, D.63 – which are made only by government and non-profit institutions serving households *do* form part of final consumption expenditure by general government or by non-profit institutions serving households. This will be explained in the following section.

Table 6.1 shows the structure of social benefits other than social transfers in kind (that is, social benefits in cash) in the United Kingdom in 1997 paid by two sectors of the economy: general government and insurance corporations and pension funds. Payments by these two sectors together account for 97.6 per cent of social benefits in cash paid by the United Kingdom economy to residents and non-residents, so the omitted sectors in Table 6.1 are only of quantitatively minor importance.

Table 6.1 serves several purposes. First, Table 6.1 shows the application of the SNA93/ESA95 classification of social benefits, D.621, D.622, D.623 and D.624, and the footnotes to Table 6.1 show how these categories apply to the list of twelve specified risks or needs of Figure 6.3 (so that the whole of Table 6.1 including the footnotes should be studied carefully in the framework of Figure 6.3). Second, Table 6.1 demonstrates the quantitative importance of social benefits; the United Kingdom's gross domestic product in 1997 was £803 889 million, so we can see that the total of social benefits (in cash) in relative terms amounted to a redistribution of no less than one-fifth of gross domestic product. Third, Table 6.1 serves as an introduction to some of the important entries in the secondary distribution of income account, to be given for the United Kingdom in Table 6.3 and for Australia in Table 6.4 (pp. 302–3 and 316–17). Especially, Table 6.1 explains the two main sources of the social benefits received by households (as a resource) in the secondary distribution of income account.

Table 6.1 should be studied in detail even though, for reasons of space, the following remarks must be kept brief. It can be seen that social security benefits in cash, D.621, largely from the United Kingdom's National Insurance scheme, are matched in size by privated funded social benefits, D.622, but we can also see that the United Kingdom's system of social assistance benefits in cash (that is, cash benefits outside and in addition to the National Insurance scheme), D.624, is the largest single category.

The D.621 social security benefits in cash are those benefits funded by social contributions from employers, from employees and from others, and subsequently in Table 6.2 we shall see how these contributions match up against the social benefits paid.

But before we consider social contributions we need to consider social benefits in kind.

Table 6.1
Social benefits other than social transfers in kind
in the United Kingdom economy, 1997

SNA93/ESA95 identification code	SNA93/ESA95 name	£ million
S.13	**General government** [a]	
D.621	Social security benefits in cash [b]	44 582
D.623	Unfunded employee social benefits[c]	14 128
D.624	Social assistance benefits in cash[d]	57 592
D.62	Social benefits other than social transfers in kind (S.13 only)	116 302
S.125	**Insurance corporations and pension funds**	
D.622	Private funded social benefits	45 482
D.623	Unfunded employee social benefits	52
D.62	Social benefits other than social transfers in kind (S.125 only)	45 534
S.1	**UK total economy**	
D.62	Social benefits other than social transfers in kind [e]	165 809

(a) The sum of data for central government, S.1311, and local government, S.1313.

(b) Of which: £43 223 mn are National Insurance fund benefits comprising (see list in Figure 6.3): (unemployment) unemployment benefit/jobseekers' allowance, £623 mn; (sickness) statutory sick pay, £27 mn; (invalidity and so on) incapacity benefit, £7580 mn; (old age) retirement pensions; £33 458 mn; (survivors) widows and guardians' allowances, £988 mn; (maternity) statutory maternity pay, £512 mn; maternity benefit, £35 mn. Other D.621 social benefits are: (unemployment) redundancy fund benefit, £93 mn; social fund benefit, £164 mn; and benefits paid to overseas residents, £1102 mn.

(c) Comprising: payments from central government: unfunded pensions paid, £4691 mn; notionally funded pensions paid, £7190 mn; other unfunded employee benefits, £253 mn; and payments from local government: unfunded pensions paid, £1603 mn; and other unfunded employee benefits; £391 mn.

(d) Comprising (see list in Figure 6.3): payments from central government: (old age, survivors) war pensions and allowances, £1311 mn; (family) family benefits, £9339 mn; (general neediness) income support, £12 050 mn; other social security benefits, £15 467 mn; other grants to households, £2986 mn; income tax reliefs, £2494 mn; and payments from local government: (housing) rent rebates, £5485 mn; rent allowances, £5866 mn; and (education) student grants, £2594 mn.

(e) This total includes, in addition to the sub-total for general government, S.13, and the sub-total for insurance corporations, S.125, above, the following sectoral sub-totals (see Table 6.3 below): non-financial corporations, S.11, £2872 mn; financial corporations other than S.125, £204 mn; households and non-profit institutions serving households, S.14 + S.15, £897 million. Note as memorandum items that for the rest of the world, S.2, £615 million of D.62 social benefits was paid and £1179 million of D.62 social benefits was received.

Sources: Office for National Statistics, *United Kingdom National Accounts The Blue Book 1999 edition*, tables 1.7.4, 4.4.4, 5.24S, and 5.34S; pp. 62–3, 166, 187 and 197; also Table 6.3 below.

6.4   Social benefits in kind and general government final consumption

We now consider social benefits in kind and their relation to final consumption expenditure by general government and by non-profit institutions serving households. In the SNA93/ESA95 social benefits in kind are called *social transfers in kind*, D.63 (Figure 6.2). The official definition of 'social transfers in kind' is:

> Social transfers in kind (D.63) consist of *individual* goods and services [goods and services consumed by individuals and not collectively] provided as transfers in kind to individual [that is, particular] households by government units and NPISHs [non-profit institutions serving households], whether purchased on the market [by government units or NPISHs] or produced as non-market output by government units or NPISHs. They [the transfers in kind of individual goods and services] may be financed out of taxation, other government income or social security contributions, or out of donations and property income in the case of NPISHs (*ESA95*, para. 4.104, italics added and with my clarifying interpolations in square brackets).

In this definition a key technical word to note is the italicised occurrence of 'individual'; this distinguishes the goods and services thus provided from the *collective* services provided to the community as a whole. The meaning of the words 'individual' and 'collective' (as opposites to each other) will be explained fully in this section. Note also that these individual goods and services are provided free of charge, or at prices not economically significant, to households. Note further that the only providers of individual goods and services as social transfers in kind are (1) general government, and (2) non-profit institutions serving households. We continue with the explanation of the categories in Figure 6.2 (but refer also to Figure 6.3).

There are two main sub-categories of social transfers in kind, *social benefits in kind*, D.631, and *transfers of individual non-market goods and services*, D.632. As I shall explain, the classification category of transfers of individual non-market services is a residual category, and may cover more than strictly social benefits.

Social benefits in kind, D. 631, are social transfers in kind which relieve households of one or more of the twelve specified needs or risks. These transfers are subdivided into three sub-sub-categories.

First, *social security benefits, reimbursements*, D.6311, consist of reimbursements to a household by a social security fund of an approved expenditure made by the household; under this convention, the household acquiring the approved good or service is treated as an agent of the social security fund in securing the provision of the approved good or service, and consequently the approved good or service is treated as a benefit in kind provided by the social security fund. Such approved expenditures usually concern expenditures on medical or dental treatments, medicines, hospital bills, and so on. D.6311 is a class of benefits in the second column of Figure 6.3, but there are other benefits in this column which do not come under D.6311.

Second, *other social security benefits in kind*, D.6312, are social transfers in kind, other than reimbursements, made by social security funds to households. These are services provided by market or non-market producers directly to households, but paid for by the social security fund. Again, the provision of these benefits mainly concerns medical etc. treatment. D.6312 is another class of benefits in the second column of Figure 6.3.

You can appreciate that there is not a great deal of difference between the situation where a social security fund acts directly to procure such services for a household (D.6312) or the situation where the household acts as an agent of the social security fund to procure the service and is reimbursed for its approved expenditure (D.6311). However, the difference may be important to the household which has greater freedom of choice under the reimbursement arrangement.

Third, *social assistance benefits in kind*, D.6313, are social transfers in kind, provided to households by government units, that are similar to social security benefits in kind (D.6312) but are not provided by a social security fund. Often these benefits are those made available to those in the community who are not within the scope of a social security scheme. Sometimes D.6313 benefits are made available to supplement D.6312 benefits (that is, D.6313 benefits are over and above the D.6312 benefits normally available to a household within a social security scheme). Examples of such D.6313 social assistance benefits in kind are housing, dwelling allowance, day nurseries (*ESA95*, para. 4.105). The D.6313 social benefits are a class of benefits occurring in the last column of Figure 6.3.

The second sub-category of social transfers in kind is *transfers of individual non-market goods and services*, D.632. This is a residual category. The official definition of 'transfers of individual non-market goods or services' is (in part):

> Transfers of individual non-market goods or services (D.632) consist of goods or services provided to individual households free or at prices which are not

economically significant, by non-market producers of government units or NPISHs (*ESA95*, para. 4.106).

This is a residual category which covers all of general government individual consumption expenditure that is not covered by social benefits in kind, D.631, and this statement will be explained shortly.

With regard to transfers of individual non-market goods and services, individual services consist mainly of education services and medical services, but within the rubric of social welfare other services such as housing are also included, and furthermore, outside the scope of the twelve specified risks or needs services such as sport and recreation, cultural services and the collection of household refuse are classified as social transfers in kind, and are therefore included under the heading social benefits.

In order to understand this, it is necessary to explain with the aid of Figure 6.4 the connection between social transfers in kind, D.63, and individual consumption expenditure, P.31, by general government and by non-profit institutions serving households. To anticipate, one of the two main purposes of Figure 6.4 is to explain that individual consumption expenditure, P.31, by general government is equal (by definition) to social transfers in kind, D.63, by general government, and that individual consumption expenditure, P.31, by non-profit institutions serving households is equal (by definition) to social transfers in kind, D.63, by non-profit institutions serving households.

The reason for these equalities (namely, P.31 = D.63 for each of general government and non-profit institutions serving households) is very straightforward and is as follows. In order to be able to make these D.63 transfers (or distributions) in kind to households, general government and non-profit institutions serving households have first to obtain the individual goods and services so distributed, and the way of obtaining them is through P.31 final consumption expenditure.

The other main purpose of Figure 6.4 is to explain the difference between actual individual consumption [by households], P.41, and final consumption expenditure [by households], P.31.

Figure 6.4 (adapted from *ESA95*, p. 52) shows, across the top, the three sectors with which we are presently concerned in relation to the expenditures with which we are presently concerned, and also, at the right, a column for the row totals. Down the left are the two sorts of final consumption expenditures (transactions in goods and services) with which we are presently concerned, and also, at the bottom, a row for the column totals. This gives a four column by three row matrix, with, at the intersection of each row and column, a category of final consumption expenditure.

In Chapter 3 we gave the definition of 'final consumption expenditure' as expenditure incurred by resident institutional units on goods or services that are used for the direct satisfaction of individual needs or wants or the collective needs of the members of the community. Chapter 3 also explained briefly the distinction between individual consumption expenditure, P.31, and collective consumption expenditure, P.32.

Individual consumption expenditure is to meet the needs of individuals who could in principle be identified or singled out by name as benefitting from the expenditure (for example, government expenditure on education), while collective consumption expenditure is to meet the needs of the community collectively, where there is in principle no sensible way in which the beneficiaries of the expenditure could be identified or singled out by name (for example, government expenditure on street lighting). Note that the division individual/collective applies only to current final consumption expenditure; it is not applied to gross capital formation (this is probably because such a division does not in practice occur in relation to capital formation; for example, in theory it is possible that general government could build new dwellings for transfer to households without charge (that is, the freehold or ownership of the dwelling being transferred) but this sort of arrangement generally does not occur).

The official definition of 'goods and services for individual consumption' is as follows:

> Goods and services for individual consumption ('individual goods and services') are *acquired* by a household and used to satisfy the needs and wants of members of that household. Individual goods and services have the following characteristics:
>
> a) it must be possible to observe and record the acquisition of the good or service by an individual household or member thereof and also the time at which it [the acquisition] took place;
>
> b) the household must have agreed to the provision of the good or service and take whatever action is necessary to make it possible, for example by attending a school or clinic;
>
> c) the good or service must be such that its acquisition by one household or person, or possibly by a small, restricted group of persons, precludes its acquisition by other households or persons (*ESA95*, para. 3.82, italics added and with my clarifying interpolation in square brackets).

	Sector making expenditure			Total acquisitions (row sum)
	General government, S.13	Non-profit institutions serving households, S.15	Households, S.14	
Individual consumption expenditure, P.31/P.41	Individual consumption expenditure by general government, P.31 *equals* Social benefits in kind, D.631 *plus* Transfers of individual non-market goods and services, D.632 *which together comprise* Social transfers in kind, D.63	Individual consumption expenditure by NPISHs, P.31 *equals* Social benefits in kind, D.631 *plus* Transfers of individual non-market goods and services, D.632 *which together comprise* Social transfers in kind, D.63	Individual consumption expenditure by households, P.31	Households' actual individual consumption, P.41
Collective consumption expenditure, P.32/P.42	Collective consumption expenditure, P.32	Not applicable	Not applicable	General government's actual collective consumption, P.42
Total (column sum)	General government's final consumption expenditure, P.3	NPISHs' final consumption expenditure, P.31	Households' final consumption expenditure, P.31	Actual final consumption, P.4 = Final consumption expenditure, P.3

Figure 6.4 Final consumption expenditure and social transfers in kind

282

Note the use of the word 'acquired' which is meant to cover both acquisition by expenditure made by the household itself and also acquisition by a transfer in kind from the government or from a non-profit institution serving households.

The category of *individual* goods and services must be understood by contrast with its opposite, *collective* services. The official definition of 'collective services' is as follows:

> Services for collective consumption ('collective services') are provided simultaneously to all members of the community or all members of a particular section of the community, such as all households living in a particular region. Collective services have the following characteristics:
>
> a) they can be delivered simultaneously to every member of the community or to particular sections of the community, such as those in a particular region or locality;
>
> b) the use of such services is usually passive and does not require the explicit agreement or active participation of all the individuals concerned;
>
> c) the provision of a collective service to one individual does not reduce the amount available to others in the same community or section of the community. There is no rivalry in acquisition (*ESA95*, para. 3.83).

Each of individual goods and services and collective services has to be obtained by final consumption expenditure, hence there are two categories of final consumption expenditure: *individual consumption expenditure*, P.31, and *collective consumption expenditure*, P.32. Individual consumption expenditure can be made by households, by general government and by non-profit institutions serving households (and these are the only sectors in the economy to which such final consumption expenditure is ascribed). Collective consumption expenditure can be made only by general government.

All household final consumption expenditure is, by definition, on individual goods and services. If you study the definitions and especially the criteria laid down in the definitions, you will appreciate that the goods and services involved in household final consumption expenditure satisfy all three criteria laid down in the definition of 'individual goods and services' and, by strong contrast, meet none of the three criteria laid down in the definition of 'collective services'.

The goods and services provided by non-profit institutions serving households are all by convention treated as individual, largely because, although the provision may be to a group (the members of the non-profit institution), the services are far more likely fully to meet the three criteria laid down in the definition for 'individual goods and services' than they are fully to meet the three criteria laid down in the definition for 'collective services'.

General government also makes expenditures on goods and services intended for use by individual households (or members thereof). Typically, such expenditures by general government are expenditures on education and health. Although the expenditure may be incurred directly by the general government, so making it count as final consumption expenditure ascribed to the sector of general government (to the sector directly incurring the expenditure), because of the transfer of the individual good or service to individual households we can also note that these goods and services are *acquired* by those households (even though those households have not themselves paid for the goods and services). Schematically:

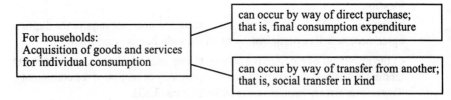

The important economic characteristic of an individual good or service is that its acquisition by one household, person or group of persons (whether by way of direct purchase or by way of social transfer) usually brings no, or relatively little, benefit to others in the community. This means that when a government or non-profit institution serving households incurs expenditure on obtaining and transferring an individual good or service 'it must decide not only how much to spend in total but how to allocate, or distribute, the goods or services among individual members of the community. From the point of view of economic and social policy, the way in which they [government-provided individual goods or services] are distributed may be as important as the total amount spent' (*SNA93*, para. 9.82, with my clarifying interpolation in square brackets).

The following are the types of expenditure which government makes in order to obtain individual goods and services:

Categories of general government final consumption expenditure treated as government individual consumption expenditure
(Classification of the Functions of the Government (COFOG) identification numbers)

---

04   Education affairs and services
05   Health affairs and services
06   Social security and welfare affairs and services
07   Housing and community amenity and services*
08   Recreational, cultural and religious affairs and services*
12   Transportation and communication affairs and services*

*   Only that part of this expenditure which is transferred to individual households (for example, household refuse collection, bus passes for age pensioners).

(Note that this classification excludes expenditures related to *general* administration, regulation, or research which occurs under these headings; for example, expenditures incurred by Ministries of Health or Education at a *national* level are included in collective consumption expenditures as such expenditures are concerned with general matters of policy, standards and regulation, which are not consumed by any identifiable households; on the other hand overhead expenses connected with the administration or functioning of *particular* hospitals or schools are included in individual expenditures – *SNA93*, para. 9.86; also para. 9.87, and pp. 599–600, or *ESA95*, para. 3.85 and pp. 301–2 or *UK NACSM*, pp. 497–501, for the listed categories in the Classification of the Functions of the Government (COFOG).)

In Figure 6.4, we can see, in the first three columns of the first row of the matrix, that individual consumption expenditure, P.31, is made by general government, by non-profit institutions serving households, and by households. But in the case of both general government and non-profit institutions serving households these expenditures on individual goods and services are made for the purpose of transferring these as D.63 social transfers in kind to households. Consequently, households (as a sector) actually obtain, or actually benefit from, more than their own P.31 individual consumption expenditure; they benefit from the P.31 individual consumption expenditure by general government and by non-profit institutions serving households ('NPISHs'). Accordingly, Figure 6.4 shows in the last column the 'total acquisitions' of individual goods and services by households, where total acquisitions of individual goods and services by households is defined as:

Total acquisitions of individual goods and services by households	=	P.31 Final consumption expenditure by households	+	P.31 Final consumption expenditure by general government (= D.63 Social transfers in kind by general government to households)	+	P.31 Final consumption expenditure by NPISHs (= D.63 Social transfers in kind by NPISHs to households)

The total acquisitions of individual goods and services by households is called *actual individual consumption*, P.41.

To illustrate for the United Kingdom in 1997 (with data from the *Blue Book 1999 edition*, tables 1.6.0 (for P.31), 1.7.5 and 1.7.6 (for D.63 and P.41), pp. 39, 64–7):

$$
\begin{array}{l}
\text{Actual individual} \\
\text{consumption,} \\
\text{P.41}
\end{array}
= \underset{\text{(P.31 Households)}}{£498\ 307\ \text{mn}} + \underset{\substack{\text{(P.31 Government)} \\ \text{= D.63 Government)}}}{£87\ 721\ \text{mn}} + \underset{\substack{\text{(P.31 NPISHs} \\ \text{= D.63 NPISHs)}}}{£18\ 725\ \text{mn}}
$$

$$
= \underset{\text{(P.41 Households)}}{£604\ 753\ \text{mn}}
$$

To illustrate for Australia in 1997–98 (with data from *Australian System of National Accounts 1997*–98, tables 2.15, 2.20, 2.21, pp. 55 and 60–61, but where data on non-profit institutions serving households is simply included with households, so the first number in the equation is for households and NPISHs' P.31 and the second number is for general government's P.31):

$$
\begin{array}{l}
\text{Actual individual} \\
\text{consumption,} \\
\text{P.41}
\end{array}
= \underset{\text{(P.31 Households and NPISHs)}}{\$332\ 311\ \text{mn}} + \underset{\substack{\text{(P.31 Government} \\ \text{= D.63 Government)}}}{\$51\ 878\ \text{mn}}
$$

$$
= \underset{\text{(P.41 Households)}}{\$384\ 189\ \text{mn}}
$$

In the United Kingdom, individual final consumption expenditure by households is augmented by 17.6 per cent by individual final consumption expenditure by general government (transferred to households as D.63 social transfers in kind), and is augmented by a further 3.8 per cent by individual final consumption expenditure by non-profit institutions serving households (transferred to households as D.63 social transfers in kind), making a total augmentation of 21.4 per cent. In Australia, individual consumption expenditure by households and non-profit institutions serving households is augmented by 15.6 per cent by individual consumption expenditure by general government (transferred to households as D.63 social transfers in kind). This demonstrates the considerable quantitative significance of the D.63 social transfers in kind to the welfare of households.

Conversely, and self-evidently by the transfer of *all* their individual consumption expenditure to households, the sector of general government records, in principle, no *actual* individual consumption, and the sector of non-profit institutions serving households records, in principle, no *actual* individual consumption. Only the household sector has actual individual consumption.

What is the reason for distinguishing, in the case of households, between P.31 final consumption expenditure and P.41 actual final consumption? The SNA93 explains:

> The term "consumption" on its own can be ambiguous and misleading. Sometimes it is used by economists to refer to consumption *expenditures*, sometimes to *acquisitions* of consumption goods and services and sometimes to the *physical use* of the goods and services for the direct satisfaction of human needs or wants. By distinguishing between consumption expenditure and actual final consumption, such ambiguity can be avoided. When consumption is recorded on an expenditure basis, the purpose is to identify the institutional units that incur the expenditures and hence control and finance the amounts of such expenditures. When consumption is recorded on an acquisitions basis, the purpose is to identify the units that actually acquire the goods and services and benefit from their use, either immediately or subsequently. The value of total final consumption is the same, however, whichever basis is used (*SNA93*, para. 9.74, italics added).

Returning to Figure 6.4, collective consumption expenditure, P.32, is ascribed only to general government and is not applicable in the case of either non-profit institutions serving households or households. Furthermore of course and by definition, collective consumption expenditure, although benefitting the community collectively, is not 'transferred' to households in the way that general government final consumption expenditure on individual goods and services is. Consequently, *actual collective consumption*, P.42, is always equal to *collective consumption expenditure*, P.32. The following are the types of expenditure which government makes in order to provide collective services:

Categories of general government final consumption expenditure treated as collective consumption expenditure

(Classification of the Functions of Government (COFOG) identification numbers)

01	General public services
02	Defence affairs and services
03	Public order and safety affairs
07	Housing and community amenity and services*
08	Recreational, cultural and religious affairs and services*
09	Fuel and energy affairs and services
10	Agriculture, forestry, fishing and hunting affairs and services
11	Mining and mineral resource affairs and services, other than fuels; manufacturing affairs and services; and construction affairs and services
12	Transportation and communication affairs and services*
13	Other economic affairs and services
14	Expenditures not classified by major group

* Excluding that part of this expenditure which is identifiably transferred to individual households.

(Note that in the case of expenditures which benefit both enterprises and households *and* where it is not possible to separate the services which benefit households from the services which benefit enterprises, then these expenditures are classified as collective final expenditure – *SNA93*, para. 9.88.)

For general government, final consumption expenditure, P.3, in total is equal to the sum of individual consumption expenditure, P.31, and collective consumption expenditure, P.32, and this is shown by summing down the first column of Figure 6.4 and giving the result in the last row (this is why general government *total* final consumption expenditure has to be identified by the overall code P.3).

Because of the non-applicability of collective consumption to either of non-profit institutions serving households or households, their total final consumption expenditure is simply their P.31 individual consumption expenditure.

Total final consumption expenditure in the economy as a whole is the same whether it is measured as the sum of all the P.31 individual consumption expenditures and the P.32 collective consumption expenditure (that is, measured as a P.3 total) or whether it is measured as the sum of the P.41 actual individual consumption and the P.42 actual collective consumption (that is, measured as a P.4 total). This is shown in the bottom right of Figure 6.4.

The discussion of D.63 social transfers in kind will be concluded in Section 6.7.

6.5 Social contributions and compensation of employees

Social contributions are contributions made to a social insurance scheme in order to secure entitlement to social benefits. These contributions may be paid by the employer (on behalf of an employee), by the employee, by a self-employed person, and (occasionally) by a non-employed person. Non-resident institutional units may also pay social contributions. In relation to employees, social contributions paid by the employer form part of compensation of employees:

> Employers' actual social contributions on behalf of their employees are usually paid directly to social security funds, insurance companies or pension funds. The underlying economic reality is that the contribution is part of the remuneration package. This is represented in the accounts by recording the amount firstly as part of compensation of employees (in the generation of income account) and secondly as a current transfer from the household (along with employee contributions) to the social security fund or whatever (in the secondary distribution of income account) (*UK NACSM*, para. 5.64).

In the preceding chapter we saw that in the household sector's balance of primary incomes, *compensation of employees*, D.1, was a large resource on the allocation of primary income account. Most households derive most of their primary income by working as employees. The employment relationship exists when there is an agreement of some sort between an enterprise and a person for the person to work for the enterprise in return for remuneration; the dividing line between an employee and an independent sub-contractor, or self-employed person, is sometimes expressed in the law relating to employment by saying that an employee works under a contract *of service*, with the employer having the right to command and the employee having the duty to obey, while a self-employed person works under a contract *for services*, with the self-employed person having only an obligation to do a certain job or jobs rather than generally to perform required duties.

We need to consider the definition and structure of compensation of employees. The official definition of 'compensation of employees' is:

> Compensation of employees (D.1) is defined as the *total* remuneration, in cash or in kind, payable by an employer to an employee in return for work done by the latter during the accounting period (*ESA95*, para. 4.02, with italics added to indicate that the SNA93/ESA95 takes an inclusive and broad view of the compensation package to cover all benefits which the employee derives from employment).

What is meant by 'total remuneration'? The structure of compensation of employees is shown in Figure 6.5.

We can see that total remuneration covers four types of remuneration: wages and salaries in cash; wages and salaries in kind (but the SNA93/ESA95 does not record the distinction between wages and salaries in cash and wages and salaries in kind); employers' actual social contributions; and employers' imputed social contributions. Each of these needs to be well understood and each will be explained in turn.

First, we discuss wages and salaries in cash. This discussion raises the important accounting convention used in the SNA93/ESA95 of *rerouting*. Rerouting is used in the SNA93/ESA95 whenever it is necessary 'to bring out the economic substance *behind* the transaction' (*ESA95*, para. 1.39, italics added). With regard to wages and salaries in cash, rerouting applies as follows.

Wages and salaries in cash is measured *before* deduction of income tax payable by the employee and the whole amount is to be credited as (before tax) income of the employee. However, in the income tax systems of most countries, the method of taxing compensation of employees is the 'pay as you earn' (or PAYE) system, whereby the employer deducts from each employee's periodic (before tax) wage or salary an amount to cover income tax due on that remuneration and the employer then sends this tax deduction *directly* to the government (or more precisely, the income tax authority). Consequently the employer actually pays to each employee the net of income tax wage or salary. The routing of the transactions/payments which *actually* occurs under this arrangement can be depicted as follows:

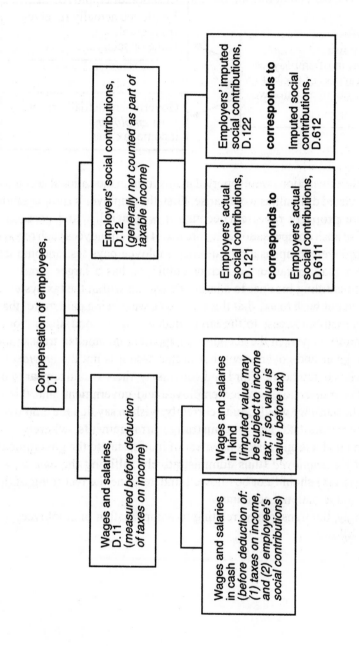

Figure 6.5 Composition of compensation of employees

Actual route of transactions

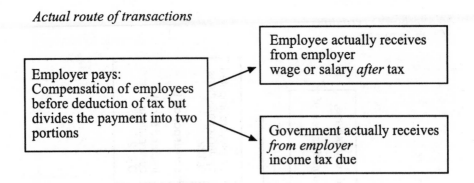

However, if the transactions were reported in this form in the national accounts, then several related difficulties would arise. First, the employee's compensation would not be properly reported because it is generally, and correctly, understood that such compensation is before tax. If two employees each receive the same employee compensation but one employee pays less income tax than the other (say, because the former employee has a larger family of dependants so entitling him/her to a larger deduction within the tax system), then we would not wish to say that this employee was 'being paid more' than the employee without access to the larger deductions. Second, there would rather awkwardly appear in the accounts an apparent income tax transaction between employer and government, but in this case it is not the *employer's* income which is being taxed. Third and conversely, there would appear to be no income tax transaction between employee and government, and this is quite wrong because we would, quite correctly, wish to say that the employee was paying income tax. The administrative arrangements, whereby the employer first deducts and makes payment of income tax to the government, *on behalf of the employee* (thus administratively fulfilling the *employee's* liability to pay tax) should not be allowed to determine the recording of the transactions in the national accounts.

Accordingly, the transactions relating to compensation of employees are *rerouted* as follows:

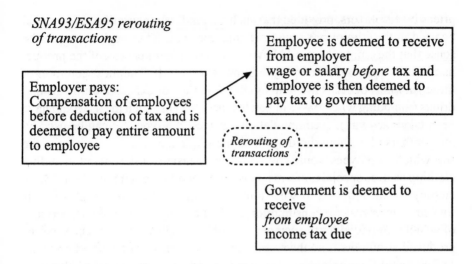

SNA93/ESA95 rerouting of transactions

> **Employer pays:**
> Compensation of employees before deduction of tax and is deemed to pay entire amount to employee

> Employee is deemed to receive from employer
> wage or salary *before* tax and employee is then deemed to pay tax to government

> *Rerouting of transactions*

> Government is deemed to receive
> *from employee*
> income tax due

The practice of rerouting accords with 'the economic substance behind the transaction'.

Wages and salaries in cash includes, besides basic wages and salaries payable at regular intervals (and measured before deduction of income tax), the following sorts of items *paid in cash* (and the list is not to be taken as exhaustive of all possibilities): overtime pay; nightwork pay; pay for working in hazardous circumstances; cost of living allowances; local allowances; expatriation allowances; bonuses (of various sorts); allowances for transport to and from work (but not including allowances or reimbursement of travelling expenses incurred *in the course of* the employee's duties – this 'in the course of duty' expenditure is treated as intermediate consumption expenditure by the employer); holiday pay; housing allowances paid in cash; tips, commissions, and gratuities received by employees.

Tips and so on are another example of a rerouted transaction. Usually a tip is paid directly by a customer to an employee. But what is the economic substance of a tip? The SNA93 argues, quite correctly, that 'these [tips] should be treated as payments for services rendered by the enterprise employing the worker, and should therefore also be included in the output and gross value added of the employing enterprise' (*SNA93*, para. 7.33). Subsequently, the tip can be recorded as compensation of employees.

Second we discuss wages and salaries in kind. Wages and salaries in kind consist of goods and services, or other benefits, provided free or at reduced prices by employers, provided that such 'in kind' compensation can or could be used in the employee's own time and represents additional income in the sense that the employee would have had to pay a market price if the product had been bought by the employee himself or herself. The most common of these 'in kind' benefits are (and again the list is not exhaustive): meals and drinks (including when travelling on business because such meals would have been taken anyway); accommodation services of a type that can be used by all members of the household to which the employee belongs; clothing of the sort which employees would choose to wear outside work (but not including clothing such as special uniforms, worn as a condition of employment, which employees are required to wear under a contract of employment – this is treated as intermediate consumption expenditure by the employer); services of vehicles provided for the personal use of the employee; goods and services produced as outputs from the employer's own processes of production (such as free travel for employees of railways or airlines); the provision of sports, recreation or holiday facilities for employees and their families; transportation to and from work; crèches for the children of employees; bonus shares distributed to employees; the value of interest forgone by the employer when providing a loan at a reduced or zero rate of interest.

Such 'in kind' goods and services are to be valued at basic prices when produced by the employer and at purchasers prices when purchased by the employer.

Wages and salaries do not include expenses of employment which are more properly treated as intermediate consumption by the employer. For example, if the nature of the work requires medical examinations to be performed on employees, then the cost of those medical examinations is intermediate consumption, not 'in kind' compensation of employees. If the employees are accommodated at the place of work in accommodation such as cabins or dormitories which cannot be used by the households to which the employees belong, then the cost of such accommodation is intermediate consumption. If the employee is paid an allowance for the purchase of tools, equipment or special clothing needed exclusively or primarily for undertaking the work for which employed, then any such allowance is intermediate consumption expenditure.

Next we discuss *employers' social contributions*, D.12. The term 'social contributions' is a new term in national accounting and needs to be explained and understood side by side with social benefits. Social contributions are those payments made to secure entitlement to social benefits. Social contributions made by employers may be actual or imputed.

The official definition of 'employers' actual social contributions' is (in part):

> Employers' actual social contributions (D.121) consist of the payments made by employers for the benefit of their employees to insurers ... [insurers comprise] social security funds, insurance enterprises or autonomous as well as non-autonomous pension funds administering social insurance schemes to secure social benefits for their employees (*ESA95*, paras 4.09 and 4.92, with my clarifying and joining interpolation in square brackets).

Employers' actual social contributions, D.121, recorded as part of compensation of employees, D.1, corresponds identically to employers' actual social contributions, D.6111, recorded as part of social contributions and benefits, D.6 (first see Figure 6.5 and then see Figure 6.2). In Figure 6.3, D.6111 social contributions may occur in any of the first four columns (see the identification codes at the top of the columns in Figure 6.3).

The official definition of 'employers' imputed social contributions' is (in part):

> Employers' imputed social contributions (D.122) represent the counterpart to unfunded social benefits ... paid directly by employers to their employees or former employees and other eligible persons without involving an insurance enterprise or autonomous pension fund, and without creating a special fund or segregated reserve for the purpose (*ESA95*, para. 4.10).

Employers' imputed social contributions, D.122, recorded as part of compensation of employees, D.1, corresponds identically to imputed social contributions, D.612, recorded as part of social contributions and benefits, D.6 (first see Figure 6.5 and then see Figure 6.2). In Figure 6.3, D.612 contributions occur only in the fifth column.

In principle, employers' imputed social contributions should be calculated on an actuarial basis of the amount of contributions necessary to secure the entitlement to the social benefits obtainable. In practice, employers' imputed social contributions are often measured simply by 'the unfunded social benefits payable by the enterprise during the same accounting period ... [which] provide sufficient estimates of the contributions and associated imputed remuneration' (*ESA95*, para. 4.99).

Although employers' actual social contributions are paid directly to the social insurance scheme (of whatever sort), the rerouting convention in the

SNA93/ESA95 is different in order to reflect the economic substance behind these payments:

Actual route of transactions

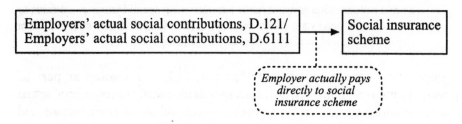

SNA93/ESA95 rerouting of transactions

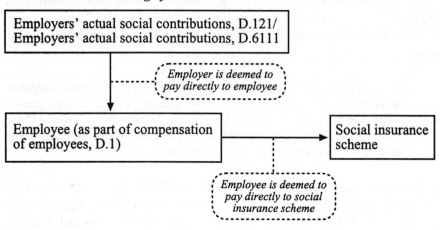

In addition to employers' actual social contributions and imputed social contributions, there are two other types of social contributions (Figure 6.2). Employees' social contributions, D.6112, are social contributions payable by employees to social security schemes, to private funded schemes and to unfunded schemes (if any such payments are made). Social contributions by self-employed and non-employed persons, D.6113, are social contributions payable, *for their own benefit*, by persons who are not employees to schemes which count as social insurance schemes (and which are distinct from individual policies).

In Figure 6.3, D.6112 social contributions may occur in any of the first four columns, while D.6113 social contributions may occur only in the first three columns.

Table 6.2 gives some data on social contributions in the United Kingdom economy in 1997. Table 6.2 serves several purposes. First and foremost, Table 6.2 is intended to emphasise the fact that employers' social contributions are part of compensation of employees – that is, these D.121 (= D.6111) social contributions are rerouted through households. It is an important function of Table 6.2 to show that the SNA93/ESA95 categories D.121 and D.6111 refer to the same transactions. Because of this rerouting, these social contributions form part of the balance of primary incomes, gross, for households. It is very important that this point be fully understood. Second, Table 6.2 demonstrates the application of the SNA93/ESA95 classification categories to real world data, but at the same time shows that although these categories apply, national accounts may use their own names if the latter fit in better with the social insurance schemes applying. Third, Table 6.2 shows how the burden of contributing to social insurance schemes is shared between employers and employees. Fourth, Table 6.2 shows the source for some of the social benefits which were given in Table 6.1.

Table 6.2 should be studied in detail even though, for reasons of space, the following remarks must be kept brief. Table 6.2 shows that employers' social contributions are a quantitatively important part of compensation of employees (13.1 per cent in 1997). This is an important fact to be kept in mind about the SNA93/ESA95 concept of compensation of employees, D.1; the concept is much more than simply the (before tax) pay packet.

Table 6.2 can also be used to see that National Insurance contributions (comprising employer's D.6111 (= D.121) National Insurance social contributions and employees' D.6112 National Insurance contributions together) total £48 758 million; so we can understand the funding of the National Insurance fund social benefits of £43 223 million in Table 6.1 (footnote (*b*)). We can see in this the Beveridge principle of 'benefit in return for contributions' – the basic principle of social *insurance* – and also the principle that in the case of employees there be a 'joint contribution' shared by employee and employer (*Social Insurance and Allied Services*, Report by Sir William Beveridge, November 1942, Cmd. 6404, paras 21 and 355).

We can also see in Table 6.2 the very substantial amount of contributions by employees and by employers to those private funded schemes run by insurance corporations and pension funds where the contributions totalled £61 172 million in 1997. These are likely to be largely contributions to 'occupational' pension schemes.

Table 6.2

Social contributions and compensation of employees in the United Kingdom economy, 1997

SNA93/ESA95 identification code	SNA93/ESA95 name or UK National Accounts name [a]	£ million	Percentage of D.1
D.11	Wage and salaries	375 643	86.9
D.12/D.6111+D.612	Employers' social contributions *Of which (identifiable items only):*	56 828	13.1
D.121/D.6111	Employers' National Insurance contributions [b]	27 200	6.3
D.121/D.6111	Employers' actual social contributions [to S.125] [c]	18 384	4.3
D.121/D.6111	Employers' actual social contributions [other] [d]	2 127	0.5
D.121/D.6111	Employers' actual social contributions [total]	47 711	11.0
D.122/D.612	Employers' imputed social contributions [e]	4 712	1.1
D.1	Compensation of employees	432 471	100.0
	Memorandum items		
D.6112	Employees' National Insurance contributions	21 558	—
D.6112	Employees' social contributions [to S.125] [c]	42 788	—
D.6112	Employees' social contributions [other] [d]	2 563	—
D.6112	Employees' social contributions [total]	66 909	—
D.6113	Social contributions by self-and non-employed persons [all National Insurance contributions [f]]	1 848	—
D.61	Social contributions [g]	125 379	—

'—' means not required.

(a) For social contributions a country may have its own name depending on its social insurance scheme.

(b) 'National Insurance' is the name of the United Kingdom's social insurance scheme originally devised by Sir William Beveridge (*Social Insurance and Allied Services*, Report by Sir William Beveridge, November 1942, Cmd.6404); the Beveridge Report is described in my book *Introduction to Economics Theory and Data* (Macmillan, 1982), pp. 98–105.

(c) 'S.125' is Sector 125, Insurance corporations and pension funds.

(d) Calculated as a residual.

(e) Comprising: pension increase payments to notionally funded schemes, £1627 mn; and employers imputed contributions to unfunded central government and local authorities pension schems, £3085 mn.

(f) No. D.6113 social contributions are recorded for S.125 in UK National Accounts (table 4.4.4, p. 166).

(g) Note that this total, comprising the amounts above, includes £107 mn of social contributions paid by non-residents (see Table 6.3, pp. 302–3) and needs an (unexplained) adjustment of £206 mn.

Source: Office for National Statistics, *United Kingdom National Accounts The Blue Book 1999 edition*, tables 1.7.3, 1.7.4, 4.4.4, 5.24S and 6.14S; pp. 60, 62, 166, 187 and 209.

All up, D.61 social contributions in the United Kingdom economy in 1997 totalled £125 379 million (including £107 million of social contributions paid by non-residents), and this is a figure we will see again in the secondary distribution of income account in Table 6.3, pp. 302–3.

6.6 Secondary distribution of income account and gross disposable income

Apart from the balancing items, the secondary distribution of income account contains only *unrequited* current transactions in cash (thus distinguishing this account from the primary distribution of income account which, apart from balancing items, contains only *requited* current transactions).

The secondary distribution of income account, Account II.2, shows, for each resident sector and for the economy as a whole, how the balance of primary incomes is added to by current transfers in cash receivable (alternatively 'secondary income receivable') – recorded in the SNA93/ESA95 under the heading 'Resources' – and is subtracted from by current transfers in cash payable (alternatively, 'secondary income payable') – recorded in the SNA93/ESA95 under the heading 'Uses'. The balancing item on the secondary distribution of income account is called 'disposable income' and disposable income may be measured gross or net depending upon whether the balance of primary incomes is measured gross or net. In other words, for the resident sectors and for the economy as a whole:

$$\begin{array}{c} \text{Disposable} \\ \text{income} \end{array} = \begin{array}{c} \text{Balance of} \\ \text{primary} \\ \text{incomes} \end{array} + \begin{array}{c} \text{Current transfers} \\ \text{receivable (in cash)} \end{array} - \begin{array}{c} \text{Current transfers} \\ \text{payable (in cash)} \end{array}$$

For the economy as a whole, gross national disposable income is gross national income *plus* current transfers receivable from non-residents *minus* current transfers payable to non-residents. As we shall later explain, gross national disposable income can be calculated either by this aggregate method using gross national income, or by a method of summing the resident sectors' gross disposable incomes, or by a method which uses the total resources for all resident sectors on the secondary distribution of income account (each of these methods being algebraically equivalent, as we shall demonstrate).

For the rest of the world, the secondary distribution of income account gives only the current transfers received (from residents) and the current transfers paid (to residents), and my presentation in Table 6.3 departs from the SNA93/ESA95 presentation by giving, in the second last entry, the balance of these current transfers, because this is helpful for the explanation.

Table 6.3 gives the secondary distribution of income account for the sectors of the United Kingdom economy in 1997. The account starts, in the first row, with the balance of primary incomes, gross, B.5g, brought down as the balancing item from the primary distribution of income account (this is for the resident sectors and the whole economy only). The next six rows in Table 6.3 show how the balance of primary incomes may be added to by various types of current transfers receivable. The seventh row gives the total of D.73, D.74 and D.75 current transfers. The eighth row gives the total resources on the secondary distribution of income account comprising the balance of primary incomes, gross, and the total of current transfers. For the rest of the world the total resources comprises only the total of current transfers. Note that, by an agreed convention of national accounting, all current transfers in kind between residents and non-residents are treated as if they were transfers in cash, and are allocated to D.62 social benefits other than social transfers in kind or to D.74 current international cooperation, as appropriate (*ESA95*, paras 4.108 and 4.121; *SNA93*, paras 8.16 and 8.92).

Current taxes on income, wealth, etc., D.5, is a current transfer receivable only by the sector of the resident general government (which can tax the income of residents and the income of non-residents which arises in the UK) and by the rest of the world – that is by non-resident governments (because non-resident governments can and do tax the primary income of UK residents which arises in their countries). Consequently, in Table 6.3, current taxes on income, wealth, etc. is recorded as a resource only under general government and the rest of the world.

The official definition of 'current taxes on income, wealth, etc.' is (in part):

> Current taxes on income, wealth, etc. (D.5) cover all compulsory, unrequited payments, in cash or in kind, levied periodically by general government and by [general governments in] the rest of the world on the income and wealth of institutional units … (*ESA95*, para. 4.77).

D.5 taxes are divided between taxes on income, D.51, comprising taxes on the income of individuals and households (including on the income of the owners of unincorporated enterprises), taxes on the income or profits of corporations, taxes on holding gains (capital gains taxes), and taxes on winnings from lotteries or gambling, and other current taxes, D.59, comprising periodic or regular taxes on capital, poll taxes (levied per adult or per household independently of wealth), taxes on the total expenditures of persons or households, payments by households for licences to own or use vehicles, boats or aircraft (not used for business purposes), and taxes on international transactions (excluding taxes payable by producers and import duties paid by households). Current taxes on income, wealth, etc. do not include inheritance taxes, death duties or taxes on gifts, because this latter group of (non-periodic or non-regular) taxes is treated separately as capital taxes, D.91. Current taxes on income, wealth, etc. excludes taxes on land, buildings or other assets owned and used by enterprises for production, because this latter group of taxes is treated separately as other taxes on production, D.29.

In the 'Uses' part of Table 6.3 we can see the sectors which paid these D.5 taxes on income: in 1997, the household sector paid about three-quarters of all income taxes paid to general government. So here we see a redistribution of income from households to general government.

The 'in and out' nature of the total for any given category of current transfers (that is, the total over the whole of the economy *and* the rest of the world) can be illustrated by current taxes on income, wealth, etc. From Table 6.3 we can see the following for the UK economy in 1997:

Current taxes on income, wealth, etc., D.5, £ million

	Received by	Paid by
Residents	121 209	120 864
Non-residents	3 863	4 208
Total received/paid	125 072 ←——(*In and out*)——→ 125 072

In principle, this 'in and out' equality for the totals in any category of current transfers will apply unless there are differences in recording between transfers received and transfers paid.

We can see in the 'Uses' part of Table 6.3 that all social contributions are paid by resident households, with a small amount of social contributions coming from non-residents. This is a consequence of the rerouting convention for social contributions adopted in the SNA93/ESA95. Social contributions received as a resource was given by type of payment in Table 6.2. In Table 6.3

Table 6.3

Secondary distribution of income account and disposable income, gross, in the United Kingdom economy, 1997

SNA93/ESA95 identification code	SNA93/ESA95 name	£ million						
		Non-financial corporations, S.11	Financial corporations other than S.125	Insurance corporations & pension funds, S.125	General government, S.13	Households and NPISHs, S.14 + S.15	UK total economy, S.1	Rest of the world, S.2
II	DISTRIBUTION AND USE OF INCOME ACCOUNTS							
II.2	SECONDARY DISTRIBUTION OF INCOME ACCOUNT							
	Resources							
B.5g	Balance of primary incomes, gross	110 719	13 531	2 393	93 313	592 505	812 461	[...] (a)
D.5	Current taxes on income, wealth, etc.	...	...	...	121 209	...	121 209	3 863
D.61	Social contributions	2 872	204	61 224	60 652	427	125 379	—
D.62	Social benefits other than social transfers in kind	...	...	...	...	165 245	165 245	1 179
D.71	Net non-life insurance premiums	...	...	23 774	...	...	23 774	5
D.72	Non-life insurance claims	9 538	581	232	349	10 259	20 959	2 820
D.73 to D.75	Other current transfers	557	—	—	61 721 (b)	20 478	82 756	6 794
Total	Total resources	123 686	14 316	87 623	337 244	788 914	1 351 783	[14 661] (c)

Uses

							Total	
D.5	Current taxes on income, wealth, etc.	28 031	2 143	1 912	...	88 778	120 864	4 208
D.61	Social contributions	...	...	...	...	125 272	125 272	107
D.62	Social benefits other than social transfers in kind	2 872	204	45 534	116 302	897	165 809	615
D.71	Net non-life insurance premiums	9 538	581	232	349	10 259	20 959	2 820
D.72	Non-life insurance claims	...	...	23 774	...	...	23 774	5
D.73 to D.75	Other current transfers	402	66	—	75 564 [b]	9 067	85 099	4 451
B.6g	Disposable income, gross	82 843	11 322	16 171	145 029	554 641	810 006	[2 455] [c][d]
Total	Total uses	123 686	14 316	87 623	337 244	788 914	1 351 783	[14 661] [c]

NPISHs = Non-profit institutions serving households; ... = Not applicable to sector (by definition of item); — = Nil or less than £0.5 million.

(a) Entry not required in this account.
(b) Of which £59 506 million is D.73 current transfers within general government from central government to local government.
(c) Entry not made in SNA93/ESA95 account.
(d) Net secondary income to non-residents or balance of current transfers.

Source: Office for National Statistics, *United Kingdom National Accounts The Blue Book 1999 edition*, tables 1.7.4, 5.2.4 and 5.3.4; pp. 62–3, 186 and 196.

we can see the same total as in Table 6.2 and we can also see the sectors receiving the social contributions as resources. The two main receiving sectors are S.13 general government (which receives the National Insurance social contributions) and S.125 insurance corporations and pension funds (which receives both employers' and employees' contributions to funded schemes). The social contributions received by the other sectors are mainly the imputed contributions which occur because of unfunded social benefits paid by those sectors.

Turning to social benefits, the make-up of social benefits other than social transfers in kind was given by type of benefit in Table 6.1. In Table 6.3 we can see the same total of social benefits as in Table 6.1 and we can see the two sectors receiving these social benefits: households and non-resident institutional units (probably mainly pensions paid to persons living abroad). The sectors paying social benefits are mainly the insurance corporations and pension funds (paying funded benefits), and general government (paying National Insurance benefits and social assistance benefits in cash).

In the 'Uses' part of Table 6.3, we can see that in 1997 general government paid £116 302 million in social benefits, and this makes up 70 per cent of the £165 245 million of social benefits in cash received by households. So here we see a redistribution of income from general government to households. Of course, what we cannot see in the national accounts is that the redistribution of income occurring between government and households is 'really' the taxation of higher-income households and the payment of social benefits to lower-income households.

In order to see this intra-sector redistribution of income, which is the microeconomic reality behind the sector macroeconomic data of the secondary distribution of income account, we have to look to other data. We have the following picture from the United Kingdom's Office for National Statistics, *Family Spending A Report on the 1996–97 Family Expenditure Survey* (table 8.3, p. 129 and notes on pp. 5, 172 and 176; this survey is a detailed sample survey of 6415 households between April 1996 and March 1997, so there are 1283 households in each income group of fifths (or 'quintiles') over which the averaging is done – in order to understand the 'quintiles' simply imagine the households lined up in strict ascending order of household income, the lowest income household on the extreme left, the highest income household on the extreme right, the line-up being 6415 households long, then divide the households into groups at each one-fifth mark, starting from the left: the 1283rd household for the lowest quintile (that is, households 1 to 1283 inclusive), the 2566th household for the second lowest quintile (that is, households 1284 to 2566 inclusive), and so on, then average the household income and so on in each group; household income is weekly cash income before deduction of income tax, National Insurance (N.I.) contributions, and other deductions at source; other sources of income not given below are: investments, annuities and pensions other than social security benefits, and other sources; 'social security benefits' below excludes housing benefit and council tax benefit):

Income group	Average for group, £ per week		Percentage of income derived from:	
	Household income	Income tax and N.I. contributions	Employment or self-employment	Social security benefits
Lowest fifth	84.84	0.97	4.9	83.7
Second lowest fifth	178.57	10.25	29.3	51.8
Middle fifth	313.68	45.93	65.1	17.5
Second highest fifth	488.77	93.74	82.6	6.3
Highest fifth	918.43	209.83	87.6	2.3

We can see that relatively little is paid in income tax and National Insurance contributions by the two lowest income groups of households, and that considerable amounts are paid by the two highest income groups. The lowest income group derives most of its income from social security benefits, while social security benefits are a negligible part of the income of the highest income groups; these high-income groups derive most of their income from employment or self-employment. It is this redistribution between households, largely mediated by the government, which is the microeconomic reality behind much of what we see in Table 6.3.

This illustration for the United Kingdom is, of course, an illustration of a general or typical pattern, which occurs in most developed economies, and which would explain much of any country's Account II.2: Secondary distribution of income account.

We now consider transfers other than income tax and social contributions and social benefits.

When an individual takes out an insurance policy in his or her own name, on his or her own initiative independently of a requirement by employer or government, then the policy does not count as *social* insurance, even when the risk or need against which insurance is taken falls within the list of specified risks or needs. There are three such classes of individual policies. First, there is endowment life insurance; second, there is term life insurance; and third, there is all other insurance. Here the SNA93/ESA95 terminology needs to be carefully understood because the recommended principles of the SNA93/ESA95 are generally not followed (more exactly, are not yet able to be followed) in the practices of the national accounts. We can use the following schematic diagram:

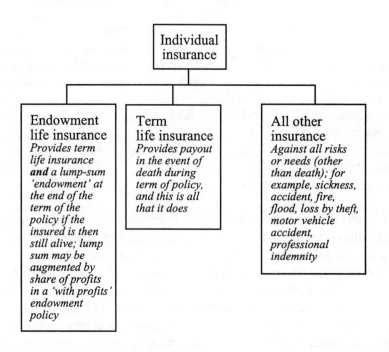

Both term life insurance and endowment life insurance provide insurance against the contingency of death, but endowment insurance is unique among insurance policies in providing a lump sum on the maturity of the policy in the event that there has been no insurance payout during the term of the policy. *Endowment* life insurance can be thought of as a scheme for saving (for financial asset accumulation) with life insurance integrally attached. *Term* life insurance is not a scheme for saving and is simply 'pure' insurance against the risk of death. (The annual payments from the insured, for the same amount of coverage, will be very much larger in an endowment life insurance scheme than in a term life insurance scheme.) (Note that an endowment policy need not be confined to a fixed sum; some endowment policies may have the endowment enhanced by a share of the profits made by the insurance company and in this case is known as a 'with profits' [endowment] policy.)

The strict recommendation of the SNA93/ESA95 is that (1) endowment life insurance policies be treated separately from all other insurance policies with the premiums paid counting as the accumulation of a financial asset and that (2) term life insurance policies be treated along with other insurance policies because in all of these policies the premiums are purely to secure insurance against a specified contingency (death, accident, fire, and so on). Conversely, in all these policies, the premiums do *not* secure a lump sum payment on the the maturity of the policy if there has been no payout during the term of the policy. The SNA93/ESA95 uses the terms 'non-life insurance policies', 'non-life insurance premiums' and 'non-life insurance claims' to refer to this second group of policies, premiums and claims.

As the SNA93 explains, a term life insurance policy 'that provides a benefit in the case of death within a given period [the term of the policy] but in no other circumstances … is [where 'is' means 'should be'] regarded as *non-life insurance* because as with other non-life insurance, a claim is payable only if a specified contingency [death] occurs and not otherwise' (*SNA93*, Annex IV, para. 1, p. 569, italics added and with my explanatory interpolations in square brackets).

However, in practice it is generally not possible (at least at present) for the national accounts statisticians to distinguish between endowment life insurance business and term life insurance business. If this is so, then term life insurance is included with endowment life insurance, with the premiums paid being counted as the accumulation of a financial asset and the claims paid being counted as the decumulation of a financial asset. Accordingly, the payment of premiums and the receipt of claims are recorded subsequently, as we shall see, in the financial account. Conversely, in the secondary distribution of income account the terms 'net non-life insurance premiums' and 'non-life insurance claims' refer only to all other insurance (see the schema above). This seems to be the practice in most countries' national accounts, but the reader interested in these premiums specifically is strongly advised to make diligent enquiry as to the precise practice adopted (and practices may change in the future because the recommendations of the SNA93/ESA95 provide a blueprint as to how the national accounts statisticians should improve the reporting and recording of life insurance data so as to conform with what is the most theoretically appropriate treatment of this data).

In the case of an independent *individual* non-life insurance policy (generally, in practice, meaning all insurance other than life insurance), the 'premiums' paid (as the annual payments made by the insured are called) do not count as social contributions and any claim paid does not count as a social benefit; rather, each is classified as a current transfer paid or received and, in the secondary distribution of income account, each is recorded separately from social contributions and social benefits as *net non-life insurance premiums*, D.71 or as *non-life insurance claims*, D.72, respectively.

In the term 'net non-life insurance premiums', the word 'net' signifies that the premiums are recorded net of (or after deduction of) the 'service charges' (or, as I sometimes call them, the 'administrative costs') of the insurance enterprises arranging the insurance. (The calculation of service charges is a complex matter but, with considerable simplification, the essence of the calculation is that service charges are the difference between total premiums paid by all insured institutional units *minus* total claims paid to all insured institutional units (*SNA93*, p. 573, para. 18, and *ESA95*, p. 269, para. 15 and p. 271, para. 27).) The reasons for separating out the service charges from the premiums paid by the insured are twofold.

First, 'the service charges constitute purchases of services by the policyholders and are recorded as intermediate [consumption by enterprises] or final consumption [expenditure by households or government or non-profit institutions serving households], as appropriate' (*SNA93*, para. 8.86, with my clarifying interpolations in square brackets). This treatment of service charges (or administrative costs) is necessary because incomes – compensation of employees and gross operating surplus (that is, the administrative costs) – are earned by the insurance enterprises from these service charges which thus involve production of services.

Second, the net amount of the premiums is the amount available to be redistributed to those suffering loss from the contingencies insured against; in other words, the *net* premiums and the claims are the 'pure' transfers involved. Consequently, for the economy as a whole plus the rest of the world, the total of the D.71 net non-life insurance premiums *paid* (by all the insured) necessarily equals the total of the D.72 non-life insurance claims *received* (by those of the insured who make claims).

In Table 6.3, we can see this equality as follows. In the 'Resources' part of Table 6.3, total D.71 net non-life insurance premiums received by S.125 insurance corporations and pension funds were, in 1997 in the UK, £23 774 million (note the obvious point that no other resident sector *receives* net non-life insurance premiums as a resource) with a further £5 million received by non-resident insurers from residents, making a total of £23 779 million of premiums received by the insurers. This is the 'pure' amount (net of service charges) available for distribution, as a current transfer, to those insured persons suffering loss during the year from whatever contingency they had insured against. Correspondingly, in the 'Uses' part of Table 6.3, we can see the *same* total, £23 779 million, paid out to residents as non-life insurance claims, D.72, by the S.125 resident insurance corporations and pension funds and by the S.2 non-resident insurers. Returning to the 'Resources' part of Table 6.3, we can see, in the row for D.72 non-life insurance claims, the sectors receiving the non-life insurance payouts: mostly the household sector (£10 259 million) and the sector of non-financial corporations (£9538 million) but all the other sectors receive payouts as well, including the rest of the world (£2820 million – and see the corresponding counter-entry in the D.71 'Uses' row) because insurers resident in the United Kingdom have (as is obvious) a large international component to their business. Note carefully for yourself that the total along this D.72 'Resources' row is £23 779 million.

In Table 6.3, for the sake of streamlining, I have grouped the remaining D.7 current transfers together (that is, D.73 to D.75 inclusive). The D.7 category is *other current transfers*. This category comprises: *net non-life insurance premiums*, D.71 (already explained); *non-life insurance claims*, D.72 (ditto); *current transfers within general government*, D.73; *current international cooperation*, D.74; and *miscellanous current transfers*, D.75 (which also includes transfers between residents and non-residents).

Current transfers within general government are quite common: in the United Kingdom, central government, S.1311, makes large current transfers to local government, S.1313; in Australia, central government, S.1311, makes large current transfers to state governments, S.1312; in each case, out of centrally collected tax revenue. In the United Kingdom in 1997, the central government transferred £59 506 million to local government (the *Blue Book 1999 edition*, tables 5.2.4 and 5.3.4, pp. 186 and 196). This payment makes up the largest part of resources (to local government) and uses (by central government) in Table 6.3's column for general government.

Current international cooperation includes all transfers in cash and kind between general government and governments or international organisations in the rest of the world (*ESA95*, para. 4.121). Note that capital transfers are excluded, because these are recorded elsewhere. These D.74 transfers are also recorded in the external accounts for the rest of the world. In Table 6.3, we can see that the rest of the world received £6794 million and paid £4451 million of D.74 and D.75 transfers.

Miscellaneous current transfers, D.75, is a residual category for current transfers not classified elsewhere. There are six main sub-categories in this miscellaneous category.

First, there are current transfers to non-profit institutions serving households, such as subscriptions and donations by households to non-profit institutions serving households (trade union dues, gifts in cash or kind to charities) and assistance and grants from general government (for purposes other than financing capital expenditure). In Australia, the government makes considerable current transfers to non-government, religious-denomination schools (non-profit institutions serving households) to help them with their current running costs, and these transfers are included here. In the United Kingdom, these transfers form a considerable part of the resources for non-profit institutions serving households.

Second, there are current transfers between households. These particularly concern remittances made or received between a resident household and a non-resident household (for example, remittances by parents to children studying abroad, remittances by persons working abroad to family members).

Third, there are fines and penalties which are treated as compulsory current transfers (but excluding penalties for tax evasion or late payment of taxes because these penalties cannot usually be distinguished from the tax payments themselves).

Fourth, there are payments for, and winnings from, lotteries and gambling (excluding a service charge, or administrative cost, element in such payments). Exclusive of service charges, the losses and winnings from lotteries and gambling are regarded as current transfers taking place directly between the households participating in lotteries and gambling (paying for the chance of winning is regarded as not a sufficiently specific quid pro quo, so the payment and the winnings count as unrequited transfers). Non-resident households may also be involved in lottery and gambling current transfers.

Fifth, there are payments of compensation, either compulsory (ordered by a court of law) or voluntary (such as settlements out of court but covering other transfers as well), generally for injury to persons or damage to property, but excluding payments of non-life insurance claims. This covers payments, usually made by general government, in compensation for damage suffered by natural disasters.

Sixth, there are other current transfers such as transfers from non-profit institutions serving persons to the rest of the world (charitable aid) and scholarships from enterprises to household members.

Having briefly described all the categories of current transfers, we can consider the calculation of the balancing item, gross disposable income, B.6g. For each resident sector this balancing item can be calculated as total resources on the secondary distribution of income account *minus* the total of current transfers paid as uses.

To illustrate for the sector of households and non-profit institutions serving households in the United Kingdom in 1997, total resources on the secondary distribution of income account was £788 914 million and the total of current transfers paid as uses was £234 273 million; accordingly for 1997:

Household sector
(inc. NPISHs)
gross disposable   =   £788 914 mn   –   £234 273 mn
income, B.6g

                     =   £554 641 mn

For the economy as a whole, gross national disposable income, B.6*g, can be calculated in any of three algebraically equivalent methods.

First, gross national disposable income can be calculated as the sum of the resident sectors' gross disposable incomes. In Table 6.3, this is simply the total of the first five numbers in the B.6g row. Accordingly:

Gross national
disposable   =   £82 843 mn + £11 322 mn
income, B.6*g
                    + £16 171 mn

                    + £145 029 mn + £554 641 mn

                =   £810 006 mn

I shall refer to this first method as the method of the sum of resident sectors' gross disposable incomes (because it uses the balancing item, disposable income, gross, B.6g, of each of the resident sectors).

Second, gross national disposable income can be calculated as the economy's (that is, all resident sectors, or S.1) total resources on the secondary distribution of income account *minus* the economy's S.1 total current transfers paid as uses on the secondary distribution of income account. Accordingly:

$$
\begin{aligned}
\text{Gross national} & & \text{S.1 total} & & \text{S.1 total current} \\
\text{disposable} & = & \text{resources on} & - & \text{transfers (paid)} \\
\text{income, B.6*g} & & \text{Account II.2} & & \text{on Account II.2}
\end{aligned}
$$

$$= \text{£1 351 783 mn} \quad - \quad \text{£541 777 mn}$$

$$= \text{£810 006 mn}$$

I shall refer to this second method as the total resources method (because it starts from total resources on the secondary distribution of income account).

Third, gross national disposable income can be calculated as gross national income *plus* current transfers received from the rest of the world (equivalently, current transfers paid as uses by the rest of the world), £12 206 million, *minus* current transfers paid to the rest of the world (equivalently, current transfers received as resources by the rest of the world), £14 661 million. Accordingly:

$$
\begin{aligned}
\text{Gross national} & & \text{Gross} & & \text{Total current} & & \text{Total current} \\
\text{disposable} & = & \text{national} & + & \text{transfers received} & - & \text{transfers paid} \\
\text{income, B.6*g} & & \text{income,} & & \text{from the rest of} & & \text{to the rest of} \\
& & \text{B.5*g} & & \text{the world on} & & \text{the world on} \\
& & & & \text{Account II.2} & & \text{Account II.2}
\end{aligned}
$$

$$= \text{£812 461 mn} \quad + \quad \text{£12 206 mn} \quad - \quad \text{£14 661 mn}$$

$$= \text{£810 006 mn}$$

I shall refer to this third method as the gross national income method (because it starts from gross national income, B.5*g).

The algebraic equivalence of the three methods can be demonstrated but for this we need to make a distinction between current transfers by residents to residents and current transfers by residents to non-residents (a distinction which is only partially made or recorded in the SNA93/ESA95). Demonstrating this algebraic equivalence is important because it elucidates the internal structure, or 'logic', of the secondary distribution of income account.

We have the following schema for current transfers with illustrative 1997 data for the United Kingdom from Table 6.3:

Current transfers paid by:	Current transfers received by:		
	Residents	Non-residents	Total
Residents	X ?	Y £14 661 mn	$X + Y$ £541 777 mn
Non-residents	Z £12 206 mn	Not applicable	Z £12 206 mn
Total	$X + Z$ £539 322 mn	Y £14 661 mn	

The amount designated by X is the annual amount of current transfers paid by residents to residents; this is not recorded as such in the SNA93/ESA95, so the above schema puts a question mark here. The amount designated by Y is the annual amount of current transfers paid by residents to non-residents; this is recorded in the SNA93/ESA95 and appears as the total of current transfers (received) by the rest of the world in Table 6.3 as £14 661 million, so the schema inserts this amount as an illustration.

The total amount of current transfers paid by residents (to both residents and non-residents) is recorded in the SNA93/ESA95 and can be calculated in Table 6.3 as the total of current transfers (paid) by the UK total economy as £541 777 million, so the schema inserts this amount as an illustration. But this S.1 total amount of current transfers paid by residents must be $X + Y$, and because we know Y we are able to calculate X, as follows:

$$(X + Y) - Y = X$$

So, for the 1997 UK data:

$$(£541\ 777\ mn) - £14\ 661\ mn = £527\ 116\ mn = X$$

The amount designated by Z is the annual amount of current transfers paid by non-residents to residents; this is recorded in the SNA93/ESA95 and can be calculated in Table 6.3 as the total of current transfers (paid) by the rest of the world as £12 206 million, so the schema inserts this amount as an illustration.

The total amount of current transfers received by residents (from both residents and non-residents) is recorded in the SNA93/ESA95 and can be calculated in Table 6.3 as the total of current transfers (received) by the UK total economy as £539 322 million, so the schema inserts this amount as an illustration. But this S.1 total amount of current transfers received by residents must be $X + Z$, and because we know Z we are able to calculate X, as follows:

$$(X + Z) - Z = X$$

So, for the 1997 UK data:

$$(\text{£539 322 mn}) - \text{£12 206 mn} = \text{£527 116 mn} = X$$

The algebraic equivalence of the last two methods of calculating gross national disposable income, B.6*g, can now be explained as follows.

For the total resources method of calculating gross national disposable income (this applies to the S.1 total economy column in Table 6.3):

$$\begin{array}{l}\text{S.1 total} \\ \text{resources on} \\ \text{Account II.2}\end{array} = \begin{array}{l}\text{Gross} \\ \text{national} \\ \text{income, B.5*g}\end{array} + (X + Z)$$

$$\begin{array}{l}\text{S.1 total current} \\ \text{transfers (paid)} \\ \text{on Account II.2}\end{array} = (X + Y)$$

Total resources method

$$\begin{array}{l}\text{Gross national} \\ \text{disposable} \\ \text{income, B.6*g}\end{array} = \begin{array}{l}\text{S.1 total} \\ \text{resources on} \\ \text{Account II.2}\end{array} - \begin{array}{l}\text{S.1 total current} \\ \text{transfers (paid)} \\ \text{on Account II.2}\end{array}$$

$$= \begin{array}{l}\text{Gross} \\ \text{national} \\ \text{income, B.5*g}\end{array} + (X + Z) - (X + Y)$$

$$= \begin{array}{l}\text{Gross} \\ \text{national} \\ \text{income, B.5*g}\end{array} + Z - Y$$

$$= \begin{array}{l}\text{Gross} \\ \text{national} \\ \text{income, B.5*g}\end{array} + \begin{array}{l}\text{Total current} \\ \text{transfers received} \\ \text{from the rest of} \\ \text{the world on} \\ \text{Account II.2}\end{array} - \begin{array}{l}\text{Total current} \\ \text{transfers paid} \\ \text{to the rest of} \\ \text{the world on} \\ \text{Account II.2}\end{array}$$

Gross national income method

The algebraic equivalence of each of these two methods to the first method, the method of the sum of the resident sectors' gross disposable incomes, can be shown as follows.

Gross disposable income, B.6g, for any sector i is, and this applies to any ith resident sector column in Table 6.3 (designating a sector amount by the use of brackets thus {} with a subscript i to indicate the sector involved):

$$\{\text{Gross disposable income}\}_i = \{\text{Total resources on Account II.2}\}_i + \{\text{Total current transfers (paid) on Account II.2}\}_i$$

The sum of resident sectors' gross disposable income is, where the summation is over all the i resident sectors:

$$\Sigma\,\{\text{Gross disposable income}\}_i = \Sigma\left[\{\text{Total resources on Account II.2}\}_i - \{\text{Total current transfers (paid) on Account II.2}\}_i\right]$$

$$= \Sigma\,\{\text{Total resources on Account II.2}\}_i - \Sigma\,\{\text{Total current transfers (paid) on Account II.2}\}_i$$

$$= \underbrace{\text{S.1 total resources on Account II.2} - \text{S.1 total current transfers (paid) on Account II.2}}_{\textit{Total resources method}}$$

$$= \text{Gross national disposable income, B.6*g}$$

The secondary distribution of income account for the Australian economy in 1997–98 is given in Table 6.4. This has much the same structure as Table 6.3, but there are some differences in terminology (reflecting the terms used in the Australian System of National Accounts). One main difference is that the Australian system of social security has no social contributions, except for workers' compensation premiums (for insurance against injury at work), because all the social benefits in Australia are financed out of general taxation and so count as social *assistance* benefits.

Table 6.4
Secondary distribution of income account and disposable income, gross, in the Australian economy, 1997–98

$ million

SNA93 identifi- cation code	Australian System of National Accounts name	Non- financial corpor- ations, S.11	Financial corporations, S.12	General govern- ment, S.13	Households and NPISHs, S.14 + S.15	Australian total economy, S.1	Rest of the world, S.2
	Income						
B.5g	Balance of primary incomes, gross	67 029	13 887	73 428 [a]	390 007	544 351	[...] [b]
D.5	Current taxes on income, wealth, etc.	...	...	98 389	...	98 389	48
D.62	Social benefits receivable						
D.621, D.6.22	Workers compensation	...	...	...	5 100	5 100	—
D.624	Social assistance benefits	...	...	...	46 281	46 281	—
D.71	Net non-life insurance premiums	...	22 468	...	...	22 468	1 760 [c]
D.72	Non-life insurance claims	3 142	...	...	13 843 [d]	16 985	...
D.73 to D.75	Other current transfers	17	—	2 168	10 906 [d]	13 091	2 117
D.5 to D.7	Total current transfers (received)	3 159	22 468	100 557	76 130	202 314	3 925
Total	Total income	70 188	36 355	173 985	466 137	746 665	[3 925] [e]

Use of income

Code	Use of income						
D.5	Current taxes on income, wealth, etc.	17 427	7 370	...	72 536	97 333	1 056
D.611	Social contributions for workers' compensation	...	...	...	5 019	5 019	...
D.624	Social assistance benefits in cash to residents	...	...	46 281	...	46 281	...
D.71	Net non-life insurance premiums	4 472	...	...	12 410	16 882	...
D.72	Non-life insurance claims	...	22 640	...	...	22 640	1 772 (c)
D.73 to D.75	Other current transfers	1 806	—	11 129 (a)	1 389	14 324	932
D.5 to D.7	Total current transfers (paid)	23 705	30 010	57 410 (a)	91 354	202 479	3 760
B.6g	Gross disposable income	46 483	6 345	116 575	374 783	544 186	[165] (e)(f)
Total	Total use of income	70 188	36 355	173 985	466 137	746 665	[3 925] (e)

NPISHs = Non-profit institutions serving households; ... = Not applicable to sector (by definition of item); — = Nil or not recorded.

(a) In calculation, subtracting $7321 million of subsidies from taxes on production and imports.

(b) Entry not required in this account.

(c) Non-life insurance transfers.

(d) Includes $9951 million of current transfer to non-profit institutions, nearly all of which is from general government under Australia's system of transfers to private non-profit (religious denomination) schools.

(e) Entry not made in SNA93/ESA95 account.

(f) Net secondary income *to* non-residents; negative of net secondary income *from* non-residents (see table 1.12).

Sources: Table 5.11, p. 261; Australian Bureau of Statistics, *Australian System of National Accounts 1997–98*, Catalogue No. 5204.0 tables, 1.12, 2.1, 2.9, 2.14, 2.20 and 2.27; pp. 32, 41, 49, 54, 60 and 67; I have ascribed the SNA93 identification codes as these are not used in the published accounts.

317

Again, in Table 6.4 we can see the redistribution of income from households to government via income tax and from government to households via social assistance benefits.

For the Australian economy, gross national disposable income can be calculated in either of the three methods described (as the reader should verify).

What is the economic significance of gross disposable income for a sector and what is the economic significance of gross national disposable income for the economy?

Gross disposable income is basically a measure of a sector's command over resources, and gross national disposable income is basically a measure of the economy's command over resources. To understand this, let us go back to Chapter 5's explanation, using the model economy, of the economic significance of gross national income and let us focus on the whole economy. We explained in Chapter 5 that gross national income represents the 'physical products for sustenance' available to residents of the economy after sharing some of their products with non-residents (on account of primary incomes being paid to non-residents) and after sharing some of non-residents' products (on account of primary incomes being received from non-residents). All of this relates only to production and requited transactions.

However, following our discussion of unrequited transactions – current transfers, specifically – we can see that there is a further element to the availability of physical products for sustenance, because residents can *transfer* some of their claims (arising out of production) to non-residents (let us consider this as 'foreign aid' from a wealthy country to a less wealthy country). In this way, the residents of the wealthy country diminish their claims on goods and services, and transfer those claims to the residents of a less wealthy country. But this is a *redistribution* of a flow of goods and services resulting from production, and has nothing to do with production itself (in the way that primary income claims are connected with production itself).

Consequently, if one wanted to consider the standard of command over resources of the population of an economy, then an appropriate measure is gross national disposable income per head of population. However, there is a further consideration in relation to disposable income, and this is the very significant concept of disposable income, *net*. Net disposable income is disposable income after making allowance for the consumption of fixed capital, and this will be explained in the last section of this chapter.

What is true for the economy as a whole is true for a sector within an economy. The purpose of current transfers is to affect the disposable income of a sector, and a portion of these current transfers are concerned with social welfare and are effected through general government to the benefit of households.

However, gross disposable income for a sector is only a part measure of the result of the process of redistribution among the resident sectors in the economy; there is a further important aspect of internal redistribution concerning transfers in kind. Accordingly, our next task is to consider the impact of social transfers in kind in the redistribution of income in kind account, Account II.3.

6.7   Redistribution of income in kind account and adjusted gross disposable income

In addition to making current transfers in cash to augment the command over resources of needy households, general government also makes individual consumption expenditure, P.31, which is transferred to households as *social transfers in kind*, D.63. Taking account of these social transfers in kind leads to *adjusted disposable income, gross*, B.7g. The adjustment is quite straightforward and is recorded in Account II.3: Redistribution of income in kind account. Table 6.5 gives a simplified version of Account II.3 for the United Kingdom in 1997 and for Australia in 1997–98, using only the two sectors affected by the adjustment.

For the United Kingdom in 1997, we can see that household sector gross disposable income is augmented by the addition of £87 721 million of D.63 social transfers in kind (= P.31 individual consumption expenditure by general government). Conversely, general government gross disposable income is diminished by the subtraction of of £87 721 million of D.63 social transfers in kind.

In Australia in 1997–98, household gross disposable income is augmented by $51 878 million of D.63 social transfers in kind and conversely general government gross disposable income is diminished by $51 878 million of D.63 social transfers in kind.

For households, the percentage augmentation to gross disposable income by social transfers in kind is 16 per cent in the United Kingdom and 14 per cent in Australia. This demonstrates the quantitative importance to households' resources of the social transfers in kind.

Using the memorandum item of the balance of primary incomes, gross, in Table 6.5, we can see that, in both economies, the overall impact of *all* current transfers (in cash and in kind) on households is to increase their command over resources: by 8.4 per cent in the United Kingdom in 1997 and by 9.4 per cent in Australia in 1997–98.

6.8   Consumption of fixed capital and net disposable income

Consumption of fixed capital is an imputed requited transaction which measures, in monetary terms, the cost incurred during a period of using fixed capital in the process of production. Consumption of fixed capital is thus a provision, set aside from sales receipts or other income, in order to make up for the decline in the (second-hand) value of a fixed asset, the decline being due to the using up of part of the asset's limited working life.

To use the illustration of Chapter 1 (Section 1.5), if a vehicle used as a fixed asset has a working life of four years and zero scrap value and has an acquisition cost when new of £20 000, then consumption of fixed capital can be imputed at a rate of £5000 per annum (= £20 000/4 years). Conversely, the second-hand value of the fixed asset would be £15 000 at the end of one year of working, £10 000 after two years of working, and so on.

In consequence of this, the only way for the 'wealth' of the owner of the fixed asset to be maintained constant over time is for the provision set aside for the consumption of fixed capital to be invested in other assets. To illustrate using the case of the owner of a vehicle, if the first year's consumption of fixed capital is invested in an asset worth £5000 then at the end of the first year the owner's wealth is equal to £15 000 (value second-hand of the fixed asset) *plus* £5000 (asset acquired with first year's provision for the consumption of fixed capital) *equals* £20 000. And so on for the second and all subsequent years. In this way the vehicle owner's wealth is maintained intact at £20 000.

The important point of this is that investing the provision for the consumption of fixed capital has only the potential to *maintain* wealth intact; conversely, investing the provision for the consumption of fixed capital has no potential to *add to* wealth.

The income of an institutional unit can be defined as the maximum amount by which an institutional unit could increase its wealth during a period (providing the institutional unit made no final consumption expenditure during the period). In other words, income is that which has the potential to add to wealth. It follows that, because provisions for the consumption of fixed capital have no potential to add to wealth, provisions for the consumption of fixed capital should not be counted as part of income (in the strict theoretical sense of the word 'income').

In other words, income (in the strict theoretical sense) should always be measured *net* of the provisions for the consumption of fixed capital. Despite this, we often use gross income because it is a measure of the cash flow available to an institutional unit, even though 'gross income' is, in strict theory, a contradiction in terms.

It follows that, viewed as the potential to add to wealth, *net* disposable

Table 6.5
Redistribution of income in kind account

SNA93/ ESA95 identific- ation code	SNA93/ESA95 name	United Kingdom 1997, £ million		Australia 1997–98, $ million	
		General govern- ment, S.13	House- holds inc. NPISHs, S.14+S.15	General govern- ment, S.13	House- holds inc. NPISHs, S.14+S.15
II.3	REDISTRIBUTION OF INCOME IN KIND ACCOUNT				
B.6g	Disposable income, gross	145 029	554 641	116 575	374 783
D.63	Social transfers in kind[a]	–87 721	+87 721	–51 878	+51 878
B.7g	Adjusted disposable income, gross	57 308	642 362	64 697	426 661
	Memorandum item				
B.5g	Balance of primary incomes, gross	93 313	592 505	73 428	390 007

(a) Recorded as minus if paid by sector and as plus if received by sector. These D.63 social transfers in kind are also the P.31 individual consumption expenditure by general government; see Table 3.1, p. 119 above.

Sources: United Kingdom: Table 6.3 and Office for National Statistics, *United Kingdom National Accounts The Blue Book 1999 edition*, table 1.7.5, p. 65; Australia: Table 6.4 and Australian Bureau of Statistics, *Australian System of National Accounts 1997–98*, Catalogue No. 5204.0, tables 2.15 and 2.21, pp. 55 and 61.

income, as measured in the SNA93/ESA95 is the balancing item closest to the theoretically strict concept of income (*SNA93*, para. 8.15). Accordingly, *net national disposable income*, B.6*n, is the most appropriate measure for analysing the country's command over resources, because it is the 'command' *after* allowing for the using up of fixed capital in the process of production. Net national disposable income is the maximum a country could consume during the period (in the event that it made no *addition* to its wealth during the period); alternatively, net national disposable income is the maximum a country could add to its wealth (in the event that it made no final consumption expenditure during the period); and, finally, net national disposable income represents the maximum of combinations of additions to wealth and final consumption expenditure during the period.

Table 6.6 gives, for the United Kingdom economy in 1997 and the Australian economy in 1997–98, the net disposable income, B.6n, by sector and for the whole economy. The United Kingdom's net national disposable income in 1997 was £724 172 million and Australia's net national disposable income in 1997–98 was $456 170 million.

One important point about Table 6.6 is that in all cases, consumption of fixed capital is large relative to gross disposable income; in other words, providing for the consumption of fixed capital is a quantitatively major adjustment. For the United Kingdom economy as a whole in 1997, consumption of fixed capital was 11 per cent of gross national disposable income, B.6*g; for the Australian economy as a whole in 1997–98, consumption of fixed capital was 16 per cent of gross national disposable income, B.6*g.

We can usefully end this chapter by recapitulating on what we have learned so far in this book. This is a useful summary because it displays part of what I call 'the family of national income concepts', because it is always useful to bear in mind that there is not just one national income concept, but a family of related concepts each of which has its own appropriate use, depending on the purposes of the analysis being undertaken. (Note that this is not a complete list of all the national income concepts because we treat mainly gross concepts, deducting consumption of fixed capital only at the final stage; however, consumption of fixed capital can be deducted at other stages.) This also shows the relationship between the various national income concepts. The recapitulation is shown in the following tabulation illustrated with data from the United Kingdom and Australia (all the data can be found in the preceding tables of this book, and it is a useful exercise to learn the sequence of the row

Table 6.6
Consumption of fixed capital and net disposable income

SNA93/ESA95 identification code	SNA93/ESA95 name	Non-financial corporations, S.11	Financial corporations, S.12	General government, S.13	Households inc. NPISHs, S.14+S.15	Total economy, S.1
	United Kingdom, 1997, £ million					
B.6g	Disposable income, gross	82 843	27 493	145 029	554 641	810 006
K.1	Consumption of fixed capital	53 343	4 145	9 283	19 063	85 834
B.6n	Disposable income, net	29 500	23 348	135 746	535 578	724 172
	Australia, 1997–98, $ million					
B.6g	Disposable income, gross	46 483	6 345	116 575	374 783	544 186
K.1	Consumption of fixed capital	42 215	3 754	10 932	31 115	88 016
B.6n	Disposable income, net	4 268	2 591	105 643	343 668	456 170

Sources: Office for National Statistics, *United Kingdom National Accounts The Blue Book 1999 edition*, table 1.7.4, pp. 62–3; Australian Bureau of Statistics, *Australian System of National Accounts 1997–98*, Catalogue No. 5204.0, tables 1.12, 2.1, 2.9, 2.14 and 2.20, pp. 32, 41, 49, 54 and 60.

headings by heart according to the exact and complete wording including the SNA93/ESA95 identification codes):

	United Kingdom 1997 £ million	Australia 1997–98 $ million
Gross domestic product, B.1*g	**803 889**	**564 705**
minus Balance of primary incomes of the rest of the world[a]	–8 572	18 794
minus Statistical discrepancy between income component and GDP, di	—	1 560
Gross national income, B.5*g	**812 461**	**544 351**
minus Balance of current transfers of the rest of the world[b]	2 455	165
Gross national disposable income, B.6*g	**810 006**	**544 186**
minus Consumption of fixed capital	85 834	88 016
Net national disposable income, B.6*n	**724 172**	**546 170**

(*a*) Primary incomes are: D.1 + (D.2 – D.3) + D.4.

(*b*) Current transfers (in cash) are: D.5 + D.6 (exc. D.63) + D.7.

Having summarised some national income concepts (in bold typeface) and their relationship to each other, we must now consider the use of gross disposable income so that we can understand the important balancing item of saving, gross, and the use of that saving to finance the accumulation of assets. This is the task of the next chapter.

7 Gross Saving and the Accumulation of Assets

7.1 Introduction

This chapter explains the two main concepts basic to the accumulation of assets: gross saving; and net lending (+)/net borrowing (−). The two concepts are related because net lending (+) is part of gross saving. Despite this, net lending (+)/net borrowing (−) has in its own right a significant economic meaning and is important for economic analysis.

The accumulation of assets is recorded in the SNA93/ESA95 accumulation accounts, and Section 7.2 explains these accounts.

The concepts of gross saving and net lending (+)/net borrowing (−), and the relationship between the two, will be fully explained in Sections 7.3 to 7.6. A provisional explanation of the concept of gross saving is that gross saving is what is left over from gross disposable income after consumption expenditure (if any). (This explanation is provisional in two ways: first, it is subordinate to, and is subject to qualification by, the technically correct general definition of 'saving' which will be given in Section 7.4; second, it is not applicable without qualification to all sectors of the economy. Nevertheless, the provisional explanation does express the substance of the concept of gross saving, especially in relation to the total economy where (apart from a very minor adjustment item) gross national saving is equal to gross national disposable income *minus* total consumption expenditure.) Alternatively (but also provisionally), gross saving is what remains from all current transactions received after all current transactions paid (*SNA93*, para. 2.133). Gross saving is the balancing flow used for the acquisition of *assets*, both non-financial assets (which are mostly real assets in the form of 'things' such as machinery and buildings) and financial assets (such as intangible assets in the form of 'claims' – for example, money in the bank or shares).

Net lending (+)/net borrowing (−) is the balancing item remaining from gross saving after the acquisition of *non-financial* assets and this chapter explains how this balancing item relates to the net acquisition of *financial* assets and liabilities.

(When attached to 'saving', the adjectives 'gross' and 'net' mean, respectively, 'before deduction of consumption of fixed capital' and 'after deduction of consumption of fixed capital'; when attached to either 'lending' or 'borrowing', the adjective 'net' has an entirely different meaning which is explained in Section 7.3; when attached to either 'acquisition of financial assets' or 'acquisition of financial liabilities', the adjective 'net' has yet another meaning which is explained in Section 7.6. The adjective 'net' also occurs in other terms and its specific meaning, again different, in these other terms will be apparent from the meaning of the term.)

Sections 7.7 and 7.8 explain some very important national accounting identities relating to gross saving and net lending (+)/net borrowing (−), and shows how an economy's current account surplus or current account deficit and foreign lending or foreign borrowing arises. These national accounting identities are absolutely basic to macroeconomics and thence to macroeconomic policy.

At the end of the SNA93/ESA95 sequence of national accounts, the balance sheet of assets and liabilities records the wealth of the nation in the form of the monetary value of the various assets and liabilities which exist at a given date and which have been accumulated over past years. In this context 'wealth' should be understood technically as 'net worth', where 'net worth' is defined as the difference between assets (of all types) owned and financial liabilities owed. Section 7.9 (Table 7.12) gives the 30 June 1998 balance sheet for, and the net worth of, the sectors of the Australian economy and the total Australian economy (at the time of writing, a complete balance sheet had not been published for the United Kingdom economy).

7.2   The accumulation accounts

Gross saving is the flow which links the current accounts with the accumulation accounts (*SNA93*, para. 9.19; and see Figure 1.6, pp. 24–5). The accumulation accounts are the accounts which record changes in assets and liabilities, and thence changes in net worth. The structure of the accumulation accounts is shown in Figure 7.1.

The accumulation accounts of the SNA93/ESA95 are devised to give a comprehensive accounting record of changes in assets and liabilities. Assets

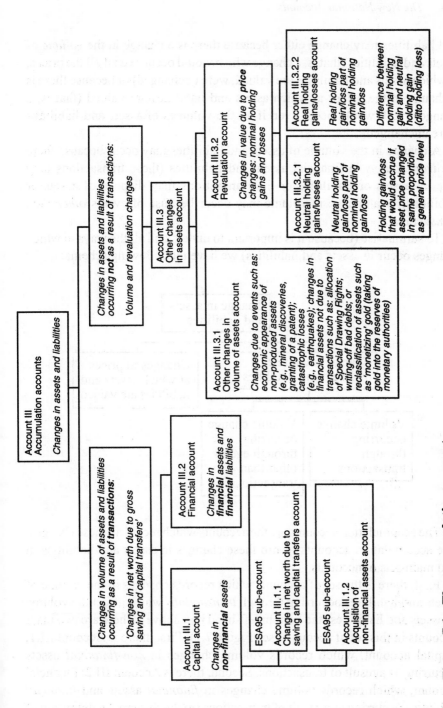

Figure 7.1 The accumulation accounts

327

and liabilities may change either because there is a change in the *volume* of assets and liabilities (that is, a change which would occur even if all the prices, at which assets and liabilities are valued, were unchanged) or because there is a change in the *prices* at which assets and liabilities are valued (that is, a change which would occur even if all the volumes of assets and liabilities were unchanged).

A change in the volume of assets and liabilities may occur because there are *transactions* in financial assets and liabilities (these transactions may acquire assets or liabilities or the transactions may dispose of assets or liabilities) or a change in volume may occur because of events *other than transactions*.

To summarise (because it is important to understand all the ways in which changes occur in assets and liabilities) we have the following schema:

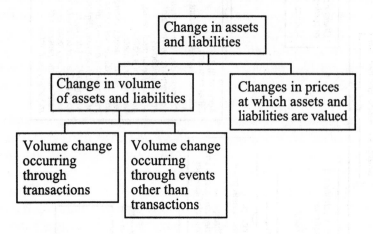

The accumulation accounts are the accounts which record all these changes. The accumulation accounts record these changes in assets and liabilities in two main sets of accounts.

First, there is the set of accounts which records changes in the volume of assets and liabilities occurring through *transactions* which affect the volume of assets and liabilities (the bottom left-hand box above). There are two main accounts in this set of accounts (see Figure 7.1). First, there is Account III.1: Capital account, which records volume changes in *non-financial* assets occurring as a result of transactions. Second, there is Account III.2: Financial account, which records volume changes in *financial* assets and *financial* liabilities occurring as a result of transactions (in the System the definition of 'liability' is a financial claim (*SNA93*, para. 13.1) so it is superfluous to attach the adjective 'financial' to the noun 'liability', but we must always keep in mind that assets can be both non-financial and financial). The changes in assets and liabilities recorded in these two accounts are the most important changes both from an economic point of view and also quantitatively (unless inflation is extreme).

Second, there is the set of accounts which records changes in assets and liabilities occurring *not* because of transactions, but which occur because of events other than transactions. This set of accounts covers all the other boxes in the schema; that is, these accounts record volume changes occurring through events other than transactions and value changes occurring because prices, at which assets and liabilities are valued, change. Figure 7.1 shows that the main account here is Account III.3: Other changes in assets account, but (following the schema) this account is divided by the SNA93/ESA95 according to the origin of these non-transaction changes in assets and liabilities (note that in the names of these accounts, the term 'assets' is to be understood as indicating that the account covers liabilities as well).

If the change is a volume change (not arising from transactions), then the change is recorded in Account III.3.1: Other changes in volume of assets account (see Figure 7.1), and this account deals with changes due to events such as: the economic appearance of non-produced assets (for example, the event of a mineral discovery or the granting of a patent); the catastrophic loss of assets (for example, the event of an earthquake or hurricane, and so on); the allocation or cancellation of Special Drawing Rights; the writing-off of bad debts by creditors (this is debt cancellation which does not occur by mutual agreement); or to reclassifications among assets. Note that these events causing changes in assets and liabilities can all be described as changes not arising from transactions (*SNA93*, paras 12.4–12.12).

If the change is due only to a change in price (the quantity or volume of the asset or liability being constant), then the change is recorded in Account III.3.2: Revaluation account (see Figure 7.1), and this account deals with nominal holding gains and losses. (To simplify, the following considers only a holding gain on an asset; parallel considerations apply to liabilities (which are included in this account) and to holding losses.) The nominal holding gain is the difference between the monetary value of the asset at a later point in time *minus* the monetary value of the asset at an earlier point in time (*SNA93*, para. 12.69).

Any nominal holding gain may be apportioned between a neutral holding gain and a real holding gain. To explain this, suppose that at the beginning of the period you held 1000 shares in Acme Foods plc/ltd valued on the stock exchange at a price of €2 per share, then your opening balance sheet would record the value of your AF.5 share assets (a quantity or volume of 1000 shares) as €2000. Suppose that at the end of the period the shares were valued on the stock exchange at a price of €3 per share; your closing balance sheet would record the value of your AF.5 share assets (the same quantity or volume of 1000 shares) as €3000. This change of €1000 during the year (in the value of the same quantity or volume of shares), due to the change in the *price* at which your asset is valued, is known as a 'nominal holding gain' and your Account III.3.2: Revaluation account would record, under the heading 'Changes in assets: K.11 Nominal holding gains (+)/losses (–)' an 'AF.5 Shares and other equity' nominal holding gain of €1000 per annum. This change, which is (NB) not due to a transaction, would then account for the difference in the value of your AF.5 assets between the opening balance sheet and the closing balance sheet.

Note that nominal holding gains can apply not only to financial assets but also to non-financial assets (inventories especially). In the SNA93/ESA95 holding gains are strictly not regarded as part of income, and are specifically kept separate from income; gross operating surplus especially is calculated excluding the holding gain on inventories (*UK NACSM*, paras 12.57–12.60 and 15.128–15.142, and especially para. 15.136). Note also that in order to be recorded in the revaluation account a holding gain does *not* need to be 'realised' (a holding gain is said to be 'realised' when the asset is sold at the higher price).

Any nominal holding gain can be partitioned between a 'neutral holding gain' and a 'real holding gain' (*SNA93*, para. 12.74). Suppose that the general price level, as measured by an appropriate price index, had increased by 10 per cent during the year or by a multiplicative factor of 1.10 (the SNA93 notes that a consumer price index meets most of the requirements of an appropriate and readily-available comprehensive price index – *SNA93*, para. 12.75). A neutral holding gain is defined as the holding gain that would have occurred if the asset price had also increased in the same proportion as the general price level; that is, by 10 per cent per annum, or by a multiplicative factor of 1.10 per annum. The neutral holding gain is thus an analytical construct. Accordingly, the *neutral* holding gain in the example of 1000 shares in Acme Foods plc/ltd can be defined and calculated as:

Neutral holding gain during year on 1000 shares in Acme Foods plc/ltd	=	Closing value of 1000 shares if share price had increased during year in same proportion as general price level	−	Opening value of 1000 shares

$$= \ 1000 \text{ shares} \ \times \ \text{€2 per share} \ \times \ 1.10 \text{ p.a.}$$
$$\quad - 1000 \text{ shares} \ \times \ \text{€2 per share}$$

$$= \ 1000 \text{ shares} \ \times \ \text{€2 per share} \ \times \ (1.10 \text{ p.a.} - 1)$$

$$= \ \text{€200 p.a.}$$

A *real* holding gain is then defined and calculated as the nominal holding gain *minus* the neutral holding gain; in the example, the real holding gain is: €1000 per annum – €200 per annum = €800 per annum (*SNA93*, paras 12.63–12.92; *ESA95*, paras 6.35–6.48).

The economic significance of a neutral holding gain is that it is 'the value of the nominal holding gain needed to preserve the real value of the asset intact' (*SNA93*, para. 12.74). The economic significance of a real holding gain (or a real holding loss) is that it may influence the economic behaviour of the owner of the asset: 'Real holding gains [and real holding losses] are important economic variables in their own right that need to be taken into account as well as income for purposes of analysing consumption or capital formation. It can be argued that real holding gains [and losses] ought to be assimilated with income as defined in the System [in order] to obtain a more comprehensive measure of income ... it is clear that information on real holding gains [and losses] needs to be made available to users [of national accounts], analysts and policy makers' (*SNA93*, para. 12.81, with my interpolations in square brackets).

Having briefly explained the changes in assets occurring not as a result of transactions, this chapter considers only those accounts which record volume changes in assets and liabilities occurring because of transactions (namely, Account III.1: Capital account and Account III.2: Financial account). The chapter does not consider the set of accounts dealing with other changes in assets and liabilities (largely because these accounts have not at the time of writing been, but will eventually be, implemented in the United Kingdom national accounts (*UK NACSM*, paras 8.1 and 11.53) and in the Australian National Accounts (Australian Bureau of Statistics, *Information Paper: Implementation of Revised International Standards in the Australian National Accounts*, Catalogue No. 5251.0, para. 10.22, also p. 78 and Table A8, pp. 88–9)).

The SNA93/ESA95 capital account records the acquisition, through transactions, of non-financial assets (out of gross saving and net capital transfers). Separately, the SNA93/ESA95 financial account records the net acquisition, through transactions, of financial assets out of the remaining part of gross saving supplemented by net capital transfers (if the combined amount is positive) called 'net lending (+)'. If this remaining part is negative it is called 'net borrowing (–)', and net borrowing (–) results in the net acquisition of liabilities. Note that it is possible for gross saving itself to be negative (for example, if gross disposable income is less than consumption expenditure (if any), or (equivalently) if all current transactions received (in) sum to less than all current transactions paid (out), and in this case the remaining part will be net borrowing (–). ('Net capital transfers' is calculated as capital transfers receivable *minus* capital transfers payable, and may be positive or negative. Net capital transfers tends to be relatively small and is not an essential part of the explanation of the acquisition of assets, so net capital transfers will initially be ignored in the following basic explanations. Once the basic concepts and principles are understood, it is an easy matter to show how and where capital transfers fit in (see Figure 7.2, p. 372).)

The SNA93/ESA95 is careful to record transactions in non-financial assets in an account (the capital account) entirely distinct and separate from the account in which transactions in financial assets and liabilities are recorded (the financial account). Why so? The answer is that non-financial assets are, in many sorts of ways, different in nature from financial assets. I discuss only three of the more important reasons for having distinct and separate accounts.

The first important reason concerns the following difference between financial and non-financial assets. Financial assets (apart from monetary gold and Special Drawing Rights) always imply a corresponding and matching financial liability – known as 'asset/liability symmetry' and meaning that someone's claim is another's liability. Consequently, among residents taken as a group each liability within the group 'cancels' its corresponding claim within the group.

(Monetary gold is gold held by monetary authorities as a financial asset and as a component of foreign reserves (because of gold's international acceptability); monetary gold is treated as a financial asset even though there is no corresponding financial claim over another institutional unit. Special Drawing Rights are reserve assets issued by the International Monetary Fund and are 'not considered liabilities of the IMF, and IMF members to whom SDRs are allocated do not have an actual (unconditional) liability to repay their SDRs allocations' (*SNA93*, para. 11.67).)

Apart from monetary gold and SDRs, the only way residents (taken as a group) can accumulate wealth, or net worth, in the form of financial assets is to acquire financial claims on non-residents in excess of non-residents' claims on residents.

With non-financial assets it is quite otherwise. Residents taken as a group can accumulate wealth in the form of non-financial assets simply by producing (or importing) and holding these non-financial assets. Ultimately, the wealth of the nation consists of its stock of non-financial assets *plus* its stock of monetary gold and SDRs *plus* the excess of residents' claims on non-residents over non-residents' claims on residents (or *minus* the excess of non-residents' claims on residents over residents' claims on non-residents).

The second important reason arises from the fact that non-financial assets are acquired in order to use these assets physically in the process of production, so generating gross value added, while financial assets are acquired in order to generate a property income and to hold as a store of value (including 'liquid' financial assets held in order to be able to make payments as and when bills fall due for payment). Acquiring non-financial assets and financial assets may each be referred to as 'investment' – an ambiguous word generally best avoided – because each involves a current outlay in return for a stream of future benefits to the owner of the asset. But the economic reasons behind investment in non-financial assets are very different from the economic reasons behind investment in financial assets.

The third reason for having a capital account distinct from the financial account is that (ignoring capital transfers) the balance between gross saving on the one hand and the acquisition of non-financial assets on the other hand determines what has to happen to the balance between the net acquisition of financial assets on the one hand and the net acquisition of financial liabilities on the other hand. For example in plain and simple terms, if your expenditure on non-financial assets during a period (say, a dwelling) is bigger than your gross saving during that period, then you have either to borrow or to use (that is, dispose of) financial assets previously accumulated (or a mixture of both). It is obviously important to know the extent of the difference between your gross saving and your expenditure on non-financial assets. The balance between gross saving and the acquisition of non-financial assets is known as 'net lending (+)/net borrowing (–)' and is the balance which is calculated, or struck, on the capital account. The capital account is therefore kept as a distinct account from the financial account precisely and expressly in order to derive this net lending (+)/net borrowing (–) balancing item, which is a balancing item essential to comprehensive economic analysis (*SNA93*, para. 2.136).

For these (and other) reasons, it is very necessary to treat transactions in non-financial assets separately from transactions in financial assets, and the SNA93/ESA95 does this by having two separate accounts: Account III.1: Capital account; and Account III.2: Financial account (see Figure 7.1 – the ESA95 division of the SNA93 Account III.1 into two sub-accounts will be discussed subsequently). Together with Account II.4.1: Use of disposable income account, the capital account and the financial account are the accounts with which we shall be mainly concerned in Sections 7.3 to 7.6.

7.3   The relationship between gross saving and net lending (+)/net borrowing (–)

Sections 7.4 and 7.5 explain the technically correct definition and derivation of gross saving, B.8g, as the balancing item on Account II.4.1: Use of disposable income account, the last account in the sequence of current accounts. Gross saving is then carried down to Account III.1: Capital account, the first account in the sequence of accumulation accounts. Gross saving thus links the current accounts and the accumulation accounts. It is then the function of the capital account to record the transactions on acquiring *non-financial* assets which are financed in whole or in part from gross saving. The capital account also records capital transfers as a source of finance; these transfers will be discussed subsequently, and are for the moment ignored. The capital account concludes by calculating and recording the balancing item: net lending (+)/ net borrowing (–), B.9. (Note that when using the term 'net lending (+)/net borrowing (–)', I always include '(+)' and '(–)', even though this is not the invariable practice of the SNA93/ESA95.)

Before explaining gross saving, it is helpful to have a map of where are about to go, and this section provides that map in the form of a series of explanatory (and simplified) schemas, and we also explain fully the meaning of the adjective 'net' in the term 'net lending (+)/net borrowing (–)'.

If we simplify by ignoring capital transfers (which will be considered subsequently), then we can devise some simplified schemas which show the basic relationship between gross saving and net lending (+)/net borrowing (–) as it looks to a single institutional unit such as a household or an enterprise. In all schemas it is necessary carefully to bear in mind the distinction between flows and stocks, because in the capital and financial accounts we are dealing with (flow) changes in the volume of stocks occurring because of transactions. (Where appropriate, the balancing item of net lending (+)/net borrowing (–) is shown with shading in the schemas.)

The first schema shows two things: (1) that net lending (+) is the excess of (positive) gross saving over the acquisition, through transactions, of non-financial assets (and hence is a part of gross saving); and (2) that this excess can be used to acquire, through transactions, financial assets or (equivalently) to repay debt (that is, reduce financial liabilities – various synonymous terms are used to refer to the reduction of financial liabilities – 'repay debt', 'redeem debt', 'liability redemption'):

Net lending (+), B.9, is the positive difference between (positive) gross saving and the acquisition, through transactions, of non-financial assets

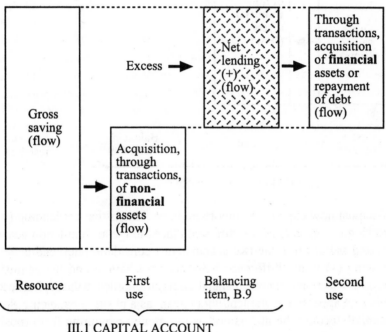

III.1 CAPITAL ACCOUNT

Conversely, net borrowing (–) can be depicted as the excess of the acquisition, through transactions, of non-financial assets over (positive) gross saving. (The negative sign for net borrowing (–) arises because the balancing item net lending (+)/net borrowing (–) is (ignoring capital transfers) always calculated as: gross saving *minus* acquisition of non-financial assets.) This second schema shows that net borrowing (–) must be financed by the acquisition, through transactions, of financial liabilities or by the reduction, through transactions, of financial assets held:

Net borrowing (–), B.9, is the negative difference between (positive) gross saving and the acquisition, through transactions, of non-financial assets

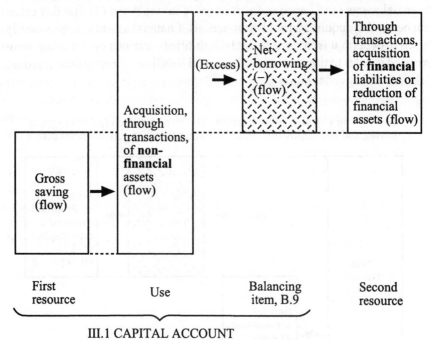

III.1 CAPITAL ACCOUNT

We must now explain an important point. This is that net lending (+)/net borrowing (–) appears in *two* different places in the accumulation accounts. First, and as shown in the two schemas just considered, net lending (+)/net borrowing (–) is the difference between gross saving and the acquisition, through transactions, of non-financial assets as recorded in the capital account. In this first appearance, net lending (+) can, as a positive balancing flow on the capital account, be understood as the money remaining from (positive) gross saving after the acquisition, through transactions, of non-financial ('real') assets (assuming the former is greater than the latter) and available to be used for the acquisition, through transactions, of financial assets, while net borrowing (–) can, as a negative balancing flow on the capital account, be understood as finance which must be obtained, through transactions, in order to make good the shortfall of gross saving over the acquisition, through transactions, of non-financial ('real') assets (assuming the former is less than the latter). This first appearance of net lending (+)/net borrowing (–) in the capital account has the SNA93/ESA95 identification code B.9, and may be referred to as 'net lending (+)/net borrowing (–) from the capital account' (see the *Blue Book 1999 edition*, table 1.7.8, p. 72 – the *Blue Book* omits the definite article).

Net lending (+) can be used either to acquire financial assets or to repay debt (that is, reduce the stock of financial liabilities outstanding). Conversely, net borrowing (–) can be met (that is, the finance can be obtained) either by increasing the stock of financial liabilities outstanding (that is, by 'borrowing' in the broadest sense of the word) or by reducing the stock of financial assets held. (The most appropriate definition of 'finance' is 'the provision of money at the time it is wanted' (F.W. Paish and R.J. Briston, *Business Finance*, Fifth Edition, Pitman, 1978, p. 1).) You can understand that, from the point of view of the overall financial standing of the institutional unit, acquiring financial assets has the same effect as repaying debt, and conversely, acquiring financial liabilities has the same effect as reducing a stock of (previously accumulated) financial assets. As explained in Chapter 1's Section 1.7, the picture we should have of net lending (+) is either of the two following (or a mixture of both):

Net lending (+) can be used either to increase financial assets or to reduce financial liabilities (repay debt)

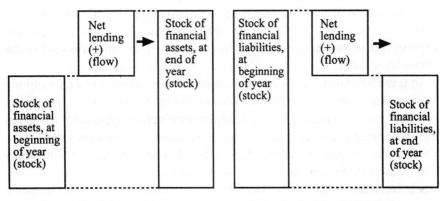

Acquisition of financial assets means volume change in stocks occurring through transactions

Reduction in financial liabilities outstanding means volume change in stocks occurring through transactions

Conversely, the picture we should have of net borrowing (–) is either of the two following (or a mixture of both):

Net borrowing (–) can be met either by increasing the stock of financial liabilities outstanding or by reducing the stock of financial assets held

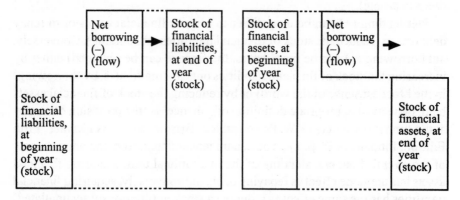

Acquisition (or 'incurrence') of liabilities means volume change in stocks occurring through transactions

Reduction in financial assets means volume change in stocks occurring through transactions

The point about these two schemas is expressed in the words 'means volume change in stocks': volume change in stocks of financial assets and/or volume change in stocks of financial liabilities has to happen (through transactions) in consequence of net lending (+)/net borrowing (–), B.9. This leads to the second appearance of net lending (+)/net borrowing (–). Thus we must now explain this second appearance of net lending (+)/net borrowing (–) in the financial account.

It is the function of the financial account to record transactions on acquiring or disposing of financial assets (of various types) and transactions on acquiring or repaying ('redeeming') financial liabilities (of various types). For any given category of financial asset or liability, these transactions are recorded net (in the meaning of 'net' which will be explained in Section 7.6 and which may for the moment be ignored).

In the financial account, net lending (+)/net borrowing (–) is the balancing item calculated as the difference between the total net acquisition, through transactions during a period, of financial assets and the total net acquisition (or 'incurrence'), through transactions during the same period, of financial liabilities. In the United Kingdom national accounts this second appearance of net lending (+)/net borrowing (–) has the identification code B.9f, where the useful suffix 'f' is added for financial account, and is referred to as 'net lending (+)/net borrowing (–) from the financial account'.

Institutional units do not, of course, have to make an either/or choice between increasing financial assets and reducing financial liabilities on the one hand (in the case of net lending (+)) or an either/or choice between increasing financial liabilities and reducing financial assets on the other hand (in the case of net borrowing (–)). It is quite possible for an institutional unit simultaneously to acquire financial assets and to incur liabilities (for example, an institutional unit could borrow from the bank in order to buy shares). It is the function of the financial account to record all these financial transactions.

If we assume that, during any period, there are positive changes in the stocks of financial assets *and* positive changes in the stocks of financial liabilities outstanding, then we may draw the following two schemas for net lending (+) and for net borrowing (–) from the financial account and this is the second appearance of net lending (+)/net borrowing (–) in the accumulation accounts (with shading to signify balancing item):

Net lending (+) and net borrowing (–) as the balancing item, B.9f, from the financial account

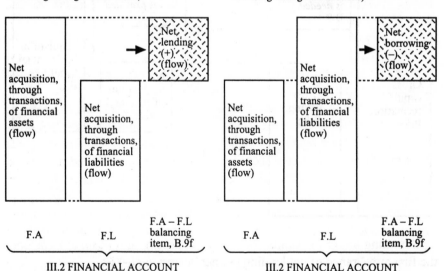

Net lending (+) (flow) is the difference between two volume changes in stocks (changes occurring through transactions)

Net borrowing (–) (flow) is the difference between two volume changes in stocks (changes occurring through transactions)

III.2 FINANCIAL ACCOUNT   III.2 FINANCIAL ACCOUNT

In the financial account, net lending (+) is the (positive) balance of the net acquisition, through transactions, of financial assets over the net acquisition (or net 'incurrence'), through transactions, of financial liabilities, and net borrowing (–) is the (negative) balance of the net acquisition, through transactions, of financial liabilities over the net acquisition, through transactions, of financial assets.

The meaning of the adjective 'net' in the term 'net lending(+)/net borrowing (–)', B.9f, can now be explained. In the schema just shown, 'net lending (+)' means the net acquisition of financial assets *net* of the net acquisition of financial liabilities, while 'net borrowing (–)' means the net acquisition of financial liabilities *net* of the net acquisition of financial assets, but always calculated as the net acquisition of financial assets *minus* the net acquisition of financial liabilities, hence the minus sign in 'net borrowing (–)'.

The term 'net lending (+)/net borrowing (–)' is used for the B.9 balancing item on the capital account because of the relation between B.9 and B.9f, as we can show in a simplified schema for net borrowing (–), taking net borrowing (–) and gross capital formation, P.5, because this is easier to understand as the relation between 'why finance (additional to gross saving) is needed' and 'how finance (additional to gross saving) is provided':

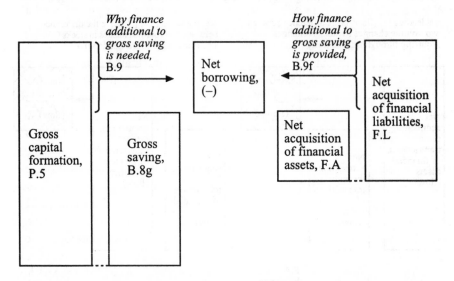

Summing up, in the capital account (and assuming no capital transfers), the first appearance of net lending (+)/net borrowing (–) is:

Net lending (+)/ net borrowing (–), B.9 = Gross saving – Acquisition, through transactions, of non-financial assets (i.e., P.5)

And in the financial account, the second appearance of net lending (+)/net borrowing (–) is the difference between two changes in stocks:

Net lending (+)/ net borrowing (–), B.9f	=	Net acquisition, through transactions, of financial assets, F.A	–	Net acquisition, through transactions, of financial liabilities, F.L

In principle, net lending (+)/net borrowing (–) calculated as the B.9 balancing item in the capital account is the same amount as net lending (+)/ net borrowing (–) calculated as the B.9f balancing item in the financial account. This is because, as we have shown for the case of net borrowing (–), net lending (+)/net borrowing (–), B.9, is the source for/cause of *the difference* between the net acquisition, through transactions, of financial assets and the net acquisition, through transactions, of financial liabilities, this difference being net lending (+)/net borrowing (–), B.9f. In practice, errors of recording and omissions may lead to B.9f being recorded as different from B.9. If this happens, then a statistical discrepancy item is needed to reconcile B.9f with B.9.

In this chapter, each of gross saving and net lending (+)/net borrowing (–), B.9 and B.9f, is explained both by the method of using a simplified 'model' account for a household and also by discussion of the relevant SNA93/ESA95 accounts for the United Kingdom and Australia.

Throughout this chapter I focus on gross saving (that is, saving before deduction of, or including, the consumption of fixed capital) partly because gross saving is the flow which finances (in whole or in part) gross capital formation and partly because gross saving is the variable most appropriate for 'Keynesian' macroeconomics. This also follows the actual presentation of the United Kingdom and the Australian national accounts in recording consumption of fixed capital as a (distinct) *positive* item under sources of finance in the capital account – together, net saving and consumption of fixed capital make up *gross* saving (*UK NACSM*, paras 6.5, 15.2–15.4 and 15.11; Australian Bureau of Statistics, *Information Paper: Implementation of Revised International Standards in the Australian National Accounts*, Catalogue No. 5251.0, para. 11.16). This may be called the 'gross presentation'. This differs from the recommended practice of the SNA93/ESA95 of recording consumption of fixed capital as a *negative* item under changes in assets in the capital account and recording *net* saving under the sources of finance side of the account (*SNA93*, paras 2.137, 6.201–6.203, 10.27 and 10.118). This may be called the 'net presentation'.

The problem arises from the dual role of consumption of fixed capital but 'both the net and gross presentations are valid, provided that both saving and fixed capital formation are dealt with consistently' (*UK NACSM*, para. 15.7).

The gross presentation (which should preferably report consumption of fixed capital as a distinct and separate item) focuses on the financing role of consumption of fixed capital; the net presentation focuses on the decline-in-value-of-fixed-assets, or cost of production, role of consumption of fixed capital. Whichever presentation is adopted, the result for net lending (+)/net borrowing (–) is the same (see footnote (*b*) to Table 7.6, pp. 366–7).

It is common in national accounts for the unqualified word 'saving' to be used to refer only to *net* saving. The best rule to apply, and one that I will try to follow, is never to use the word 'saving' without attaching either the adjective 'gross' or 'net' as required unless there is a very specific reason for referring to 'saving' generally. In other contexts, if you see the word 'saving' without a requisite adjective, you are advised to ascertain immediately whether 'gross saving' or 'net saving' is meant.

The reason why national accounts often focus attention on net saving is that (ignoring capital transfers and changes in assets and liabilities due to things other than transactions) it is net saving which finances an increase in net worth. To explain this, let us focus upon non-financial assets (because this is the essential part of the problem). Consider gross saving as the sum of its two parts: net saving and the consumption of fixed capital. The potential of the consumption of fixed capital, in its dual role as an *imputed* cost of production and as a set-aside or provision from sales receipts or other revenue, is only to make good the decline in the value of fixed assets due to depreciation resulting from use in production (*SNA93*, paras 6.179, 6.182, 6.183 and 6.193). Therefore, if gross fixed capital formation is exactly equal to the amount of the consumption of fixed capital, there is no change in the value of non-financial assets held and no change in net worth. Consequently, that part of gross fixed capital formation financed by that part of gross saving which is consumption of fixed capital does not add to wealth (net worth) but only maintains wealth constant. In strong contrast, the potential of net saving is, so to speak, to continue on from where consumption of fixed capital left off (maintaining wealth constant) and so net saving has the potential to add to wealth. Hence *net* saving is the source from which an increase in wealth is financed (*SNA93*, para. 13.94). The increase in the wealth of the nation arises from net saving rather than from gross saving. This is why the national accounts pay considerable attention to net saving.

7.4   Meaning and measurement of household gross saving

The concept of the gross saving of an institutional unit is quite straightforward in principle, although (as will here be explained) the measurement of gross saving for the household sector is quite complex in practice. For purposes of explanation, we will take the case of a single institutional unit, such as a household (here called the 'model household' because the case is imaginary, simplified and hypothetical), which engages in final consumption expenditure, P.3, in the form of individual consumption expenditure, P.31. We start by calculating gross disposable income (so it is essential that the reader begin this section with a clear understanding of gross disposable income from Tables 6.3 and 6.4). We have said that gross saving can be provisionally understood as what is left over from gross disposable income after consumption expenditure has been met (if any). Alternatively (but also provisionally), gross saving is what remains from all current transactions received after all current transactions paid.

(For any institutional unit which does not (in principle) undertake final consumption expenditure, such as non-financial corporations, gross saving is (and must be in principle) equal to gross disposable income (*SNA93*, para. 9.4). For this reason, the explanation of gross saving as the difference between the total of current transactions received and the total of current transactions paid is a more general explanation.)

Gross saving can be positive or negative; positive gross saving means that the total of all current transactions received is greater than the total of all current transactions paid; conversely, negative gross saving means that the total of all current transactions received is less than the total of all current transactions paid. The ESA95 explains:

> [Gross] Saving is the (positive or negative) amount resulting from [all] current transactions which establishes the link with accumulation. If [gross] saving is positive, non-spent [disposable gross] income is used for the acquisition of assets [both non-financial and financial] or for paying off liabilities. If [gross] saving is negative, certain assets are liquidated [sold, disposed of in return for cash] or certain [financial] liabilities increase (*ESA95*, para. 8.43, with my clarifying interpolations in square brackets).

Technically, 'saving' can only be correctly and generally defined as the balancing item on Account II.4.1: Use of disposable income account (*SNA93*, paras 9.5–9.6 and 9.17; *UK NACSM*, para. 14.16; and see Table 7.2, p. 354).

If disposable income is taken gross of consumption of fixed capital, then the balancing item is *gross saving*, B.8g; if disposable income is taken net of consumption of fixed capital, then the balancing item is *net saving*, B.8n. Alternatively, net saving can be calculated as gross saving minus consumption of fixed capital, K.1. The implication of the technically correct definition is that in order to understand the meaning of the word 'saving', one first has to understand Account II.4.1: Use of disposable income account and the items in it. For sectors which in principle do not undertake final consumption expenditure, Account II.4.1 is simply a 'dummy account' that contains no entries for final consumption expenditure (*SNA93*, para. 9.4).

However, the correct measurement of gross saving for households as the balancing item on Account II.4.1 is complicated. The complication concerns contributions to private pension funds, comprising private funded schemes (see Figure 6.3, p. 270). The complication will now be explained with the aid of Table 7.1, because understanding the complication, and its solution, is an essential prerequisite to understanding the application of Account II.4.1 to the household sector of the economy (and also to understanding the contra-entry for the sector of insurance corporations and pension funds, S.125). This matter is important because of the relative magnitude of household sector gross saving in any economy: to illustrate, in the United Kingdom in 1997 the gross saving of the household sector (including NPISHs) contributed 37 per cent of the economy's total gross saving, while in Australia in 1997–98 the corresponding figure was 39 per cent (Table 7.9, pp. 382–3).

Table 7.1 is effectively in three parts. The purpose of Part One is to recapitulate previous explanations of the calculation of disposable income (this gives us a secure foundation and a point of departure for the explanation). The purpose of Part Two (with its two columns) is to explain how to measure gross saving correctly, and in order to explain what the correct procedure it is best to begin by explaining an incorrect procedure; this is because once one understands why the simple and 'obvious' procedure for measuring household gross saving is incorrect, it is then an easy step to understand how to devise the correct procedure for measuring household gross saving. The purpose of Part Three of Table 7.1 is to explain, with reference to financial assets acquired, why it is that the incorrect procedure is, in fact, incorrect and gives a 'wrong' or 'inappropriate' measure of gross saving.

Table 7.1 relates to a model household taken as a single institutional unit. Table 7.1 uses simple imaginary numbers, all in € per annum (in order to avoid fractions in subsequent tables, the numbers used are in the realm of the tens up to one hundred). In Table 7.1, I give the SNA93/ESA95 identification

Table 7.1
The problem of measuring household gross saving correctly; model household

SNA93/ESA95 identification code		Model household [a], € per annum	
PART ONE: MEASURING DISPOSABLE INCOME			
	Resources		
D.11	Wage/salary	90	
D.12	Employer's social contribution to private pension fund	10	
D.1	Compensation of employee	100	
Total	Total resources	100	
	Uses		
D.6111	Employer's actual social contribution (= D.12 above)	10	
D.6112	Employee's social contribution to (same) private pension fund	10	
B.6g	Disposable income, gross	80	
Total	Total uses	100	
	PART TWO: MEASURING GROSS SAVING	INCORRECT	CORRECT
	Resources		
B.6g	Disposable income, gross	80	80
—	INCORRECT: Total resources	×80	...
	CORRECT, add:		
D.8	Adjustment for the change in net equity of household in pension fund's reserves	...	20
Total	CORRECT: Total resources	...	100 ✓
	Uses		
P.31	Individual consumption expenditure	70	70
—	INCORRECT: Saving, gross	×10	...
—	INCORRECT: Total uses	80	...
B.8g	CORRECT: Saving, gross	...	30 ✓
Total	CORRECT: Total uses	...	100
	PART THREE: FINANCIAL ACCOUNT		
F.22	Acquisition of financial assets: change (increase) in bank deposit		10
F.612	Acquisition of financial assets: change (increase) in net equity of household in private pension fund		20
F.A	Total acquisition of financial assets.		30

should be, but is not, equal

should be, and is, equal

'...' means not applicable in order to illustrate the case; note that SNA93/ESA95 identification codes are not given for items illustrating incorrect procedure.

(a) Note that in this simplified account there is: (1) no acquisition of non-financial assets (no capital formation), and (2) no acquisition of financial liabilities.

Source: numbers hypothetical and explained in Section 7.4.

codes but I use some abbreviated, easy-to-remember names, not the proper SNA93/ESA95 names (which are introduced at a later stage).

Part One of Table 7.1 goes further back than the secondary distribution of income account (for example, see the household sector column in Table 6.3), because it is useful to begin at the very origins of household sector primary income. We imagine that the model household receives a primary income which is in large part a wage or salary from employment (a member of the household works as an employee); the amount of this D.11 wage or salary primary income is €90 per annum. But for reasons explained in Chapter 6, Table 7.1 records another part of compensation of employees as the *employer's* social contribution to a private pension fund on behalf of the employee; the amount of this D.12 employer's social contribution is €10 per annum. This makes up the household's total 'compensation of employee' income, D.1, of €100 per annum. The household in Table 7.1 receives, and pays, no other primary income, so its total resources, given in the fourth row, is its balance of primary income.

The next section of Part One of Table 7.1 gives the Uses segment of the secondary distribution of income account (see Table 6.3, household sector column). In this simplified example, there are only two uses, because it is these two uses that we need to consider especially. Specifically, in Table 7.1 there is assumed to be no payment by the household of current taxes on income, because income tax is not relevant to the problem being considered. However, what is relevant to the problem to be considered is the D.61 social contributions, which are, in this example, confined to: (1) the employer's actual social contribution, D.6111, to the private pension fund (note that this is identical to the D.12 social contribution included in the compensation of the employee – to be quite explicit, this is identically the same D.12 item which is here being reported, as D.6111, under a different heading) and amounting to €10 per annum; and (2) the employee's social contribution, D.6112, to the same private pension fund, which is assumed also to be €10 per annum (that is, in the model, employer and employee are each assumed to make equal and matching annual social contributions to the private pension fund).

These two social contributions to the private pension fund are the only transfers paid on the model household's secondary distribution of income account and no transfers are received on this account. Accordingly, the model household's gross disposable income can be calculated as:

| Gross disposable income, B.6g | = | Total resources, or compensation of employee | − | Total social contributions, D.61 |

$$= \text{€}100 \text{ p.a.} - \text{€}20 \text{ p.a.}$$

$$= \text{€}80 \text{ p.a.}$$

It is useful at this juncture to consider the cash flows involved. (As a general methodological matter when trying to understand the accumulation accounts, it is helpful to keep a watch on the cash flows because these provide a basis for understanding the items in the accounts. For this reason, I refer below to the cash flows at critical points in the explanation.) The model household has received, in cash, €90 per annum as a wage/salary (remember our assumption of no income tax); the household has paid, in cash, €10 per annum as the employee's social contribution, D.6112; this leaves the household with €80 per annum 'cash in hand'. We have also taken into consideration the fact that, by a different actual route, the employer has paid a D.12 (= D.6111) social contribution, on behalf of the employee, to a private pension fund, but the SNA93/ESA95 reroutes this payment (as shown in Table 7.1) to reflect the fact that the employee is benefitting (that is, will upon retirement benefit) from the employer's social contributions (accumulated) as well as from the employee's own social contributions (accumulated). But we can see that the gross disposable income is 'cash in hand' for the model household.

Unfortunately, if we confine our attention to this 'cash in hand' gross disposable income we will fall into error when it comes to measuring the model household's gross saving. The purpose of Part Two of Table 7.1 with its two columns is to demonstrate the nature of this error.

Suppose that we proceed to measure the model household's gross saving as the difference between its B.6g disposable income of €80 per annum and its P.31 individual consumption expenditure of €70 per annum. This procedure follows the provisional explanation of gross saving as the difference between gross disposable income and consumption expenditure, but (as we are about to explain) the provisional explanation of gross saving needs to be qualified in the case of households. We would then prepare an incorrect version of Account II.4.1: Use of disposable income account, as shown in the column in Table 7.1 labelled 'INCORRECT'.

First we would report gross disposable income, B.6g, as a resource on Account II.4.1. This is correct so far as it goes. Then we would report that gross disposable income was the only, and therefore the total, resource on Account II.4.1; and here we would fall into error. Accordingly, in Table 7.1 I have marked this occurrence of €80 per annum as the *total* resource for the model household with a cross to indicate that this is an incorrect procedure. In order to understand why this procedure is incorrect, we need to continue with the account, persisting in the error, because we shall then find that we have been led to an unacceptable result.

The uses on Account II.4.1 are: (1) individual consumption expenditure by the model household, P.31, amounting to €70 per annum; and (2) the balancing item of gross saving. In the 'INCORRECT' column we calculate the model household's gross saving (incorrectly) as the difference between gross disposable income and individual consumption expenditure in accordance with our provisional explanation of the concept of gross saving (in this case the explanation is not applicable without qualification):

$$\begin{array}{rcl} \text{Gross saving} & = & \text{Gross disposable} \quad - \quad \text{Individual consumption} \\ \text{(incorrect)} & & \text{income, B.6g} \qquad \text{expenditure, P.31} \\[1em] & = & \text{€80 p.a.} - \text{€70 p.a.} \\[0.5em] & = & \text{€10 p.a.} \end{array}$$

However, this result of €10 per annum for the model household's gross saving is incorrect (because, as we shall show, this result is unacceptable), so this result is also marked with a cross. Of course, we are tempted to accept this result for gross saving because we know that out of the €90 per annum cash in hand wage/salary and after payment of €10 per annum employee's social contribution to the private pension fund and after €70 per annum individual consumption expenditure, the model household is left with €10 per annum 'cash in hand' which thus appears at first sight to be the household's gross saving (but this is incorrect, as we shall show).

The next step in the explanation is to explain why this (apparently reasonable) way of measuring the model household's saving is incorrect, in the sense of leading to an unacceptable result. For this we need to consider Part Three of Table 7.1, the financial account, which deals with the model household's acquisition of financial assets. (For the sake of keeping the example as simple as possible, it is assumed that the model household undertakes no expenditure on non-financial, or real, assets during the year and acquires, with its gross saving, only financial assets.)

The model household acquires, during the year, *two* financial assets. This is key to all that follows and needs to be well understood.

In the first place, assuming that the model household has a bank deposit and places all its cash in the bank deposit, the model household increases its bank deposit by €10 during the year. Remember the cash flow situation of this household: (1) cash inflow received of €90 per annum as wage/salary; (2) cash outflow paid (by household) of €10 per annum of employee's social contribution to pension fund; and (3) cash outflow paid (by household) of €70 per annum of consumption expenditure; (4) leaving €10 per annum cash remaining. It is this leftover cash which is deposited in the bank as a change (increase) in a bank deposit financial asset, F.22.

If we (incorrectly) confined our attention to this change in a bank deposit financial asset we would encounter no problem with measuring household gross saving as €10 per annum, because we could simply say that the household gross saving had led to an increase in its bank deposit financial asset.

The problem is that this view of household financial asset acquisition is incomplete. Why so? The answer is very simple.

In the second place, during the year, the model household has increased its claim on a private pension fund by €20 (the total amount of the social contributions which have been paid into the pension fund by and/or on behalf of the employee). This is the second financial asset which the household acquires during the year. Although the model household does not have control over this private pension fund (in the way that it has control over its bank deposit), and although the model household will not obtain the benefits from the private pension fund until that future date at which the employee in the household retires, it is nevertheless an economic reality that this household is 'benefitting', year by year, from these D.61 social contributions to the private pension fund and that the household relies on these accumulating contributions, held in what are called the 'pension fund's reserves', to provide an income in retirement.

As the SNA93 explains:

> The reserves of private funded pension schemes are treated in the System as being collectively owned by the households with claims on the funds. The payments of pension contributions [by both employers and employees] into the funds ... constitute the acquisition ... of financial assets [by the households] (*SNA93*, para, 9.14, with my clarifying interpolations in square brackets).

This means that in the balance sheets these reserves, held in the pension funds, are treated as assets owned by or belonging to households and 'this reflects the underlying economic reality [of these reserves and contributions thereto]' (*UK NACSM*, para. 20b.9, p. 460, with my clarifying interpolation in square brackets).

This is important not only in theory but also in practice. In Table 7.12, pp. 398–400, we will see that these assets constitute a significant part of household sector financial assets in Australia.

Consequently, it is important that the reasonableness of this argument about, or view of, social contributions to private pension funds be thoroughly appreciated because it is absolutely the key to everything that follows. The reserves of private pension funds are the financial assets of the contributing households; during the year, the model household has social contributions totalling €20 paid in to the private pension fund; therefore we must record an increase in its financial assets, or (eventual) claims on the private pension fund, of this amount of €20 per annum.

(In the real world, the calculation is a little more complicated than this because the calculation must include, in addition to the total value of the actual social contributions to the private funded pension schemes, the following three items: (1) the property income (interest) earned on accumulated (past) contributions and attributed to holders of pension rights ('insurance policy holders'), which increases households' claims; (2) the service charges, or administration costs, which diminish households' claims; and (3) the total value of the pensions paid out as social insurance benefits, which reduces households' claims (*SNA93*, para. 9.16; *ESA95*, para. 4.142). However, these three items are matters of detail, not of basic principle, and will be ignored in Table 7.1.)

Accordingly, in Part Three of Table 7.1, we must record, under acquisition of financial assets, a change (increase) in the net equity of the household in (meaning 'claims by the household on') [private] pension funds, F.612. This F.612 item in Table 7.1's financial account is €20 per annum.

At this juncture it is helpful to know about the following SNA93/ESA95 categories of (flow) transactions in financial instruments (net acquisition of financial assets/net incurrence of liabilities, F.; full definitions of these items are given in *ESA95*, paras 5.98 to 5.119, but for present purposes we need only a knowledge of the names and identification codes of the items):

Transactions in financial instruments (net acquisition of financial assets/net incurrence of liabilities, F. (in part)
F.6 Insurance technical reserves
F.61 Net equity of households in life insurance reserves and in pension funds' reserves
F.611 Net equity of households in life insurance reserves
F.612 Net equity of households in pension funds' reserves
F.62 Prepayments of insurance premiums and reserves for outstanding claims

There is an exactly corresponding SNA93/ESA95 classification of the *stocks* of financial assets:

Financial assets/liabilities, AF. (in part)
AF.6 Insurance technical reserves
AF.61 Net equity of households in life insurance reserves and in pension funds' reserves
AF.611 Net equity of households in life insurance reserves
AF.612 Net equity of households in pension funds' reserves
AF.62 Prepayments of insurance premiums and reserves for outstanding claims

Note that in F.612 and AF.612 the term 'pension funds' reserves' means *private* pension funds' reserves (according to the explanation on pp. 271–2 above; see also *ESA95*, para. 5.98).

Consequently in Table 7.1, the model household's total acquisition of financial assets, F.A, during the year is €30 (= €10 increase in bank deposits, F.22 + €20 increase in its claim on [private] pension fund, F.612). This is a reasonable view to take of what has happened, in terms of financial assets, to the model household's wealth during the year. (To keep the example simple, Table 7.1 assumes that no financial liabilities are incurred during the year, so this €30 per annum increase in financial assets is all that we have to consider.)

But if this is a reasonable view of the model household's increase in financial assets during the year, then the immediate, and inescapable, consequence is that the calculation of household gross saving as €10 per annum is, and must be, incorrect, because gross saving is (in this simple example) the sole source of finance for the acquisition of financial assets, and therefore gross saving (in this simple example) must be equal to the total acquisition of financial assets. As indicated in Table 7.1, this equality does not hold, and as €30 per annum is the correct figure for financial asset acquisition, then €10 per annum must be an incorrect figure for gross saving.

How may this problem be resolved? The answer is that, although the payment of €20 per annum of social contributions (the combined payment by the employer and employee) to the private pension fund leaves the model household with €80 per annum of gross disposable income, the €20 per annum of social contributions nevertheless constitutes a *resource* for the household from which the financial asset (of the claim on the private pension fund) is to be acquired. Accordingly, in the 'CORRECT' column for measuring saving in Part Two of Table 7.1, to gross disposable income we must add, as a further resource, the SNA93/ESA95 item: Adjustment for change in net equity of household in pension fund's reserves, D.8.

The D.8 item adjustment for the change in net equity of households in pension funds' reserves is identically the same item as the F.612 financial transactions item net equity of households in pension funds' reserves (see the classification scheme for the flow transactions in financial assets).

This D.8 adjustment then gives, as the total resources on the use of disposable income account, the correct amount of €100 per annum, accordingly marked with a tick. It is from this total resources that the household (1) meets its consumption expenditure and (2) has gross saving (correctly measured), as a balancing item, with which to acquire financial assets.

Accordingly, if we deduct €70 per annum of consumption expenditure from the total resources of €100 per annum, we correctly obtain the balancing item of gross saving amounting to €30 per annum, also marked with a tick. We can then see that this is the correct measure of gross saving, B.8g, because the balancing item so calculated on Account II.4.1 is exactly equal to the total acquisition of financial assets of €30 per annum. (This is why the only technically correct and generally applicable (without qualification) definition of 'saving' is that saving is the balancing item on Account II.4.1 and why the explanation of gross saving as what is left over from gross disposable income after consumption expenditure has to be described as a provisional and subordinate explanation, not applicable to all sectors without qualification, albeit an explanation that does express the substance of the concept of gross saving.)

The D.8 adjustment item resolves the problem of how to measure household gross saving 'correctly', in the sense of giving a result for gross saving consonant with the household's acquisition of financial assets (including the increase in the claim on the private pension fund).

The adjustment (to calculate household sector gross saving correctly) requires also a contra-entry in the account to calculate the gross saving of S.125 insurance corporations and pension funds. This is by reason of the fact that if the incorrect procedure in Table 7.1 understates household sector gross saving, then the incorrect procedure would matchingly overstate the gross saving of the private pension funds; consequently, when we correct for the former we must matchingly and conversely correct for the latter. In other words, aggregate saving across sectors is not affected because two D.8 adjustments are made, one an *addition* under 'Resources' in the household sector's Account II.4.1, the other a *subtraction* under 'Uses' in the insurance corporations and pension funds sector's Account II.4.1.

(Note that the D.8 adjustment item (= F.612) may also apply to households in the rest of the world (*UK NACSM*, para. 24.37, also 18.216). The D.8 adjustment item in relation to the rest of the world, S.2, is the very minor adjustment item referred to at the beginning of this chapter; S.2's D.8 adjustment item can be negative if households in the rest of the world are drawing down their claims on resident private pension funds (for example, retirees living outside the country and drawing their pensions from a resident private pension fund). Without the D.8 adjustment item for (households in) the rest of the world, we can without qualification apply the national accounting identity: Gross national saving *equals* Gross national disposable income *minus* Final consumption expenditure. With the D.8 adjustment item for (households in) the rest of the world, this national accounting identity has to be amended to: Gross national saving *equals* Gross national disposable income *minus* Final consumption expenditure *minus* S.2's Adjustment for the change in net equity of households in pension funds' reserves.)

Finally, because the reserves of pension funds are treated as the AF.612 *assets* of the household sector, S.14, so, matchingly, these reserves are treated as the AF.612 *liabilities* of the insurance corporations and pension funds, S.125 (included in financial corporations, S.12). This we shall see in Table 7.12, pp. 398–400. In other words, in the System the insurance corporations and pension funds are treated only as managers (not as owners) of the reserves (*ESA95*, paras 5.100 and 5.101; *SNA93*, paras 11.93 and 13.76; *UK NACSM*, paras 18.216, 20.100 and 22.130).

Now that we understand in principle how to calculate a household's gross saving correctly, we can consider, for the United Kingdom and Australia, the household sector Account II.4.1: Use of disposable income account, shown in Table 7.2.

Table 7.2 illustrates the correct procedure for calculating gross saving for the household sector (including non-profit institutions serving households). An important point to observe in Table 7.2 is the illustration of the technically correct definition of 'saving' as the balancing item on Account II.4.1: Use of disposable income account. (Non-profit institutions serving households, or NPISHs, are included with the household sector only because these national accounts have not, at the time of writing, separated out the transactions of

Table 7.2
Gross saving of households,[a]
United Kingdom and Australia

SNA93/ ESA95 identifi- cation code	SNA93/ESA95 name	Households and NPISHs, S.14 + S.15	
		United Kingdom 1997, £ million	Australia 1997–98, $ million
II.4	USE OF INCOME ACCOUNT		
II.4.1	USE OF DISPOSABLE INCOME ACCOUNT		
	Resources		
B.6g	Disposable income, gross	554 641	374 783
D.8	Adjustment for the change in net equity of households in pension funds' reserves	15 692	n.a. [b]
Total	Total resources	570 333	374 783
	Uses		
P.31	Individual consumption expenditure	517 032	332 311
B.8g	Saving, gross	53 301	42 472
Total	Total uses	570 333	374 783

(a)   Including non-profit institutions serving households.

(b)   'n.a.' means 'not available'; D.8 adjustment item not yet implemented in the Australian System of National accounts which still includes adjustment item in gross disposable income (so gross saving is correctly measured in the Australian System of National Accounts; but, conversely, gross disposable income is here not measured according to SNA93 principles). The SNA93 recommendation may eventually be implemented in the Australian System of National Accounts; see Australian Bureau of Statistics, *Information Paper: Implementation of Revised International Standards in the Australian National Accounts*, Catalogue No. 5251.0, September 1997, paras 5.82 and 5.83.

Sources: Office for National Statistics, *United Kingdom National Accounts The Blue Book 1999 edition* table 6.1.6, p. 210; Australian Bureau of Statistics, *Australian System of National Accounts 1997–98*, Catalogue No. 5204.0, table 2.20, p. 60.

NPISHs from the transactions of households, but this will be done eventually (*UK NACSM*, para. 10.203; Australian Bureau of Statistics, *Information Paper: Implementation of Revised International Standards in the Australian National Accounts*, Catalogue No. 5251.0, paras 5.67–5.68 and Table A9, p. 90).)

In the United Kingdom in 1997, the resources of households (including NPISHs) on Account II.4.1 were twofold. First, there is disposable income, gross, B.6g, of £554 641 million (see Table 6.3, pp. 302–3, column for the household (including NPISHs) sector, second last row, for the B.6g balancing item to ensure that you fully understand the calculation of disposable income from the balance of primary incomes, gross, B.5g). Second, there is the item *adjustment for the change in net equity of households in pension funds' reserves*, D.8, of £15 692 million. As explained for the correct procedure in Table 7.1, this has to be added to gross disposable income to get the correct total resources on Account II.4.1 of £570 333 million.

The uses on Account II.4.1 were individual consumption expenditure, P.31, of £517 032 million (see Table 3.1, p. 119), and the balancing item, *gross saving*, B.8g, for households (including NPISHs) is accordingly calculated for 1997 as £53 301 million (= £570 333 million – £517 032 million). This exemplifies the technically correct definition, and the correct calculation, of gross saving for the household sector.

In the Australian System of National Accounts the gross disposable income of households (including NPISHs) includes the adjustment item (although this may in future be excluded from gross disposable income in line with the SNA93 recommendation; in terms of the illustration of Table 7.1, the 1997–98, but possibly-to-be-changed, procedure of the Australian System of National Accounts is not to deduct the D.6111 and D.6112 items as uses on the secondary distribution of income account before calculating gross disposable income, which, for the model household, the Australian System of National Accounts would report as €100 per annum). Accordingly, for 1997–98, the Australian System of National Accounts calculates household (including NPISHs) sector gross saving (correctly) as gross disposable income (including the adjustment item), $374 783 million *minus* household final consumption expenditure, $332 311 million, *equals gross saving* $42 472 million.

In the United Kingdom in 1997, household (including NPISHs) sector gross saving was 9.3 per cent of total resources on the household (including NPISHs) use of disposable income account (the average over the preceding eight years having been 9.2 per cent), and in Australia in 1997–98, household (including NPISHs) sector gross saving was 11.3 per cent of household (including NPISHs) gross disposable income (the average over the preceding eight years having been 13.7 per cent).

7.5   Gross saving by other sectors of the economy and by the rest of the world

For the sectors of non-financial corporations and financial corporations excluding insurance corporations and pension funds, gross saving is simply gross disposable income (Tables 6.3 and 6.4). For the sector of insurance corporations and pension funds, S.125, gross saving is gross disposable income adjusted by subtracting the contra-entry D.8 adjustment for the change in the net equity of households in pension funds' reserves. The technically correct definition of 'saving' still applies.

Table 7.3 gives gross saving for these sectors of the economy in the United Kingdom in 1997 and in Australia in 1997–98. Review Tables 6.3 and 6.4 (pp. 302–3 and 316–17) to understand the starting points in Table 7.3. Because these sectors do not in principle make any final consumption expenditure, their gross disposable income has no deductions, apart from the D.8 contra-entry adjustment for S.125. The SNA93 explains:

> Corporations do not make final consumption expenditures. They may purchase the same kinds of goods or services as households use for final consumption – e.g., electricity or food – but such goods or services are either used for intermediate consumption or provided to employees as remuneration in kind. ... Apart from the adjustment item for pension funds ... *the gross or net saving of corporations must be equal to their gross or net disposable ... incomes.* In other contexts, the saving of corporations is often described as the "retained earnings" or "undistributed incomes" of corporations (*SNA93*, para. 9.4, italics added).

The sector of general government, S.13, does make final consumption expenditure, both individual consumption expenditure and collective consumption expenditure. Accordingly, the gross saving of general government has to be calculated as general government gross disposable income *minus* general government total consumption expenditure. For this sector the provisional explanation of gross saving applies without qualification.

Table 7.4 gives the gross saving of general government in the United Kingdom in 1997 and in Australia in 1997–98. For each country, the general government's gross disposable income has been calculated in Tables 6.3 and 6.4 respectively. The individual consumption expenditure, P.31, and the collective consumption expenditure, P.32, has each been seen and explained in Chapters 3 and 6.

Table 7.3
Gross saving of non-financial corporations and financial corporations, United Kingdom and Australia

SNA93/ ESA95 identification code	SNA93/ESA95 name	Disposable income, gross, B.6g	Adjustment for the change in net equity of households in pension funds' reserves, D.8	Saving gross, B.8g
	United Kingdom 1997, £ million			
S.11	Non-financial corporations	82 843	...	82 843
S.12 (exc.S.125)	Financial corporations	11 322	...	11 322
S.125	Insurance corporations and pension funds	16 171	15 690 (a)	481
	Australia 1997–98, $ million			
S.11	Non-financial corporations	46 483	...	46 483
S.12	Financial corporations	6 345	n.a. (b)	6 345

'...' means not applicable in principle.

(a) This D.8 adjustment is a subtraction and is the contra-entry to the entry in the household sector account (an addition) in Table 7.2 of £15 692 million; the remaining –£2 million of this latter contra-entry is for the rest of the world (see footnote (c) Table 7.5).

(b) Adjustment not yet made in the Australian System of National Accounts.

Sources: Office for National Statistics, *United Kingdom National Accounts The Blue Book 1999 edition*, table 1.7.6, pp. 66–7; Australian Bureau of Statistics, *Australian System of National Accounts 1997–98*, Catalogue No. 5204.0, tables 2.1 and 2.9, pp. 41 and 49.

In the United Kingdom in 1997 general government gross saving was negative, –£2 744 million; in Australia in 1997–98 general government gross saving was positive, $12 994 million.

The negative saving for general government in the United Kingdom indicates that in 1997 the government needed to borrow money simply to cover the excess of its P.3 consumption expenditure over its B.6g gross disposable income; in other words, the United Kingdom general government in 1997 was in a position of having to borrow money even before consideration was given to gross capital formation by general government. This situation had been the case in each year between 1992 and 1997 inclusive.

Table 7.4
Gross saving of general government, United Kingdom and Australia

SNA93/ ESA95 identification code	SNA93/ESA95 name	General government, S.13	
		United Kingdom 1997, £ million	Australia 1997–98, $ million
II.4	USE OF INCOME ACCOUNT		
II.4.1	USE OF DISPOSABLE INCOME ACCOUNT		
	Resources		
B.6g	Disposable income, gross	145 029	116 575
Total	Total resources	145 029	116 575
	Uses		
P.3	Final consumption expenditure		
P.31	Individual consumption expenditure	87 721	51 878 [a]
P.32	Collective consumption expenditure	60 052	51 703
P.3	Total [final consumption expenditure by general government]	147 773	103 581
B.8g	Saving, gross	–2 744	12 994
Total	Total uses	145 029	116 575

(a)   Called 'Outlays in kind: Transfers of individual non-market goods and services' in the Australian System of National Accounts.

Sources: Office for National Statistics, *United Kingdom National Accounts The Blue Book 1999 edition*, table 1.7.6, p. 67 or table 5.1.6, p. 178; Australian Bureau of Statistics, *Australian System of National Accounts 1997–98*, Catalogue No. 5204.0, tables 2.14 and 2.15, pp. 54–5.

In Australia, general government has also had years of negative gross saving (1991–92 to 1995–96 inclusive), so the phenomenon of 'lax' fiscal policy is not uncommon, but reasons of space preclude further analysis of government fiscal policy. The purpose of these paragraphs is to indicate how the national accounts can be used to describe fiscal policy.

Finally, we need to consider 'gross saving' by the rest of the world, S.2, *vis-à-vis* its current transactions with residents. Here I put the words 'gross saving' in quotation marks, because the proper SNA93/ESA95 name for this item is not 'gross saving' but is 'current external balance', B.12. However, as the SNA93 explains:

the current external balance ... plays a role in the structure of the System equivalent to [gross] saving for [resident] institutional sectors (*SNA93*, para. 2.167, with my clarifying interpolations in square brackets).

What does this mean and what is the current external balance? The current external balance is calculated *from the point of view of non-residents* (or, technically, the rest of the world, identified as Sector S.2) and the current external balance comprises the sum of all their (S.2) current transaction income received from residents (S.1) *minus* the sum of all their (S.2) current transaction payments paid to residents (S.1). Accordingly, the current external balance is calculated in a way that is *exactly equivalent* to the calculation of gross saving for resident sectors (allowing for the correct procedure to calculate household gross saving and the corresponding contra-entry).

For convenience, we shall sometimes refer to non-residents or the rest of the world as 'S.2' – but remembering that this reference is always and only in regard to their transactions or holding of assets and liabilities with residents – and we shall sometimes refer to residents taken as a group, or the *total economy*, as 'S.1' (also referred to as the 'whole economy' or the 'national economy').

The rest of the world accounts for S.2's current and other transactions and so on are called 'external accounts' and are identified by the SNA93/ESA95 prefix of the roman numeral 'V', followed by a full point, in front of the account number (for example, 'V.I'). The prefix 'V.' to an account must always be understood as signifying an external account, whether or not the word 'external' is used in the name of the account. In the external accounts, the SNA93/ESA95 convention is that:

> The rest of the world sector [S.2 accounts] records transactions, flows and economic relationships between residents of all sectors of the economy combined (i.e. non-financial and financial corporations, non-profit institutions serving households, households and general government) [these sectors comprise S.1] and non-resident institutional units [these institutional units, *in their transactions vis-à-vis resident units*, comprise S.2]. The total economy [S.1] is defined in terms of resident units. ... Resident units engage in transactions with non-resident units i.e. units which are resident in other economies. These transactions are the *external transactions* of the economy and are grouped in the rest of the world [S.2] accounts. ... [and because] the rest of the world plays a role in the accounting structure similar to that of an institutional sector, its account [the S.2 account] is viewed *from the point of view of the rest of the world*. A resource for the rest of the world is a use for the total economy and vice versa. If the [external] balance is positive, it means a

surplus for the rest of the world and a deficit for the whole economy and the reverse if the balance is negative (*UK NACSM*, paras 24.2 and 24.3, italics added, and with my clarifying interpolations in square brackets; take particular note of the last sentence).

The rest of the world (S.2) is a grouping of units without any characteristic functions and resources; it consists of non-resident units insofar as they are engaged in transactions with resident institutional units, or have other economic links with resident units. Its accounts provide an overall view of the economic relationships linking the national economy with the rest of the world. ... These accounts are drawn up from the point of view of the rest of the world. Thus, what is a resource for the rest of the world is a use for the total economy and vice versa. By the same token, a financial asset held by the rest of the world is a liability for the total economy and vice versa (except monetary gold and special drawing rights) (*ESA95*, paras 2.89 and 8.67).

This accounting convention is applied to the following SNA93/ESA95 accounts:

Account V.I: External account of goods and services
Account V.II: External account of primary incomes and current transfers
Account V.III: Accumulation accounts
Account V.III.1: Capital account
ESA95 Account V.III.1.1: Change in net worth due to saving and capital transfers account
ESA95 Account V.III.1.2: Acquisition of non-financial assets account
Account V.III.2: Financial account
Account V.III.3: Other changes in assets accounts
Account V.III.3.1 Other changes in volume of assets account
Account V.III.3.2: Revaluation account
Account V.III.3.2.1: Neutral holding gains/losses account
Account V.III.3.2.2: Real holding gains/losses account
Account V.IV: External assets and liabilities account
Account V.IV.1: Opening balance sheet
Account V.IV.2: Changes in balance sheet
Account V.IV.3: Closing balance sheet

Where relevant, the balancing item on any of these SNA93/ESA95 V. accounts is a balancing item presented from the point of view of non-residents, S.2.

(For reference beyond this book, it is important to note that, in balance of payments accounts compiled according to the BPM5, credit entries and debit entries are recorded from the point of view of the compiling economy (that is, from the point of view of S.1); this convention is the *reverse* of the convention used in the SNA93/ESA95 national accounts. Consequently, balances presented in the BPM5 balance of payments accounts have the reverse sign to external balances presented in SNA93/ESA95 national accounts (*BPM5*, paras 19 and 36 and Appendix I; *SNA93*, fn. 2, p. 342 and Annex II).)

It is usual to group current transactions into their three distinct categories: goods and services; primary incomes; and current transfers. In order to understand this we need to consider Table 7.5 which shows the calculation of the current external balance, B.12, for the United Kingdom (that is, 'for' S.2's transactions with S.1) in 1997 and for Australia (ditto) in 1997–98. The purpose of Table 7.5 is to show how the concept of 'gross saving' applies to S.2 *vis-à-vis* S.2's current transactions with S.1.

In Table 7.5, imports of goods and services, P.7, represent income receivable by non-residents from residents because of their (non-residents) supply of goods and services to residents; conversely, exports of goods and services, P.6, represent income payable by non-residents to residents because of their (non-residents) purchases of goods and services from residents. This is the convention of the SNA93/ESA95 applied to this external account. The balance recorded on Account V.I: External account of goods and services and calculated as: Imports of goods and services, P.7, *minus* Exports of goods and services, P.6, is the *external balance of goods and services*, B.11. The external balance of goods and services in the balance of payments accounts is called the 'balance of trade in goods and services' or the 'balance on goods and services' (but this balance is presented from the viewpoint of S.1 and is calculated with exports as a credit entry and imports as a debit entry thus: P.6 *minus* P.7).

For transactions in goods and services with the United Kingdom economy in 1997, non-residents earned income of £228 822 million and spent £229 326 million. Accordingly, the external balance of goods and services was –£504 million (= £228 822 million – £229 326 million). Thus we can see that, in relation to trade in goods and services during 1997, non-residents, S.2, earned less than they spent with residents, S.1. Put the other way round, the balance of payments accounts description of this would be that the United Kingdom had a surplus on the balance of trade in goods services of £504 million during 1997.

For transactions in goods and services with the Australian economy in 1997–98, non-residents earned income of $118 510 million and spent $114 203 million. Accordingly, the external balance of goods and services was $4307 million (= $118 510 million – $114 203 million). Thus we can see that during 1997–98 non-residents, S.2, earned more than they spent with residents, S.1.

Table 7.5

'Gross saving' of the rest of the world *vis-à-vis* the United Kingdom and Australia

SNA93/ESA95 identification code	SNA93/ESA95 account name[b]	Rest of the world, S.2 [a], *vis-à-vis*:	
		United Kingdom 1997, £ million	Australia 1997–98, $ million
V.I	EXTERNAL ACCOUNT OF GOODS AND SERVICES		
P.7	Imports of goods and services	228 822	118 510
P.6	Exports of goods and services	229 326	114 203
B.11 (= P.7 – P.6)	External balance of goods and services	–504	4 307
V.II	EXTERNAL ACCOUNT OF PRIMARY INCOMES AND CURRENT TRANSFERS		
D.1 + (D.2 – D.3) + D.4	Primary income paid to non-residents	99 333	28 889 [e]
D.1 + (D.2 – D.3) + D.4	Primary income received from non-residents	107 905	10 095 [f]
	External balance of primary incomes	–8 572	18 794
D.5 + D.6 + D.7 + D.8	Current transfers paid to non-residents	14 659 [c]	3 925 [g]
D.5 + D.6 + D.7 + D.8	Current transfers received from non-residents	12 206	3 760 [h]
	External balance of current transfers	2 453	165
B.12	Current external balance [d] [or 'gross saving' of non-residents *vis-à-vis* all current transactions with residents]	–6 623	23 266

(a) Transactions and balancing items are here entered from the point of view of non-residents (for example, imports of goods and services represent a resource (or income) for non-residents). Note that the items 'External balance of primary incomes' and 'External balance of current transfers' do not appear as items in the official template SNA93/ESA95 accounts.

(b) The account names are proper SNA93/ESA95 names; only the items P.7, P.6, B.11 and B.12 have their proper SNA93/ESA95 names; the other item names are given for the purpose of the explanation and this table.

(c) Including –£2 million of a D.8 adjustment (see footnote (a), Table 7.3).

(d) Calculated as the sum of : (1) external balance of goods and services; (2) external balance of primary incomes; and (3) external balance of current transfers (all viewed from non-resident viewpoint).

(e) Called 'Total primary income receivable' in the Australian System of National Accounts 'External income account'.

(f) Called 'Total primary income payable' in the Australian System of National Accounts 'External income account'.

(g) Called 'Total secondary income receivable' in the Australian System of National Accounts 'External income account'.

(h) Called 'Total secondary income payable' in the Australian System of National Accounts 'External income account'.

Sources: Office for National Statistics, *United Kingdom National Accounts The Blue Book 1999 edition*, tables 7.1.0 and 7.1.2, pp. 225–7; Australian Bureau of Statistics, *Australian System of National Accounts 1997–98*, Catalogue No. 5204.0, table 2.27, p. 67.

Put the other way round, the balance of payments recording of this would be that Australia had a balance of trade in goods and services of –$4307 million during 1997–98 or a *deficit* in the balance on goods and services.

But transactions in goods and services are not the only current transactions which non-residents have with residents; there are also the current transactions of primary incomes and the current transactions of current transfers. Primary incomes comprise: compensation of employees, D.1; taxes on production and imports, D.2, less subsidies [on production and imports], D.3; and property income, D.4. In the United Kingdom in 1997 more primary income was received from non-residents than was paid to non-residents so S.2's external balance of primary incomes with the United Kingdom was negative at –£8572 million. In sharp contrast, in Australia in 1997–98 more primary income was paid to non-residents than was received from non-residents so S.2's external balance of primary incomes with Australia was positive at $18 794 million. As we shall see in Section 7.9, this is a consequence of Australia's relatively large 'foreign debt' – meaning by 'foreign debt' the total of financial liabilities (of all types) owed to non-residents by residents *minus* the total of financial liabilities (of all types) owed to residents by non-residents. This is a non-technical use of the term 'foreign debt' which accords with popular usage. The technically correct term for what we are calling the 'foreign debt' is 'net international investment position'.

Current transfers in this context comprise current taxes on income, wealth, etc., D.5, social contributions and benefits, D.6, other current transfers, D.7, and the adjustment for the change in net equity of [non-resident] households in pension funds' reserves, D.8 (which is here included with current transfers). In regard to these current transfers, non-residents had relatively small positive external balances of current transfers *vis-à-vis* their transactions both with the United Kingdom in 1997 and with Australia in 1997–98. (Note that neither the term 'external balance of primary incomes' nor the term 'external balance of current transfers' is an official SNA93/ESA95 term; the SNA93/ESA95 template accounts simply do not calculate and report these two balancing items.)

The total of the external balance of goods and services, the external balance of primary incomes, and the external balance of current transfers constitutes the *current external balance*, B.12. When the current external balance is positive 'it signifies a surplus of the rest of the world on current transactions with the total economy (a deficit of the total economy), while a negative [current external] balance denotes a deficit of the rest of the world on current transactions (a surplus of the total economy)' (*SNA93*, para. 14.87, with my clarifying interpolation in square brackets).

In 1997, non-residents had a negative current external balance with the residents of the United Kingdom because S.2's negative external balance of primary incomes and S.2's negative external balance of goods and services outweighed the positive external balance of current transfers. By contrast, in 1997–98, non-residents had a relatively large positive current external balance with Australia, because S.2's very large positive external balance of primary incomes was augmented by S.2's positive external balance of goods and services. In Australia, the current external balance, B.12, is popularly referred to as the 'current account deficit' (taking the viewpoint of Australian residents, S.1).

Table 7.9, pp. 382–3, gives each sector's gross saving and the current external balance in both the United Kingdom (1997) and Australia (1997–98) as a starting point for calculating each sector's net lending (+)/net borrowing (–). But before this we must fully explain the concept of net lending (+)/net borrowing (–), building upon Sections 7.3 and 7.4.

7.6   Meaning and measurement of net lending (+)/net borrowing (–)

In order to explain net lending (+)/net borrowing (–), I will continue with the model household of Table 7.1, but with the changed assumption that this model household acquires some non-financial assets; in other words, has some gross capital formation, P.5. For the purposes of explaining more about what goes on in the financial account, I will also make some changes to the acquisition of financial assets and will assume some changes in financial liabilities. The explanation uses two scenarios, the first of which explains net lending (+), the second of which explains net borrowing (–). Table 7.6 gives the requisite data.

Table 7.6 shows that the model household has €30 per annum of gross saving (as derived correctly in Table 7.1). Table 7.6 continues with the simplifying assumption of no capital transfers (it is quite an easy matter to show where these fit in and we will do so in Table 7.7). Accordingly, gross saving is the only item to be considered in the first part of Account III.1.2: Acquisition of non-financial assets account; gross saving is the only receipt on this account. Gross saving is the source of finance for changes in assets through transactions, recorded in the second part of the account. (For the reasons explained in Section 7.3, this presentation follows the gross presentation of the United Kingdom and Australian national accounts, but it should be noted that this is a departure from the net presentation recommended by the SNA93/ESA95.)

Now that we understand the structure and terminology of the accumulation accounts and to save repetition, in all of what follows the word 'acquisition' and its cognates ('acquired', and so on) should be understood always to mean 'acquisition *through transactions*'. Most importantly, this also applies to the SNA93/ESA95 (*SNA93*, para. 10.15 (*b*)). Consequently, as we go through these accounts note that all changes in assets, non-financial and financial, and changes in liabilities, occur through transactions (for a few paragraphs I will remind you of this by mentioning 'transaction' in brackets).

In accordance with the strict separation of non-financial asset acquisition from financial asset acquisition, Account III.1.2 (gross presentation) is concerned only with the P.5 item gross capital formation and with the K.2 item, acquisitions less disposals of non-produced non-financial assets (not included in the simplified account of Table 7.6). In other words, Account III.1.2 is concerned only with the acquisition of *non-financial* assets. The other item is the capital account's balancing item, *net lending (+) /net borrowing (–)*, B.9. Indeed, the *raison d'être* of the distinct capital account is to derive this B.9 balancing item.

The first scenario explains net lending (+). In the first scenario, the model household has gross capital formation, P.5, of €6 per annum (a transaction); when subtracted from gross saving of €30 per annum, this leaves the model household with net lending (+), B.9, of €24 per annum. Appearing on the capital account, this is the *first* appearance of the balancing item net lending (+)/net borrowing (–), and so it has the identification code B.9.

In Table 7.6's first scenario we assume that the model household acquires during the year two financial assets. First, it acquires, as before, its claim on the pension funds, F.612, of €20 per annum (through the transactions of the D.6111 and D.6112 social contributions – see Table 7.1).

Second, the household has some transactions in acquiring shares. The household's net acquisition of shares is reported in Table 7.6 as €40 per annum. At this point it is necessary to explain and illustrate the meaning of the word 'net' in the term 'net acquisition of financial assets' (see the row heading in bold in Table 7.6).

In the term 'net acquisition of financial assets', the word 'net' is applied in respect of a given category of financial assets or of (financial) liabilities, and means that, *within a given category*, this is the total, or gross, acquisition of financial assets (in that category) *minus*, or net of, the total disposals of financial

Table 7.6
To explain net lending (+)/net borrowing (–) using two different scenarios for the model household

SNA93/ESA95 identification code		Model household using loans (ie., acquiring financial liabilities), € per annum	
		Scenario 1: Net lending (+) (positive)	Scenario 2: Net borrowing (–) (negative)
III	ACCUMULATION ACCOUNTS		
III.1	CAPITAL ACCOUNT		
III.1.2[a]	ACQUISITION OF NON-FINANCIAL ASSETS ACCOUNT[a]		
	Changes in liabilities and net worth		
B.8g	Saving, gross[b]	30	30
	Changes in assets		
P.5	Gross capital formation[c]	6	35
B.9	Net lending (+)/net borrowing(–)[d]	+ 24	–5
III.2	FINANCIAL ACCOUNT		
F.A	**Net acquisition of financial assets**		
F.5	Shares[e]	40	40
F.612	Change in net equity of household in pension funds	20	20
F.A	Total net acquisition of financial assets	60	60
F.L	**Net acquisition of financial liabilities**		
F.4	Loans	36	65
F.L	Total net acquisition of financial liabilities	36	65
B.9f	Net lending (+)/net borrowing (–)[f]: F.A – F.L	+ 24	–5

(a) This is a sub-account specific to the ESA95 (sub-dividing the SNA93 Account III.1: Capital account) and is not in the SNA93, which reports these items in (an undivided) Account III.1: Capital account. The presentation here is the gross presentation, not the net presentation recommended by the ESA95.

(b) This is the gross presentation adopted by the United Kingdom and Australian national accounts (but here simplified because the gross presentation should report net saving and consumption of fixed capital each as a distinct item). This is different from the SNA93/ESA95 recommended net presentation, which would report in this row *net* saving, B.8n, with consumption of fixed capital, K.1, reported as a *negative* item following P.5 gross capital formation (or following P.51 gross fixed capital formation) in the Changes in assets part of the account. To illustrate for assets (in that category) (*SNA93*, para. 11.1; the principles of netting in this context are explained in *SNA93*, paras 11.50–11.51).

To explain and illustrate this netting within a given category, suppose that the household has bought, during the year, 1000 shares (a given category of financial asset, viz., AF.5) in Beta Computers plc/ltd at a price of €3.04 per share, giving it a total, or gross, acquisition of shares of €3040 per annum; suppose also that, in order to help it partly to finance this purchase of shares, the household sells (or 'disposes of') 1000 shares (a financial asset of the same given category) in Acme Foods plc/ltd for a price of €3 per share, giving it a total, or gross, disposal of shares of €3000 per annum. Consequently, the household's *net* acquisition of this category of financial assets (namely, shares) is: €3040 per annum (gross acquisition) – €3000 per annum (gross disposal) = €40 per annum (net acquisition). It is this €40 per annum which is reported in Table 7.6 as the *net* acquisition of shares, F.5, during the year. This explains and illustrates the application of the word 'net' in the term 'net acquisition of

---

consumption of fixed capital, K.1, of, say, €2 per annum, the net presentation would be, for Scenario 1 (all figures in € per annum):

	Changes in liabilities and net worth	
B.8n	Saving, net	28
	Changes in assets	
P.5	Gross capital formation	6
K.1	Consumption of fixed capital	–2
B.9	Net lending (+)/net borrowing (–)	24

In either presentation, the value for net lending (+)/net borrowing (–) is the same.

(c) Note that this entry represents a change in the assumptions of Table 7.1, which assumed no acquisition of non-financial assets.

(d) This is net lending (+)/net borrowing(–) calculated as the balancing item on the ESA95 Account III.1.2 Acquisition of non-financial assets account and has the SNA93/ESA95 identification code B.9.

(e) To illustrate the meaning of the word 'net' in the term 'net acquisition of financial assets', the model household has, during the year, bought 1000 shares in Beta Computers plc/ltd at a price of €3.04 per share, giving it a total, or gross, acquisition of shares of €3040 per annum, and has sold 1000 shares in Acme Foods plc/ltd at a price of €3 per share, giving it a total, or gross, disposal of shares, of €3000 per annum; consequently, the household's *net* acquisition of shares is: €3040 per annum (gross acquisition) – €3000 per annum (gross disposal) = €40 per annum (net acquisition).

(f) This is net lending (+)/net borrowing (–) calculated as the balancing item on Account III.2 Financial account and in the United Kingdom national accounts has the identification code B.9f.

Source: numbers hypothetical and explained in Section 7.6.

financial assets', and we see how the netting is *within* a given category of financial asset.

Together with the change in the net equity of the household in the pension fund, the model household's total net acquisition (through transactions) of financial assets, F.A, is €60 per annum.

Now, the household's B.9 net lending (+) balance from the capital account was only €24 per annum, so the household has acquired financial assets (net) in excess of its positive net lending balance. Table 7.6 assumes that the model household finances its net acquisition of shares in part by borrowing €36 per annum, so accordingly the financial account shows, under the net acquisition of financial liabilities, a net incurrence of loan liabilities, F.4, of €36 per annum (through a transaction). Here, 'net' likewise refers to the gross incurrence of liabilities (in a given category) *minus*, or net of, any repayment, or 'redemption', of liabilities (in that same category).

In order to understand the amount of this borrowing, it helpful to consider the cash flows; this household has cash in hand of €10 per annum left over from its €90 per annum wage/salary cash in hand after paying its D.6112 social contributions of €10 per annum and its P.31 consumption expenditure of €70 per annum. Some of this €10 per annum cash in hand is used to pay (in whole) for its P.5 gross capital formation of €6 per annum, leaving the household with €4 per annum cash in hand (= €10 per annum cash in hand – €6 per annum gross capital formation). The household has to find €40 per annum of cash to finance its net F.5 acquisition of shares (we have seen how some, but not all, of the finance for the purchase of shares in Beta Computers plc/ltd comes from the sale of shares in Acme Foods plc/ltd). The household has €4 per annum left over after gross capital formation so, to finance its €40 per annum net acquisition of shares, the household has to borrow the rest, which amounts to €36 per annum.

The balancing item on the financial account, net lending (+)/net borrowing (–), B.9f, is calculated as the total net acquisition of financial assets minus the total net acquisition of financial liabilities; as follows:

$$
\begin{array}{l}
\text{Net lending (+)/} \\
\text{net borrowing (–),} \\
\text{B.9f}
\end{array}
=
\begin{array}{l}
\text{Total net acquisition of} \\
\text{financial assets, F.A}
\end{array}
-
\begin{array}{l}
\text{Total net acquisition of} \\
\text{financial liabilities, F.L}
\end{array}
$$

$$= \text{€60 p.a.} - \text{€36 p.a.}$$

$$= \text{€24 p.a.}$$

Appearing on the financial account, this is the second appearance of the balancing item net lending (+)/net borrowing (–), and so it has the identification code B.9f.

We can see in this model account (no errors of recording or omissions!) that the balancing item from the financial account is equal to the balancing item, differently calculated, from the capital account. But of course, if you consider the cash flows involved, you will see how it is, and how it must be, that the two are equal.

The second scenario explains net borrowing (–). In the second scenario, the model household has gross saving of €30 per annum (as before) but now has gross capital formation of €35 per annum; when gross capital formation is subtracted from gross saving, this leaves the household with net borrowing (–), B.9, of – €5 per annum.

In Table 7.6's second scenario we assume that the model household acquires during the year two financial assets. First, it acquires, as before, its claim on the pension funds, F.612, of €20 per annum. Second and as in the first scenario, it has a net acquisition of shares, F.5, worth €40 during the year. Accordingly, the model household's total net acquisition of financial assets is €60 per annum.

Now, the model household's net borrowing (–) balance from the capital account, B.9, was – €5 per annum. In other words, the model household had a need for finance to pay for its excess of gross capital formation over its gross saving, even before its net acquisition of financial assets is considered. Assume that the model household meets all its needs for finance by borrowing €65 per annum; accordingly the financial account shows, under the net acquisition of financial liabilities, an incurrence of loans, F.4, of €65 per annum.

In order to understand the amount of this borrowing, it helpful to bear in mind the cash flows; this household has cash in hand of €10 per annum left over from its €90 per annum wage/salary cash in hand after paying its social contribution of €10 per annum and its €70 per annum consumption expenditure. This cash in hand is used to pay part of its gross capital formation of €35 per annum, leaving the household short of €25 per annum (= €35 per annum gross capital formation – €10 per annum cash in hand). Additionally, the household has to find €40 per annum of cash to finance its net acquisition of shares. In total then, the model household has to borrow €65 per annum (= €25 per annum + €40 per annum).

In both scenarios, the net lending (+)/net borrowing (–) balancing item from the financial account may be calculated as the total net acquisition of financial assets, F.A, *minus* the total net acquisition of financial liabilities, F.L:

Scenario 1

Net lending (+)/
net borrowing (–),   =   Total net acquisition of   _   Total net acquisition of
B.9f   financial assets, F.A   financial liabilities, F.L

=   €60 p.a. – €36 p.a.

=   €24 p.a.

Scenario 2

Net lending (+)/
net borrowing (–),   =   Total net acquisition of   _   Total net acquisition of
B.9f   financial assets, F.A   financial liabilities, F.L

=   €60 p.a. – €65 p.a.

=   – €5 p.a.

Now that we understand the capital account and the financial account in an 'in principle' way, we can consider the capital account and the financial account for the household sector in each of the United Kingdom (1997) and Australia (1997–98). Tables 7.7 and 7.8 give the requisite data.

Table 7.7 starts with the balancing item on Table 7.2 – with household sector gross saving (correctly measured). In the real world we have to take account of capital transfers received and paid. What are capital transfers? Figure 7.2 answers this question (also see Figure 6.1, p. 265; for full discussion of capital transfers see: *SNA93*, paras 10.131–10.141; *ESA95*, paras 4.145–4.166; and *UK NACSM*, paras 6.30–6.34, 15.12–15.16, and 21.101–21.105).

Figure 7.2 shows the classification of *capital transfers*, D.9, into the three main SNA93/ESA95 categories: *capital taxes*, D.91; *investment grants*, D.92; and *other capital transfers*, D.99. Figure 7.2 gives examples of investment grants and other capital transfers, but these examples are illustrative and are not to be taken as exhaustive of all possibilities.

Households pay capital taxes largely in the form of inheritance taxes (sometimes called 'estate duties' and popularly referred to as 'death duties'); households may receive investment grants from government in relation to the construction, purchase or improvement of dwellings, and non-profit institutions

Table 7.7
Household[a] capital account, United Kingdom and Australia

SNA93/ESA95 identific- ation code	SNA93/ESA95 name	United Kingdom 1997, £ million	Australia 1997–98, $ million
		Households and NPISHs, S.14 + S.15	
III	ACCUMULATION ACCOUNTS		
III.1	CAPITAL ACCOUNT		
III.1.1[b]	CHANGE IN NET WORTH DUE TO SAVING AND CAPITAL TRANSFERS ACCOUNT[b]		
B.8g	Saving, gross	53 301	42 472
D.9	Capital transfers receivable	4 482	2 501
– D.9	*less* Capital transfers payable	–2 193	–1 083
B.10.1g	Total change in liabilities and net worth	55 590	43 890 [c]
III.1.2[b]	ACQUISITION OF NON-FINANCIAL ASSETS ACCOUNT[b]		
B.10.1g	Total change in liabilities and net worth	55 590	43 890 [c]
	Changes in assets		
P.5	Gross capital formation	33 536	51 368
K.2	Acquisition *less* disposals of non-produced non-financial assets	250	—
B.9	Net lending (+)/net borrowing (–)	21 804	–7 478

'—' means category not recorded.
(a) Including non-profit institutions serving households.
(b) This is a sub-account specific to the ESA95 (sub-dividing the SNA93 Account III.1: Capital account) not in the SNA93, which reports these items in (an undivided) Account III.1: Capital account. The presentation is the gross presentation.
(c) Called 'Gross saving and capital transfers' in the Australian System of National Accounts 'Household capital account'.

Sources: Office for National Statistics, *United Kingdom National Accounts The Blue Book 1999 edition*, table 6.1.7, p. 211; Australian Bureau of Statistics, *Australian System of National Accounts 1997–98*, Catalogue No. 5204.0, table 2.22, p. 62.

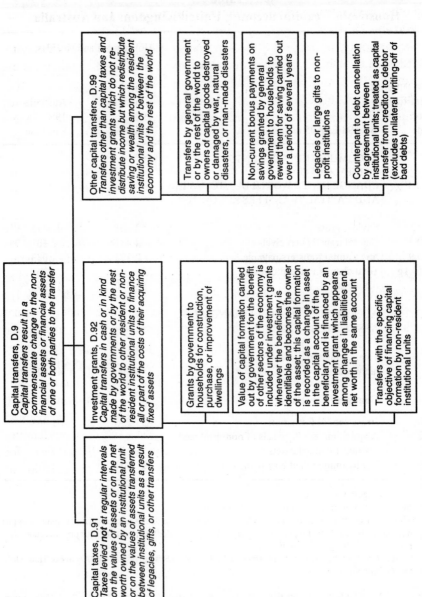

Capital transfers, D.9
Capital transfers result in a commensurate change in the non-financial assets or financial assets of one or both parties to the transfer

Capital taxes, D.91
*Taxes levied **not** at regular intervals on the values of assets or on the net worth owned by an institutional unit or on the values of assets transferred between institutional units as a result of legacies, gifts, or other transfers*

Investment grants, D.92
Capital transfers in cash or in kind made by governments or by the rest of the world to other resident or non-resident institutional units to finance all or part of the costs of their acquiring fixed assets

Grants by government to households for construction, purchase, or improvement of dwellings

Value of capital formation carried out by government for the benefit of other sectors of the economy is included under investment grants whenever the beneficiary is identifiable and becomes the owner of the asset; this capital formation is recorded as a change in asset in the capital account of the beneficiary and is financed by an investment grant which appears among changes in liabilities and net worth in the same account

Transfers with the specific objective of financing capital formation by non-resident institutional units

Other capital transfers, D.99
Transfers other than capital taxes and investment grants which do not re-distribute income but which redistribute saving or wealth among the resident institutional units or between the economy and the rest of the world

Transfers by general government or by the rest of the world to owners of capital goods destroyed or damaged by war, natural disasters, or man-made disasters

Non-current bonus payments on savings granted by general government to households to reward them for saving carried out over a period of several years

Legacies or large gifts to non-profit institutions

Counterpart to debt cancellation by agreement between institutional units; treated as capital transfer from creditor to debtor (excludes unilateral writing-off of bad debts)

Figure 7.2   Capital transfers

372

serving households receive investment grants from the general government and other capital transfers from other institutional units (*UK NACSM*, paras 22.100 and 22.103).

Accordingly, in Table 7.7 we see that in 1997 households (including NPISHs) in the United Kingdom received £4482 million of capital transfers and paid £2193 million of capital transfers, so net capital transfers was (positive) £2289 million (not shown in Table 7.7). In 1997–98 households (including NPISHs) in Australia received $2501 million of capital transfers and paid $1083 million of capital transfers, so net capital transfers was (positive) $1418 million (not shown in Table 7.7).

Note that the ESA95 divides the SNA93 Account III.1: Capital account into two sub-accounts (see Figure 7.1), which are here given in the gross presentation used in the United Kingdom national accounts.

First, a sub-account which is the ESA95 Account III.1.1: Change in net worth due to saving and capital transfers account; this account (in its gross presentation) records capital transfers receivable, D.9, and capital transfers payable, D.9, in addition to gross saving, B.8g, giving a total item called in the *Blue Book 1999 edition* 'total change in liabilities and net worth', B.10.1g; this changes the SNA93/ESA95 name for B.10.1 which is 'changes in net worth due to saving and capital transfers' (this name also being used in the *Blue Book 1999 edition*); subsequently we shall use the simpler (and more descriptive) name for B.10.1g adopted in the Australian System of National Accounts of 'Gross saving and capital transfers'. Account III.1.1 has to include capital transfers because these affect the ability of the institutional unit to finance the acquisition of assets, but (and this is an important 'but') capital transfers involve (by their very nature and definition) no simultaneous liability (so in this respect a capital transfer received is absolutely different from, for example, a loan liability incurred, although each finances the acquisition of assets). Consequently, capital transfers must always be kept separate from financial transactions.

Second, a sub-account which is the ESA95 Account III.1.2: Acquisition of non-financial assets account; this account (in its gross presentation) records B.10.1g brought down from Account III.1.1, and against this records gross capital formation, P.5, and acquisitions less disposals of non-produced non-financial assets, K.2, with the balancing item net lending (+)/net borrowing (–), B.9, where B.9 is calculated as B.10.1g *minus* P.5 and *minus* K.2. The SNA93 simply reports all these items in one account, Account III.1: Capital account, but the balancing item B.9 remains the same, regardless of how the accounts are arranged (*ESA95*, paras 8.48–8.49; *UK NACSM*, paras 6.2, 11.54–

11.55, 15.3–15.4, 15.10 and 15.26; *SNA93*, paras 10.20 and 10.29).

The balancing item in ESA95 Account III.1.2 is the balancing item *net lending (+)/net borrowing (–)*, B.9. However, despite the complications of detail in the real world, you can readily see, by looking at Table 7.7's B.8g and P.5 rows, that the B.9 balancing item is (very largely) gross saving *minus* gross capital formation. We may put the calculations of Table 7.7 into the form of equations (because these equations need to be thoroughly understood and note that each equation can be applied, in the gross presentation, either in the context of the ESA95 accounts or in the context of the SNA93 account). First (in the terminology of the *Blue Book 1999 edition*):

| Total change in liabilities and net worth, B.10.1g | = | Gross saving, B.8g | + | Capital transfers receivable, D.9 | – | Capital transfers payable, D.9 |

Second:

| Net lending (+)/ net borrowing (–), B.9 | = | Total change in liabilities and net worth, B.10.1g | – | Gross capital formation, P.5 | – | Acquisitions less disposals of non-produced non-financial assets, K.2 |

$$= \text{Total change in liabilities and net worth, B.10.1g} - \left[\text{Gross capital formation, P.5} - + \text{Acquisitions less disposals of non-produced non-financial assets, K.2} \right]$$

Applying the equations, we have for the household (including NPISHs) sector in the United Kingdom in 1997:

| Total change in liabilities and net worth, B.10.1g | = £53 301 mn + £4 482 mn – £2 193 mn |
| | = £55 590 mn |

| Net lending (+)/ Net borrowing (–), B.9 | = £55 590 mn – £33 536 mn – £250 mn |

$$= £55\ 590\ \text{mn} - [£33\ 536\ \text{mn} + £250\ \text{mn}]$$

$$= £21\ 804\ \text{mn}$$

And for the household (including NPISHs) sector in Australia in 1997–98, and switching to the Australian System of National Accounts' terminology of 'Gross saving and capital transfers' for B.10.1g:

Gross saving and capital transfers, B.10.1g	$= \$42\ 472\ \text{mn} + \$2\ 501\ \text{mn} - \$1\ 083\ \text{mn}$
	$= \$43\ 890\ \text{mn}$

Net lending (+)/ net borrowing (−), B.9	$= \$43\ 890\ \text{mn} - \$51\ 368\ \text{mn}$
	$= -\$7\ 478\ \text{mn}$

So the household (including NPISHs) sector in the United Kingdom in 1997 was able to acquire financial assets (net), or repay outstanding debt (or a mixture of both) with the positive net lending balance from the capital account, while the household (including NPISHs) sector in Australia in 1997–98 was required to incur financial liabilities (net), or to run down stocks of financial assets (or a mixture of both) in order to finance the negative net borrowing balance from the capital account. (A negative net borrowing balance is, in fact, unusual for the household sector, and the situation is a result of a downward trend in household sector gross saving relative to gross disposable income which afflicted the Australian economy in the 1990s.)

We can now turn to the second appearance of net lending (+)/net borrowing (−) in the financial account. Table 7.8 shows the SNA93/ESA95 Account III.2: Financial account for the household (including NPISHs) sector in the United Kingdom in 1997 and in Australia in 1997–98.

The financial account first records the types of financial assets acquired net (see Chapter 1, Section 1.6 and Figure 1.7, pp. 38–9). It is possible for a net acquisition of financial assets entry in the financial account to be negative as well as positive; a negative entry occurs when financial assets are disposed of (gross) in excess of financial assets acquired (gross). The signs occurring in the financial account should cause no difficulty if you bear in mind that the account records changes (net) in *stocks* of financial assets and liabilities and that these stocks can decrease as well as increase.

Table 7.8
Household[a] financial account, United Kingdom and Australia

SNA93/ ESA95 identification code	SNA93/ESA95 name	Households and NPISHs, S.14 + S.15	
		United Kingdom 1997, £ million	Australia 1997–98, $ million
III.2	FINANCIAL ACCOUNT		
F.A	**Net acquisition of financial assets**		
F.2	Currency and deposits	38 400	16 293
F.3	Securities other than shares	−1 267	−4 866
F.4	Loans [b]	−332	960
F.5	Shares and other equity	−2 217	8 068
F.6	Insurance technical reserves	32 974 [c]	27 835
F.7	Other accounts receivable	4 249	—
F.A	Total net acquisition of financial assets	71 807	48 290
F.L	**Net acquisition of financial liabilities**		
F.3	Securities other than shares	137	176
F.4	Loans[b]	38 830	39 766
F.7	Other accounts payable	2 417	—
F.L	Total net acquisition of financial liabilities	41 384	39 942
B.9f	Net lending (+)/net borrowing (−), from the financial account (= F.A − F.L) [d]	30 423	8 348
dB.9f	Statistical discrepancy [e]	−8 619	15 826
B.9	Net lending (+)/net borrowing (−), from the capital account	21 804	−7 478

'—' means nil.

(a) Including non-profit institutions serving households.
(b) Called 'Loans and placements' in the Australian System of National Accounts.
(c) This amount includes the D.8 adjustment item from Table 7.2 of the change in the net equity of households on pension funds of £15 692 million, but the F.6 item of insurance technical reserves includes, besides the D.8 item, the increase in claims on life assurance reserves and the prepayments of insurance premiums and reserves for outstanding claims.
(d) Called 'net change in financial position' in the Australian System of National Accounts.
(e) Called 'net errors and omissions' in the Australian System of National Accounts with converse sign.

Sources: Office for National Statistics, *United Kingdom National Accounts The Blue Book 1999 edition*, table 6.1.8, pp. 212–13; Australian Bureau of Statistics, *Australian System of National Accounts 1997–98*, Catalogue No. 5204.0, table 2.23, p. 63.

Second, the financial account records the types of financial liabilities acquired (net). It is likewise possible for a net acquisition of financial liabilities entry in the financial account to be negative as well as positive; a negative entry occurs when financial liabilities are repaid or 'redeemed' (gross) in excess of financial liabilities incurred (gross).

Limitations of space preclude a full discussion of all the types of financial assets and liabilities acquired by the households (including NPISHs) sector in each economy (see Figure 1.7). We can see that households (including NPISHs) in both countries increased their holdings of currency and (bank) deposits (net) during the year, but that households (including NPISHs) in the United Kingdom during 1997 reduced their holdings of shares (net) while households (including NPISHs) in Australia during 1997–98 increased their holdings of shares (net). One important feature which we should note is that in both countries transactions in the financial asset *insurance technical reserves*, F.6, is one of the biggest single categories of net acquisition of financial assets and this is a result of households' participation in private pension schemes and in endowment life insurance which leads each year to substantial increases in claims on pension funds and on life assurance reserves. (Consequently, these assets form a quantitatively important part of households' holdings of *stocks* of financial assets. In the balance sheet for Australia (Table 7.12, pp. 398–400) we shall see that the households' (including NPISHs) stock of AF.6 insurance technical reserves amounts to 43 per cent of households' (including NPISHs) holdings of financial assets, AF.A; while in the United Kingdom at the end of 1997 this percentage was 53 per cent (the *Blue Book 1999 edition*, table 6.1.9, p. 214).)

The main category of financial liabilities incurred (net) by households (including NPISHs) in both countries is *loans*, F.4. This would include loans for the purchase of dwellings ('mortgages') and loans to finance consumer spending. In both the United Kingdom and Australia, nearly all household financial liabilities are in the form of loans.

Net lending (+)/net borrowing (−) from the financial account, B.9f, may be calculated as the total net acquisition of financial assets, F.A, *minus* the total net acquisition of financial liabilities, F.L. In theory, the balancing item so calculated should be equal to the balancing item from the capital account. In practice, there tends to be considerable errors of recording and omissions and so a statistical discrepancy item, dB.9f, is introduced to 'reconcile' the two balances. We can see in Table 7.8 that the statistical discrepancy item in the household sector account is relatively very large in both the United Kingdom and Australia (indicating that this is an area of national income accounting where improvement needs to be made, but the difficulty of collecting comprehensive and accurate information, by sector, on the acquisition of financial assets and the incurring of financial liabilities is considerable – especially for the household sector (*UK NACSM*, para. 17.43)).

Figure 7.3 provides a summary of the chapter so far and serves to illustrate all the various concepts and relationships so far explained as well as the point that (allowing for capital transfers) net lending (+)/net borrowing (–) is part of, or originates from, gross saving; more precisely, net lending (+)/net borrowing (–), B.9, is part of, or originates from, (changes in net worth due to) gross saving and capital transfers, B.10.1g.

Figure 7.3 is drawn for the household sector of the economy and illustrates the accounts in general (that is, it is not a depiction of any particular set of data). Figure 7.3 goes through all the accounts from the use of disposable income account to the financial account so that we can see how these accounts are connected (and Figure 7.3 is drawn – in the gross presentation – for the ESA95 sub-accounts III.1.1 and III.1.2). In Figure 7.3 the *height* of a bar, or any part thereof, indicates the value of an annual flow. Note that, for diagrammatic reasons of accommodating the words, Figure 7.3 is *not* to scale (for example, in the real world gross saving is always relatively much smaller than final consumption expenditure, gross capital formation is always much larger than net lending (+)/net borrowing (–), and – especially – net capital transfers is always a relatively much smaller item than net lending (+)/net borrowing (–)). Also note carefully that Figure 7.3 indicates horizontal alignment between items by broken lines which are the key to understanding how the diagram 'works'; note also that balancing items are indicated by shading, but note that capital transfers receivable *minus* capital transfers payable is not treated as a balancing item.

On the left side Figure 7.3 shows that, in Account II.4.1, gross saving, B.8g, is calculated as the difference, or balancing item, between gross disposable income, B.6g, plus the adjustment for the change in net equity of households in pension funds, D.8, on the one hand, and individual consumption expenditure, P.31, on the other hand. Gross saving is transferred to Account III.1.1: Change in net worth due to saving and capital transfers account.

In Account III.1.1, gross saving is added to by capital transfers receivable, D.9, and is subtracted from by capital transfers payable, D.9. For diagrammatic purposes, Figure 7.3 shows, for the household sector, a positive balance of capital transfers (drawing negative balances makes the diagram difficult to follow). The resulting total can be called 'gross saving and capital transfers' using the name adopted in the Australian System of National Accounts but

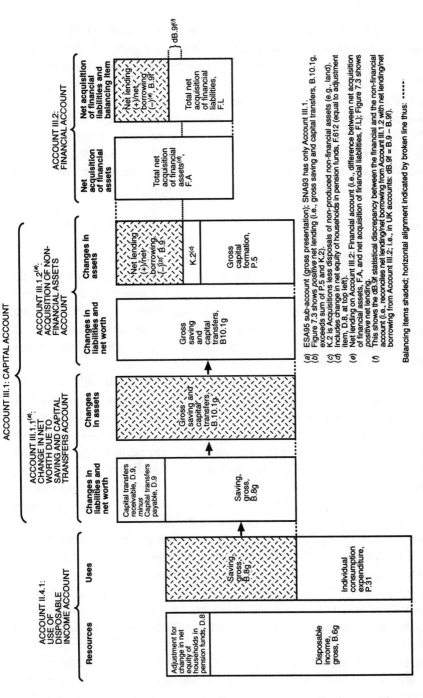

Figure 7.3 Household sector, S.14: from the use of disposable income account to the financial account

(a) ESA95 sub-account (gross presentation); SNA93 has only Account III.1.
(b) Figure 7.3 shows *positive* net lending (i.e., gross saving and capital transfers, B.10.1g, exceeds sum of P.5 and K.2).
(c) K.2 is Acquisitions less disposals of non-produced non-financial assets (e.g., land).
(d) Includes change in net equity of households in pension funds, F.612 (equal to adjustment item, D.8, at top left).
(e) Net lending on Account III.2: Financial account (i.e. difference between net acquisition of financial assets, F.A, and net acquisition of financial liabilities, F.L); Figure 7.3 shows *positive* net lending.
(f) This shows the dB.9f statistical discrepancy between the financial and the non-financial account (i.e., reconciles net lending/net borrowing from Account III.1.2 with net lending/net borrowing from Account III.2; i.e., in UK accounts: dB.9f = B.9 − B.9f).

Balancing items shaded; horizontal alignment indicated by broken line thus: ------

with the SNA93/ESA95 identification code B.10.1g (because B.10.1g has the same composition whichever name we use). In Figure 7.3, this is shown as a shaded balancing item because it so largely comprises gross saving.

The B.10.1g item is transferred to Account III.1.2: Acquisition of non-financial assets account, and this account then shows, under the heading 'Changes in assets', the acquisition of *non-financial* assets both in the form of P.5 gross capital formation and also in the form of K.2 acquisitions less disposals of non-produced non-financial assets. (Note the SNA93/ESA95 separation of the acquisition of non-financial assets, recorded in this account or in the SNA93 capital account, from the net acquisition of financial assets, recorded in the next account, III.2.)

An important function of Account III.1.2 is to derive the balancing item on the capital account; namely, net lending (+)/net borrowing (–), B.9. Figure 7.3 shows a positive balance of net lending (again for the same diagrammatic reason). This appearance on the capital account is the first appearance of net lending (+)/net borrowing (–), and, as explained, because this is the balancing item from the *capital* account, it has the SNA93/ESA95 identification code B.9. It is an important point of Figure 7.3 that we can very clearly see that, and in what way, net lending (+)/net borrowing (–), B.9, is the balancing item on the capital account.

The next account in sequence is the SNA93/ESA95 Account III.2: Financial account. Figure 7.3 shows the total net acquisition of financial assets, F.A, and the total net acquisition of financial liabilities, F.L. For diagrammatic/ explanatory purposes, the total net acquisition of financial assets is aligned horizontally *with the top* of the preceding B.9 net borrowing (+); and the downward extent of the total net acquisition of financial assets is simply whatever is needed to represent the total net acquisition of financial assets. The total net acquisition of financial liabilities is then horizontally aligned *with the bottom* of the total net acquisition of financial assets.

The balancing item calculated as the total net acquisition of financial assets, F.A, *minus* the total net acquisition of financial liabilities, F.L, is the balancing item from the financial account: net lending (+)/net borrowing (–), B.9f. This appearance on the financial account is the second appearance of net lending (+)/net borrowing (–), and as explained, because this is the balancing item from the *financial* account, it is helpful to give this the distinctive identification code B.9f.

In principle, net lending (+)/net borrowing (–), B.9f, should be equal to (because arising from) net lending (+)/net borrowing (–), B.9. But in practice (in real world national accounts), the recorded value of B.9f may differ from the recorded value of B.9. Using dotted lines, Figure 7.3 shows the statistical discrepancy item as the difference, or discrepancy between the financial account and the non-financial account, with the identification code dB.9f and calculated as B.9 *minus* B.9f (using the UK accounts sign conventions).

(Incidentally, note that in Figure 7.3 the adjustment for the change in net equity of households in pension funds, D.8, shown at the top left, is included in the net acquisition of financial assets (as the F.612 item net equity of households in pension funds' reserves, which forms part of F.A), but to keep the diagram simple Figure 7.3 does not depict this linkage explicitly.)

Now that we have an overall perspective on the accounts linking gross saving to net lending (+)/net borrowing (–) in each of its two appearances, we can consider, through the capital account, each sector's gross saving and net lending (+)/net borrowing (–), B.9, in the United Kingdom (1997) and in Australia (1997–98).

Using the gross presentation, Table 7.9 shows the capital accounts for each of the S.1 sectors of the economy (S.11, S.12, S.13 and S.14 + S.15) and for the rest of the world, S.2. For the total economy, the S.1 total is simply the total of all resident sectors' entries.

For the resident S.1 sectors, Table 7.9 starts with each sector's gross saving, B.8g, and then adds on that sector's net capital transfers to get each sector's gross saving and capital transfers – the item identified as B.10.1g whichever name we use.

For the rest of the world sector, S.2, Table 7.9 starts with the current external balance, B.12, and then adds on S.2's net capital transfers to get S.2's 'gross saving' (that is, current external balance) and capital transfers, B.10.1. (For future reference, note that I shall call S.2's net capital transfers the 'external balance of capital transfers', although this is not an official SNA93/ESA95 term. Note also that because consumption of fixed capital, K.1, is not applicable to the rest of the world, the suffix 'g' is not strictly required on 'B.10.1' for S.2.)

From each resident sector's B.10.1g total, Table 7.9 subtracts the total of gross capital formation, P.5, plus the acquisitions less disposals of non-produced non-financial assets, K.2, in order to arrive at the net lending (+)/ net borrowing (–), B.9, balancing item on each sector's capital account.

The rest of the world, S.2, cannot, in principle, engage in P.5 gross capital formation. A non-resident can, of course, own a resident institutional unit which itself engages in gross capital formation, but this gross capital formation is ascribed to the resident institutional unit, with the non-resident institutional unit acquiring a corresponding financial claim on the resident institutional unit. The SNA93 explains:

Table 7.9
The net lending (+)/net borrowing (−) balances for the sectors of the economy; the United Kingdom and Australia

	Gross saving, B.8g	Net capital transfers, D.9(in) − D.9(out)	Gross saving and capital transfers, B.10.1g	Gross capital formation, P.5	Acquisitions less disposals of non-produced non-financial assets, K.2	[Total acquisition of non-financial assets], P.5 + K.2	Net lending (+)/net borrowing (−), B.9
United Kingdom 1997, £ million							
S.11 Non-financial corporations	82 843	2 459	85 302 [a]	89 945	195	90 140	−4 838
S.12 Financial corporations	11 803	–	11 803 [a]	5 087	−39	5 048	6 755
S.13 General government	−2 744	−3 910	−6 654 [a]	10 012	−372	9 640	−16 294
S.14 + S.15 Households and NPISHs	53 301	2 289	55 590 [a]	33 536	250	33 786	21 804
S.1 Total economy	145 203	838	146 041 [a]	138 580	34	138 614	7 427
S.2 Rest of the world	−6 623 [b]	−838	−7 461	...	−34	−34	−7 427

Australia 1997–98, $ million

S.11	Non-financial corporations	46 483	1 353	47 836	66 122	703	66 825	−18 989
S.12	Financial corporations	6 345	50	6 395	4 435	1	4 436	1 959
S.13	General government	12 994	−1 724	11 270	12 418	−734	11 684	−414
S.14 + S.15	Households and NPISHs	42 472	1 418	43 890	51 368	—	51 368	−7 478
S.1	Total economy	108 294	1 097	109 391	134 343	−30	134 313	−24 922
								−2 783 (c)
S.2	Rest of the world	23 266 (b)	−1 097	22 169	...	30	30	22 139 (d)

'—' means nil; '...' means not applicable in principle.

(a) Called 'Total change in liabilities and net worth' in the United Kingdom national accounts.
(b) Current external balance, B.12.
(c) This is the statistical discrepancy and here it is calculated as the statistical discrepancy between expenditure components and GDP, de, or 'Statistical discrepancy (E)' of −$1223 million less the statistical discrepancy between income components and GDP, di, or 'Statistical discrepancy (I)' of $1560 million equals 'statistical discrepancy' of −$2783 million.
(d) Equals net borrowing (−) of total economy with sign reversed *plus* statistical discrepancy.

Sources: Office for National Statistics, *United Kingdom National Accounts The Blue Book 1999 edition*, table 1.7.7, pp. 68–9; Australian Bureau of Statistics, *Australian System of National Accounts 1997–98*, Catalogue No. 5204.0, tables 1.13, 2.2, 2.10, 2.16, 2.22 and 2.28; pp. 33, 42, 50, 56, 62 and 68; Table 7.9 follows the gross presentation of the capital account used in both sources.

An unincorporated enterprise that operates in a different economy from the one in which its owner resides is considered to be a separate entity [from its non-resident owner]; that [separate] entity is a resident of the economy where it operates rather than of the economy of its [non-resident] owner. All assets, non-financial as well as financial, attributed to such an enterprise are to be regarded as foreign *financial assets* for the [non-resident] owner of the [unincorporated] enterprise (*SNA93*, para. 14.133 (b), italics added and with my clarifying interpolations in square brackets).

A non-resident can, of course, buy a capital good from the economy for use outside the country, but this counts as a P.6 export of a good, not as P.5 gross capital formation which relates solely to the accumulation of capital *within* the country. A non-resident institutional unit can make the K.2 transaction acquisitions less disposals of non-produced non-financial assets (such as the purchase of land (but transactions in land between residents and non-residents applies only where foreign governments or international organisations are involved), patent rights, copyrights, and so on – *ESA95*, paras 6.06–6.13; *BPM5*, paras 51, 312 and 358). Note that the K.2 amount for non-residents is the same as, but with an opposite sign to, the K.2 transactions totalled for the resident sectors of the economy S.1; this is because the non-residents must be buying the K.2 assets from, or selling the K.2 assets to, residents, so the two are simply the opposite sides of the same total of K.2 transactions.

Allowing for the statistical discrepancy (if any), the net lending (+)/net borrowing (–) of the total economy, S.1, is equal to, but has the opposite sign of, the net lending (+)/net borrowing (–) of the rest of the world, S.2. This is because the economy, as a whole, can only lend to, or borrow from, the rest of the world. In other words, for the United Kingdom economy in 1997, S.1's net lending (+) of £7427 million was S.2's net borrowing (–) of –£7427 million, while for the Australian economy in 1997–98, S.1's net borrowing (–) of –$24 922 million was S.2's net lending (+) of $22 139 million (allowing for the statistical discrepancy). So in the B.9 balancing item for S.1, we see either the economy's annual net acquisition of foreign assets (if positive – United Kingdom 1997) or the economy's annual net acquisition of foreign liabilities (if negative – Australia 1997–98).

In order to understand how foreign lending or foreign borrowing arises we need to consider another basic identity of national accounting. This is the identity that the sum of total gross saving by resident sectors, S.1, and the current external balance of S.2 is, and must be, equal to the total gross capital formation in the economy (allowing, if necessary, for the statistical discrepancy). This very important national accounting identity for the whole economy, S.1, is explained in the next section.

7.7 The national accounting identity for the total economy: gross saving plus the current external balance equals gross capital formation

Table 7.10 illustrates the equality between the sum of gross saving by the total economy plus the current external balance on the one hand and gross capital formation by the total economy on the other hand (allowing if necessary for the statistical discrepancy).

For the United Kingdom in 1997, the sum of the economy's gross saving and the current external balance was £138 580 million. The United Kingdom national accounts recorded no statistical discrepancy for 1997, so this sum was straightforwardly equal to the economy's gross capital formation of £138 580 million.

For the Australian economy in 1997–98, the sum of the economy's gross saving and the current external balance was $131 560 million. Australia's gross capital formation during 1997–98 was $134 343 million, and if we add to this the statistical discrepancy of –$2783 million, we arrive at the same total of $131 560 million.

The reason for this very important national accounting identity (for the total economy) between the sum of gross saving and the current external balance on the one hand and gross capital formation on the other hand (allowing for any statistical discrepancy), can be explained with the aid of Figure 7.4, which brings together much of what we have learnt in this book.

Figure 7.4 illustrates the SNA93/ESA95 accounts in general, and has seven numbered bars with subdivisions, where any height represents the monetary amount of an annual flow; for diagrammatic reasons, all amounts reported are positive (even though in the real world some of the external balance amounts may be negative); horizontal alignments between items are indicated by broken lines and dotted lines are used to indicate horizontal alignments which go through bars. In order to simplify the horizontal reading of the diagram, Figure 7.4 dispenses with the use of shading to show balancing items. Note that Figure 7.4 is not to scale (for example, final consumption expenditure is always much larger than gross capital formation, and intermediate consumption is larger than either of these).

On the left-hand side, Bars (1) and (2) represent Account 0: Goods and

Table 7.10

Gross saving, the current external balance and gross capital formation in the United Kingdom and Australia

SNA93/ESA95 identification code		United Kingdom 1997, £ million	Australia 1997–98, $ million
B.8g	Gross saving by total resident sectors, S.1	145 203	108 294
B.12	Current external balance, rest of the world, S.2	–6 623	23 266
Total	Total gross saving, S.1 + S.2	138 580	131 560
P.5	Gross capital formation[(a)], S.1	138 580	134 343
	Statistical discrepancy	—	–2 783
Total	Total gross capital formation and statistical discrepancy	138 580	131 560

'—' means nil.

(a)   Gross capital formation is, in principle, undertaken only by resident sectors making up S.1.

Source: Table 7.9.

services account. (As explained and illustrated in Chapters 3 and 5, the goods and services account can be compiled only for the total economy, S.1.) In Figure 7.4, Bar (1) shows the total use of goods and services in the economy – the sum of intermediate consumption, P.2, final consumption expenditure, P.3, gross capital formation, P.5, and exports of goods and services, P.6. Bar (2) shows the availability of goods and services to the economy. This bar consists of output, P.1, at basic prices; taxes on products less subsidies on products, D.21 – D.31 (for the reasons explained in Chapter 4); and imports of goods and services, P.7.

Bar (2) is, and must be, equal in height to Bar (1). This equality holds because the total uses of goods and services in the economy (valued at market prices) must be matched by an equal total availability of goods and services to the economy.

Bar (3) shows two amounts. First, Bar (3) shows gross domestic product as equal to the total of output, P.1, and taxes on products less subsidies on products, D.21 – D.31 (both from Bar (2)) minus intermediate consumption, P.2 (from Bar (1)). Parts of Bars (2) and (3) form a representation of Account I: Production account for S.1.

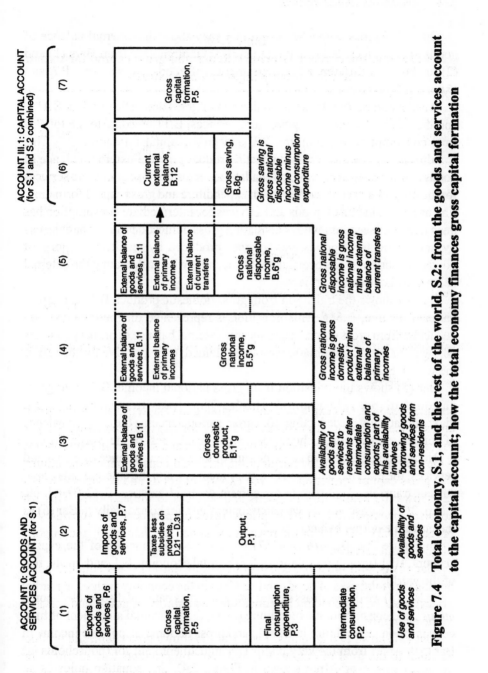

Figure 7.4 Total economy, S.1, and the rest of the world, S.2: from the goods and services account to the capital account; how the total economy finances gross capital formation

387

On top of gross domestic product we may show the external balance of goods and services, B.11, using the horizontal alignment from Bars (1) and (2) to show the difference between imports of goods and services, P.7, and exports of goods and services, P.6.

It is most important to note that the sum of gross domestic product, B.1*g, and the external balance of goods and services, B.11, is equal to the total of final consumption expenditure, P.3, and gross capital formation, P.5. This equality holds because gross domestic product *plus* the external balance of goods and services represents the availability to residents of goods and services for the purposes of final consumption expenditure and gross capital formation. The use by residents of goods and services for intermediate consumption has been taken into account when calculating gross domestic product; and the use by non-residents of goods and services produced by residents (exports of goods and services) has been taken into account when calculating the external balance of goods and services.

Bar (4) shows the transition from gross domestic product, B.1*g, to gross national income, B.5*g. This transition is represented diagrammatically by deducting from gross domestic product the external balance of primary incomes (shown, for the diagrammatic reasons explained, to be positive for the rest of the world, S.2).

Bar (5) shows the transition from gross national income, B.5*g, to gross national disposable income, B.6*g. This transition is represented diagrammatically by deducting from gross national income the external balance of current transfers (also shown as positive for the rest of the world, S.2).

Note that in Bar (5) we have the sum of the external balance of goods and services, the external balance of primary incomes, and the external balance of current transfers. This sum is the current external balance, B.12 (see Table 7.5, p. 362). Consequently we can transfer this sum horizontally to Bar (6) as the current external balance, B.12.

In Figure 7.4, Bars (6) and (7) represent a combination of the capital account, III.1 (gross presentation), for the total economy, S.1, and for the rest of the world, S.2.

In Bar (6) we derive gross saving, B.8g, as gross national disposable income *minus* final consumption expenditure (using the horizontal alignment of final consumption expenditure in Bar (1) and gross national disposable income in Bar (5)). Apart from the very minor D.8 adjustment item for (households in) the rest of the world (not shown in Figure 7.4), this equation holds as an important national accounting identity.

Consequently, Bar (6) taken in its entirety represents the sum of gross saving, B.8g, for the total economy and the current external balance, B.12; this is a combination of the capital accounts for S.1 and S.2.

We may now note that Bar (6) is exactly horizontally aligned, top and bottom, with gross capital formation, P.5, in Bar (1). Just to make this absolutely explicit (because this is the main point of the entire diagram), Bar (7) brings gross capital formation, P.5, over to the right-hand side of the diagram.

We can now see that, for the whole economy, gross capital formation is, and must be, equal to the sum of gross saving and the current external balance. (In real world national accounts an allowance might have to be made for a statistical discrepancy but this is not material to the principle of Figure 7.4.) It is this equality between Bar (6) and Bar (7) which is illustrated in Table 7.10, and which is an important identity of national accounting for the total economy.

There is an extremely important macroeconomic/national accounting truth in Bars (6) and (7) of Figure 7.4. The truth is this. If an economy has gross saving that is less than gross capital formation, then the economy must 'finance' the excess of gross capital formation over gross saving by drawing on the (positive) 'gross saving' of S.2 – that is, the economy must have a current account deficit. Gross saving which is persistently less than gross capital formation is the macroeconomic origin of persistent current account deficits.

7.8   Net lending (+)/net borrowing (–) by the total economy, S.1, and by the rest of the world, S.2

The national accounting identity, gross saving *plus* the current external balance *equals* gross capital formation, is important because, among other things, it can be used to explain how, for the total economy, annual 'foreign borrowing' or annual 'foreign lending' arises. I put the terms 'foreign borrowing' and 'foreign lending' in inverted commas because these are not official SNA93/ESA95 terms; the official SNA93/ESA95 terms are simply 'net borrowing (–)' and 'net lending (+)' respectively but applied to the S.1 total economy (that is, the total of the resident sectors of the economy). The purpose of this section is to explain that (ignoring the statistical discrepancy, if any):

S.2 Net lending (+)/net borrowing (–) = –[S.1 Net lending (+)/net borrowing (–)]

Table 7.11 illustrates this equation for the United Kingdom (1997) and Australia (1997–98) and it is necessary to approach Table 7.11 through Table 7.9.

During 1997, the United Kingdom's net lending (+) was £7427 million.

This is calculated in Table 7.9 by taking the United Kingdom's (S.1's) changes in net worth due to gross saving and capital transfers, B.10.1g, and subtracting the sum of the United Kingdom's gross capital formation, P.5, plus acquisitions less disposals of non-produced non financial assets, K.2.

The United Kingdom's net lending (+) is equal, but opposite in sign, to the net borrowing (–) of the rest of the world. In Table 7.9 the rest of the world's net borrowing (–) is calculated by taking the sum of the current external balance, B.12, plus the external balance of capital transfers and subtracting S.2's acquisitions less disposals of non-produced non-financial assets, K.2.

During 1997–98, Australia's net borrowing (–) was –$24 922 million. This is calculated in Table 7.9 by taking Australia's (S.1's) changes in net worth due to gross saving and capital transfers, B.10.1g, and subtracting the sum of Australia's gross capital formation, P.5, plus acquisitions less disposals of non-produced non financial assets, K.2.

Allowing for the statistical discrepancy, Australia's net borrowing (–) is equal, but opposite in sign, to the net lending (+) of the rest of the world. In

Table 7.11

Net lending (+)/net borrowing (–) by S.1 and S.2 in the United Kingdom and Australia

SNA93/ESA95 identification code		United Kingdom 1997, £ million	Australia 1997–98, $ million
B.9	Net lending (+)/net borrowing (–) by S.1	7 427	–24 922
	Statistical discrepancy	—	–2 783
Total	Net lending (+)/net borrowing (–) by S.1 *minus* statistical discrepancy	7 427 [a]	–22 139 [b]
B.9	Net lending (+)/net borrowing (–) by S.2	–7 427	22 139

'—' means nil.

(a) Annual (1997) 'foreign lending' by the United Kingdom economy; 'lending by' the economy is indicated by the (silent) plus sign.

(b) Annual (1997–98) 'foreign borrowing' by the Australian economy; in the national capital account of the Australian System of National Accounts, this is called 'net lending to non-residents' and that it constitutes borrowing by the economy is indicated by the minus sign.

Source: Table 7.9.

Table 7.9 the rest of the world's net lending (+) is calculated by taking the sum of the current external balance, B.12, plus the external balance of capital transfers and subtracting S.2's acquisitions less disposals of non-produced non-financial assets, K.2.

In order to make the comparisons more easily, Table 7.11 brings these figures on net lending (+)/net borrowing (−) by each of S.1 and S.2 together. We can clearly see that (allowing for the statistical discrepancy) the economy's net lending (+)/net borrowing (−) is equal, but opposite in sign, to net lending (+)/net borrowing (−) by the rest of the world. This is an important national accounting identity, with a very simple macroeconomic meaning. If an economy has to borrow, then it has to borrow from the rest of the world (the case of Australia in 1997–98); if an economy is lending (or acquiring financial assets net), then it has to lend to the rest of the world (the case of the United Kingdom in 1997).

Figure 7.5 explains how this all comes about. Figure 7.5 shows the capital account (gross presentation) for S.1. In order to simplify the diagram slightly (and because the relative amount is almost negligible) Figure 7.5 omits the detail of the acquisitions less disposals of non-produced non-financial assets, K.2.

Figure 7.5 is a continuation of Figure 7.4 (but on an enlarged scale to make it easier to read), so the numbering of the bars is continued in sequence. Bar (6a) is a version of Bar (6) in Figure 7.4, except that the three external balances are given as a reminder of where we are starting from.

Bar (8) shows that the external balance of capital transfers (taken as positive for the rest of the world; that is, the rest of the world receives a greater amount of capital transfers from residents than residents receive from the rest of the world) is to be subtracted from (or diminishes) gross saving. (Note that the term 'gross saving' is always and only used to refer to gross saving by resident S.1 sectors of the economy and by the S.1 total economy; likewise for 'gross capital formation'; in other words, it is superfluous to attach 'S.1' to either of these terms; and in this section, of course, we are dealing only with S.1's gross saving and S.1's gross capital formation.)

The transition from Bar (8) to Bar (9) is important in two respects. First, the sum of the current external balance, B.12, and the external balance of capital transfers is S.2's net lending (+)/net borrowing (−), B.9. (Remember that, following the conventions of the external accounts in the SNA93/ESA95, this balancing item is calculated from the viewpoint of non-residents.) Second, gross saving minus the external balance of capital transfers is S.1's gross saving and capital transfers, B.10.1g.

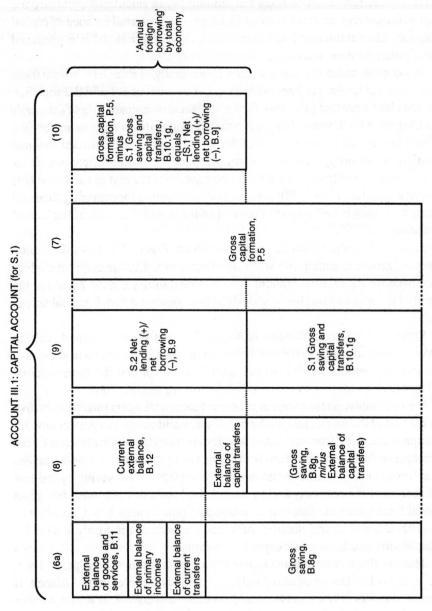

Figure 7.5 Total economy, S.1: the capital account and how annual foreign borrowing arises

Gross capital formation (equal to the total of the current external balance and gross saving), or Bar (7) from Figure 7.4, may now be brought into the diagram. The reason for this is that we can use Bar (7) to show, in Bar (10), gross capital formation minus S.1's gross saving and capital transfers, B.10.1g. We do this because:

$$\begin{matrix} \text{S.1 Net lending (+)/} \\ \text{net borrowing (-),} \\ \text{B.9} \end{matrix} = \begin{matrix} \text{S.1 Gross saving and} \\ \text{capital transfers,} \\ \text{B.10.1g} \end{matrix} - \begin{matrix} \text{Gross capital} \\ \text{formation, P.5} \end{matrix}$$

So that:

$$\begin{matrix} \text{Gross capital} \\ \text{formation, P.5} \end{matrix} - \begin{matrix} \text{S.1 Gross saving and} \\ \text{capital transfers, B.10.1g} \end{matrix}$$

$$= - \left[\begin{matrix} \text{S.1 Gross saving} \\ \text{and capital} \\ \text{transfers, B.10.1g} \end{matrix} - \begin{matrix} \text{Gross capital} \\ \text{formation, P.5} \end{matrix} \right]$$

$$= - \begin{matrix} \text{S. 1 Net lending (+)/} \\ \text{net borrowing (-),} \\ \text{B.9} \end{matrix}$$

Consequently, Bar (10) represents the negative of the economy's net lending (+)/net borrowing (–), B.9. However, and this is the main point of Figure 7.5, we can see by the horizontal alignment between Bar (9) and Bar (10) in Figure 7.5 that Bar (10) is equal to the rest of the world's net lending (+)/net borrowing (–), B.9, in Bar (9). This shows how it comes about that the economy's net lending (+)/net borrowing (–) is equal, but opposite in sign, to the rest of the world's net lending (+)/net borrowing (–).

The fundamental point of Figure 7.5 is quite straightforward. Loosely, annual foreign borrowing occurs in an economy if the economy's gross capital formation, P.5, shown in Bar (7), is greater than the economy's gross saving, B.8g, shown in Bar (6a), allowing for the impact of the external balance of capital transfers, shown in Bar (8). More precisely, annual foreign borrowing occurs if the economy's gross capital formation is greater than the sum of the economy's gross saving and capital transfers, B.10.1g.

However, because the external balance of capital transfers is nearly always relatively small, the fundamental national accounting origin of annual foreign borrowing for the total economy is gross saving by the economy (that is, by all the resident sectors of the economy) which is less than gross capital formation by the economy. This is why a decline in saving by any one of the resident sectors is a serious matter for macroeconomic policy.

Conversely, if an economy is to be able to accumulate foreign assets (net) or to repay outstanding foreign debt then it must achieve gross saving which is greater than gross capital formation. Consequently, in an economy with foreign debt, achieving gross saving which is greater than gross capital formation becomes an important goal of macroeconomic policy.

7.9   The wealth of the nation

Finally in this book we may consider the upshot of all the transactions we have explained in terms of the nation's holdings of stocks of assets and liabilities. The closing balance sheet completes the sequence of SNA93/ESA95 accounts (Figure 1.6, pp. 24–5). What is a balance sheet? *United Kingdom National Accounts Concepts, Sources and Methods 1998 Edition* explains:

> Balance sheets are statements of the value of assets and liabilities at a particular point of time, and can be drawn up for institutional units, sectors or the whole economy. The balancing item is 'net worth' or, in the case of the whole economy, 'national wealth' – the aggregate of non-financial assets and net claims on the rest of the world (*UK NACSM*, para. 9.1).

We need to note five points about this.

First, balance sheets record stocks existing (and valued) at a moment in time. For example, the Australian economy's balance sheet, to be considered in Table 7.12, is drawn up for the date 30 June 1998. It is important to note this, because so far all the accounts considered in this book have been accounts which record *flows* during a period of time (such as a year). The distinction between stocks and flows was explained in Section 1.2.

Second, we should initially focus upon a single institutional unit, because we can quite properly talk about an institutional unit owning assets and liabilities (that is, it is the institutional unit which is recognised in law as the entity which is the owner of the asset or which is the entity legally responsible for meeting the obligations under the liability). It is only an institutional unit which can exercise legal rights and sue (or be sued) in a court of law.

Third, we understand that a sector is an aggregate of institutional units according to type of institutional unit (Figure 1.2, p. 9); and we understand that the economy is an aggregate of the resident sectors (that is, the aggregate of resident institutional units). Consequently, *but only metaphorically*, we can talk of assets 'owned by' or 'belonging to' a sector or the economy, and we can talk of the liabilities 'owed by' a sector or the economy. But we must always remember that this is only metaphorical talk: neither a sector nor the economy can exercise legal rights and sue or be sued in a court of law. (We do not discuss those cases where the nation, acting through its government, is regarded as a legal person under international law.) So, when we say that a sector owns such-and-such assets, we mean that the institutional units comprising that sector own the assets. This being said, I continue the discussion in terms of an institutional unit, and the (metaphorical) extension of the concept of ownership can be applied as appropriate.

Fourth, a balance sheet is a comprehensive, all-inclusive, record of *all* the assets, non-financial and financial, owned by an institutional unit, and likewise for the liabilities owed by an institutional unit. The classification of economic assets was given in Figure 1.7, pp. 38–9, and the classification of financial liabilities is the same as the classification for financial assets with the exception that, as financial assets, monetary gold and Special Drawing Rights do not have counterpart financial liabilities. By convention, the SNA93/ESA95 recognises shares and other equity as a financial liability, except that, as explained in Chapter 1, shares constitute (and are devised to constitute) a financial liability of a peculiar and distinctive type.

Fifth, a balance sheet has a balancing item, known in the SNA93/ESA95 as *net worth*, B.90. The following is the definitional equation for 'net worth':

$$\text{Net worth, B.90} = \begin{array}{c}\text{Total of non-}\\\text{financial}\\\text{assets owned,}\\\text{AN}\end{array} + \begin{array}{c}\text{Total of}\\\text{financial}\\\text{assets owned,}\\\text{AF.A}\end{array} - \begin{array}{c}\text{Total of}\\\text{financial}\\\text{liabilities}\\\text{owed, AF.L}\end{array}$$

In the first instance, it is best to understand this definitional equation in terms of a single institutional unit. The concept and the calculation of the balancing item can be applied to a sector or to the economy (bearing in mind what was said previously about the metaphorical meaning of 'owned' or 'owed' in such a context).

When the equation is applied to the resident sectors of the economy taken as a whole (that is, applied to S.1), net worth so calculated can be called 'the wealth of the nation' or 'national wealth'.

It is also possible to calculate a sub-part of net worth, called in the United Kingdom national accounts 'net financial assets (+)/net financial liabilities (–)' and given the identification code BF.90, where 'F' stands for financial. The following is the definitional equation for 'net financial assets (+)/net financial liabilities (–)':

Net financial assets (+)/   Total financial   Total financial
net financial liabilities (–), =   assets owned,   –   liabilities
BF.90   AF.A   owed, AF.L

Comparing this equation with the equation for net worth, you can readily see that net financial assets (+)/net financial liabilities (–), BF.90, is a part of net worth, B.90.

All this can be illustrated by the balance sheet for the sectors of the Australian economy at 30 June 1998 given in Table 7.12. Note that, unlike all the other tables in this book, the units of measurement in Table 7.12 are in $ billion (where 'billion' means 'thousand million'). Table 7.12 exemplifies much (but not all) of the classification scheme for economic assets given in Figure 1.7, but the Australian System of National Accounts has some sub-categories of its own and has not yet recorded the category of valuables, AN.13.

Limitations of space preclude any extended discussion of Table 7.12; indeed, it is clear that any such discussion could readily take up a book of its own. The row headings of Table 7.12 give the various categories of assets. The balance sheet begins with all the non-financial assets, and studying these gives you an understanding of what is meant in the SNA93/ESA95 by the term 'non-financial assets'. Non-financial assets are divided between produced assets and non-produced assets, and in turn produced assets are divided between fixed assets and inventories.

A few relevant points from Table 7.12. Insurance technical reserves, AF.6, constitutes 43 per cent of the total financial assets of households ($421.8 billion/$983.6 billion = 0.4288), and constitutes 23 per cent of the total wealth of households ($421.8 billion/$1849.1 billion = 0.2281). These insurance technical reserves include the AF.612 claims on pension funds ('net equity of households in pension funds' reserves'), so we can infer that the claims on pension funds are an important part of households' financial assets (but until we have a breakdown of AF.6 into AF.611 (net equity of households on life insurance reserves) and AF.612 (net equity of households in pension funds' reserves) we cannot say precisely how important).

We can see in Table 7.12 that non-financial corporations hold as financial assets a further $18.3 billion of insurance technical reserves, AF.6.

Consequently, the total of financial assets held in this form in the economy is $440.1 billion (= $421.8 billion + $18.3 billion).

Corresponding to these AF.6 insurance technical reserves as assets of $440.1 billion, there is a matching *liability* of the insurance corporations and pension funds, S.125 (included in financial corporations, S.12), of $440.1 billion. This illustrates how financial assets held within the group of residents are 'matched' and 'cancelled' by financial liabilities also held within the group of residents.

Households in Australia owned $474.0 billion worth of dwellings, and this category of non-financial assets is the only category of asset greater than household claims on insurance technical reserves.

In the case of financial assets, the Australian System of National Accounts departs from the conventions of the SNA93, and reports for the Australian total economy, S.1, only the financial assets held as claims against non-residents; likewise for financial liabilities. The convention of the SNA93/ESA95, followed in the United Kingdom national accounts is to report under S.1, the aggregate of financial assets for S.11, S.12, S.13 and S.14 + S.15; likewise for financial liabilities.

Taking Table 7.12 under the Australian reporting convention, Australia's total non-financial assets at 30 June 1998 amounted to $2599.9 billion. Australia's gross domestic product during the preceding year was $564.705 billion, so that we can see that the Australian economy required 4.6 units (dollars) of non-financial assets (by value) to produce 1 unit (dollar) per annum of gross value added (or gross domestic product). Put the other way round, for every $1 worth of non-financial assets which the Australian economy held, the economy produced 21.7 cents per annum of gross value added.

Gross value added is not, of course, the same thing as gross operating surplus/gross mixed income, because the compensation of employees and taxes less subsidies on production and imports are both included in gross value added. Gross operating surplus/gross mixed income, B.2g + B.3g, in the Australian economy in 1997–98 was $228.095 billion, and if we regard the Australian economy as an enterprise, we could make the following estimate of the 'rate of profit' made by the total economy:

$$\frac{\text{Gross operating surplus/gross mixed income p.a.}}{\text{Stock of non-financial assets}} = \frac{\$228.095 \text{ bn p.a.}}{\$2\,599.9 \text{ bn}}$$

$$= 0.088 \text{ p.a.}$$

$$= 8.8 \text{ per cent p.a.}$$

Table 7.12
Account IV: Balance sheet, Australia, 30 June 1998

SNA93/ESA95 identification code	Australian System of National Accounts name	30 June, 1998, $ billion					
		Non-financial corporations, S.11	Financial corporations, S.12	General government, S.13	Households and NPISHs, S.14 + S.15	Australian total economy[a], S.1	Rest of the world, S.2
	Assets						
AN	**Non-financial assets**						
AN.1	Produced assets						
AN.11	Fixed assets						
AN.111	Tangible fixed assets						
AN.1111	Dwellings	30.7	—	3.4	474.0	508.1	...
AN.1112	Other buildings and structures	349.7	44.2	193.1	42.2	629.2	...
AN.1113	Machinery and equipment	197.4	10.8	17.5	79.2	304.9	...
AN.1114	Cultivated assets						
AN.11141	Livestock — fixed assets	1.3	—	—	15.3	16.7	...
AN.112	Intangible fixed assets						
AN.1122	Computer software	8.5	1.3	2.7	2.0	14.5	...
AN.1123	Entertainment, literary or artistic originals	0.1	—	0.1	0.1	0.3	...
AN.11	Total fixed assets	587.8	56.3	216.8	612.8	1 473.6	...
AN.12	Inventories						
—	Private non-farm stocks	67.3	—	—	7.5	74.8	...
—	Farm stocks	0.7	—	—	6.0	6.6	...
—	Public marketing authorities	1.7	—	—	—	1.7	...
—	Other public authorities	0.2	—	0.2	—	0.3	...
—	Livestock—inventories	0.7	—	—	4.8	5.6	...
—	Plantation forests	1.0	—	4.5	1.6	7.0	...
AN.12	Total inventories	71.6	—	4.6	19.9	96.1	...
AN.1	Total produced assets	659.3	56.3	221.4	632.7	1 569.7	...

AN.2	Non-produced assets						
AN.21	Tangible non-produced assets						
AN.211	Land	146.6	32.3	—	590.0	769.0	...
AN.212	Subsoil assets	—	—	258.5	—	258.5	...
AN.213	Native forests	0.2	—	2.1	0.4	2.7	...
AN.21	Total non-produced assets	146.9	32.3	260.6	590.4	1 030.2	...
AN	Total non-financial assets	806.2	88.5	482.0	1 223.1	2 599.9	...
AF	**Financial assets**						
AF.1	Monetary gold and SDRs	—	1.3	—	—	1.3	—
AF.2	Currency and deposits	87.4	16.7	5.8	232.9	20.0	31.1
AF.3	Securities other than shares	20.2	189.2	0.8	20.0	39.9	241.4
AF.4	Loans and placements	12.2	638.6	24.0	9.8	38.9	58.2
AF.5	Shares and other equity	63.7	260.8	180.2	156.9	146.0	241.7
AF.6	Insurance technical reserves	18.3	—	—	421.8	—	—
—	Unfunded superannuation claims	—	4.8	—	122.8	—	—
AF.7	Other accounts receivable	55.5	46.6	30.4	19.3	14.2	9.6
AF.A	Total financial assets	257.3	1 158.0	241.3	983.6	260.3	582.0
Total	Total assets	1 063.5	1 246.5	723.2	2 206.6	2 860.2	582.0

Table 7.12
Account IV: Balance sheet, Australia, 30 June 1998 (continued)

30 June, 1998, $ billion

SNA93/ESA95 identification code	Australian System of National Accounts name	Non-financial corporations, S.11	Financial corporations, S.12	General government, S.13	Households and NPISHs, S.14 + S.15	Australian total economy(a), S.1	Rest of the world, S.2
Liabilities							
AF	**Financial liabilities**						
AF.1	Monetary gold and SDRs	...	...	...	...	...	1.3
AF.2	Currency and deposits	—	352.2	1.6	—	31.1	20.0
AF.3	Securities other than shares	119.0	203.0	107.3	2.5	241.4	39.9
AF.4	Loans and placements	243.8	55.1	50.1	355.0	58.2	38.9
AF.5	Shares and other equity	588.7	168.6	—	—	241.7	146.0
AF.6	Insurance technical reserves	—	440.1	—	—	—	—
—	Unfunded superannuation claims	—	—	127.6	—	—	—
AF.7	Other accounts payable	73.6	60.0	13.7	—	9.6	14.2
AF.L	Total liabilities	1 025.1	1 279.0	300.3	357.5	582.0	260.3
B.90	Net worth	38.4	-32.5	422.9	1 849.1	2 278.2	321.7 (b)
Total	Total liabilities and net worth	1 063.5	1 246.5	723.2	2 206.6	2 860.2	582.0

'—' means nil; '...' means not applicable.

(a) For financial assets/liabilities, this column records 'Financial assets with the rest of the world' and 'Financial liabilities to the rest of the world'; for financial assets and financial liabilities this column is *not* the row total of S.11 + S.12 + S.13 + (S.14 + S.15); this recording is a convention of the Australian System of National Accounts and is a departure from the convention of the SNA93/ESA95 where the recording is for the row total.

(b) In the Australian System of National Accounts external balance sheet this is called the 'net financial position'; this is the total of what Australian residents *owe* to non-residents net of Australian residents' claims on non-residents; it is the broadest measure of Australia's 'foreign debt', and is officially called Australia's 'net international investment position' in the Australian Bureau of Statistics, *Balance of Payments and International Investment Position Australia 1997–98*, Catalogue No. 5363.0, table 2, p. 19.

Source: Australian Bureau of Statistics, *Australian System of National Accounts 1997–98*, Catalogue No. 5204.0, tables 1.15, 2.4, 2.12, 2.18, 2.24 and 2.30, pp. 35, 44, 52, 58, 64 and 70; rounding discrepancies may result in reported totals differing from sum of components.

This is an approximation (under certain assumptions) to an 'internal rate of return' (see my book *Profitability, Mechanization and Economies of Scale*, Chapter 3, for an explanation of this approximation).

The value of the rest of the world's, or S.2's, financial assets, or claims on residents, minus the value of the rest of the world's, or S.2's, financial liabilities, or liabilities to residents, is a measure of the Australian economy's 'foreign debt', in the broadest sense of the word 'debt' – that is, including shares and other equity in the coverage of 'foreign debt'. We have to be careful at this juncture because the Australian Bureau of Statistics officially uses the technical term 'net foreign debt' to refer only to non-equity liabilities minus non-equity assets; equity liabilities minus equity assets are officially called 'net foreign equity' or 'net equity liabilities', and what we are calling, in a non-technical and popular use of the term, 'foreign debt' the Australian Bureau of Statistics calls Australia's 'net international investment position' (Australian Bureau of Statistics, *Balance of Payments and International Investment Position Australia 1997–98*, Catalogue No. 5363.0, p.10 and table 2, p. 19).

From Table 7.12, Australia's net international investment position, or loosely 'foreign debt', at 30 June 1998 was:

$$\text{Total financial assets, S.2} - \text{Total liabilities, S.2} = \$582 \text{ bn} - \$260.3 \text{ bn}$$

$$= \$321.7 \text{ bn}$$

Australia's 'foreign debt' thus amounted to 57 per cent of annual gross domestic product (= \$321.7 bn [30 June 1998]/\$564.705 bn [1997–98]). This is, of course, the reason for the rest of the world's large positive external balance of primary incomes.

Finally, Australia's net worth at 30 June 1998 is the total non-financial assets *plus* total financial assets *minus* total financial liabilities:

$$\text{S.1 net worth, B.90} = \text{Total non-financial assets, AN} + \text{Total financial assets, AF.A} - \text{Total financial liabilities, AF.L}$$

$$= \$2\,599.9 \text{ bn} + \$260.3 \text{ bn} - \$582.0 \text{ bn}$$

$$= \$2\,278.2 \text{ bn}$$

Australia's net worth at 30 June 1998 can also be understood as the total value of non-financial assets *minus* the 'foreign debt':

$$
\begin{array}{rcl}
\text{Net worth,} & = & \text{Total value of} \\
\text{B.90, of S.1} & & \text{non-financial} \quad - \quad \text{'Foreign debt'} \\
& & \text{assets, AN}
\end{array}
$$

$$= \$2\,599.9 \text{ bn} - \$321.7 \text{ bn}$$

$$= \$2\,278.2 \text{ bn}$$

The economic significance of the balance sheet is that:

> For an institutional unit or sector, the balance sheet provides *an indicator of economic status* – i.e., the financial and non-financial resources at its disposal that are summarized in the balancing item net worth (*SNA93*, para. 13.2, italics added).

Australia's population in 1997–98 was 18.637 million (*Australian System of National Accounts 1997–98*, table 1.1, p. 21); consequently, the 'economic status' of the average Australian in terms of the net worth of assets 'available' (including assets collectively 'owned' by the community through the general government, such as roads and bridges and also making an allowance for the 'share' of households in Australia's 'foreign debt') was \$122 241 per person; this translates into £48 707, €73 772 or US\$77 537 per person (using the average of buy and sell exchange rates at 1 September 1999).

Index

direct foreign investment 234–5
disposable income, gross, B.6g 24, 31–2, 262, 299, 303, 311, 315, 317–25, 345, 347–8, 354–8, 378–9
distributed income of corporations, D.42 232–3, 254–5
distribution and use of income accounts 302
distributive transactions 100
dividends, D.421 232–4, 239–45, 260–61
domestic product *see* gross domestic product
domestic servants 95, 131–2
double-counting 62, 64–6, 85, 149
dwellings, AN.1111 38, 40, 397–8

economic activity 48–9, 120, 123, 132–4
economically significant prices 76, 92–3, 95–6, 123
economic assets 33–4, 38, 395
employees' social contributions, D.6112 268, 270, 296–8, 345–9
employer/employee relationship 289
employers' actual social contributions, D.121 (= D.6111) 268, 270, 289–91, 294–9, 345–7
employers' imputed social contributions, D.122 291, 295, 298
employment 120, 132–3
endowment life insurance 306–7
enterprises 48–9, 51–3, 55–6, 58
entertainment, literary or artistic originals, AN.1123 38, 41, 398
entrepreneurial income, B.4 236
establishments 51, 55
estimated values 15–18, 93–4, 124
exports of goods and services, P.6 108, 111–12, 118–20, 136–9, 159, 161, 168, 219–28, 361–2, 384, 386–8
export taxes, D.213 166
external accounts 11, 359–62
external balance of goods and services, B.11 224, 361–4, 387–8, 392
externalities 89
external transaction 10–11, 205, 359

final consumption expenditure, P.3 24, 32, 108, 111–16, 118–19, 136, 139–41, 152–3, 155–62, 174, 177–9, 190–92, 281, 284–8, 343, 386–8
final expenditure 47, 108–12, 118–20, 134–50, 153, 155–62, 182–5, 192–3, 210–19, 223–8

financial account 25, 44, 327–8, 331–4, 338–41, 348, 366, 368–70, 375–80
financial assets/liabilities, AF 34, 39, 325–8, 332–4, 337–9, 349–51, 377, 395, 399–401
financial corporations, S.12 9, 11–15, 356–7
financial intermediation services indirectly measured (FISIM), P.119 254–5
finished goods, AN.123 37–8, 76–81, 126
fixed assets, AN.11 37–8, 40, 396, 398
flow 6–7, 394
f.o.b. *see* free on board
foreign debt *see* net international investment position
free on board 207, 209

general government, S.13 9, 12–15, 113–19, 124, 262, 267, 271, 277–8, 301–4, 316–19, 321, 323, 356–8
goods 89–90
goods and services account 22, 109, 151–61, 177–80, 190–91, 212–17, 221–2, 224–7, 385–7
goods and services tax (GST) *see* value added type taxes (VAT), D.211
goods for resale, AN.124 38, 40, 172
gross 28, 326
gross capital formation, P.5 25, 43, 108, 111, 116, 118–19, 159, 161, 224–8, 340, 364–9, 371–5, 379–94
gross domestic product, B.1*g 7, 20, 25, 47, 58, 67–8, 83–4, 86–8, 97–8, 105–7, 109, 143, 157–62, 180–85, 191–200, 210–13, 216–18, 220–24, 226–8, 237, 242, 247–52, 257–9, 324, 386–8, 397, 401
gross fixed capital formation, P.51 29, 42, 111–12, 116, 118–19, 127–9, 136, 141–2, 172
gross mixed income, B.3g 7, 24, 30, 58, 99–107, 157, 195–8, 200, 203–4, 229–30, 241–2, 254, 260
gross national disposable income, B.6*g 262, 299, 303, 311–12, 314–15, 317–18, 322, 324–5, 387–8
gross national income, B.5*g 229–30, 236–9, 243, 246–7, 249–52, 255–61, 299, 312, 314, 316, 324, 387–8
gross operating surplus, B.2g 7, 20, 24, 30, 58, 99, 100–107, 157, 188, 195–7, 200, 203, 229–30, 241–2, 253–4, 260
gross saving, B.8g 7, 24, 27, 32–3, 43–4, 325–